Independent
Mexico

The Mexican Experience | William H. Beezley, series editor

Independent
Mexico

The *Pronunciamiento*
in the Age of Santa
Anna, 1821–1858

WILL FOWLER

University of Nebraska Press | Lincoln & London

© 2016 by the Board of Regents of the University of Nebraska

All rights reserved
Manufactured in the United States of America

Library of Congress
Cataloging-in-Publication Data
Fowler, Will, 1966– author.
Independent Mexico: the pronunciamiento in the age of Santa Anna, 1821–1858 / Will Fowler.
pages   cm.—(The Mexican experience)
Includes bibliographical references and index.
ISBN 978-0-8032-2539-8 (pbk.: alk. paper)
ISBN 978-0-8032-8467-8 (epub)
ISBN 978-0-8032-8468-5 (mobi)
ISBN 978-0-8032-8469-2 (pdf)
1. Mexico—Politics and government—
1821–1861. 2. Government, Resistance to—
Mexico—History—19th century. 3. Coups
d'état—Mexico—History—19th century.
4. Revolutions—Mexico—History—
19th century. 5. Mexico—History—1821–1861.
I. Title.
F1232.F69 2016
972'.04—dc23
2015031797

Set in Adobe Garamond Pro by L. Auten.

For Caroline

"... the absurd events of a land incapable of tranquility, enamored of convulsion."

—CARLOS FUENTES, *The Death of Artemio Cruz*
(translated by Sam Hileman; Harmondsworth:
Penguin Books, 1979 [1962]), 37

"When a law is unfair, the correct thing to do is to disobey."

—Banner displayed in the Zócalo during a demonstration
in Mexico City on 7 July 2012, *El País*, 8 July 2012

"When the unjust becomes the law, rebellion becomes a duty."

—Banner displayed outside Mexican
Senate, *La Jornada*, 2 October 2012

Contents

Maps

Preface

This book is about *pronunciamientos* and a phenomenon I have chosen to term "mimetic insurrectionism." It is about an insurrectionary practice that became widespread in Independent Mexico whereby garrisons, initially, but eventually also town councils, state legislatures, and a whole array of political actors, groups, and communities took to petitioning the government aggressively at both a national and a local level to address their grievances during what amounted to a period of considerable constitutional uncertainty. Albeit often translated as a revolt or a coup d'état, the pronunciamiento was a complex form of insurrectionary action that relied, in the first instance, on the proclamation and circulation of a plan that listed the *pronunciados'* demands and, thereafter, on its endorsement by significant enough a number of copycat pronunciamientos *de adhesión* or allegiance to force the authorities, be they national or regional, to the negotiating table.

It is a study that has its origins in a paper I gave at the then Institute of Latin American Studies in London in May 1997 on civil conflict in Independent Mexico and that builds on the subsequent research and publications that were developed ten years later as part of the University of St. Andrews "Pronunciamiento in Independent Mexico" project, which was funded by an incredibly generous grant from the UK-based Arts and Humanities Research

Council (AHRC). It was while preparing an overview of civil conflict in Independent Mexico back in 1997 for the Nineteenth-Century History Workshop that Eduardo Posada Carbó organized "On the Origins of Civil Wars in Nineteenth-Century Latin America" that I was first struck by the fact that the literally hundreds of pronunciamientos recorded in Mexico following its achievement of independence from Spain in 1821 were not strictly speaking revolts and that their threats of violence were seldom actually carried out. Once the Pronunciamientos Project got under way in 2007, it became more than evident that there was much more to the pronunciamiento phenomenon than I had ever anticipated.

In the first of the four volumes to arise from our AHRC-funded project, *Forceful Negotiations: The Origins of the* Pronunciamiento *in Nineteenth-Century Mexico* (Lincoln: University of Nebraska Press, 2010), the contributors established that the pronunciamiento became a common phenomenon in the Hispanic world in the nineteenth century. We argued that it was a practice (part petition, part rebellion) that sought to effect political change through intimidation and that was adopted to negotiate forcefully. We showed, moreover, that the pronunciamiento developed alongside Mexico's constitutions and formal political institutions and was resorted to, time and again, to remove unpopular politicians from positions of power, put a stop to controversial policies, call for a change in the political system, and promote the cause of a charismatic leader and/or the interests of a given region, corporate body, or community. We concluded that the pronunciamiento became *the* way of doing politics.

In the second edited volume of our pronunciamiento tetralogy, *Malcontents, Rebels, and* Pronunciados: *The Politics of Insurrection in Nineteenth-Century Mexico* (Lincoln: University of

Preface

Nebraska Press, 2012), we explained why this was the case. The process whereby the pronunciamiento went from originally being a military-led practice to one that was endorsed and employed by civilians, priests, indigenous communities, and politicians from all parties was traced through the study of a rich variety of pronunciamientos stretching from Tlaxcalan pueblo political activities in the late colonial period to a socialist *levantamiento* (uprising) with anarchist overtones in Chalco in 1868, with the stress being on individual and collective motivation.

In the third edited volume in the series, *Celebrating Insurrection: The Commemoration and Representation of the Nineteenth-Century Mexican* Pronunciamiento (Lincoln: University of Nebraska Press, 2012), we focused on how Mexicans tried to come to terms with this practice, how they attempted to legitimize it by celebrating it and including it in their repertoire of civic fiestas, and how these fiestas came to reflect the ambivalence people felt toward the pronunciamiento. We sought to explain how pronunciamientos were celebrated, remembered, commemorated, and represented. In so doing, what emerged was a striking interpretation of a phenomenon that was characterized by its duality and ambivalence, one that was experienced as a necessary evil, celebrated yet criticized, reluctantly justified, and the heroes of which were both damned and venerated.

In this current fourth and final volume I have set out to provide a comprehensive overview of the pronunciamiento practice in Independent Mexico, with the emphasis being on national pronunciamientos. It is a book concerned with the dynamics of the pronunciamiento and, in turn, with how a given form of insurrectionary action can spread and become adopted by growing numbers of groups and individuals. It is also a study that highlights the extent to which this given model of political contestation evolved between 1821 and 1858, in terms of who pronounced, and why and how they did so, while paying attention to the shift that was also experienced in the kind of demands pronunciamientos set out to address. Therefore I provide in chapter 1 a critical review of the relevant literature while offering a detailed analysis of the nature of the pronunciamiento as a political-insurrectionary practice. I go on to define and explore in the following chapter the dynamics of mimetic insurrectionism. Here I provide an interpretation of how the pronunciamiento, as a phenomenon, became such an emulation-worthy practice on the back of the successful pronunciamientos of Cabezas de San Juan in Spain, on 1 January 1820, and of Iguala, on 24 February 1821, but also because of the context of severe constitutional crisis in which it originated. Chapter 3 then addresses how the pronunciamiento started to spread in the first decade following independence, and I argue that a key factor in its proliferation was the manner in which regional elites used it to renegotiate their political power with the center. As becomes evident in chapter 4, by the 1830s it was not just high-ranking officers in collusion with the *hombres de bien* who were pronouncing but the disenfranchised and a veritable plethora of subaltern political actors. The political demands of the pronunciamientos also changed, something that becomes evident as the book progresses from one chapter to the next. However, despite the proliferation of pronunciamientos, or perhaps because of it, the Mexican political class proved unable to consolidate a long-lasting constitutional order. As argued in chapter 5, the pronunciamiento, as may be the case wherever mimetic insurrectionism arises, had the tendency to generate more pronunciamientos. The retaliatory nature of these, in turn, meant that by the mid-1840s, they were no longer so much about forceful negotiation but about overthrowing the government, and this, paradoxically, put an aggressive end to pronunciamiento politics. In the end, the result of more than three decades of pronunciamiento politics would be the extremely sanguinary Civil War of the Reforma, 1858–60, and the ensuing French Intervention, 1862–67. Given the frequency and importance of the pronunciamiento, and how many of the main events and changes of this period were the result of pronunciamiento pressure, this book is also, almost by default, a concise political history of Independent Mexico.

Acknowledgments

In June 2007 I was the recipient of a major Arts and Humanities Research Council research grant amounting to more than
£610,000, which funded the three-year project on "The *Pronunciamiento* in Independent Mexico, 1821–1876" (2007–2010). It paid
for the salaries of two research fellows and a database developer
and covered the cost of two PhD studentships. It also funded the
research team's travel expenses to and from Mexico, including
expenses incurred in the organization of three major conferences
held at St. Andrews in June 2008, 2009, and 2010. This generous
award allowed me to put together a vibrant research team focused
on producing a major online relational database that includes
transcriptions of more than 1,500 pronunciamientos (see http://
arts.st-andrews.ac.uk/pronunciamientos/) and on publishing four
volumes (three edited and one monograph) on different aspects
of this phenomenon. The first volume came out in 2010, focused
on the origins, nature, and dynamics of this practice. The second was published in 2012 and concentrated on who adopted this
form of insurrectionary politics and why, noting how it evolved
from 1821 to 1868. The third also appeared in 2012, highlighting
how pronunciamientos were celebrated and represented, in turn
showing how most Mexicans condemned the practice and yet
adopted it when they deemed it necessary.

Needless to say, I am extremely grateful to the Arts and Humanities Research Council. Without the AHRC's funding, this extraordinary project would never have taken place. Thanks are due to all the people who were involved in the project in some capacity, both directly and indirectly: the research fellows who worked on the database, the numerous academics, including my PhD students, who participated in the conferences held at St. Andrews and who generously discussed the project findings with me, either as part of the AHRC-funded events or outside them, as I tried out my ideas on countless patient scholarly audiences in Mexico, the United States, and Spain. In alphabetical order I hereby record my gratitude to Andrea Acle Aguirre, José Antonio Aguilar Rivera, Aquiles Alencar Brayner, Shara Ali, Catherine Andrews, Timothy Anna, Jaime del Arenal Fenochio, Linda Arnold, Bill Beezley, David Brading, Melissa Boyd, Matthew Brown, Zachary Brittson, Raymond Buve, Sergio Cañedo Gamboa, John Charles Chasteen, Hannah Clarke, Brian Connaughton, Christopher B. Conway, the late Michael P. Costeloe and his wife Eleanor, Manuel Chust, Catherine Davies, Sean Dooley, Rosie Doyle, Michael Ducey, Rebecca Earle, Francisco A. Eissa Barroso, Antonio Escobar Ohmstede, Eduardo Flores Clair, Josep M. Fradera, Ivana Frasquet, Paul Garner, Elspeth Gillespie, Andrew Ginger, Brian Hamnett, Mark Harris, Sam W. Haynes, Jesús Hernández Jaimes, Daniela Ibarra López, Jason Irwin, Alan Knight, Marco Antonio Landavazo, Iona MacIntyre, Erika Madrigal, Germán Martínez Martínez, Kerry McDonald, His Excellency Eduardo Medina Mora, Luis Medina Peña, Leonidas Kymon Megas, Humberto Morales Moreno, Rodrigo Moreno, Leticia Neria, K. Aaron Van Oosterhoot, Abdiel Oñate, Juan Ortiz Escamilla, Erika Pani, Gabriel Paquette, Francisco Parra, Natasha Picot, Antonia Pi-

Acknowledgments

Suñer Llorens, Eduardo Posada Carbó, Ana Romero Valderrama, Terry Rugeley, Flor de María Salazar Mendoza, Pedro Santoni, José Antonio Serrano Ortega, Alison Sinclair, Natalia Sobrevilla Perea, Reynaldo Sordo Cedeño, Miguel Soto, Brian Stauffer, Trevor Stack, Anne Staples, Marcela Terrazas, Guy Thomson, Deborah Toner, Andrew J. Torget, Eric Van Young, José Varela Ortega, Josefina Zoraida Vázquez, Richard Warren, and Verónica Zárate Toscano. I am also incredibly grateful to the two anonymous readers who peer reviewed the manuscript for the University of Nebraska Press and whose comments were most helpful, resulting in a punchy and far snappier final text.

As always I would like to thank my friends and colleagues in the Department of Spanish and the School of Modern Languages at the University of St. Andrews for their unwavering support and collegiality. Professor Louise Richardson, principal and vice-chancellor of the university, has been tremendously supportive and kindly launched the web-based "Pronunciamientos Database," accompanied by His Excellency the Mexican Ambassador Eduardo Medina Mora, in September 2010. My colleague and cartographer Graeme Sandeman swiftly prepared the maps of Mexico contained herein. Thanks are also due to Salvador Rueda Smithers and Hilda Sánchez at the Museo Nacional de Historia in Mexico City and the Instituto Nacional de Antropología e Historia for authorizing the use of the image *Plaza Mayor de la Ciudad de México* on the cover of the present volume. And I am indebted to the Tenorio family for their hospitality and warm friendship.

As ever, I must thank Bridget Barry and her first class editorial team at the University of Nebraska Press, in particular Sally E. Antrobus, Sabrina Ehmke Sergeant, and Joeth Zucco. It was a real pleasure to work with Nebraska on my *Santa Anna of Mexico* (2007), *Forceful Negotiations* (2010), *Malcontents, Rebels, and Pronunciados* (2012), and *Celebrating Insurrection* (2012). I am delighted that we continue to work together and that we do so in such a friendly fashion. I thank Bridget, in particular, for believing in this project, and for supporting the publication of the books it has generated.

Last but not least my gratitude extends to my family—to my wife, Caroline and our children, Tom, Edd, and Flo; to my parents, my late father, W. S. Fowler, and my mother Dr. Rosa María Laffitte Figueras, and to my parents-in-law, Peter and Susan Wilkes. They have all been incredibly patient and supportive over the years. And it is fitting that in completing the manuscript of this book in 2014, twenty-five years after Caroline and I married, I dedicate it to her.

Acknowledgments

Chronology of Main Events and Pronunciamientos, 1821–1858

1810–1821	WAR OF INDEPENDENCE

1821

24 February	Agustín de Iturbide launches the Plan of Iguala
24 August	Iturbide and Viceroy O'Donojú sign the Treaty of Córdoba
27 September	War ends with the Army of the Three Guarantees' march into Mexico City

1822–1823	FIRST EMPIRE

1822

19 May	Pronunciamiento is launched in Mexico City to crown Iturbide, who becomes Emperor Agustín I
26 August	Iturbide imprisons nineteen members of Congress
22 September	Pronunciamiento of Felipe de la Garza in Soto la Marina, Tamaulipas
31 October	Iturbide closes down Congress

2 December	Santa Anna launches Pronunciamiento of Veracruz, which inspires the follow-up Plan of Veracruz of 6 December and the Plan of Casa Mata of 1 February 1823

1823

1 February	Plan of Casa Mata
2 February	Santa Anna joins the Plan of Casa Mata
23 February	Federalist Plan of Jalisco
19 March	Iturbide abdicates and goes into exile in Europe

1823–1824	THE TRIUMVIRATE
	The Federal Constitution is drafted; triumvirate is made up initially of generals Guadalupe Victoria, Nicolás Bravo, and Pedro Celestino Negrete

1823

5 June	Santa Anna pronounces the federalist Plan of San Luis Potosí

1824

23 January	Anti-Spanish pronunciamiento of José María Lobato, Mexico City
19 July	Agustín de Iturbide is executed in Padilla, Tamaulipas, following his return from exile

1824–1835	FIRST FEDERAL REPUBLIC
1824–1829	Guadalupe Victoria, president

1827

19 January	Father Joaquín Arenas's pro-Spanish Conspiracy is uncovered and dismantled
10 May	First anti-Spanish Expulsion Laws
20 December	Second Expulsion Laws
23 December	Plan of Montaño is pronounced in Otumba; Vice President General Nicolás Bravo joins Montaño's *escocés*-pronunciados in Tulancingo

1828

7 January	Battle of Tulancingo; Bravo and *escoceses* are defeated
September	The moderate General Manuel Gómez Pedraza wins presidential elections
16 September	Santa Anna pronounces in Perote proclaiming Vicente Guerrero the rightful president; Plan of Perote is followed up by Santa Anna's Oaxacan-based pronunciamientos of 5 and 20 November
30 November	Revolt of La Acordada barracks in Mexico City results in unrest
4 December	Unrest escalates to Parián Market Riot
27 December	Manuel Gómez Pedraza escapes and goes into exile

1829 Vicente Guerrero, president

26 July	Isidro Barradas's expedition lands in Tampico to reconquer Mexico for Spain

11 September	Santa Anna defeats Barradas's expedition
6 November	Centralist pronunciamiento in Campeche; results, unwittingly, in Yucatán seceding from Mexico for two years
4 December	Pronunciamiento of Jalapa; which, followed by
23 December	Pronunciamiento of Mexico City garrison, results in
31 December	General Anastasio Bustamante taking over the national government in Mexico City; deposed President Guerrero leads War of the South against the government in present-day State of Guerrero
1830–1832	Anastasio Bustamante, president (also known as the Alamán Administration)

1831

14 February	Vicente Guerrero is executed; War of the South ends soon after

1832

2 January	Plan of Veracruz, calling for removal of centralist ministers
March–December	Civil War spreads across central Mexico
3 March	Battle of Tolome: government troops achieve initial victory against Santa Anna
27 April	Plan of Lerma
5 July	Pronunciamiento of Veracruz and San Juan de Ulúa

10 July	Plan of Zacatecas
14 July	Plan of Guadalajara
18 September	Battle of El Gallinero: government troops win again
29 September	Santa Anna wins battle of El Palmar
6 December	Battle of Rancho de Posadas
December	Convenios de Zavaleta bring an end to Bustamante's regime

1833

January	Manuel Gómez Pedraza, president (as agreed in Zavaleta, Gómez Pedraza returns to complete his interrupted term in office while elections are held)
1 April	Santa Anna elected president; however, he does not take up the post immediately, leaving Vice President: Valentín Gómez Farías in charge

1833–1834	Gómez Farías "Radical" Administration
26 May	Pronunciamiento de Morelia
1 June	Plan of Durán
8 June	Plan of Huejotzingo calling for an end to Congress's radical reforms and for Santa Anna to become dictator
June–October	Santa Anna dedicates himself to quelling pronunciamiento cycle of Escalada–Durán–Arista
November	Santa Anna returns to Mexico City but does not stay long and retires to Manga de Clavo

1834

25 May — Plan of Cuernavaca starts a series of pronunciamientos against the anti-clerical reforms of the Gómez Farías Administration; Santa Anna intervenes and annuls most of the reforms

1835

January — Gómez Farías is stripped of his vice-presidential office

1835–1836 — Santa Anna, president; however, due to his absence the presidency is taken by

28 January — Miguel Barragán, president

February — Federalists revolt in Zacatecas against the rise of the centralists

11 May — Santa Anna quells the revolt in the Battle of Guadalupe

19 May — Pronunciamiento of Orizaba calls for change to centralism

29 May — Pronunciamiento of Toluca does so as well

22 June — Revolt in Texas begins

23 October — The Federal Constitution is abolished and Mexico becomes a central republic

1835–1846 — THE FIRST CENTRAL REPUBLIC

1836

27 February — José Justo Corro, president (following Barragán's death)

6 March — Battle of the Alamo

21 April	Battle of San Jacinto (Santa Anna is taken prisoner the following day)
29 December	The Siete Leyes (the 1836 Constitution) adopted, consolidating a centralist political system and limiting the suffrage

1837–1841 Anastasio Bustamante, president

1837

February	Santa Anna returns from the United States in disgrace
April	Anastasio Bustamante, president (after winning elections)
14 April	Federalist pronunciamiento of San Luis Potosí
16 September	Pronunciamiento of Sonora
1 December	Federalist Pronunciamiento of Aguililla

1838

March	French fleet starts blockade of port of Veracruz
May	Santiago Imán revolt in Yucatán begins
27 November	French Pastry War begins with the bombardment of Veracruz
5 December	Santa Anna forces the French to retreat and loses one leg in battle

1839

April	José Antonio Mejía and José Urrea start federalist pronunciamiento in Tamaulipas
May–June	Santa Anna acts as interim president

3 May	Battle of Acajete; Santa Anna defeats pronunciados; Mejía is executed
29 May	Pronunciamiento of Tizimín, Yucatán

1840

14 February	Pronunciamiento of Mérida, resulting in temporary secession of Yucatán
15 July	Federalist pronunciamiento in the capital; Bustamante is taken prisoner in the National Palace but escapes
27 July	Revolt ends and Bustamante is restored to power

1841

August–October	Triangular Revolt (also called Revolución de Jalisco) overthrows Bustamante's regime with pronunciamientos of 8 August (Guadalajara), 4 September (the Ciudadela Barracks in Mexico City), and 9 September (Perote)
1841–1844	Santa Anna, president
October	Bases de Tacubaya approved: Santa Anna has "almost absolute power"
22 December	Pronunciamiento of Valladolid

1842

9 December	Pronunciamiento in San Luis Potosí demanding closure of Congress in rejection of draft 1842 Constitution

11 December	Pronunciamiento in Huejotizingo also demanding closure of Congress in rejection of draft 1842 Constitution
19 December	Congress is closed down
1843	
8 June	Bases Orgánicas adopted; ultimate *santanista* constitution is approved and sworn in on 13 June
1844	
2 November	Pronunciamiento of Guadalajara is launched by General Mariano Paredes y Arrillaga against Santa Anna
6 December	Revolt of Las Tres Horas overthrows Santa Anna's regime in the capital
1845	José Joaquín de Herrera, president
June	Santa Anna goes into exile to Cuba
7 June	Pronunciamiento of Guardia Nacional, Mexico City, results in short-lived capture of the National Palace with President Herrera in it
14 December	Pronunciamiento of General Mariano Paredes y Arrillaga in San Luis Potosí leads to fall of Herrera's government
23 December	Pronunciamiento of Veracruz
1846	Paredes y Arrillaga's dictatorship
April	War with the United States begins

4 August	Plan de la Ciudadela overthrows Paredes y Arrillaga and replaces the Centralist Republic with the restored Federal Republic; Santa Anna returns invited by the Federalists
5 August	Pronunciamiento of Toluca
August	José Mariano Salas, temporary president while elections are held
1846–1853	SECOND FEDERAL REPUBLIC
December	Santa Anna elected president; however, due to the War with the United States, Valentín Gómez Farías acts as president again

1847

February	Pronunciamientos of Los Polkos against Gómez Farías and anti-clerical measures
23 February	Battle of Angostura–Buena Vista
9 March	General Winfield Scott arrives in Veracruz
21 March	Santa Anna ends Gómez Farías's administration again
18 April	Battle of Cerro Gordo
July	Caste War begins in Yucatán
11 August–15 September	Campaign of the Valley of Mexico
August	Sierra Gorda peasant rebellion begins
14 September	Government leaves Mexico City to become established in Querétaro

15 September	U.S. Army takes Mexico City
September	Manuel de la Peña y Peña, president, forms new government

1848

2 February	Treaty of Guadalupe Hidalgo grants half of Mexico's national territory to the United States

1848–1851	José Joaquín de Herrera, president
4 June	Pronunciamiento of Tomás Mejía
15 June	Pronunciamiento of Mariano Paredes y Arrillaga

1849

11 February	Pronunciamiento of Leonardo Márquez
14 March	Pronunciamiento of Eleuterio Quiroz
1851–1853	Mariano Arista, president

1852

26 July	Plan of Blancarte
13 September	Second Plan of Blancarte
20 October	Plan del Hospicio

1853

January–February	Arista resigns and is replaced as president by Juan Bautista Ceballos, who also resigns in favor of
February	Manuel María Lombardini, president
April	Santa Anna returns from exile and is proclaimed dictator

1853–1855	SANTA ANNA'S DICTATORSHIP

1854

| 1 March | Revolution of Ayutla begins |
| 11 March | Plan of Acapulco |

1855

| 8 August | Santa Anna's last regime falls |

1855–1876	REFORM PERIOD
4 October	Juan Álvarez, president
22 November	Ley Juárez

| 1855–1858 | Ignacio Comonfort, president |

1856

January	Six-day siege of Puebla
February–March	Siege of Puebla
11 April	Ley Iglesias
25 June	Ley Lerdo
October–December	Third siege of Puebla

1857

| 5 February | Federal Constitution published |
| 17 December | Coup d'etat of Tacubaya |

1858

| 11 January | Pronunciamiento in Mexico City Félix Zuloaga, president of Rebel Conservative Government (Mexico City) |

| 1858–1860 | CIVIL WAR OF THE REFORMA |

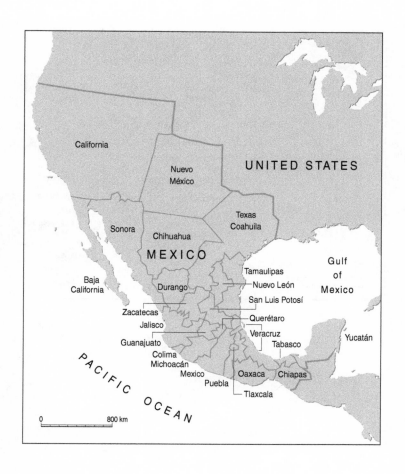

1. Mexico in 1824. Map by Graeme Sandeman.

2. Central Mexico. Map by Graeme Sandeman.

1. "Soft" Coups, Occupations, and "Gestures of Rebellion"

The Pronunciamiento, Past and Present Interpretations

On 23 February 1981, at 6:22 in the early evening, Guardia Civil Lieutenant Colonel Antonio Tejero Molina stormed into the Spanish parliament at the head of his paramilitary forces. His men fired several rounds of ammunition over the heads of the assembled politicians while he ordered them to remain still, waved a gun in the air, and shouted at them to "sit down, damn it" ("*¡Se sienten, coño!*"). With the exception of the outgoing prime minister Adolfo Suárez, the sixty-nine-year-old minister of defense General Manuel Gutiérrez Mellado, and the chain-smoking leader of the Spanish Communist Party, Santiago Carrillo, the more than three hundred politicians, gathered that day to vote over Leopoldo Calvo Sotelo's prime ministerial accession, flung themselves to the floor.[1] With the television cameras still rolling, Spain would subsequently get to see the first thirty minutes of what became the only coup to be staged in Spain following its transition to democracy after dictator General Francisco Franco died in 1975. This would entail witnessing such outrageous scenes as that of the strutting mustachioed Tejero actually trying, but failing, to wrestle the aging lanky minister of defense to the ground.[2] And while Tejero held Spain's entire political class hostage in Madrid, General Jaime Milans del Bosch ordered the tank division Maestrazgo Num. 3, stationed in Valencia, to roll out into the streets, to intimidate the civilian population into accepting the outcome of the coup.

I was fourteen years old at the time, living in Barcelona. I found out about the coup in the dressing rooms of the sports center where I used to go, just as I came out of my Monday Tae Kwon Do lesson. I remember running back home to tell my parents, who refused to believe me until they switched on the radio and discovered, much to their horror, that the national radio station in Prado del Rey was playing only military marches, having been occupied by troops from the Saboya Regiment. My father went down to the nearby *colmado* (corner shop) and stocked up on basics, "just in case,"—bread, milk, cigarettes—and as we sat down to dinner in the kitchen, with my parents barely touching their food, I listened to them discuss the possibility of our heading to Perpignan and leaving Spain the next day. We feared, as most people did on that long winter night, that Spain was about to experience the kind of brutal repression countries to which Chile, Argentina, and Uruguay had been subjected since the early to mid-seventies when likeminded army officers had overthrown the existing governments by force.

On paper, Tejero's assault and capture of the Spanish Cortes in 1981 was intended as a straightforward coup d'état. As I have argued elsewhere, a coup d'état aims to overthrow the government without involving the population at large.[3] It is typically carried out by members of the armed sector of the state against its own state's leadership. The successful coup is that which in one fell swoop takes out the government or certain individuals within the government by assaulting the National Palace and arresting, exiling, or killing the incumbent president and cabinet. As Eric Carlton has pointed out, it is "a high-risk, low-cost

"Soft" Coups, Occupations, "Gestures of Rebellion"

strategy" that does not require the "mobilization of large forces" and does not rely on "the uncertainties of recruitment and continued popular support."[4] Textbook coups d'état could include the military action in Chile of 11 September 1973 and, more recently, that in Honduras of 28 June 2009. In Chile a junta made up of four generals, including Augusto Pinochet, overthrew Salvador Allende's elected socialist government by bombarding the Palacio de la Moneda and using mass executions, torture, and disappearances to quell any voices of dissent. In Honduras the forces led by Lieutenant Colonel René Antonio Hepburn Bueso broke into the residence of the elected president, Manuel Zelaya, escorted him onto a plane, and flew him out of the country, still in his pajamas, resulting in Roberto Micheletti becoming the de facto acting president of Honduras. In neither case was there an attempt to negotiate with the government or members within it. In neither case did the perpetrators of the coup seek to gain the support of the broader community before acting. Each was a clear-cut *golpe de estado*.[5] Members of the army simply used their military might to topple the government and replace it with one that was more to their liking.[6]

That it was Tejero's plan to carry out a similar swift and effective coup is unquestionable. According to Spanish novelist Javier Cercas, the *franquista* hardliner Tejero "aimed to bring an end to democracy, even at the cost of ending the monarchy."[7] Having said this, a closer look at the events building up to 23 February 1981 and the intentions of the other high-ranking officers who orchestrated the assault on Congress, namely Milans del Bosch and General Alfonso Armada, shows that the military action of that day could be considered, from a certain angle, as a modern day *pronunciamiento*. In Cercas's mind there were two different coups unfolding at the same time: that perpetrated by Tejero in the Spanish parliament and the one the main instigators of the movement were hoping to bring about behind the scenes. To use Cercas's definition, Tejero's was a *"golpe duro,"* a hard coup, while that of the other *golpistas* was a *"golpe blando,"* a soft coup. For them it was meant to be "a bloodless coup in which the threat alone of deploying their weapons would suffice to make the King, the political class and the Spanish people accept the golpistas' demands."[8]

For Armada, in particular, the hope was that in the context of the severe political and economic crisis in which Spain was immersed at the time, their "soft" coup would result in King Juan Carlos, as head of state, listening to and acting upon their demands by removing Adolfo Suárez from power—putting on hold the 1978 Constitution with its decentralizing "Estado de las Autonomías" (a federal state of sorts with autonomous regional governments, which grated with the golpistas' nostalgia for Franco's centralist values)—and would abolish all political parties and replace the current government with an emergency one of national unity with Armada at its head, awarding the army the power to crush the Basque terrorist group ETA effectively by whatever means. Both the Manifesto Tejero read out over the phone, to be inserted in the right-wing newspaper *El Alcázar* the following day, and Milans del Bosch's edict of 23 February 1981 ended with them professing their obedience and loyalty to the king.[9] Had the soft coup unfolded as Armada intended, other commander generals and garrisons across Spain would have followed in Milans del Bosch's steps, ordered their troops onto the streets, and issued copycat statements of support and allegiance. The king would have realized that Armada's demands had the

"Soft" Coups, Occupations, "Gestures of Rebellion"

best interests of Spain at heart as well as the backing of the army and, in complying with them, would have avoided a bloodbath. Had Armada's coup been successful, like a pronunciamiento, it would have resulted in a forcefully negotiated change of government while retaining King Juan Carlos as Spanish head of state.

As it happens, King Juan Carlos had other ideas. After forces loyal to him regained control of the Spanish radio and television studios at Prado del Rey, the king addressed the nation at 1:14 a.m. on February 24, stating in unequivocal terms: "The Crown, symbol of the permanence and unity of the Patria, cannot tolerate, in any form, the actions and behavior of people who intend to interrupt by force the democratic process that was put in place by the Constitution the Spanish people voted for."[10] Following the king's intervention, my parents and I stayed glued to our television during the early hours of the 24th, waiting for news, incongruously watching Bob Hope and Bing Crosby in *The Princess and the Pirate* (1944) dubbed in Spanish. As time went by it became obvious to Armada, Tejero, Milans del Bosch, and the other officers who joined the attempted coup that theirs was a lost cause and that they had little choice but to turn themselves in, which they did by midmorning.

The reason I have started a book on pronunciamientos in nineteenth-century Mexico by discussing the failed Spanish golpe of 23 February 1981 is because by adopting Cercas's notion of a soft coup, it is possible to begin to clarify what is meant here by a pronunciamiento. This is important given that common wisdom would still have us believe a pronunciamiento was nothing other than, to quote a popular source such as *Wikipedia*, "a form of military rebellion or coup d'état peculiar to Spain and the Spanish American republics, particularly in the 19th century."[11]

The pronunciamientos of Independent Mexico, with some notable exceptions in the 1840s, were *not* coups d'état; or if they were,
they were precisely that: soft coups d'état. They were meant to
be bloodless, and they were meant to negotiate political change
forcefully, by use of threats and intimidation but without necessarily overthrowing the entire government or the head of state. In
this sense a pronunciamiento was a "gesture of rebellion," to quote
Miguel Alonso Baquer, whereby a garrison declared its insubordination to the government and threatened to use violence if the
authorities did not attend to its grievances; town councils and state
legislatures also made such declarations against national and/or
regional government.[12] Unlike a "hard" coup d'état, the pronunciamiento relied heavily on receiving *pronunciamientos de adhesión*: copycat pronunciamientos of allegiance from other garrisons
and communities. In publicly coming out in support of the original "gesture of rebellion" by defiantly occupying their respective
villages, municipalities, or cities and refusing to obey the authorities until their own demands were heard, the other communities
gave force and legitimacy to the original pronunciados' demands.

It is because of this that at another level—in terms of the
dynamic of most nineteenth-century pronunciamiento cycles
in Mexico, especially once the practice was adopted by civilians and a whole range of subaltern groups in the 1830s—these
soft coups d'état also shared a great deal in common with the
cycles of protests that spread from town to town in 2011 as part
of the so-called Arab Spring and Spain's 15 May *indignado* movement.[13] Also similar were the U.S. "Occupy" Wall Street protests
that broke out in New York, Chicago, Boston, Memphis, New
Orleans, Las Vegas, Philadelphia, Austin, Louisville, Atlanta,
and seventy other cities.[14] The dynamic was the same, whether it

was to bring an end in Tunisia to President Zine al-Abidine Ben Ali's twenty-three-year dictatorial government through a constellation of simultaneous peaceful protests in Sidi Bouzid, Menzel Bouzaiene, al-Ragab, Miknassi, Kairouan, Sfax, Ben Guerdane, Tunis, Sousse, Monastir, Chebba, Thala, Kasserine, and Regeb, or to force the Spanish government to reform a whole range of laws through the peaceful occupation—*acampadas*—of the main squares of seventy-three Spanish cities, from A Coruña to Zaragoza. Peaceful acts of defiance and insubordination that started in one town were soon seconded in others, until in the case of Tunisia and later Egypt, it became impossible for the authorities to ignore the protestors' demands or their claim to represent the will of their aggrieved nations.[15]

As would be the case with those nineteenth-century pronunciamiento cycles that succeeded in Mexico, the success of Tunisia and Egypt's constellations of protests and town square occupations relied on the governments' weakness and the willingness on the part of key military officers within them to back the protestors' (or pronunciados') demands. Events in Libya, Syria, and Bahrain would take a very different course: their respective governments—and in particular their armed forces—did not shy away from opening fire on the protestors repeatedly, resulting either in the outbreak of civil war, as in Libya and Syria, or in the government staying in place at the time of writing, as with Sheikh Salman bin Hamad bin Isa al-Khalifa in Bahrain.

In other words, the dynamic of the Mexican pronunciamiento cycle was one in which after the initial *grito* (cry) was launched there was the hope and expectation, on the part of the pronunciados, that other communities (garrisons and town councils) would second their demands (circulated in a signed petition or plan) with copycat pronunciamientos of allegiance. The idea was that should there be a significant number of these statements of adherence (*actas de adhesión*), the government would see the sense of listening to the "pronounced ones" and would back down on, retract, or change its unpopular policies, ministers, congress, and/ or constitution. In the same way that the Occupy movements that spread across the world in 2011 claimed to represent the voice of the aggrieved majority—"We are the 99 percent"—the constellations of pronunciamientos de adhesión that mushroomed around Mexico's nineteenth-century original gritos were meant to prove, in themselves and because of their abundance, that the pronunciados' demands actually reflected the legitimate voice of an ignored general, national, and/or popular will.

Comparing the Mexican pronunciamiento to Armada's intended soft coup of 1981 and the waves of protests that spread across the world thirty years later against "corporate greed and financial mismanagement" in different forms should serve to highlight the complex nature of this nineteenth-century insurrectionary practice. It denotes how misleading it is to categorize the pronunciamiento as little other than a "coup d'état peculiar to Spain and the Spanish American republics." It is also a way of drawing attention to the relevance of studying how and why Mexicans adopted this particular practice to effect meaningful political change. Although the circumstances have changed, and today's "pronunciados" use information technology and social networking websites to communicate their grievances and organize their "gestures of rebellion," it remains the case that people, past and present, have been drawn to employing extra-constitutional means when all other legal avenues have been exhausted. Studying the Mexican pronunciamiento allows us, first and foremost, to understand the country's political culture following the consummation of independence in 1821, but it also offers us the chance to reflect more broadly on how, when, and why people rebel—sometimes violently, yet peacefully at other times.

As can be gathered already, a practice that shares similarities with such ostensibly different actions as a military-led soft coup and the coordinated popular protests of 2011 has proven difficult to define to date. Historian Michael P. Costeloe admitted as much in one of the earlier studies to engage with the subject of the nineteenth-century Mexican pronunciamiento:

> The *pronunciamiento* in early nineteenth century Mexico is difficult to define for practical purposes of analysis. Variable in size, objective, cause and effect, it became an established and recognized means of seeking change. Often but not always accompanied by the threatened use of military force, it was used by leading politicians of all parties to demand change at the national political level but it also provided the opportunity for ambitious military officers to achieve promotion, dissatisfied merchants to obtain the repeal of laws, the poor to augment their income with loot, and bandits to legitimize their trade.[16]

From the perspective of the nineteenth century it is clear that the term *pronunciamiento* was applied to a wide array of insurrectionary activities. They ranged from soft coups d'état, such as the military action in Mexico City of 19 May 1822, to peaceful declarations of principles, such as the Acta (de adhesión) of Tlalmanalco of 6 June 1834, to note but two very different examples of how the word was used at the time.[17] The coup of 19 May 1822 resulted in liberator Agustín de Iturbide becoming Emperor Agustín I, in defiance of article 4 of the Plan of Iguala (24 February 1821).[18] It likewise contravened article 3 of the Treaty of Córdoba (24 August 1821).[19] Both had conditioned the independence of Mexico from Spain by noting that either Ferdinand VII or a Bourbon prince would sit on the Mexican throne; for the perpetrators their action was, by the officers' own confession, a "*pronunciamiento* that was followed by the most lively demonstrations of joy and enthusiasm on the part of the people of this capital, who are gathered still in its streets."[20] In contrast, the strictly civilian Acta of Tlalmanalco of 6 June 1834 detailed how the town council, parish priest, and "honorable neighbors of this municipality" gathered together and reached the decision of offering their support and allegiance to the Plan of Cuernavaca of 25 May 1834 with their "effective cooperation" (since they had no garrison in the vicinity to back the movement with armed force).[21] The appointed minute-taking secretary in Cuernavaca, Tomás Pliego, was perfectly happy to define their public statement of allegiance as a "*pronunciamiento* which was applauded by everybody present at our multitudinous meeting with repeated calls of: Long live our Christian religion! Long live the Constitution! And long live the Excelente Señor Presidente."[22] One way or another, although Mexicans described different kinds of insurrectionary activity as pronunciamientos, there was a general understanding of what they broadly entailed and what they were meant to achieve, namely: political change at a regional and/or national level by forcing the authorities to bow down and comply with the pronunciados' demands following the concerted orchestration of numerous simultaneous acts of insubordination, which, accompanied by the circulation of petitions outlining the grievances that needed to be addressed, employed intimidating tactics to get their point across (i.e., the threat of violence—"you do as we say or else").

"Soft" Coups, Occupations, "Gestures of Rebellion"

Having said this, there were different types of pronunciamientos, depending on what they specifically set out to achieve. For the sake of categorization there were what I call start-up pronunciamientos—that is, those initiating the expected pronunciamiento cycle with their initial grito—including the *Acta* recording how it had come to pass that the pronunciados had chosen to pronounce, and the petition-like Plan setting out their demands and threats. These were the parent pronunciamientos that started up a given pronunciamiento constellation, such as the *impulso* de Veracruz of 2 January 1832, which condemned the government's centralist ministers and called for their resignation.

There were then pronunciamientos or actas de adhesión that came out in support of the original pronunciamientos. These could be either reactive or reactive-cum-proactive. By reactive pronunciamientos de adhesión I mean one of two kinds. Some limited themselves to cut and paste the original pronunciamiento's demands and threats (such as the Acta of the Veracruz garrison and fortress of San Juan de Ulúa of 12 January 1832, which copied and pasted the four articles, word for word, that had figured in the start-up Plan of Veracruz).[23] Others stated that they backed the original in its entirety without bothering to repeat the articles from its plan (such as the Acta of the Alvarado garrison of 6 January, which limited itself to stating that its men fully backed the Plan of Veracruz).[24]

By reactive-cum-proactive pronunciamientos de adhesión I mean, in contrast, those that reiterated all or a selection of the original pronunciamiento's demands and threats and then included new additional demands. Depending on the nature of the additions or corrections made to the original pronunciamiento, the reactive-cum-proactive pronunciamiento de adhesión could alter the course of a given pronunciamiento cycle at a national level. For instance, the Plan of Lerma of 27 April 1832 backed the Plan of Veracruz as long as the constitutional government that had been overthrown in 1828 was restored.[25] It would be as a result of the Plan of Lerma that what started as a pronunciamiento calling for certain centralist-sympathizing ministers to step down became a more general movement to overthrow Anastasio Bustamante's government and bring back exiled president Manuel Gómez Pedraza.[26]

Moreover, quite often the reactive-cum-proactive pronunciamiento de adhesión became an original start-up pronunciamiento of sorts at a regional level. It became common, in provincial Mexico, for garrisons, town councils, and state legislatures or departmental juntas to use the upheaval provoked by a given pronunciamiento cycle from elsewhere in the republic to address different yet very concrete local concerns. In Acapulco, in the present-day state of Guerrero, the forces stationed in the fortress of San Diego pronounced on 11 August 1832 in favor of the Plan of Veracruz *and* added an article that called upon Juan Álvarez to become commander-in-chief of the region.[27] Such proactive pronunciamientos de adhesión were then capable of inspiring their own separate constellation of reactive pronunciamientos de adhesión within their given state or province. In the case of the Plan of the fortress of San Diego it inspired the garrison of Acapulco to pronounce on the following day to offer their support and allegiance to the 2 January 1832 pronunciamiento of Veracruz on behalf of the South of Mexico, *and* to proclaim Juan Álvarez commander-in-chief of the forces of the region. Recent research carried out by Shara Ali, Rosie Doyle, and Kerry McDonald, centered on reactive-cum-proactive pronunciamientos de adhesión in Yucatán, Jalisco, and San Luis Potosí, has demonstrated, in fact, that most acts of allegiance or defiance launched in response to national pronunciamientos were, essentially, focused on addressing strictly local concerns. From a regional perspective, the reactive-cum-proactive pronunciamiento de adhesión therefore had a tendency to hijack pronunciamientos from elsewhere to reorder the local political scene.[28]

Of course, not everybody felt compelled into supporting a pronunciamiento cycle, and as a result there were also counter-pronunciamientos or *pronunciamientos de rechazo* whereby a garrison or community publicly pronounced in favor of the government and against a given pronunciamiento wave. The Plan of Veracruz of 1832 provoked a significant cluster of pronunciamientos de rechazo in the states of Mexico, Guerrero, and Michoacán from January through to March as General Francisco Hernández went from village to village at the head of a military squadron seeking to ensure the region remained loyal to the government.[29]

Beyond these types of pronunciamientos, there were also follow-up pronunciamientos in which a community that had already pronounced did so again, in order to modify, improve, or edit their original demands in response to how the national and/or regional authorities as well as other pronunciamientos and counter-pronunciamientos had reacted to their original forceful petition. In the case of the 1832 series, Santa Anna and his supporters, most notably Ciriaco Vázquez, ended up adopting the proposal to bring back the overthrown 1828 administration, made in the Plan of Lerma of 27 April, in their follow-up pronunciamiento of the garrison of Veracruz and fortress of San Juan de Ulúa of 5 July.[30]

Last but not least, there were *despronunciamientos*, i.e. pronunciamientos in which a given community publicly repented from having previously pronounced, claiming, more often than not, that they had been coerced into pronouncing in the first place, as was the case with the despronunciamiento of Tancahuitz of 1 June 1832, in which the pronunciados publicly repented for having pronounced in favor of the Plan of Veracruz on 8 April.[31]

The pronunciamiento's potential for violence (absent in a straightforward petition), paired with the fact that it was extra-constitutional and unlawful (pronunciados did not wait until the next round of elections to vote out whoever it was they opposed) explain why most Mexicans were, at best, ambivalent about the practice and, at worst, highly critical of it. As early as 1830, not yet ten years since the pronunciamiento of Iguala had resulted in independence, repentant *escocés* pronunciado General Miguel Barragán, conveniently forgetting that he had backed the Iguala movement as well as a conspiracy to overthrow Iturbide in 1822, and the Plan of Montaño of 23 December 1827, described the pronunciamiento as a "system," and distanced himself from engaging in such unlawful activity: "I am far from making the mistake of endorsing the pronunciamiento system." Of interest to us here is that he was at pains to show that the "respectful petition" he circulated from San Pedro, in his home province of San Luis Potosí, on 17 November was *not* a pronunciamiento. As he explained, his petition did not challenge the government, it did not use intimidating politics, it did not call for an act of insubordination, and nor did it make any threats of rebellion. Moreover, it was not supported by a given garrison or division (i.e., it was a personal initiative). And it did not aim to have a legislative or executive quality (i.e., it did not forcefully propose a change in the law; it simply made a proposal for discussion and consideration).[32] Evidently what set a pronunciamiento apart from a petition or representation was precisely its threat of violence. This would be one of the main problems with the practice from the perspective of most of its critics. As was minuted in the Acta del Ayuntamiento de San Juan Bautista (present-day Villahermosa) of 1 February 1832, the town council condemned the Plan of Veracruz of 2 January 1832 and all pronunciamientos because they undermined the authority of the law as well as the republic's prestige. In the view of these *tabasqueño* town councilors a petition made with a gun in one hand could never be considered legal, since that would threaten the rule of law and public peace.[33]

Needless to say, the repeated waves of pronunciamientos that spread across Mexico from 1821 to 1858 made governance particularly difficult, preventing any of the constitutions that were drafted in 1824, 1836, 1842, and 1843 from lasting long enough to establish resilient roots. In the case of the 1842 Constitution the pronunciamiento cycle of San Luis Potosí and Huejotzingo of 9 and 11 December 1842 actually prevented it from even being implemented. As a result, for many Mexicans pronunciamientos became indicative of the country's backwardness, proof that they were unable to govern themselves, the most obvious expression of the young republic's chronic political turmoil and unrest, both a cause *and* an effect of endemic instability. According to a reasoned critique of the pronunciamiento practice that was published in the *Diario del Gobierno* on 17 October 1838, despite the pronunciados' customary rhetorical flourishes about wanting to instigate what was best for the nation, all that pronunciados were really after was plunder:

> We all know about the need to justify the motives that excuse or legalize such a reprehensible action, especially when it results in killings, abuses, and the kind of political disturbances that undermine the

establishment, and which occur whenever there is an armed insurrection. The authors of our pronunciamientos have conveniently gone on believing that they are authorized to do what they please as long as they have the forceful arguments to justify their hostile attitude towards the sovereign [government], attracting in so doing the support of the ignorant classes by tricking them. . . . If, among the authors of our republic's many pronunciamientos, just one had been genuinely convinced of the justice of his cause, he would have demonstrated this without doubt by not disregarding the possibility of making a rational representation [to the government] rather than rely time and again on the support of the bayonets.[34]

Most nineteenth-century foreign travelers would concur with this interpretation, depicting the pronunciamiento in equally negative terms.[35] As would be noted somewhat bluntly by U.S. Consul General David Hunter Strother (aka Porte Crayon), writing at a time when pronunciamientos had all but vanished from the political scene, these were "nothing more than schemes for plunder and power."[36] The actual term *pronunciamiento* would go on to figure in European novels such as Marcel Proust's *Remembrance of Things Past* (1913–1927) as representative of Latin America's political chaos and barbarism. Proust has his character M. de Norpois tell Bloch in book three, *The Guermantes Way* (1920): "Heaven be praised, France is not a South American Republic, and the need has not yet been felt for a military pronunciamiento."[37]

And yet, as was recently argued by Melissa Boyd after studying the way a selection of leading Mexican intellectuals and politicians viewed the pronunciamiento at the time, they may very well have been "unanimous in their condemnation of pronunciamientos, but [. . .], when it suited their purpose or benefited

"Soft" Coups, Occupations, "Gestures of Rebellion"

them, they were quite happy to look the other way and even to instigate the actions."[38] The ambivalence Mexicans felt toward the practice stemmed from the fact that pronunciamientos could ultimately result in positive outcomes (e.g., independence in 1821, restoration of constitutional order, the end of the abuses of a given despotic government). There was also the painful reality that initially and during much of the early national period, Mexico's political institutions—new, poorly funded, and with officials lacking in experience—were incapable of inspiring the respect and obedience and authority mustered among the population by other government branches that had been in place for decades, such as an elected executive, legislature, and judiciary. Unlike the Chilean coup of 1973, which came as a complete shock at least to some, considering Chile's long democratic tradition— (novelist Isabel Allende, in an attempt to help Britons and Americans grasp what the experience was like, stated that it was as if "the army rolled up in full battle gear to attack the White House or Buckingham Palace, and in the process caused the deaths of thousands of citizens")—the Mexican pronunciamiento surfaced at a time of contested legitimacies and uncertain political processes on the back of an eleven-year civil war that had politicized the army and militarized society.[39] Just because a group of *criollo* politicians in Mexico City decided the independent country would be governed as a monarchy with Agustín I at its head in 1822, as a Triumvirate in 1823, and as a Federal Republic in 1824, this did not mean that in remote Yucatán or in the Sierra Gorda, for the sake of argument, people ceased to obey those men who had established themselves over time as the "natural" leaders of their given communities.[40] At independence and for many years to come the real wielders of power at a local level, simply because there was continuity to their presence, were local *caciques*; constituted authorities such as the *ayuntamientos* (town councils) that still lingered in some form or other, having come and gone in 1812–14 and 1820–21 when the 1812 Cádiz Constitution was in place; self-proclaimed *jefes políticos* or warlords who had come to prominence during the War of Independence; the odd charismatic parish priest; or the main patriarchal *hacendados* or landowners of the area.[41] To quote Karen D. Caplan, "All in all, continuity in local administrations outweighed change."[42] As long as Mexico's new and often temporary authorities were improvising, experimenting, and inventing new political systems as they sought to forge workable bureaucratic processes that the population at large could recognize as legitimate and deserving of their obedience, most people found themselves understandably listening to their local bigwigs much as they had done before and during the Mexican War of Independence while royalists and insurgents had gained or lost control of given towns and villages as the conflict raged on over a period of eleven long years. During the War of Independence the people of Nueva Galicia (subsequently Jalisco) took their orders not from central authority but from Brigadier José de la Cruz.[43] In the same way the people of Nuevo Santander and the Provincias Internas de Oriente (subsequently Tamaulipas and Nuevo León) obeyed Antonio López de Santa Anna's forceful mentor, General Joaquín de Arredondo.[44] Regardless of whoever was the viceroy of New Spain, the issue of who really held power at a local level once the country's independence was consummated remained a thorny issue and one that was not resolved overnight. There may well have been a document in Mexico City that a constituent congress had spent many a sleepless night agonizing over before it had been formally proclaimed as the republic's constitution, but there was no guarantee that it would be implemented consistently across the country. How could it possibly be understood and applied in the same way in each and every province? Why would people necessarily accept it as their legitimate charter when other upstarts had previously claimed to have designed the nation's constitution, only to discover several years later that after several pronunciamiento cycles, they had been forced to tear it up since it did not reflect Mexico's customs and traditions?

For those who reluctantly came out in support of pronunciamientos (which, in truth, was almost everybody who was somebody at one stage or another), this was done as a last resort, because, it was alleged, they had no other alternative. But it was done also with a sense of patriotism and revolutionary pride. As was explained in an editorial of *El Aguila Mexicana* on 9 September 1828, before the Perote–Oaxaca–La Acordada cycle of pronunciamientos broke out, resulting in Manuel Gómez Pedraza's self-imposed exile and his presidential electoral victory being disallowed:

> The greatest tragedy for a nation is when its elections produce such mistaken results that it falls upon unworthy men to fill the [government] posts the people have granted them. When such a calamity happens, it is important that we resign ourselves to waiting until their constitutional term in office comes to an end. However, should the patria become endangered because these empowered men are addicted to the scandalous and treacherous conduct of our former oppressors, and are obstinate in pursuing a path that is exclusively centered on revenge, ignoring public opinion, . . . then yes, the people have an unquestionable right to remove them without delay from posts they are not worthy of occupying any longer.[45]

Thus those who endorsed the practice would do so because, to quote serial pronunciado Santa Anna, "When people realize they are oppressed: when their most treasured desires are focused exclusively on preserving their adored freedom, and when their most just outcries have been completely ignored . . . they have no other choice but to make use of their sacred right of insurrection."[46] As a Yucatecan newspaper would admit, as early as 1832, "Each country is governed more by customs than by laws: and so it is that for us pronunciamientos and gritos are becoming our fundamental law."[47]

It is important to remember as well that while the potential for violence cannot be ignored, few pronunciamientos actually degenerated into civil wars or significant fighting.[48] The more than 1,500 pronunciamientos launched between 1821 and 1876 were in reality comparatively peaceful, with the exception of the sanguinary civil wars of 1832, 1854–55, and 1858–60 (and not including international conflicts, such as the 1829 Barradas Expedition, 1835–36 Texan Revolution, 1838 French Pastry War, 1846–48 Mexican-U.S. War, the French Intervention of 1862–67, or caste wars like the one that spread across Yucatán in 1847–52).[49] The nineteenth-century Spanish writer Benito Pérez Galdós humorously depicted the pronunciamiento as one of Spain's most successful exports.[50] In his novel *Fortunata and Jacinta* (1887) his character Pepe Izquierdo is mocked for describing the 1789 French Revolution as a "pronunciamiento," precisely because a pronunciamiento was not understood as a violent revolution.[51] Rather, to quote Scottish eyewitness Fanny Calderón de la Barca, a pronunciamiento was more like "a game at chess, in which kings, castles, knights, and bishops are making different moves, while the pawns are looking on or taking no part whatever."[52]

Until recently the pronunciamiento was a phenomenon that had received scant attention in the historiography. While several groundbreaking works have been dedicated to agrarian violence, rural riots, and revolts for this period, the pronunciamiento in comparison has been overlooked as a separate political practice with its own particular dynamic and set of objectives.[53] Caught up in what Timothy E. Anna defined as the "chaos school of history," pronunciamientos were thrown in with rebellions, coups, and revolutions.[54] They were part of a guiding narrative that, in Edmundo O'Gorman's words, presented the period as:

> a spectacle of unspeakable sadness: . . . a rosary of pronunciamientos and golpes de Estado which seem to demonstrate nothing more than the congenital incapacity of our people to govern themselves and to establish the basis of a civilized life together. That, in effect, has been and continues to be an interpretation much touted as true by foreign historiographers and one that finds adherents even today among our resentful and less intelligent reactionaries.[55]

Research on the pronunciamiento in Spain, while not substantial, preceded that on its Mexican counterpart, with the publication of four key volumes by José Luis Comellas, Stanley Payne, Julio Busquets, and Miguel Alonso Baquer.[56] Comellas focused mainly on the 1814–20 period, the years under Ferdinand VII when the pronunciamiento first came into being, analyzing the failed attempts of Francisco Espoz y Mina (1814), Juan Díaz Porlier (1815), Vicente Richart (1816), Luis de Lacy (1817), and Joaquín Vidal (1819) that paved the way for Rafael del Riego's first successful and explicitly self-termed pronunciamiento (1820). Comellas argued that it was an exclusively nineteenth-century Spanish military practice, which originated in Masonic lodges where liberal officers—most of whom had been veterans of the Peninsular War (1808–1813) and had become disgruntled by the way the regime had failed to reward them with promotions—conspired against Ferdinand VII's absolutist reign following his abolition of the 1812 Cádiz Constitution. Worthy of note was Comellas's view that for nineteenth-century Spaniards, pronunciamientos became the expression of an essentially liberal political project.[57] The project was shared by a supposed majority of "sensible men" (in reality a restless minority) who felt compelled to rebel in the face of what was consistently depicted as an "unbearable, dishonorable tyranny."[58]

Payne took a broader look, reaching the beginning of the Spanish Civil War in 1936. Although his study was not specifically about the pronunciamiento practice, in focusing on the liberal politics of the Spanish Army and its political participation in the long nineteenth century, Payne inevitably engaged with the topic and came up with the idea that the period spanning from 1814 to 1868 deserved the title of "the era of the pronunciamientos" because of their frequency. As for the pronunciamiento itself, for Payne it was ordinarily "a revolt by one section of the Army—sometimes a very small section—which raised the flag of rebellion in its district and hoped that its example would lead other units to rally around, or would at least break the government's nerve."[59]

Both Busquets and Baquer, interestingly, wrote their books in the wake of the 23 February 1981 coup discussed at the beginning of this chapter and made reference to it in their studies. Busquets, like Payne, took the long view, with his work reaching as far as 1981, and focused entirely on the pronunciamiento/coup phenomenon. For Busquets, though, the term *pronunciamiento* was little other than a euphemism: "[adopted] so as not to employ

    "Soft" Coups, Occupations, "Gestures of Rebellion"

another term, which is rude [*malsonante*] and denotes a criminal act: rebellion."[60] As a result, his study did not necessarily distinguish between a golpe and a pronunciamiento, and resulted in his somewhat misleadingly including in his list of the eleven successful Spanish pronunciamientos of all time (1814–1936) such different military actions as Riego's pronunciamiento of 1 January 1820 and Franco's *levantamiento* of 18 July 1936.[61]

Of these four precursor authors it was Baquer who provided the most nuanced interpretation of the Spanish pronunciamiento. In his seminal 1983 study Baquer highlighted a number of characteristics of what he termed the pronunciamiento "model," which subsequently informed much of this project's initial view on the subject. As noted earlier, Baquer coined the idea of a pronunciamiento being "a gesture of rebellion" and defined the practice as "an act of rebellion on the part of professional commanders, that is endorsed by political groups who are convinced that the officers' gesture of rebellion, in counting with the support of public opinion, will result in social peace and political reform without risk or damage."[62] Moreover, he argued that it was a practice needing time to be successful, because for a given grito to work it required the number of pronunciamientos de adhesión to escalate meaningfully for a government (which had to be weak rather than tyrannical for a pronunciamiento series to work) to buckle before its demands. Baquer made the valid point that most successful pronunciamientos were launched from the periphery rather than from the capital precisely because they needed the time and space for other garrisons to pronounce in their favor. Consequently, it was an indirect action; that is, (unlike a coup) it did not seek direct confrontation with the government. Those that were staged in the capital were less likely to succeed given that the government could crush them more speedily, or at least before news spread of their demands and they mustered the kind of support the pronunciados could later claim was proof that they represented the "general will." Unlike Busquets, Baquer was adamant that a pronunciamiento was not a coup. A coup could be staged in the capital because it was a practice with the purpose of removing the government by force. The pronunciamiento sought instead to intimidate it into changing its policies. In this sense, the pronunciado did not set out to win (*vencer*) but to convince (*convencer*).[63]

Baquer also saw in the pronunciamiento model a set of recognized albeit unstated rules. He argued that those involved, both pronunciados and counterpronunciados, applied a certain prescriptive theory of games to the process once a pronunciamiento was launched. The pronunciados knew they had to establish contact with their adversaries so as to challenge them and make them aware of the grievances and demands. The government authorities, in turn, knew that depending on how fast the start-up pronunciamiento gained adherents, they had a chance of resisting, crushing the pronunciados, or delaying their response. Baquer was convinced that the "game" was never meant to result in bloodshed and that when a given cycle degenerated into civil war it was an aberration. He also gave great importance to words, to the written text that was quite literally "pronounced" (*pronunciado*) in garrisons and public squares when the pronunciados launched their pronunciamiento. The texts that circulated in every pronunciamiento were a characteristic trait of this insurrectionary model, not only because plans and addresses were drafted and disseminated whenever there was a pronunciamiento (unlike whenever there was a coup, revolt, or riot, in which cases aggressive petitions were not "mandatory") but also because they appealed to public opinion. The pronunciamiento text thus not only legitimized the practice—it transformed what could be deemed as a simple act of insubordination into an expression of the "general will." Those pronunciamientos that succeeded became, in retrospect, institutionalized processes that had led to a change in government or government policy. Last but not least, Baquer was of the view that the Spanish pronunciamiento evolved (something I argue was also the case in Mexico). He identified four different stages with different kinds of pronunciamiento in Spain: the liberal and royalist pronunciamientos of the "time of revolution" (1815–40), the military pronunciamientos of the "regime of the generals" (1841–60), the revolutions and coups of the "restoration" (1868–98), and the national insurrections and uprisings of the "era of dictatorships" (1926–39).[64]

Although Baquer recognized that the pronunciamiento created a space where soldiers and civilians could join forces for political motives, eventually becoming a hybrid political movement of sorts, like Comellas, Payne, and Busquets he believed that the participation of the army in pronunciamientos was all important. Regardless of however many popular expressions of support a pronunciamiento received, if it did not have the backing of the army, it was doomed to failure.[65] Such a view remains entrenched in most of the studies that have been dedicated to the Spanish pronunciamiento, including José Cepeda Gómez's more recent monographs on the subject.[66] Yet a number of studies on Ferdinand VII's turbulent reign—including the so-called *década ominosa* in Spain (1823–33), which witnessed several failed pronunciamiento cycles—namely those written by Josep Fontana, Irene Castells, and Roberto L. Blanco Valdés, while not denying the importance of the army and the liberal ideas that fuelled the twice-abolished 1812 Cádiz Constitution, presented the pronunciamiento as a joint military-civilian endeavor.[67]

In the case of the Mexican pronunciamiento no monograph has been dedicated to the topic, neither in English nor Spanish. This is the first such study to do so. However, prior to the launch of the 2007–10 AHRC-funded project that generated the three volumes I edited on the phenomenon, a number of seminal essays as well as critical editions including collections of actas, plans, or pronunciamiento texts had been published between the late 1980s and 2010.

A leading voice in the study of the pronunciamiento has no doubt been Josefina Zoraida Vázquez, who headed the project in Mexico that resulted in the publication of several anthologies of pronunciamiento texts.[68] Vázquez also wrote two highly suggestive essays on the pronunciamiento.[69] Like Baquer she argued that a pronunciamiento was not a coup because "it calls on public opinion to legitimize the movement."[70] Focusing on Mexico she came to the conclusion that although there were around one hundred start-up pronunciamientos in the first half of the nineteenth century (with more than one thousand actas of allegiance), only fifteen plans impacted upon the national stage, spreading beyond the territorial limits of their regions.[71] Notwithstanding this, Vázquez became convinced that there was an urgent need to study Mexico's pronunciamientos, given that they were the expression of the beliefs and ideas of the factions and political parties of their day, that they became the means whereby news circulated— politicizing the population in the process—and that they consistently and paradoxically sought to "constitute the nation" despite undermining the existing institutional order. In the same way

"Soft" Coups, Occupations, "Gestures of Rebellion"

that Baquer stressed the nonviolent nature of most Spanish pronunciamientos, Vázquez also argued that most Mexican ones did
not result in violence. Instead almost all of them ended guaranteeing an "olvido general" (general amnesty) whereby once the
given pronunciamiento cycle had come to an end, everybody was
allowed to return to their everyday lives as if nothing had happened. Although for Vázquez pronunciamientos were military-led,
she did recognize that that there was significant civilian involvement, either because it was civilians (politicians, businessmen,
merchants, tobacco planters) who instigated and/or funded these
ventures, using the army to defend or further their interests, or
because the military pronunciados themselves needed the civilians' support and endorsement to legitimize their actions.[72]

The other two scholars who wrote about the pronunciamiento
phenomenon in nineteenth-century Mexico before the St. Andrews
project got under way were Barbara A. Tenenbaum and François-
Xavier Guerra.[73] Tenenbaum was quick to recognize that "scholars
of nineteenth-century Mexico generally have ignored the phenomenon of the pronunciamiento" and highlighted, for the first
time, the fact that by the mid-1830s, Mexicans throughout the
country were gathering in juntas, studying the pronunciamientos that were doing the rounds, and deciding whether to join
them or not. Although she made a point of noting that "historians should not look at these plans as some subtle form of
representative democracy in action," she found commonalities
between a pronunciamiento and "a mass demonstration today,
where people principally gather to protest some event and listen
to a great number of speeches." Tenenbaum's unequivocal view
that as "a thorough reading of the plans conclusively shows, Mexicans throughout the country were passionately interested in pol-

itics and in political ideas," and that "it would be a serious error to dismiss their obvious involvement in such questions as meaningless," is a view I fully endorse.[74]

In François-Xavier Guerra's mind it was evident that because of its recurrence, the pronunciamiento was "one of the most important political practices of the nineteenth century." Regardless of the fact that most pronunciamientos failed to achieve their aims, it was clear to Guerra as well that "all of the political changes of this period, including the constitutional ones, had their origin in pronunciamientos, starting with independence itself." What is more, he saw in the pronunciamiento a practice that allowed communities to engage with politics as corporate bodies, that elicited active popular participation, and that offered Mexicans the opportunity to consult directly and without intermediaries what the true general will of the people actually was. For Guerra the prevalence and preponderance of the pronunciamiento phenomenon were proof that for most nineteenth-century Mexicans the Federal Congress did not really represent the nation. Instead it was seen as an assembly that was ultimately accountable to a people who could withdraw their support or recognition the moment they thought it had acted against their will, or broken an imagined social pact whereby the sovereign people allowed the government to rule in exchange for it safeguarding the Patria's so-called sacred rights. When a government supposedly violated those rights, the people could cease to recognize its authority and constitute the nation by pronouncing. The state, therefore, and by inference the government, did not incarnate or embody the nation for most Mexicans following the achievement of independence. Rather the nation was constituted by the pueblos, and the pronunciamiento became the way in which they, in turn, were able to express their political beliefs.[75]

"Soft" Coups, Occupations, "Gestures of Rebellion"

Apart from Vázquez, Tenenbaum, and Guerra's relevant journal articles and book chapters, and including the more recent historiography generated by the project, there have since been a number of individual essays dedicated to specific pronunciamientos or pronunciamiento cycles stretching from the 1821 Plan of Iguala to the 1852 Blancarte series in Jalisco.[76] Moreover, the three volumes I edited on the phenomenon, *Forceful Negotiations* (2010), *Malcontents, Rebels, and Pronunciados* (2012), and *Celebrating Insurrection* (2012) have gone some way toward correcting the manner in which the pronunciamiento was understood until recently.[77]

If I may recap the findings of all three volumes, in *Forceful Negotiations* we established that the pronunciamiento was a phenomenon that became common in the Hispanic world in the nineteenth century and that it became widespread in Mexico following the impact Rafael del Riego's pronunciamiento of 1 January 1820 and the Plan of Iguala of 24 February 1821 had in the region. Focusing on early pronunciamientos, we argued that it was a practice (part petition, part rebellion) seeking to effect political change through intimidation, and adopted to negotiate forcefully, concluding that it became *the* way of doing politics in nineteenth-century Mexico.[78] In *Malcontents, Rebels, and Pronunciados* we went on to explore why this was the case by concentrating on what inspired a selection of individuals (e.g., Felipe de la Garza, Anastasio Bustamante, Julio López Chávez) and given corporate bodies (e.g., garrisons, parish churches, town councils) to pronounce in a wide range of regions extending from Tamaulipas in the north to Yucatán in the southeast.[79] Last but not least, in *Celebrating Insurrection* we concentrated on how Mexicans tried to come to terms with this practice, how they attempted to legitimize it by celebrating it and including it in their repertoire of civic fiestas. By exploring how pronunciamientos were celebrated, remembered, commemorated, and represented, we found that it was a phenomenon characterized by its duality, one that was experienced as a necessary evil, celebrated yet criticized, reluctantly justified, its heroes both damned and venerated.[80]

In terms of my own particular journey of discovery into the subject, I was initially struck by the fact that the Mexican pronunciamiento was not an exclusively military practice as commonly thought. I argued this in the first essay I published on the pronunciamiento phenomenon by stressing that the often civilian-led pronunciamiento de adhesión was more than just a reactive statement of support; that there were a number of extremely influential town council–inspired pronunciamiento cycles (Cuernavaca, 1834; Orizaba-Toluca, 1835; and San Luis Potosí-Huejotzingo, 1842); that the great majority of so-called military pronunciamientos were actually prepared by high-ranking officers in collusion with civilians; that the Mexican regular army was still more of an informal army than a professional force, resulting in the military-civilian divide being somewhat blurred at the time; that there were no militaristic pronunciamientos during this period (i.e., with the sole concern of furthering the cause of the army); and that most pronunciamientos were launched to negotiate with, rather than overthrow, the government.[81]

In two subsequent different yet complimentary essays I traced the origins of the practice back to the impact Riego's 1820 pronunciamiento had in Mexico and developed an understanding of its dynamics, offering in a separate journal article a snapshot of the way pronunciamiento cycles developed and spread by concentrating on six pronunciamientos that randomly happened to be launched on the same day, 3 June 1834.[82] I also sought to explain the practice's appeal and popularity in my book chapter "'I Pronounce Thus I Exist,'" by analyzing its experience and multiple purposes. I argued that pronunciamientos allowed people to express and publicize their views; commune with their fellow soldiers, villagers, and parishioners; party late into the night; and advance their careers as well as effect meaningful political change. In this sense I proposed that it became part of everyday life, accepted, used, and endorsed by almost everybody regardless of the fact that it was outside the law.[83]

Following on from this, I explained what I consider to be the differences between a revolution, a coup d'état, and a pronunciamiento, in the introduction to *Malcontents, Rebels, and Pronunciados*, reflecting on why an individual and/or a given group might have opted to adopt one form of insurrectionary action rather than another. It became apparent to me that from the perspective of the pronunciados, the pronunciamiento was not about annihilating the opposition, structurally and dramatically changing society, or necessarily seizing power. It was a way of doing politics; in fact, *the* way of doing politics at a time when the nation-state was still in the making, governments were weak and ineffectual, the constitutional order lacked legitimacy and authority, and the law was a matter of opinion, there to be disobeyed, contested, and challenged by the alternative revolutionary bureaucracy of the pronunciamiento.[84] With this view in mind, I demonstrated how pronunciamiento cycles were as much, if not more, about compromise and coalition forming than they were about confrontation, by studying Santa Anna's shifts and changes during the pronunciamiento series of Veracruz–Casa Mata (1822–23), Perote–Oaxaca–La Acordada (1828), and Veracruz–Lerma–Zacatecas (1832).[85]

In a similar vein, in a book chapter I contributed to José Antonio Aguilar Rivera's volume on elections and representative government in nineteenth-century Mexico, I also interpreted the pronunciamiento as a practice that developed in the shadow of the flawed constitutional experiments of the day, becoming, in a sense, an extension of them. Studying how elections and pronunciamientos were employed, at times together or alongside each other to determine who governed Mexico, and the manner in which pronunciamientos developed their own logic of legitimacy in a context where elections could be fraudulent and suffrage was increasingly restricted to an affluent minority of *hombres de bien*, I suggested it was a practice that could be, in certain contexts as representative as if not more so than some of the constitutional systems that were put in place.[86]

I returned to the issue of the pronunciamiento's legitimacy in *Celebrating Insurrection* by focusing on how these insurrectionary acts were celebrated, commemorated, and represented in the nineteenth century and, in a separate paper, by analyzing the pronunciamientos' textual discourse and rhetoric of legitimacy.[87] The celebration and representation of the pronunciamiento certainly captured its contradictions and complexities. It was both the cause of much of Mexico's instability *and* the tool Mexicans used to ensure that the constitution was not ignored, reflecting the genuine grievances of an exploited and disenfranchised people. And it was a practice that clearly became legitimized through its constant and enthusiastic celebration.[88]

Last, analyzing the way foreign travelers depicted the pronunciamiento, I was able to highlight how although most of them failed to grasp the subtler functions, dynamics, and nature of the pronunciamiento, preferring to dwell instead on its potential for humor or to justify European/U.S. misgivings about Mexicans' ability to govern themselves, there was definitely more to it than met their eyes. I ended the third and last edited volume on the pronunciamiento arguing that it was, in a sense, a form of political vigilantism. I proposed that in the same way that vigilantes take the law into their own hands because they believe justice will not be done otherwise, because the forces of law and order are corrupt or ineffective, and because the threat posed by the criminals waiting outside is very real indeed, the pronunciados took politics into their own hands. Mexicans pronounced because they believed the constitution did not work (or was not being allowed to work); because the government or political class was corrupt, ineffective or despotic; and because the threat posed to them by their political enemies (including other pronunciados) was very real as well. Needless to say, many used the act of pronouncing to further their career prospects, improve their lot, and indulge in the occasional act of robbery. However, it became obvious to me that it is important not to ignore the pronunciamiento's bureaucratic nature with its claim to represent the "will of the nation," its dependency on receiving the support of constellations of pronunciamientos de adhesión, and its propensity to avoid bloodshed where possible, seeking to resolve problems through (forceful) negotiation. Contained within its insurrectionary drive, there was a strong belief in giving the pronunciamiento's demands a definite constitutional or institutional legitimacy. Although it remains the case that the numerous waves of pronunciamientos that spread across Mexico throughout the nineteenth century made governance extremely difficult, and that in some cases they degenerated into conflicts characterized by appalling levels of violence, they spread because, paradoxically, there was no government that succeeded in making good use of power for any significant period of time until, arguably, 1876.[89]

This book is not a *refrito* or rehash of previous publications. It is not a compilation of previously published essays of mine either. Rather it is the culmination of my sixteen-year research on the pronunciamiento phenomenon, in which I seek to show how this unlawful yet "legitimate" insurrectionary practice was used and developed in Mexico from 1821 to 1858. Although pronunciamientos continued to be staged after 1858, with the 1876 Plan of Tuxtepec having been notoriously responsible for Porfirio Díaz's rise to power, I have chosen to center my analysis on those that erupted between independence and the midcentury War of the Reforma. The reason for this, as discussed in chapters 4 and 5, is that the pronunciamiento as understood here, with its game theory, petitioning, appeal to the "general will," and controlled insurrectionary cycles, ultimately evolved into a far more radical and violent form of rebellion as of the mid-1840s. In other words, the view espoused in this study is that the period of the "classic" Mexican pronunciamiento unfolded between 1821 and 1858.

The aim of this monograph is thus to explore how and why this particular insurrectionary practice prospered in Independent Mexico, bearing in mind current and past theories of revolutionary actions and movements. I am particularly interested in how its adoption and endorsement by a wide spectrum of society impacted upon the political life of the republic, at a national and local level. Among the many questions I set out to address, the following deserve a mention, since they form of the backbone of this study. Who pronounced, where, and why? What issues gave rise to so many pronunciamientos? How did their demands change over time? What was it about Mexico's early national

"Soft" Coups, Occupations, "Gestures of Rebellion"

period that gave rise to a political culture in which an aggressive extra-constitutional practice like the pronunciamiento could become an intrinsic part of the institutional fabric of the country's incipient nation-state?

The book's other key aim is to provide, for the first time, a concise general overview of the pronunciamiento constellations that impacted upon national politics between 1821 and 1858. Given the constraints of time and space this volume is mainly concerned with national pronunciamiento cycles. For me to have attempted to analyze in equal depth the hundreds of pronunciamiento constellations that developed within or alongside the national cycles at a regional level, taking into consideration every single one of Mexico's thirty-one states, would have required several other lifetimes. As we discovered thanks to Ali, Doyle, and McDonald's theses on the pronunciamiento-prone regions of Yucatán, Jalisco, and San Luis Potosí, each state's experience of the pronunciamiento was different, with local politics having played a crucial role in determining the way they developed and the issues that gave rise to them. My hope is that providing a general overview of Mexico's national pronunciamientos will place future students of Mexican history in a better position to research and interpret how this practice developed at a regional level in states that clearly remain to be studied. By acquiring a full understanding of what the Mexican pronunciamiento was all about, it will be possible to engage with and appreciate the political issues, ideas, and grievances that polarized nineteenth-century Mexico, as well as the manner in which the not insignificant political crises of the period were negotiated and, eventually, overcome through this extra-constitutional form of effecting change.

Given that the practice evolved with time, the book is organized broadly in a chronological fashion, with chapter 2 focusing on the foundational pronunciamientos of 1820–21; chapter 3 on the early pronunciamientos of independent Mexico (1822–31); chapter 4 on those of the pronunciamiento-busy years of 1832–42; and chapter 5 on those that took place between the drafting of the 1843 Constitution and the beginning of the Civil War of the Reforma in 1858. It is a study that, on the one hand, comes to the conclusion that the retaliatory nature of mimetic insurrectionism meant that the repeated pronunciamiento cycles that spread throughout Mexico during the early national period ultimately culminated in the bloodshed of the 1858–60 Civil War. On the other hand, I argue that most of the significant political shifts the new country experienced were the result of pronunciamiento pressure. As the following pages attest, pronunciamientos were unlawful and a major source of instability, but they also offered Mexicans an effective way of addressing political injustice and challenging unconstitutional measures in a context where no single government was able to muster any meaningful degree of authority for any length of time.

2. The Origins of Mexico's Mimetic Insurrectionism

*The Foundational Pronunciamientos of Cabezas
de San Juan and Iguala, 1820–1821*

O n 7 April 1954 U.S. President Dwight Eisenhower explained the "domino theory" in an interview in the following terms: "You have a row of dominoes set up, you knock the first one, and what will happen to the last one is the certainty that it will go over very quickly. So you could have a beginning of disintegration that would have the most profound influences."[1] In the context of the Cold War, faced with the threat of communist expansionism, the domino theory would be at the heart of the U.S. foreign policy of "containment" that was adopted to prevent developing countries in Southeast Asia and Latin America from toppling "like a row of dominoes" under the influence of communism and insurrectionary politics.[2] Although the domino principle is attributed to Eisenhower's secretary of state, John Foster Dulles, as Gerard J. DeGroot reminds us it was actually first conceived of by Vladimir Illich Lenin.[3]

Lenin did not actually use the falling dominoes metaphor. What he did was develop a theory of insurrectionary contagion (notwithstanding his condemnation of the term *contagion*, as "the favourite metaphor of the bourgeoisie and the bourgeois police").[4] Under this theory it was not only possible but *inevitable* for successful revolutionary movements to find echoes elsewhere, moving from one country to another in a context where "the exploited and oppressed masses [had come to] understand the impossibility of living in the old way," *and* in which it had also become impossible for the exploiters to "live and rule in the old way."[5] He saw in Bolshevism a "*model of tactics for all*," and predicted that it would be adopted and applied by revolutionaries throughout the world.[6] Lenin's insurrectionary "contagion," he believed, had "very thoroughly permeated the [capitalist] organism and [had] completely impregnated it. If special efforts [were] made to 'stop up' one of the channels, the 'contagion' [would] find another, sometimes a very unexpected channel."[7] Critical to understanding how this had come about was ultimately the empirical value of insurrectionary action: "The poor peasants learned, not from books or newspapers, *but from life itself*."[8]

Although Marxism-Leninism undoubtedly became an extremely captivating creed for revolutionaries across the world in the twentieth century, the Soviet revolution did not spread successfully to Western Europe as Lenin believed it would. Despite this, Lenin was right in highlighting the contagious qualities of insurrectionary politics. Although Bolshevism did not triumph in Western Europe, this does not mean that it did not inspire revolutionary movements, such as those that fought in the Spanish and Greek civil wars of 1936–39 and 1946–49, respectively.[9]

A brief glance at some of the main revolutions of the last three hundred years eloquently highlights the contagious or what I term *mimetic* nature of insurrectionism. The U.S. War of Independence (1775–83) influenced events in France, leading to the 1789 Revolution, and served as inspiration for the Spanish American Wars of Independence that spread from Buenos Aires in Argentina to Dolores in Mexico from 1810 to 1826. The 1848 revolutions that witnessed middle-class liberals rebelling in Paris, Milan, Venice,

Origins of Mexico's Mimetic Insurrectionism

Naples, Palermo, Vienna, Prague, Budapest, Kraków and Berlin, against what Mike Rapport defined as "the brick-built authoritarian edifice that had imposed itself on Europeans for almost two generations," offer an equally clear example of mimetic insurrectionism at work.[10] The same can be said for the impact the 1956–59 Cuban Revolution's "*foco revolucionario*" model had in the rest of Latin America.[11] One guerrilla army after another was created in the hope of emulating the success of Ernesto "Che" Guevara's formula in their respective countries.[12] Guevara, like Lenin before him, was convinced that his revolutionary example would lead to others taking up arms in their quest for liberation:

> The example of our revolution for Latin America and the lessons it implies have destroyed all the café theories: we have shown that a small group of resolute men supported by the people and not afraid to die if necessary can take on a disciplined regular army and completely defeat it.[13]

As Chilean presidential candidate Salvador Allende would admit in 1960, only a year after Cuban dictator Fulgencio Batista had been overthrown: "The Cuban Revolution is a national revolution, but it is also a revolution of the whole of Latin America. It has shown the way for the liberation of all our peoples."[14] Then came the effervescence of student protests and insurrectionary activity that spread across university campuses all over the world in 1968.[15] The revolutions of Eastern and Central Europe came in 1989.[16] The Arab Spring of 2011 is a recent manifestation.[17] These are obvious examples of instances in which collective political acts of defiance that started in one place found themselves being replicated in multiple others, succeeding in crossing national boundaries, overcoming language and cultural barriers, and impacting the political behavior of people from different social classes.[18]

Building on Lenin's vision of revolutionary contagion while thinking of the way the Mexican pronunciamiento went viral during the early national period, it may be possible to conceive of a phenomenon I define here as "mimetic insurrectionism." By this I mean a natural tendency on the part of people in a context of acute social injustice, political oppression, and/or economic as well as racial inequality to replicate—mimic—insurrectionary tactics from elsewhere if these are seen to have worked. The nature and scale of the protests, rebellions, or revolutionary activity may vary in scope; however, what appears to be a recurrent phenomenon in contexts where a significant portion of the population is seriously aggrieved for political, social, or economic reasons is that when people are presented with an example of *successful* insurrectionary activity from elsewhere, there will invariably and repeatedly be some who will attempt to mimic it by applying its methods or model to their own particular and local context.

It is obvious that the original and subsequently mimicked form of insurrection needs to have been successful. For mimetic insurrectionism to occur the mimetic insurrectionists clearly start from the premise that "if it worked for them, it can work for us." But it also occurs in a context where success grants legitimacy to the original act of insurrection and, in so doing, offers a second but equally important premise for mimetic insurrectionists to justify the launching of their own version of the emulated action: "insurrection is legitimate when it succeeds, ergo insurrection is legitimate." To put it differently, when insurrection becomes an acceptable means of political participation—because it works, and because in having worked it is a perfectly legitimate way of going about challenging the current unjust order, even if it involves violence—there is nothing, apart from the government's force, to stop a given successful insurrectionary model from being copied again and again and again, regardless of the fact that it may not succeed anywhere else other than where it originated.

As discussed in my introduction to *Malcontents, Rebels, and Pronunciados*, for a full-scale revolution to take place, the following ingredients are crucial: (1) widespread dissatisfaction with the political, economic, and social situation (this must affect a variety of social classes); (2) widespread politicization of the people, whereby they do not blame fate or God but the government or the political system for their misfortune; (3) a generalized sense that the government is illegitimate; and (4) a belief that there is a viable and preferable alternative on offer. Interestingly not all of these ingredients need to be in place for mimetic insurrectionism to occur. With mimetic insurrectionism all that would appear to be necessary are conditions (1) and (2), widespread dissatisfaction and a politicized population. The government may be considered legitimate, but this will not prevent insurrectionary acts such as strikes, demonstrations, riots, and pronunciamientos from taking place. If collective bargaining is a strategic aim and the insurrectionists seek to negotiate forcefully with rather than to overthrow a given government, whether it is perceived as legitimate or not is ultimately irrelevant. Similarly, the mimetic insurrectionists may lack a clear alternative, but this will not stop them from attempting to replicate a successful insurrectionary model from elsewhere if they believe it may end the current source of discontent (again by intimidating the authorities into changing their policies).

It is important to note that mimetic insurrectionism as understood here is not exclusively inspired by major seismic revolutions (e.g., the 1789 French Revolution or the 1917 Russian Revolution); rather it is more likely to emerge and develop in response to "minor" yet successful insurrectionary activities. Mimetic insurrectionism is far more common when the original act of defiance has avoided violence (as much as possible) and has resulted in a perceived meaningful change that is not necessarily equated with a truly radical transformation of the existing order (e.g., the 1848 Revolutions). In fact, mimetic insurrectionism on the scale witnessed in Independent Mexico came about precisely because pronunciamientos were seen as an effective means of bringing about change that did not entail overthrowing the prevailing socioeconomic order.

After all, although major sanguinary revolutions can inspire the aggrieved to try to replicate them in their own country, they can equally act as a major deterrent, causing these people to abandon their original radical ideas. News of guillotine frenzies, mass killings, generalized acts of rape, pillage, and widespread destruction of property can dissuade even the most radical of conspirators from opening an unpredictable Pandora's box of revolutionary mayhem in their own country. If the potential revolutionaries fear their revolutionary endeavors will unleash the full horrors of revolutionary "terror" on their own population, as reportedly occurred wherever the original revolution took place, they may very well be inclined to settle for a reformist agenda and forget their early tentative support for violent political action.

The ferocious 1791 slave-led Haitian Revolution, to give just one example, resulted in Cuban *criollos* (white Spanish-Americans) interring their incipient rebellious independent impulses for a good seventy years, until the outbreak of the Ten Years' War

(1868–78), because they were terrified of finding their plantation-based colonial society destroyed by their slaves should they dare to challenge Madrid.[19] To quote historian John Lynch, "Cuba's expanding sugar economy depended on slave labour, the supply of which in turn depended on the continuation of Spanish rule. The demographic strength of the Negroes, moreover, recalling as it did the black population in Haiti, deterred the white aristocracy from promoting change and persuaded them to place their trust in a reformed colonial administration backed by strong military force."[20]

Inevitably, for any insurrectionary practice, method, or model to spread, be replicated, and prosper, the context must lend itself to revolutionary politics. To return to the aforementioned ingredients (1) and (2): there must evidently be widespread dissatisfaction and a politicized population. So what was the situation in Mexico when news of the success of Rafael del Riego's pronunciamiento of 1 January 1820 reached Veracruz on the gloriously sunny morning of 26 April that year? How widespread was New Spain's discontent? How politicized were the people?

News of the insurrectionary model of the pronunciamiento reached Mexico at the end rather than at the beginning of its revolution of independence. The various intendancies of the Kingdom of New Spain had thus witnessed, some more closely than others, the ravages of civil war for the better part of ten years. The context was one of revolutionary exhaustion and counterinsurgent fatigue. In a sense, the four conditions I have mentioned as necessary for a revolution to erupt had been in place twelve years earlier when the Napoleonic occupation of the Iberian Peninsula resulted in "the dissolution of the Spanish Monarchy," to borrow Jaime E. Rodríguez O.'s words, and the consequent political vacuum and constitutional impasse that gave way to "the revolutions of the Spanish world."[21]

That there was widespread dissatisfaction in 1808 as a result of the impact several decades of Bourbon reforms had had in the region is unquestionable. As part of enlightened bids by Charles III (1759–88) and subsequently Charles IV (1788–1808) to modernize despotically the way the Spanish Empire was run, the decades building up to the revolutionary turmoil of the 1810s were characterized by the issuing and implementation of a whole battery of profoundly unpopular laws. Bent on ensuring that the colonies were efficiently administered, that their extraordinary financial resources were exploited to the full, and that the wealth and influence of institutions such as the church, which were deemed to stand in the way of the monarchy's enlightened agenda, were accordingly corrected, Charles III initiated a particularly thorough and widespread campaign of reforms that dramatically impacted the political, economic, and social bases of Spanish America.[22]

Following the demise of the Habsburg dynasty in Spain and the Spanish War of Succession (1702–13), the Spanish Crown under the Bourbons, in particular after Charles III came to the throne, reordered the colonial structure into one of intendancies, flooding its dominions in the Americas with an army of Spanish-born bureaucrats and administrators. Criollos found themselves ousted from positions of political power and discriminated against on the grounds of not having been born in the Iberian Peninsula, as the "bureaucratic invasion" of the 1760s and '70s resulted by 1780 in 72 percent of all government officials being newcomers from Spain.[23] Nineteenth-century Mexican politician, conservative ideologue, and historian Lucas Alamán described the effects.[24] "There were sixty thousand Spaniards born in Europe residing in

New Spain in the year of 1808. They occupied all the main jobs in the administration, the church, the judiciary, and the army: they controlled commerce almost exclusively. . . . [The result] was a declared rivalry between them [the European Spaniards and their Mexican counterparts], that albeit hidden for a long time, it was feared could break out in a baneful fashion, given the chance."[25]

Bourbon economic reforms added further insult to injury. Monopolies were created that favored Spanish interests to the detriment of Mexican-born merchants and local elites. Old taxes were increased while new ones were invented. A new controlled economic model, ironically called *"comercio libre"* (free commerce), was put into place in 1778.[26] It resulted in returns from America to Spain increasing by 1,528 percent between 1778 and 1784.[27] In addition a mining boom at the end of the eighteenth century resulted in Mexico yielding two thirds of the revenue of the Spanish Empire by 1800, the profits being spent on Spain's war efforts in Europe.[28] The culmination of years of fiscal abuse, for want of a better term, on the part of the Spanish authorities came in 1805 with Viceroy José de Iturrigaray's implementation of the 1804 royal decree for the *"amortización para la consolidación de vales reales,"* whereby those who had borrowed funds from the church (i.e., most, not to say all property owners) were forced to redeem their debts and return what they owed to the ecclesiastical authorities with immediate effect so that they, in turn, could lend the money to the Crown. Although, as Margaret Chowning reminds us, Bourbon fiscal and economic measures resulted in a real drop in elite wealth of the order of 30 to 35 percent, the ruinous impact the *consolidación de vales reales* decree had on extensive sectors of society proved critical in turning people from all social classes against Spanish *"mal gobierno"* (bad gov-

last straw [handwritten annotation]

ernment).[29] Liberal Mexican priest, politician, and ideologue José María Luis Mora provided commentary.[30] For him if there was one reform that finally succeeded in destroying whatever popularity the Spanish government may have enjoyed in New Spain until then, it was this one.[31]

Yet Spanish American discontent also had a long-term popular sociocultural religious component. The generation-long assault the Spanish Crown led against the church met with fierce opposition at a popular level as devout parishioners and religious communities witnessed with horror the manner in which the Bourbon monarchs high-handedly confiscated church wealth, condemned religious practices they deemed were superstitious, and took on the Jesuit order for putting the pope before the king of Spain, expelling all its members from Spain and its colonies in 1767. As William B. Taylor has noted, "Unwittingly, the Bourbons would contribute to the national revolutions of the early nineteenth century by effectively cutting themselves loose from divine right."[32] In its drive to secularize society and do away with zealotry and backwardness, the crown attacked the church and popular Mexican piety with its autochthonous indigenous syncretic elements (e.g., hybrid religious celebrations, processions, and liturgical events involving the veneration of local Indian icons, cults, and practices).[33] As a result the crown not only lost the support of the very priests who had served as its mediators, teaching their parishioners about unity in hierarchy and the religious legitimacy of the monarch; it lost the respect of a traditionalist population who started viewing their monarchs as "*afrancesados*" (Frenchified), no longer rulers adored for their principled generosity but despots characterized by their irreligious "arbitrary and capricious demands."[34]

Origins of Mexico's Mimetic Insurrectionism

Although Lynch is probably right in noting that the "Spanish American revolutions responded first to interests" rather than ideology, it nonetheless remains the case that "this was the age of democratic revolution when ideas appeared to cross frontiers and leave no society untouched."[35] The thinkers of the Enlightenment, whether they were radical or reformist, demonstrably provided the aggrieved with arguments to challenge absolutism and the *ancien régime* as well as articulating the promise of new forms of representative constitutional government. The writings of Thomas Hobbes (1588–1679), John Locke (1632–1704), Voltaire (1694–1778), Charles de Secondat Baron de Montesquieu (1689–1755), Jean Jacques Rousseau (1712–78), Abbé Raynal (1713–96) and Thomas Paine (1737–1809), to name but a few, informed the writings and policies of a number of key liberators and insurgents.[36] To quote historian Peggy Liss, "The American Revolution [of Independence, 1775–1783] and its aftermath, together with the Enlightenment and the onset of the industrial revolution, all had a great impact on Spanish policies and Spanish Americans."[37] How could a population that was illiterate almost in its entirety have been conversant with Rousseau's views on inequality?[38] As Jaime E. Rodríguez O. noted at a conference in Veracruz in 2008 when asked this question, "People do not need to have read a given author to know about his or her key ideas."[39] In the same way that most people today have a notion of what Karl Marx or Sigmund Freud stood for without having read them, there were popular sections of the population in Mexico who had some idea of the content of key enlightened texts such as the 1789 *Declaration of the Rights of Man* in its more radical 1793 version. Evidence of this is that the right to insurrection that would be alluded to in countless pronunciamientos to justify and legitimize the pronunciados' call to arms originated in the 1793 *Declaration of the Rights of Man*, in which article 35 stated unequivocally: "When the government violates the rights of the people, insurrection is for the people and for each portion of the people the most sacred of rights and the most indispensable of duties."[40]

The politicization of the population thus came about as news spread of events in America and France, and certain ideas and key precepts of the Enlightenment found their way into the people's political imaginary. The expulsion of the Jesuits in 1767, moreover, resulted in this process of politicization acquiring a marked patriotic slant, as certain notable exiled professors, including Francisco Xavier Clavigero, set about producing works of great scholarship about the geography and history of their faraway homeland. Clavigero's *Ancient History of Mexico* was published in 1780–81 from his exile in Italy, and he described it as "a history of Mexico written by a Mexican."[41] It served to initiate an intellectual process of national reappraisal that would ultimately give way to what David Brading came to define as "creole patriotism."[42]

The third revolutionary ingredient (i.e., the need for there to be a severe crisis of legitimacy) came in 1808 in two forms. The first was the Napoleonic occupation of the Iberian Peninsula with the capture of King Ferdinand VII and the imposition of the usurper Joseph Bonaparte on the Spanish throne in May 1808.[43] The second was the coup the Spanish merchant guild launched in Mexico City on 15 September 1808, which resulted in the overthrow of Viceroy José de Iturrigaray, putting an end to the Mexico City town council's attempt to form a Mexican junta that would serve as a caretaker government in New Spain while Ferdinand VII remained captive in France.[44] With three out of the four preconditions for a revolution to erupt in place by the fall of 1808, it was

Origins of Mexico's Mimetic Insurrectionism

only a matter of time before the fourth (i.e., an alternative) came into play, finding a voice in Father Miguel Hidalgo y Costilla's 1810 *grito* of Dolores with its barely disguised call for independence.[45] In Brian Hamnett's view, "Two crucial elements need to be operative if transition to the political plane of activity is to be realised. These are (1) the availability of leadership to articulate and direct grievances, that in their origins may be local, and (2) a crisis at the centre and the existence of political uncertainty in provincial capital cities. Such elements were present in New Spain in 1808–10. The conjunction of social, economic and political factors enabled the mental transition from local grievance or sense of alienation to outright revolt."[46]

The causes of the War of Independence were therefore long term and short term, general and particular, protonational and local. On a macro level, the Bourbon reforms had over a period of fifty years generated significant discontent at all levels of New Spain's society. The language of the age of revolution with its call for equality, fraternity, and liberty had also had time to permeate political culture throughout the Atlantic world, politicizing people's response to their context of heightened crisis. With the overthrow of the legitimate monarch of Spain and that of the legitimate viceroy of New Spain, sovereignty devolved to the people, given that they could not obey a French king, imposed by Napoleon, and had no reason to support *golpistas* Gabriel de Yermo and Pedro Garibay, who in 1808 arrested the viceroy and his family and locked up Mexico City's town councilors. With independence as a possible path to liberation, events conspired so that the revolution of independence finally broke out in the early hours of 16 September 1810, when Father Hidalgo summoned his parishioners to his church in Dolores and gave the rallying cry of

"Long live the Virgin of Guadalupe! Death to bad government! Death to the *gachupines* [Spaniards]!"[47]

Notwithstanding this, the experience of the War of Independence was very different from place to place, depending on the nature of local grievances. As noted by Eric Van Young, "A central characteristic of the Mexican insurgency is that the very localist energies and diversity of circumstances that fueled the popular movements prevented them from coalescing ideologically or militarily for the capture of larger prizes, except under exceptional circumstances and for a limited period of time."[48] Having arrived in Valladolid (present-day Morelia) from Guanajuato in the autumn of 1810, Hidalgo may very well have been issuing addresses that condemned the Europeans' tyrannical rule and their overthrow of Iturrigaray, urging the Mexican people—*Americanos*—to rise up in arms to defend their religion and their liberty. In a village such as Atlacomulco (in the present-day state of Mexico) the main reason why there was a particularly violent riot on the evening of Thursday 1 November 1810 had far more to do with local grievances than it did with the larger events unfolding around them.[49] As Van Young's research attests, "Where collective political violence erupted in village Mexico, it was most often driven by local historical memory, local religious sensibility, local conflict, and local actors, and was not easily reframed in a discourse of providentialism, national or protonational political aspiration, or Enlightenment philosophical thinking."[50] The result of this was ten disjointed years of conflict, civil war, revolutionary action, and brutal counterinsurgency tactics, in which regions such as the present-day states of Guanajuato, Jalisco, Michoacán, Guerrero, and Oaxaca witnessed horrendous massacres, full-scale battles, and scenes of appalling violence and cruelty, while most other regions went comparatively unscathed.[51] Furthermore, while the countryside, in particular that of the Bajío (Guanajuato and Michoacán), became the main theater of war, life in New Spain's principal cities prior to 1820 was not affected directly by the fighting, with the exceptions of Guanajuato, Valladolid, Guadalajara, Toluca, Cuautla, Tehuacán, Orizaba, Oaxaca, and Acapulco.

Despite the shared grievances of so many criollos, the war, when it finally broke out, did not result in a clear-cut conflict between Mexicans and Spaniards either. In fact, once news spread of the atrocities committed by Hidalgo's 80,000 strong army in Guanajuato, Valladolid, and Guadalajara during the first three months of the revolution (16 September–26 November 1810), with its elements of class and racial hatred, a significant proportion of white-skinned criollos thought twice about their initial autonomist impulses and found themselves backing the royalist *"causa buena"* (good cause).[52] The war also underwent various phases. The first four years between 1810 and 1814 were the most dynamic. Under the leadership of Father Hidalgo in the first instance (1810–11), and then Father José María Morelos y Pavón (1811–14), the initial years of the War of Independence entailed major military campaigns and engagements as the insurgent army swept from the Bajío down to Oaxaca and east as far as Orizaba in the present-day state of Veracruz, tracing a crescent of revolutionary violence around the Valley of Mexico, as the cities initially taken by the revolutionaries were regained, one after another, by the royalists.[53]

To make matters more complex a particularly progressive constitution was drafted in Cádiz in 1812 by the Spanish parliament, the Cortes, assembled in the far south of the peninsula since 24 September 1810. The different juntas that surfaced in Spain claiming to represent the nation following the events of May 1808 had merged into one Central Junta, which—hounded by the French, first to Seville and then to Cádiz—gave way to the creation of the Cortes. Besieged on the Isle of León, yet protected by the British Navy, the Cortes of Cádiz brought together deputies, theoretically elected by a convoluted indirect household suffrage system, from across Spain and its dominions, including twenty-one representatives from New Spain.[54] The 1812 Constitution they produced went on to be implemented in those parts of Spanish America that had not fallen to the different insurgent or so-called patriot armies. In Mexico the implementation of the 1812 Cádiz Constitution in 1812–13 certainly divided opinion, both among the royalists and the insurgents. The absolutists in the royalist camp found that the constitution severely undermined their authority in the context of the war that had been fought since 1810. It entailed creating a constitutional monarchy in which the Cortes—that is, the legislative branch of government—was where the nation was represented. It resulted in the formation of elected town councils and provincial deputations and forged an electoral system that came close to introducing universal male suffrage. It also defended a whole range of liberal values such as freedom of speech and the press.[55] For Viceroy Francisco Javier Venegas (1810–13) the 1812 charter posed a major headache: he was demoted from viceroy of a colonial kingdom with full regal power to becoming just one more provincial political chief (*jefe político de provincia*) according to the constitution, placing him on a par with the other political chiefs of Nueva Galicia, Yucatán, San Luis Potosí, the Eastern Interior Provinces, and the Western Interior Provinces. Not surprisingly he called a *real acuerdo* in December 1812 that, as Nettie Lee Benson noted, allowed him "because of the exigencies of the time [i.e., a context of war] . . . to ignore the Con-

Origins of Mexico's Mimetic Insurrectionism

stitution in as much as possible and to continue the old order of things."[56] By the same token, creole liberals such as Lorenzo de Zavala, who sympathized with the cause of independence, albeit not on Hidalgo or Morelos's terms, came round to preferring to remain linked to a Spain governed according to the 1812 Constitution rather than back an insurgent movement led by traditionalist Catholic revolutionary priests.[57]

However, following the decisive battle of Puruarán (5 January 1814) the power and influence of the insurgency were severely damaged. The return of Ferdinand VII to the throne of Spain that year paired with his abolition of the 1812 Constitution also strengthened the hand of Viceroy Félix Calleja (1813–16). Although the insurgents issued their own Constitution of Apatzingán on 22 October 1814, they were not in a position to implement it.[58] A year on from then the independence cause appeared all but over. With Morelos captured (5 November 1815) and executed (22 December 1815), what was left of the original insurgency, significantly reduced in numbers to not more than eight thousand poorly armed men, was forced to take refuge in the countryside and the sierra and resort to guerrilla warfare and hit-and-run operations.[59] In the optimistic words of Viceroy Juan Ruiz de Apodaca (1816–21), writing to the Spanish Minister of War on 31 October 1816, there were no longer any insurgent armies left in New Spain.[60]

This notwithstanding, it is evident that ten years of insurgency, counterinsurgency, and daily threats of political violence had a major impact on New Spain's society. As historian John Coatsworth has argued, Mexican political culture was one characterized by a centuries-long tradition of resistance, dissent, riots, and revolts. During both the colonial and independent periods most Mexicans saw the government "as something foreign, if not illegitimate, one you always had to avoid and elude if possible."[61] Eighteenth-century village uprisings were common, with Taylor finding that "in central Mexico, the Mixteca Alta, and the Valley of Oaxaca [they] were alike in repertory of actions, instruments and dramatis personae. Nearly all were spontaneous, short-lived armed outbursts by members of a single community in reaction to threats from outside; they were 'popular' uprisings in which virtually the entire community acted collectively and usually without identifiable leadership."[62] However, ten years of ongoing civil war had significantly impacted the population's political and—yes, insurrectionary—behavior. As noted by Michael T. Ducey, "Political practice changed dramatically during and after independence. . . . Violence became an acceptable mechanism of political change. Rebels no longer had to disguise their willingness to take up arms as they had once done in the eighteenth century. The system of royal-judicial mediation that once existed broke down irrevocably."[63] It is a view with which John Tutino concurs when he states that "in the process, agrarian Mexicans learned much about insurrection, and those lessons proved useful as they continued to experiment with opposition to the agrarian structure during the nineteenth century."[64] As stressed by Robert H. Holden in his study on circular patterns of violence in Central America, "Violence and the threat of violence generate fear and therefore preparation for violence."[65]

Given these circumstances, it was almost inevitable that by April 1820 violence had become an expected if not an acceptable part of everyday life and political life. The cities of New Spain were in the hands of the royalists. The countryside, without being in the hands of the insurgents, provided them with the space and resources to hide from the government's counterinsurgent forces

Origins of Mexico's Mimetic Insurrectionism

and mount their ongoing and relentless hit-and-run operations, constantly interrupting the flow of trade and funds. As Peter Guardino rightly argues: "New Spain had not been pacified as of 1820. Furthermore, it could never have returned to the degree of consensus that had maintained the colonial system with very little recourse to force before 1808. The crisis that had touched off the war was unresolved, and this crisis, combined with the effects of war itself, had irrevocably damaged the legitimacy of the old colonial system."[66] In essence the war had reached a stalemate. The few insurgent guerrillas left in the field were too few to defeat the colonial administration, but there were enough of them to ensure that the royalist forces could not defeat them entirely either.

For many criollos who had backed the royalist cause out of fear of Hidalgo's revolutionary hordes or Viceroy Félix Calleja's repressive counterinsurgent measures, or out of inertia or misplaced loyalty, a sense of despair arose that peace would never be attained as long as Spain continued to rule over Mexico's destiny. News of the successes of other wars of independence also started to filter through, such as the proclamation of the independence of the United Provinces of South America (Argentina) in 1816, José de San Martín's victory at Maipú in 1818 and the subsequent independence of Chile, and Simón Bolívar's victory at Boyacá in 1819, resulting in the fall of Bogotá and Nueva Granada to the Liberator's army.[67] Moreover, in the autumn of 1819 the news that started to come from Spain gave the impression that Ferdinand VII's position as absolute king of Spain was also under threat. What is more, the fact that it became publicly known that Viceroy Apodaca was evidently desperate to silence news that members of the expeditionary army being organized in Cádiz had been discovered plotting to restore the 1812 Constitution gave the impression that the Spanish authorities in Mexico were certainly uneasy about the situation. In Zavala's mind, the fact that rumors suddenly abounded concerning the existence of an important sector of the Spanish army being intent on restoring the 1812 Constitution gave hope to the liberals in New Spain while alarming the absolutists.[68]

The change of heart of Cádiz-based Commander General Enrique José O'Donnell, Count of La Bisbal, on 8 July 1819 and his decision to turn on his fellow conspirators, officers who had been conspiring with him since March, should have represented a major blow to the liberals and, if anything, should have shown that all attempts at restoring the Cádiz Constitution were doomed. Not only did La Bisbal betray his followers; he arrested the leading officers at the head of the troops that had been mobilized to the military camp at El Palmar on the outskirts of the port of Santa María, Cádiz. However, the effect of news of the uncovering of the pronunciamiento of El Palmar was quite the opposite. On the one hand, it did not stop those who eluded capture or suspicion from persevering with their plan to pronounce. If anything, it focused their minds and strengthened their resolve.[69] On the other hand, it served to publicize the fact that leading high-ranking officers, like La Bisbal himself, were thinking about rebelling (even if in his case, he changed his mind), and it planted the thought that such a rebellion could conceivably succeed if an army like the one that was being put together in Cádiz with a view to reconquering independent South America turned against the government in Madrid.[70] By the time Rafael del Riego launched the pronunciamiento of Cabezas de San Juan, on 1 January 1820, the expeditionary army in Cádiz was made up of eighteen battalions, one squadron, and four regiments.[71]

Origins of Mexico's Mimetic Insurrectionism

News reached Mexico at the beginning of April that the Asturias battalion commanded by Riego had pronounced in Cabezas de San Juan, refusing, on the one hand, to embark to fight "an unjust war in the New World" and demanding, on the other, that the 1812 Constitution be restored.[72] Given that the pronunciamiento did not receive significant support to begin with, the first accounts of the event to reach Veracruz did not necessarily translate into a sense that Riego's movement was inevitably destined to triumph. Nevertheless, Viceroy Apodaca is known to have panicked, coming up with the idea that should the liberals succeed, Ferdinand VII could be offered asylum in Mexico.[73]

However, the copies of the *Gaceta de Madrid* of 18 March 1820 that were unloaded in Veracruz harbor on the morning of 26 April 1820 not only confirmed that Riego's pronunciamiento had actually succeeded, but they also came with King Ferdinand VII's decree calling upon his kingdom's judges to restore, and his subjects to swear an oath to abide by, the 1812 liberal charter of 9 October 1812.[74] Furthermore, given that the ship bringing this news from A Coruña had stopped in Havana along the way, it also brought tidings of how the authorities in Cuba had gone ahead and proclaimed the restoration of the 1812 Constitution without waiting to receive orders from the government in Spain.[75] Members of the liberal merchant community of the port of Veracruz, regardless of whether they were Spaniards or criollos, were ecstatic on reading the news of how Riego's pronunciamiento had been seconded by "the general movement of the provinces."[76] Pronunciamientos de adhesión had been launched in fourteen Spanish cities between 21 February and 11 March.[77] The events had resulted in King Ferdinand VII giving in to the popular demands for the restoration of the 1812 charter on 7

March.[78] What is more, they wasted no time before marching to see the commander general and provincial intendant of Veracruz, Field-Marshall José Dávila, to demand that the authorities of the port immediately swore their allegiance to the constitution. Dávila tried to dissuade the assembled crowd from forcing him to do so, arguing that it was up to the viceroy to give such an order and that for the viceroy to do so he first needed to receive orders directly from the king. He argued that one could not legislate on the basis of a newspaper report. However, faced with the threat of a major commotion, Dávila relented in the end, and the constitution was publicly sworn in that very same day, but not without his first telling the gathered merchants, "Gentlemen, you have forced me to proclaim and swear in the Constitution: now prepare yourselves for independence, because that is what is going to come of this."[79]

The authorities in Xalapa followed Veracruz's example and swore in the constitution. When news of the events in Spain and Veracruz reached Apodaca three days later, on 29 April, he was predictably horrified. He considered disobeying the royal decree of 8 March, and looked into ways of delaying the restoration of the constitution in New Spain. But there was no turning the clock back now. As Zavala observed in his 1831 account of the period: "The speed with which the new revolution led by Riego, [Antonio] Quiroga and other famous patriots, spread in Spain, made Viceroy Apodaca's plan disintegrate."[80] As noted by Roger L. Cunniff, "As the news spread inland, other villages began to establish popular councils. All this was done without the permission of the viceroy. The swift march of events put such pressure on Viceroy Juan Ruíz de Apodaca that on May 31 he found himself obliged to publish the constitution in Mexico City, although he still had received no official confirmation from Spain."[81]

The impact Riego's pronunciamiento had in New Spain was there for all to see. Each town and city publicly swore in the constitution. Elected town councils were restored. Freedom of the press was reestablished. The Inquisition was dissolved. Political prisoners were released (although the amnesty did not extend to captive insurgents). And elections to the Cortes were held in September that year, resulting in forty-nine Mexican deputies being elected to represent New Spain in Madrid in 1821.[82] From the perspective of Riego's fellow conspirator Antonio María Alcalá Galiano their pronunciamiento's success offered the world two incredibly resonant lessons: first, "The world will admire, when it finds out, how with such weak forces we were able to overthrow the huge mass of oppression that weighed upon us"; and second, "Just one voice was going to determine the fate of Spain without there being baneful disorders, the source of interminable bitter hatreds."[83] In a nutshell, it was possible to force an absolutist monarch like Ferdinand VII to listen to the general will of the nation with a pronunciamiento. Moreover, it was possible to make him change his ways, in this instance intimidating him into restoring the liberal Constitution of 1812, through coordinated acts of defiance and insubordination. Last but not least, it was possible to rebel and petition for political change, without the need for bloodshed, in a curiously orderly fashion.

Essentially the lesson drawn from the extraordinary series of events that unfolded as a result of Riego's grito of 1 January 1820 was that a pronunciamiento opened the possibility of bringing about significant political change. It also showed how participating in a pronunciamiento could bring fame and recognition. In the words of Comellas:

> Riego, commander of one of the battalions that participated in the pronunciamiento, following Quiroga's orders, and whose involvement in the conspiracy had been relatively unimportant, will become the leading hero of the venture, the incarnation and symbol of the entire period of Spanish liberalism. Riego will be the author of liberty, his person will be glorified in petitions, disseminated in illustrations, immortalized in poems; his name will become engraved in streets, and an anthem composed in his honor by one of his regiment's musicians will mark a period of Spanish history.[84]

In a context of contested authority, as observed by Josefina Vázquez, Riego's example would serve as an inspiration to liberal army officers both in Spain and in its kingdoms: "it did not take long to become a tempting example for New Spain's criollos."[85] It also served as inspiration for the mirror constitutionalist revolts that took place in Portugal, Naples, and Piedmont in the summer of 1820.[86] According to Irene Castells, after 1823 liberals remained fascinated "by the experience of 1820, given further prominence by the mythification of Riego following his execution in the Plaza de la Cebada in Madrid on 7 November 1823," and would concur "in putting in practice the general scheme of the insurrectionary pronunciamiento."[87]

Riego's achievement would be duly recorded in one Mexican pamphlet in the following resonant terms: "Europe admires the noble audacity of the commanders and soldiers who . . . proclaimed on 1 January 1820 the august code of 1812. The provinces went on to imitate the example of these brave men; . . . and became the champions of liberty throughout the entire Peninsula. . . .

Origins of Mexico's Mimetic Insurrectionism

The King finally adhered to the will of the nation . . . and thus swore before the eyes of the people his willingness to make them happy."[88] Three lessons had already been learned: a group of officers and soldiers could challenge the government with a pronunciamiento; liberty could triumph if their example and strategy were emulated by the provinces; and it was possible this way to instigate significant political change (to ensure that the "will of the nation" was respected), without bloodshed.

The impact Riego's pronunciamiento had on the Spanish and Mexican imaginary cannot be overstated. As subsequent events would show with the proliferation and popularization of the pronunciamiento in both countries, Riego's successful 1820 gesture of rebellion provided the template of what was to become the legitimate yet unlawful practice that would be used thereafter, time and again, to effect meaningful political change at a local and national level for the next five decades. The question of the pronunciamiento's legitimacy would also prove crucial, as illustrated in an article that appeared in the Puebla-based newspaper *La Abeja Poblana* on 5 April 1821 defending Agustín de Iturbide's pronunciamiento of Iguala (24 February 1821): "Who authorized Quiroga in Spain to impose laws on Ferdinand VII? He demanded these with bayonets and triumphed: he is a hero; now [the American Iturbide proclaims Ferdinand king of Independent Mexico] and he is a traitor. . . . How absurd! [¡*Qué inconsecuencias!*]."[89]

That Riego's pronunciamiento had a major impact in Mexican politics at the time is unquestionable. As can be evidenced in a letter insurgent leader Vicente Guerrero wrote to Colonel Carlos Moya on 17 August 1820, even guerrilla fighters reduced to carrying out hit-and-run operations in the remote sierras of the Tierra Caliente knew about events in Spain and were perfectly aware of what a pronunciamiento could do: "Since I consider your Excellency well instructed in the liberal revolution in the Peninsula, those disciples of the great Porlier, Quiroga, Arco-Agüero, Riego and their comrades, I will not waste time going over this [their exploits] and instead go on to state to you that this is the most precious time for the sons of this Mexican land . . . to adopt that model to become independent."[90] This is, of course, what happened, except that the man who was to take the lead in adopting the pronunciamiento model in Mexico was criollo royalist colonel Agustín de Iturbide rather than the mulatto insurgent *cabecilla* (leader) Guerrero.[91]

The Plan of Iguala was the first pronunciamiento to be launched in Mexico. Although royalist commander cum liberator Iturbide claimed that he was the sole author of the text, recent research has shown that other actors were involved in the discussions and deliberations that led to it being drafted, including a group of criollos who gathered in the clandestine salon presided over by the extremely vivacious and beautiful independence supporter María Ignacia Rodríguez de Velasco, affectionately known as *la güera* Rodríguez.[92] In this sense Iturbide's Plan of Iguala was very much made up of the collated ideas of a number of people from Mexico's urban elites.[93] Iturbide took it upon himself to consult influential officers, clerics, civilians, and even Mexican deputies to the Spanish Cortes for the greater part of 1820, following the success and impact of Riego's pronunciamiento of Cabezas de San Juan.[94] And he corresponded with his military adversary, Guerrero, following his move to lead the royalist forces in the Tierra Caliente, before he openly changed sides and issued the plan.[95] Iturbide and Guerrero did not draft the pronunciamiento document together; Guerrero came out in support of the plan after it

Origins of Mexico's Mimetic Insurrectionism

was launched.[96] But Iturbide took on board the insurgent's view that they should not discriminate against mulattos and castas in the way that the Cádiz 1812 Constitution had done, stating from the outset of the actual text that "Europeans, Africans, and Asiatics" were all Mexican.[97]

As had been the case with the pronunciamiento of Riego, Iturbide's pronunciamiento of Iguala resulted in meaningful political change—in this case, the consummation of independence—in a matter of months and with very little bloodshed, after receiving waves of pronunciamientos de adhesión from all over the country. Evidently royalists and insurgents had reached a stage where they wanted to bring the war to an end and were receptive to what the Plan of Iguala offered them. The royalist cause had also been severely weakened following the re-adoption of the 1812 Constitution. Evidence of this is that following the plan's circulation, only the *madrileño* (Madrid-born) Field Marshall Francisco Novella in Mexico City and the Spanish forces in Veracruz displayed any appetite to fight on. However, it was Iturbide's singular ability to combine the proposals and desires of his fellow conspirators and appeal to a particularly broad range of actors that accounts, in no small measure, for the speed with which his plan gained adherents, resulting in the dramatically swift fall of the royal government in Mexico City on 27 September 1821.[98]

Probably the most salient characteristic of the pronunciamiento of Iguala was its conciliatory nature. It mimicked the Spanish liberals' 1820 use of forceful negotiation or intimidating politics to bring about *consensual* change, ensuring that a meaningful political shift was effected without overthrowing the monarchy. In other words, unlike a coup that is staged to overthrow the government, or a revolution that is launched to change the government, the political system, *and* the prevailing socioeconomic order, the pronunciamiento of Iguala, like that of Cabezas de San Juan before it, was designed to promote a forcefully negotiated political change. By this I mean it sought to ensure that the current ruler, in both these cases the king of Spain, played a part in authorizing and legitimizing the pronounced or demanded political goals without being overthrown (even though in the case of the latter, Ferdinand VII would refuse to acquiesce to the pronunciados' demands). And it did so by accepting that in order to achieve a meaningful shift in the way New Spain was governed, importantly bringing the War of Independence to an end in the process, it was imperative that the aspirations of ostensibly opposed factions were satisfied. It is for this reason that Timothy Anna argued: "Iturbide understood his role to be that of consensus-maker among Mexicans and conciliator between Spain and Mexico."[99]

The pronunciamiento of Iguala thus consolidated in Mexico an insurrectionary practice that relied heavily on consensual tactics, that sought to bring about change without overthrowing the country's ultimate ruler or head of state, and that did so by offering general and concrete benefits to a wide range of political actors, in so doing overcoming seemingly irreconcilable views and interests. It also established in Mexico an insurrectionary practice in which the texts that accompanied the act or gesture of rebellion were given special importance, endowing them with a self-apportioned legislative nature. Iturbide's pronunciamiento, publicly proclaimed in the town of Iguala (present-day state of Guerrero), on 24 February 1821, included the proclamation (the pronouncement) of a document that contained an address-like preamble and a plan. The opening justificatory preamble offered an account of how and why the plan, with its corresponding act of insubordina-

Origins of Mexico's Mimetic Insurrectionism

tion, was being launched and circulated. The plan that followed these introductory words was a petition made up of a numbered list of articles indicating the changes being sought, with the notable characteristic that these were presented as though they were actual laws, outlined so as to be implemented and abided by as of the day they had been issued/pronounced. The template of the Plan of Iguala would, in effect, become that of the subsequent 1,500 pronunciamientos launched in Mexico from 1821 to 1876.[100]

The document itself was therefore made up of an opening address, twenty-three articles, and a final exhortation to the Mexican people—addressed as "Americanos." In the plan's preamble, Iturbide adopted a deliberately integrationist stance: the Americanos were *all* the people who lived in Mexico, not just those who had been born there, and without distinction of race. He also made a point of praising Spain and everything that Spain represented to Mexico on the eve of its independence: Mexico—which he referred to as "Northern America" (*la América septentrional*) —"has been nurtured for three hundred years by the most Catholic, pious, heroic, and magnanimous nation. Spain educated her, made her great, erecting those opulent cities, those beautiful pueblos, those expansive provinces and kingdoms which in the history of the universe are now to occupy such a distinguished place." Alongside his robust defense of independence as a natural and inevitable eventuality and a goal he claimed was desired by Spaniards and Americanos alike—(had not all great nations, he asked, been ruled by others at some stage and become subsequently emancipated?)—he went out of his way to appeal to the Spanish population by ensuring they appreciated that independence did not entail a rejection of Spain or Spanish values: "Who among you can say you do not descend from the Spanish? See the sweetest of chains that links us together, add the ties of friendship, the dependency of our shared interests, our education and language, and the conformity of our sentiments; and you will see they are so tight and so powerful that the happiness of our kingdom must of necessity come about through us being united in one single opinion with one single voice."[101]

He also made a point of stressing that this was a peaceful revolution. This was not like the grito of Dolores "of the year 1810 . . . which gave rise to so many misfortunes" but rather the expression of the general will.[102] The comparatively peaceful nature of the pronunciamiento—experienced first with Riego's successful movement and now with Iturbide's consensual Plan of Iguala, would clearly prove determining in inspiring the mimetic insurrectionism of early republican Mexico. It was not just that the pronunciamiento could result in meaningful change without resort to violence; because it voiced a supposedly united and uniting call, the pronunciamiento explicitly set out, somewhat paradoxically, to force change *peacefully* and *consensually*. As Iturbide stated at the end of the plan: "Astonish the nations of erudite Europe, let them see how Northern America became independent without shedding one drop of blood."[103] In the memoirs he was to write subsequently from his exile in Italy, he would return to this point: "Without bloodshed, without incendiaries, without murders, without robberies, in short, without tears and without lamentations, my country became free."[104]

The other lesson to be drawn from the experience of Iguala was that words were translated into accomplished goals. The act of pronouncing the words—"I have proclaimed the Independence of Northern America"—actually meant, from the perspective of the pronunciados in the first instance, and from that of the nation sev-

Origins of Mexico's Mimetic Insurrectionism

eral months later, that Mexico was indeed now independent from Spain. The pronunciamiento could almost be seen to have a spell-like quality. Political aspirations were announced—*pronunciadas* (pronounced)—and they became reality. Therein lay the origin of the term *pronunciamiento* (pronouncement) and a quality that clearly differentiated it from a coup or a revolt. Iturbide liberated Mexico by *stating* that Mexico was free in his pronouncement of Iguala. And bloodlessly, because his words supposedly expressed the will of all Americanos, that which was pronounced became true. It was nothing short of political sorcery.

However, the success of the pronunciamiento of Iguala was not the result of magic but of the thought that went into the twenty-three articles making up the plan. In an extraordinary display of political know-how, the Plan of Iguala really did have something for everyone. Astutely it started by appealing to the population's widespread and uniting religious fervor, proclaiming the Apostolic Roman Catholic faith to be the new country's state religion, with tolerance of none other (art. 1). It then pleased the insurgents and all those Mexicans who believed in independence by decreeing the absolute independence of "this kingdom" in article 2. Having thus taken the bold step of proclaiming Mexico's independence, the plan stated that Mexico would be a monarchy (art. 3) and that the throne would be offered to Ferdinand VII or to a member of his royal family should he decline (art. 4). This was Iturbide's way of appeasing the royalists. Yes, he was gunning for independence, but it was independence with a Spanish monarch on the throne.

Pragmatism clearly informed a number of articles in the plan. There were practical considerations, such as the declaration that a temporary junta was to be formed while the new nation's parliament or congress was constituted (art. 5). This interim junta would have the authority to govern the independent nation, and it would be independent and yet made up of *vocales* (members) who had Viceroy Apodaca's approval (art. 6). Once more, Iturbide was finding ways of softening the blow of independence to the Spanish community in Mexico. Of course, as becomes clear in the following pages, pronunciamiento texts did not always say what the pronunciados wanted, but rather what they suspected those they needed to convince wanted to hear, in order to achieve their aims. Iturbide could very well claim that Apodaca was to approve the proposed members of the junta; he knew perfectly well that the viceroy (turned-political-chief following the reintroduction of the constitution) would refuse to back independence. The same applied to his offer of the throne to Ferdinand VII. Iturbide and his fellow conspirators must have known that the king would not come to Mexico to take up the throne. Cunningly, in articles 7 and 8 Iturbide prepared for such an eventuality. The junta would rule Mexico for however long it took for Ferdinand VII to cross the Atlantic and take up the offer of the Mexican crown. If Ferdinand VII opted not to come, the so-called Junta de la Regencia (Regency Junta) would have the mandate to continue governing the newly independent country while the nation decided who should don the crown. Subsequent events, namely the crowning of Emperor Agustín I that resulted from the premeditated coup of 19 May 1822, would suggest that Iturbide was preparing the ground for such an outcome while appearing to be loyal to the king of Spain.

The mention of force, which in subsequent pronunciamientos could include an explicit or implicit threat of violence, came in article 9, where Iturbide noted that the new Mexican government

Origins of Mexico's Mimetic Insurrectionism

was to be "sustained by the Army of the Three Guarantees." The reference to an army dedicated to defending independence was clearly a way of ensuring everybody knew that behind the plan's good intentions was a mighty military force ready to fight for the newly formed independent governing junta. It was also significantly a new army, and as was explained in more detail in articles 16–19, it would be made up of former royalists *and* insurgents and all those soldiers who joined Iturbide's cause. That it was called the Army of the Three Guarantees—in reference to the rallying call of Iturbide's movement: "Religion, Independence, Union"— served to reiterate the pronunciamiento's consensual and resonant message of forging a country that was Roman Catholic and independent, in which under the banner of "union" nobody would be discriminated against or persecuted on the grounds that they were Spaniards, castas, or Indians.[105]

Bearing in mind the impact the reintroduction the Cádiz Constitution was having in Mexico, Iturbide skillfully found ways of defending yet distancing himself from the charter's liberal values and principles. According to the Plan of Iguala, Mexico would have its own "Cortes" (parliament, as termed in the 1812 Constitution), which in the long term would decide whether to replace the interim junta with a regency while waiting for the throne to be taken (art. 10).[106] These Cortes, moreover, would be charged with drafting the constitution of the Mexican Empire (art. 11), which indicated, on the one hand, that the Mexican monarchy would be a constitutional and not an absolutist one (that is, a liberal monarchy like the one established in Cádiz); but that it would abide by an entirely different constitution, reassuring, on the other hand, the more reactionary or traditionalist *borbonistas* and *serviles* who had dragged their feet over swearing in the

Cádiz magna carta that Mexico would *not* be governed according to the divisive 1812 charter. This notwithstanding, as long as the Mexican Cortes had not been convened, the Cádiz Constitution would remain in place in terms of juridical matters and criminal offenses (art. 20). However, the rules that were to dictate how the deputies of the Mexican Constituent Cortes were to be elected would be determined by the Mexican junta in another move away from the laws—in this case electoral—outlined in the 1812 charter (art. 23).

Yet another example of the plan's remarkable balancing act can be found in articles 12–15, in terms of the way it promoted major political change (independence!) while promising those who might be badly affected by such an eventuality that their interests would not be harmed. For those Mexicans who had been banned from public office by the discriminatory laws of Bourbon Mexico, Iturbide promised employment: "All the inhabitants [of the Mexican Empire], without distinction other than merit and virtue, are citizens ideally entitled to apply for any post" (art. 12). For those Spaniards who were already employed in the viceregal bureaucracy, Iturbide guaranteed that they would be allowed to continue in the public posts as long as they supported the plan (art. 15). To everybody he promised respect for and the protection of their persons and properties (art. 13). And to the members of a clergy who had suffered as a result of the Bourbon reforms and were apprehensive about the anticlerical laws the reconvened liberal Spanish Cortes in Madrid might have up their sleeve, Iturbide explicitly stated that they were to retain their properties and privileges (*fueros*; art. 14). It was a perfect recipe for mustering support. Criollos would now have access to jobs in the bureaucracy, Spaniards in post would not be removed, everybody's property

Origins of Mexico's Mimetic Insurrectionism

would be safeguarded, and the clergy's wealth and prerogatives would not be confiscated.

Last but not least, following all the consensual fireworks discussed so far, the plan contained two articles (21 and 22) serving to reinforce the tougher stance that lay hidden behind the promise of a future providing something for everybody, namely that those who conspired against independence or sought to spread discord in the new nation would be imprisoned. As would become common in most nineteenth-century pronunciamientos, alongside the bid to represent the general will through consensual demands, there would be a paradoxical flexing of muscles, which would find expression either in the threat of violence or in the announcement that those who opposed the plan would suffer the consequences (by going to prison, losing their jobs, or in a handful of extreme cases facing death or exile).

The pronunciamiento ended with a final exhortation in which Iturbide proclaimed the creation of a new Mexican empire and called upon the population to cooperate and unite behind the Army of the Three Guarantees. Given that this army was to be made up of "Europeans and Americans, royalists and dissidents [insurgents]," Iturbide was confident that peace would be attained, if nothing else because there was no longer an army there to oppose them. The grito of Iguala ended with three *vivas*: to Religion, Independence, and Union.

In Iturbide's own words:

> The plan of Iguala guaranteed the religion which we inherited from our ancestors. To the reigning family of Spain, it held out the only prospect which survived for preserving those extensive and fertile provinces. To the Mexicans, it granted the right of enacting their

own laws, and of having their government established within their own territory. To the Spaniards, it offered an asylum, which, if they had possessed any foresight, they would not have despised. It secured the rights of equality, of property, and of liberty, the knowledge of which is within the reach of every one, and the possession of which, when once acquired, every man would exert all his power to preserve. The plan of Iguala extinguished the odious distinction of castes, offered to every stranger safety, convenience, and hospitality; it left the road to advancement open to merit; conciliated the good opinion of every reasonable man; and opposed an impenetrable barrier to the machinations of the discontented.[107]

The Plan of Iguala turned out to be an incredibly seductive proposal. With the vague promise of Three Guarantees—religion, independence, and union—Iturbide brought former insurgents and royalists together, even though they opted to join forces for very different reasons. While the Spanish troops in the main garrisons of Veracruz (Orizaba, Córdoba, Alvarado, Xalapa, Perote, Veracruz, and San Juan de Ulúa) put up stiff resistance against the then as yet unknown Antonio López de Santa Anna and his liberating forces, the rest of the country let itself be seduced and charmed by the Plan of Iguala.[108] From Lorenzo de Zavala's point of view, the reason was simple:

> This was not the tumultuous cry of Dolores in 1810: [there were] no Indians armed with sickles, slings and stones, shouting confusedly and in disorder: *Death to the gachupines! Long live our Virgin of Guadalupe!* Here was a leader renowned for his valor who, supported by the national vote, with disciplined troops, spoke in the name of the pueblos, and demanded rights that were all but too well known: this

was a new generation, that had learnt in the hard school of the past revolution to respect rights and justice.[109]

Above and beyond the numerous professions of allegiance the Plan of Iguala received, it benefited from the endorsement of Juan O'Donojú, the liberal superior political chief of New Spain who arrived from Spain in August 1821. Responding to the waves of support the Plan of Iguala had received, O'Donojú actually recognized Mexico as a "sovereign and independent nation," and signed, on 24 August 1821, the Treaty of Córdoba. Regardless of the fact that Ferdinand VII would disavow the treaty and that Spain would not recognize the independence of Mexico until 1836, from the Mexican perspective of the time, the pronunciamiento of Iguala had resulted in the recently arrived representative of the Spanish government appearing to be prepared to bow down and negotiate with the pronunciados. Interestingly, in terms of nomenclature, O'Donojú referred to the Plan of Iguala as a *pronunciamiento*, in stating that "New Spain [had] pronounced for Independence" and had "an army there to sustain this pronunciamiento."[110]

The Treaty of Córdoba retained the spirit of Iguala's proposals, adding concrete details to specific aspects of the plan, such as who in the Bourbon dynasty would be offered the Mexican throne and in what order (art. 3). It also set out the rules and attributes that would govern the Junta Provisional de Gobierno. With Novella having staged a coup against a dithering Viceroy Apodaca in Mexico City on 5 July 1821, the treaty ended with O'Donojú offering to use his authority to negotiate the "bloodless exit and honorable capitulation" of the Spanish forces in the capital.[111] Novella received a copy of the Treaty of Córdoba on 30 August, and despite trying to avoid capitulation, was ultimately persuaded into it on 13 September after a six-day-long armistice. Eleven days later, on 24 September, Novella abandoned the capital at the head of two thousand Spanish troops. Apodaca followed suit the next day.[112]

With the scene set for a triumphal entrance into Mexico City, Iturbide and the Army of the Three Guarantees marched into the capital on the Liberator's thirty-eighth birthday (27 September). Iturbide famously made his army take a diversion as it processed toward the main square, so that he could wave to his inspirational and free-spirited lover, la güera Rodríguez.[113] Thus the independence of Mexico was consummated, even though Perote, the port of Veracruz, and the garrison of San Juan de Ulúa were still controlled by the royalists at the time.[114]

Independence was formally ratified on 28 September 1821 with the signing of the Acta de Independencia, which gave bureaucratic formality to the fait accompli of independence. The Acta de Independencia also legitimized the Plan of Iguala by stating that this pronunciamiento, together with the Treaty of Córdoba, had "wisely" established the bases upon which Mexico was to be constituted. In this sense, pronunciamientos would, from the very beginning, be seen as having constitutional and constitutive qualities; something a straightforward revolt or coup could never possess. Bearing in mind how pronunciamientos would result in the hero worship of their leaders and perpetrators, inspiring more than one ambitious officer hungry for fame and notoriety to attempt to emulate Riego and Iturbide's success thereafter, the Acta de Independencia did not shy away from celebrating Iturbide's personal role in the venture: "the entirely memorable enterprise of independence is consummated, that which a genius superior to all admiration and praise, love and glory of his patria, initiated in Iguala, persevered with and ultimately brought about, overcoming insurmountable obstacles."[115]

It is evident that the success of the Plan of Iguala transformed it into the role model for successive Mexican pronunciamientos. To quote Timothy Anna: "The reason the pronunciamiento became the preferred instrument for fundamental political change is that it worked; at least the first ones did."[116] There was no looking back. Cabezas de San Juan had resulted in the Spanish expeditionary army being organized in Cádiz avoiding having to cross the Atlantic to fight in South America, it had forced King Ferdinand VII to restore the 1812 Constitution, and it had transformed Riego into a much lauded liberal hero. Iguala applied the same model to the Mexican context and had an even more dramatic result: Mexico gained its independence from Spain through a process of forceful, albeit consensual, negotiation. Iturbide not only went on to be celebrated as a truly national hero; eight months later he was proclaimed emperor by another self-denominated pronunciamiento. What was to follow would be five decades of pronounced political insurrectionism as one disgruntled pronunciado after another sought to address grievances by attempting to emulate Riego and Iturbide's success. The scene was set for mimetic insurrectionism to spread like wildfire.

3. The Voice of the Provinces

The Insurrectional Contagion of Mexico's
First Pronunciamientos, 1821–1831

The consummation of independence, arising as it did from the pronunciamiento cycle that began in Iguala on 24 February 1821, albeit a truly momentous event, did not give way to a new dawn of peace, order, and prosperity. As captured by historian Javier Ocampo, the dreams and aspirations Mexicans treasured on the very day independence was achieved turned out to be tragically short-lived, being little more than, as he put it, "the ideas of one day."[1] Alexander von Humboldt's seminal 1811 study of the Kingdom of New Spain, while not predicting that with independence Mexico would fast become a world power, had argued that the colonial structure represented "an obstacle to the public prosperity" of Mexico and hinted at the potential benefits separation from Spain could bring with it. Humboldt's detailed survey of the country's mineral and natural wealth, its abundant silver mines and exuberant primary goods (vanilla, coffee, tobacco, cochineal, sugar, and bananas), certainly led those educated Mexicans who read him to believe that once they took control of and owned their own resources, the world would be their oyster.[2]

Humboldt was perceptive enough, however, to note that for the Mexican people truly to enjoy their country's wealth, they would need to overcome the social and racial inequality that characterized New Spain's society at the time: "the prosperity of the whites is intimately connected with that of the copper-colored race, and . . . there can be no durable prosperity for the two Americas till this unfortunate race, humiliated but not degraded by long oppression, shall participate in all the advantages resulting from the progress of civilization and the improvement of the social order!"[3] Social injustice, racial discrimination, and acute asymmetries of wealth would represent but just some of the truly monumental obstacles that would stand in the way of Mexico's first rulers' early attempts to give their newly independent nation respected liberal institutions, political stability, and a solid financial foundation.

To begin with, there was the legacy of a particularly violent eleven-year-long civil war. The destruction suffered by those very resources about which Humboldt had waxed lyrical and the psychological harm that had been inflicted on the people who found themselves caught up in the revolutionary whirlwind were not inconsiderable. Between 1810 and 1821 mining declined by a third, with numerous silver mines having been flooded by insurgents and royalists alike in a bid to prevent the enemy benefiting from them. Once flooded, these mines were lost for good.[4] According to Barbara Tenenbaum, not until the 1850s would the mining of silver regain the levels of profit and production it had reached on the eve of the War of Independence.[5] Furthermore, the disruption of the war severely impacted the revenue collected through taxation, which had gone from an annual average of almost 18 million pesos in 1789 to less than 3 million pesos in 1816.[6] As a result Iturbide's independent government inherited a national debt that was calculated in 1822 at 76 million pesos.[7] Much of the turmoil that would characterize the following decades would stem from the nascent country's dire straits and fiscal disarray as its new rulers desperately sought to erect on the ruins of the war-torn colonial financial system an entirely new and workable tax structure that could pay back its debts, both old and new (including the substantial loans Mexico received in 1824 from several British commercial houses) and cover the ever-increasing expenses of its army.[8]

As for the mental, emotional, and ultimately political scars the war would leave behind, although research still needs to be done on how the different sides' antagonism was played out in the early national period, it is evident from the way former criollo royalists like generals Manuel Gómez Pedraza and Anastasio Bustamante behaved toward the mulatto former insurgent leader Vicente Guerrero in the late 1820s and early 1830s that a visceral rivalry with racist undertones dating back to the war remained as potent as ever. Bustamante's government's decision to have Guerrero executed on Valentine's Day in 1831 must be understood as a vendetta carried out by former royalists on a renowned and dark-skinned insurgent commander. To a certain extent the civil conflicts of the 1820s and early 1830s would see former royalists and insurgents pitted against one another in political reruns of the military battles of the War of Independence. It would prove difficult for the open wounds of the revolution to heal, let alone scar, especially since most of the political leaders of Independent Mexico were veterans of the 1810–21 Revolution.[9]

The absence of a clear sense of national identity or consciousness did not help either. What was Mexico in 1821, after all? To begin with it was not a nation as such but an empire that included (until 1823) the present-day Central American countries of Guatemala, Nicaragua, El Salvador, Honduras, and Costa Rica, and with remote frontier posts reaching as far north as present-day

California, Nevada, and Utah. Before Mexico became Mexico it was, as defined in the Plan of Iguala, the América del Septentrión (Northern America), and subsequently, as described in the 1824 Constitution, the Estados Unidos Mexicanos (United Mexican States). Creole patriotism had resonated with certain educated Mexican intellectuals like Carlos María de Bustamante, and the war had given the army a definite patriotic rhetoric and discourse.[10] That much is true. This does not mean that there was a clear sense of what it meant to be Mexican for the majority of the population, living in remote sierras, barely speaking Spanish, with strong local, regional, and/or ethnic identities. Until independence, the people who inhabited New Spain and the Captaincy General of Guatemala owed their allegiance and obedience to the crown, not to Spain or their own nation. What were important to them were their families, neighbors, parish, and *milpas* (fields of maize). Mexico was, to quote Raymond Buve, "an archipelago of local societies."[11] Making that mental change, coming to accept that you now belonged to a country—a shared and abstract community that extended beyond your village, hacienda, or valley, that granted you rights but also expected you to fulfill certain responsibilities and obligations, expecting you to pay taxes, join its national army if you were of a certain age, and abide by its laws—would most certainly not happen overnight and would take considerable time. The country had an ethnically diverse population of around 6 million, of whom two-fifths were Indians.[12] Only an urban minority could read and write, and a uniformly accepted idea of nationhood, of what it meant to be Mexican, would not come easy.[13] By 1836, although the centralist constitution known as the *Siete Leyes* (Seven Laws) that replaced the 1824 charter made a point of denoting who qualified as a Mexican (one needed to have been born in Mexico, or have been a resident in Mexico at the time of independence in 1821, or be a naturalized foreigner), it nonetheless made a distinction between having Mexican nationality and being a Mexican citizen who could actually vote in popular elections (servants, criminals, drunks, vagrants, and people earning less than two hundred pesos per annum were excluded).[14] According to Josefina Vázquez it would take the Mexican-U.S. War of 1846–48 for Mexicans to begin to see themselves as belonging to a shared imagined community as they were pitted against another country and culture in the form of the invading U.S. Army.[15] Some would argue that it would take at least another half-century before a meaningfully shared sense of national identity was cemented. In the words of Alan Knight, Mexico in 1910 was "less a nation than a geographical expression, a mosaic of regions and communities, introverted and jealous, ethnically and physically fragmented, and lacking common national sentiments."[16]

Mexico's size and complex geography of inaccessible mountain ranges, vast deserts, and impenetrable jungles and the country's poor state of communications were also contributing factors in making governance near impossible. The very logistics of ruling Mexico were in themselves mindboggling. How could you ensure from a ventilated room in the national palace overlooking the main square in Mexico City, with its tilting *churrigueresque* (Spanish baroque) cathedral to one side and the bustling and noisy Parián market before you, that the laws you passed traveled to, reached, were understood and actually implemented almost 1,500 kilometers away in the remote Maya-speaking village of Tizimín in northeast Yucatán, for example?[17] According to English traveler William Bullock, writing in 1823, it took "four days to travel a distance an English stagecoach on English roads would have covered comfortably in twenty-eight hours, carrying double the weight."[18] By the 1850s it still took three and a half days for the stagecoach to travel from the port of Vera-cruz on the Gulf of Mexico to Mexico City. From the capital it took a further ten days for it to reach the port of San Blas on the Pacific coast.[19] As was noted by U.S. envoy Joel Poinsett follow-ing his first trip to Mexico in 1822, "Notwithstanding the labour and expense bestowed upon the roads from Vera Cruz and Aca-pulco to Mexico [City], they are still very bad, and the transpor-tation of merchandise and produce over them, will for years be difficult and costly. . . . The elevation of those plains from the ocean, opposes an insuperable obstacle to the cheap transporta-tion of its produce to the sea coast."[20]

Furthermore, the sudden absence of one established, recog-nized, and respected legal system, with a clearly outlined and accepted set of constitutional or systemic norms and political institutions, resulting from the overthrow of the colonial *ancien régime* on 27 September 1821, would arguably present Mexico's new rulers with one of the hardest challenges to be overcome. As noted, the Plan of Iguala stipulated that certain aspects of the Cádiz Constitution would remain in place while the Junta de la Regencia governed the new country, and a new constitution and legal system were drafted. In practice, this meant that from the outset there was no clear or single set of rules to govern society.

The wise men in what was for many a remote highland capi-tal gathered to determine whether Mexico should be a monarchy or a republic, whether they should adopt a federalist or a central-ist constitution, and whether they should empower the legisla-tive branch of power over the executive. They debated whether all men born and/or residing in the country should have the right to vote (or just those who made a living "decently"). They even argued over what role the indigenous population, still set apart in their *repúblicas de indios*, could possibly have as model citizens in the nation's novel order. And they wrangled over how much congressmen should be paid and how they should address one another in this new independent dawn.[21] In the meantime, who was a hypothetical cobbler in the Veracruzan mountain village of Naolinco, overlooking its spectacular eighty-meter-high waterfall, meant to obey and why? More to the point, according to what rules was he meant to obey his local mayor, town councilors, priest, landowner, or military commander? Did colonial norms and customs still apply? Which ones and when?

To provide a sense of how confusing the context was following the country's sudden independence from Spain, the clash that took place between the town council of Xalapa and Santa Anna in late September 1821 is highly illustrative. The ayuntamiento elected in 1813 and reconvened seven years later in 1820 following the reintroduction of the Cádiz Constitution while Mexico was still New Spain (ultimately as a result of Riego's pronunciamiento in Cabezas de San Juan), wanted to know why they were compelled to obey the recently arrived and somewhat demanding "Lieutenant Colonel of the Imperial Army of the Three Guarantees, Commander General of the Province of Veracruz, Sub-Inspector of its troops, and Political Chief of the same."[22] They asked Santa Anna to provide them with a copy of the order from Iturbide that confirmed he was indeed the political chief of the province, "for the belief that just being a military commander makes you a *jefe político* is not valid." In reply to their legalistic challenge, the ambitious young officer and de facto ruler of the province retorted that when he entered a village the town councils recognized him as their political chief. It was in his view that simple. Just as the rest of the kingdom had recognized Sr. Iturbide as their leading *jefe*, he argued, in Orizaba and Córdoba, mirroring national trends, Santa Anna had appointed himself or obtained the same position that Sr. Dávila had occupied under the Spanish government. If the ayuntamiento of Xalapa were not going to accept this, he asked, with which political chief or intendant were the town councils of the province going to deal? In his mind:

> Just as Sr. Dávila was the political and military head, he [Santa Anna] was so now, with it not being necessary for him to have a document stating as much; or a nomination signed by the Sr. First Jefe, for there are still many captains and officers in the Imperial Army who have not received any such written confirmations, orders, or decrees from the Sr. First Jefe; the kind of formalities that only come when a government has long been established; this does not mean that they lack power or should not be obeyed, because regularly it is the case that necessity makes the illicit licit.[23]

In the end, for Santa Anna, the fact that Iturbide addressed all military and political orders to him settled the matter. He did not need to have been elected or nominated, nor did he need a formal document to legitimate his position of authority.[24] With more than eight hundred armed men under his orders camped in the neighboring fields of Las Ánimas, it was always going to be difficult for a dozen earnest and punctilious councilors to ignore him.[25]

It would take three years, during which past and present New Spanish and Mexican military and civilian authorities competed with each other at a local level, improvising laws as they went along, before Mexico's first national constitution was finally inaugurated on 4 October 1824. Even then, as I go on to show in the present work, the constitutional and legal conundrums of independence would not be entirely resolved until the 1857 Constitution was fully restored in 1867. For the sensitive mid-nineteenth-century moderate liberal deputy and intellectual Mariano Otero, writing in 1842, one of the causes of Mexico's troubled first two decades as an independent nation lay in the fact that the country was undergoing a transition process.[26] Old laws and customs still lingered in some form or another, while new rules and institutions were in the process of being formulated and had not yet had time to become firmly established: "when [political institutions] are destroyed or have as yet to be forged, authority lacks real strength, civil war becomes the norm, and all questions are resolved on the battlefield."[27]

Colonial political norms and institutions such as the ecclesiastical and military *fueros* (legal privileges), which spared clerics and soldiers from being tried in civil courts, giving them a degree of legal immunity, remained in place for the next three decades.[28] So did *ejidos* (communal lands) and rights that dated back in some cases to the sixteenth century and which numerous indigenous groups held onto against the odds.[29] Alongside these institutions were the constitutional structures that came and went as the 1812 Constitution of Cádiz (implemented in Mexico in 1813–14 and 1820–22) was replaced with the Reglamento provisional político del Imperio Mexicano of 18 December 1822; the 1824 federal charter, with its constellation of separate state constitutions; and the centralist 1836 Siete Leyes, 1841 Bases de Tacubaya, 1843 Bases Orgánicas, 1824 Constitution restored in 1846, and *santanista* dictatorship of 1853–55. It would take the laws of the midcentury liberal governments of Juan Álvarez (1855), Ignacio Comonfort

(1855–58), and Benito Juárez (1860–63) as well as the 1857 Constitution and the bloodshed of both the War of the Reforma (1858–60) and the French Intervention (1862–67) for Mexico finally to dismantle its resilient colonial juridical legacies.[30]

The unresolved problem of legitimacy and authority was undoubtedly at the heart of much of Mexico's early unrest, and the pronunciamiento was its most obvious expression. Political legitimacy, after all, relies on faith or trust.[31] You and your community (village, province, and ultimately nation) must collectively be willing to obey a set of rules, a given government, or a particular individual for any of these to have the legitimacy and the authority to determine the way your society is run. With the one exception of charismatic domination—where, as argued by Max Weber, in a context of a severe economic, social, political, or religious crisis a group may place faith overnight in a given individual's Messianic ability (rather than in established institutions) to rule—legitimacy typically requires time.[32] As Seymour Martin Lipset reminds us, the grounds of political legitimacy rest on institutions having had the time to "engender and maintain the belief" that they are "the most appropriate and proper ones for society."[33] You can appear to invent a new legitimacy (e.g., by overthrowing an unpopular government and a whole set of institutions with a coup) and you can, initially, persuade others of the legitimacy of your actions (e.g., through military victory; claiming to represent the popular will). But crucially, you then need to "maintain" belief in this legitimacy. For this to occur your system or government needs to be effective in resolving the problems afflicting society and, critically, you need *time* to develop a "common secular political culture" (e.g., creating sites of memory through national holidays and rituals that ingrain a sense of identity, purpose, and institutional stability) that may enable your constitutional framework to resonate with the population of your country.[34] In other words, legitimacy is either born from a collective's disposition to believe in a given way of doing things, because that is the way things have been done for generations (i.e., tradition), or from its willingness to believe in the legality of a given regime/system, as a matter of principles (e.g., because people believe in democracy, republican values, the need for the rule of law, etc.). But even in the second of these two scenarios, a community's readiness to believe in a given constitutional system will come about because it works, and for it to work and prove that it has worked (i.e., for its institutions to appear as the "most appropriate and proper ones") will of necessity have required time to engender and *maintain* the aura of legitimacy.[35]

By understanding the transitory context of Mexico's early national period and appreciating the extent to which no given set of laws or institutions enjoyed sufficient time to *maintain* their engendered or recently invented legitimacies, it is possible to begin to see how the pronunciamiento, as a practice, became as much a curious constitutional stopgap measure as an obvious source of instability. In a context in which it remained unclear which laws and institutions were legitimate and had authority, the pronunciamiento flourished, developing its own form of legitimacy. Evidence of how pronunciamientos became, at times, part of the decision-making process of Independent Mexico's early constituted institutions can be found in the manner in which these overtly aggressive petitions actually inspired new legislation.

Taking just one example from the mid- to late 1820s, when the call to expel Spanish nationals from Mexico gathered momentum as a result of Spain's refusal to recognize Mexico's independence, the manner in which Jalisco's state congress ended up legislating in favor of expelling the Spanish population from the region in 1827 came about as a result of pronunciamiento pressure. The regional legislature's radical decree of 3 September 1827, giving Spaniards twenty days in which to pack their belongings and leave the state, was as much motivated by the proposals of the state congress's committee of public security of 24 August as it was by the intimidating "Plan de descoyotar en el estado de Jalisco" (Plan to free the state of Jalisco of [Spanish] coyotes) of 7 August.[36] Of particular interest is that the proposals of 24 August, drafted by the committee set up by the state legislature of Jalisco to formulate a regional-based decree in response to the moderate federal or national expulsion laws of 10 May 1827, mirrored the unlawful yet arguably legitimate extra-constitutional text of the pronunciamiento of 7 August.[37] The fact that the proposed decree of 24 August was preceded by the adjective *"Verdadero"* (true; "Verdadero decreto del Congreso de Jalisco para la salida de los españoles") is suggestive of the fact that the members of the official committee of public security, despite working for the legally constituted state legislature of Jalisco, still considered it necessary to remind the population that their proposed law was the actual "real one," as opposed to the laws that had been promoted in the unlawful "Plan de descoyotar" of 7 August.[38]

In a context in which constitutional and revolutionary bureaucracies and practices coexisted alongside and mirrored each other, with pronunciamiento texts becoming characterized by their formal legal lexicon and register, and where political measures could be informed and influenced using both lawful (constitutional) and unlawful (extra-constitutional) methods (i.e., laws were proposed by state legislature committees *and* demanded in aggressive pronunciamientos), it is evident that during the early national period it was not always obvious where authority truly lay. In a sense, legitimacy, like power itself, was up for grabs. Whoever could *maintain* their engendered or recently invented legitimacy the longer would ultimately become the legitimate authority, at a national or local level, regardless of whether they had been elected in the first instance according to one or another set of recently approved constitutional norms or had risen to power on the back of a successful (and thus legitimate) pronunciamiento cycle.

Although understanding the context of Independent Mexico certainly goes a long way toward explaining the proliferation of the pronunciamiento, we must not underestimate the importance of local and regional concerns. The pronunciamientos of Cabezas de San Juan and Iguala had certainly provided Mexicans with an insurrectionary practice that appeared to offer them a very effective and comparatively peaceful means of effecting meaningful political change in this turbulent age of democratic revolutions. However, it was the moment that it became clear that it was a practice that could work for the regions and its elites that accounts for the insurrectional contagion of Mexico's first pronunciamientos. The pronunciamiento gave the regional elites an effective tool with which to address local grievances *and* renegotiate their peripheral political power bases vis-à-vis the center.

It would be during Mexico's first decade as an independent nation, between the triumph of the pronunciamiento of Iguala in 1821 and the end of the War of South in April 1831, that the pronunciamiento as a practice would find itself replicated by increasing numbers of political actors. It became evident that not only could a pronunciamiento serve to bring about meaningful change at a national level; it could also serve to promote and defend very specific regional interests. Given the importance of the local—the fact that from the ground what mattered was who determined how your region was run rather than what might have been occurring in the distant capital—it was almost inevitable, following the success of the pronunciamientos of Cabezas de San Juan and Iguala, that mimetic insurrectionism would not take long to surface in the regional milieu and that it would give expression to the voice of the provinces.

The spread of mimetic insurrectionism in provincial Mexico can be accounted for in part by the very dynamic of the *actas de adhesión,* which entailed replicating the motions and demands of the original start-up pronunciamiento. That in itself was conducive to popularizing the practice. The experience undergone by provincial juntas and garrisons of having gathered to read, discuss, and pronounce in favor of the Plan of Iguala, throughout the spring and summer of 1821, in so doing mimicking the steps taken in Iguala on 24 February, taught Mexico's incipient political class how to effect change through pronunciamiento methods. With most of these actas de adhesión having involved the broader community through the organization of fiestas in which church bells pealed, Te Deums were sung, music was played, fireworks went off, and the population at large joined the festivities by lighting their houses overnight, or on occasion for three whole days, and hanging bunting from their windows, it is not difficult to grasp how this apparently joyous and peaceful form of insurrection caught on.[39] Zavala in recounting how Yucatán and Guatemala became independent in 1821, throwing in their lot behind the Plan of Iguala, would recall that they did so "without any support from Mexico," inspired solely by having witnessed "the brilliant example of ideas triumph."[40]

Not quite a year after Iturbide marched into Mexico City at the head of the Army of the Three Guarantees, in the northern province of Nuevo Santander (present-day Tamaulipas), a pronunciamiento was launched against him by the local governor, Felipe de la Garza. It marked the beginning of a trend toward the adoption of this particular insurrectionary practice (with its characteristic act of insubordination, issue of a written plan, and call for negotiation) to address regional grievances. This pronunciamiento was dated 22 September 1822.[41] As Catherine Andrews noted, it "has the dubious honor of being among the first military rebellions in independent Mexico."[42] Ostensibly opposed to Iturbide's growing despotic tendencies and his arrest of nineteen deputies on 26 August, it was concerned as much with national grievances as it was with preventing the center from interfering in the local political scene. In a nutshell, Garza's gesture of rebellion was spurred by his refusal to hand over the command of the province to Iturbide's appointee, Colonel Pedro José Lanuza. Albeit unsuccessful, Garza's pronunciamiento, in being used to address provincial concerns alongside national ones, signaled a crucial shift in the way this insurrectionary practice would start to be used in Mexico.

If I may reprise the point made in the previous chapter that for mimetic insurrectionism to occur, the original act of insurrection needs to have been successful—it was the eventual success of the Veracruz–Casa Mata pronunciamiento cluster of 2 December 1822–1 February 1823 that demonstrated how the regional elites could successfully bring down an interfering centralist regime and defend their local power arrangements through pronunciamiento pressure. Critical to the Plan of Casa Mata's success was its ninth article, which empowered the provincial deputation.[43] It was its defense of the powers of the Veracruz Provincial Deputation that inspired all the other provincial deputations in Mexico, resentful of the manner in which Iturbide had sought to curtail their sphere of influence, to come out with proclamations of allegiance. Although these did not actually call for the establishment of a republic, nor did they demand an end to Iturbide's rule, the emphasis was on summoning a new congress, and in view of the support the Acta de Casa Mata received, the emperor opted to restore the closed-down First Constituent Congress and abdicate on 19 March 1823, going into exile soon after. With it now proven that pronunciamientos resulted in meaningful change at a regional as well as at a national level, they started to spread. Thereafter the pronunciamiento became the favorite means used to reorder the local political scene or address local concerns, even when lip service was paid to grander remoter national matters, and it gave expression to the voice of the provinces in their power struggle with the center.

Following the success of the Plan of Iguala it did not take long for the insurrectionary model of the pronunciamiento to be adopted by other restless officers in collusion with Masonic lodges, civilian politicians, and regional/state authorities. Between 1821 and 1831 more than fifty separate individual pronunciamientos were launched, whether these were start-up pronunciamientos, pronunciamientos de adhesión, counterpronunciamientos, or *despronunciamientos*. In terms of actual pronunciamiento constellations, cycles, or series, there were more than ten distinct groups, which for analytical purposes I distinguish here in terms of five different types of pronunciamiento clusters.

First, there were those that engaged with national concerns, spread across several states or regions, and were successful. These were the Veracruz–Casa Mata series of 2 December 1822–1 February 1823 that brought an end to Agustín de Iturbide's Mexican Empire; the Perote–Oaxaca–La Acordada series of September–November 1828 that overturned General Manuel Gómez Pedraza's victory in the presidential elections in favor of *yorkino* candidate Vicente Guerrero; and the Jalapa–Mexico City constellation (December 1829) that gave way to the overthrow of Guerrero and the rise to power of General Anastasio Bustamante (inspiring, in turn, a cluster of counter-Jalapa pronunciamientos as well as the sixteen-month-long War of the South in the present-day state of Guerrero).

Second, there was one particular pronunciamiento cycle that engaged with national concerns and spread across several states or regions but failed to achieve its aims. This was the pronunciamiento cycle of Manuel Montaño or Otumba (23 December 1827), calling for the end of all secret societies, a change of cabinet, and the expulsion of interfering U.S. Minister Plenipotentiary Joel Poinsett, while upholding the 1824 Constitution and the law. It lasted more than a fortnight and spread across the present-day states of Mexico and Hidalgo, eliciting the mobilization of military forces from both the capital and the state of Veracruz, but was forcefully quelled in the battle of Tulancingo of 7 January 1828.

Third, there were pronunciamiento clusters that engaged with national concerns but, unlike the Plan of Montaño, failed to spread beyond their region of origin and were also forcefully quelled. These were the noted pronunciamiento of Felipe de la Garza in Tamaulipas of 22 September 1822 in defense of congress and its arrested deputies; the plans of Guadalajara and San Luis Potosí (May to June 1823) that were launched to lobby the authorities in Mexico City to convoke a federalist constituent congress; José María Lobato's anti-Spanish pronunciamiento of 23 January 1824 calling for the removal of all Spanish nationals from posts in the government bureaucracy; and the radical federalist plan of Guadalajara (8 June 1824) that defended the Acta Constitutiva of January that year against the watered-down version that was adopted in the form of the 1824 Constitution.

Fourth, there was one pronunciamiento cycle that engaged with national concerns and failed to spread beyond its region but succeeded in reordering the local political scene. The pronunciamiento of Campeche (6 November 1829) did not spread beyond Yucatán and failed to bring about its national demand to abolish the 1824 Federal Constitution and replace it with a new centralist charter. However it succeeded, arguably unwittingly, in Yucatán becoming a pseudo-independent state for the next two years.

The fifth and last category involves pronunciamientos that were engaged with strictly regional concerns. These did not intend to influence national politics and did not seek to elicit support from elsewhere. They were launched by local political actors with the sole purpose of reordering the local political scene or addressing very specific regional grievances. The plan of Veracruz of 31 July 1827 and that of San Juan Bautista of 29 April 1830 are but two such pronunciamientos, typically focused on reordering the local political scene; that is, removing Veracruz state governor Miguel Barragán, in the former, and the Tabasco commander general Francisco Palomino, in the latter. Before I analyze these, it might be helpful to provide a concise summary of the main events of these years, 1821–31.

The consummation of independence on 27 September 1821—albeit not consolidated in Veracruz until 28 October (with

Spanish forces hanging onto the island fortress of San Juan de Ulúa in Veracruz harbor until 17 November 1825)—was initially celebrated with "explosive enthusiasm" from California to Yucatán in what Javier Ocampo described as a veritable collective joyful ruckus.[44] An initial mood of intense hope spread across Mexico, expressed with loud festivities, breathtaking pyrotechnic displays, and an astonishing proliferation of celebratory speeches, sermons, allegorical representations, poems, and newspaper articles. However, before long a multitude of problems faced the newly constituted government, the so-called Regencia del Imperio (Imperial Regency), made up of Iturbide, Manuel de la Bárcena, Isidro Yáñez, Manuel Velázquez de León, and Spanish jefe político Juan O'Donojú (who died of a lung infection on 8 October and was replaced by the bishop of Puebla, Antonio Joaquín Pérez).

Spain and the Holy Alliance, including the Vatican, refused to recognize Mexico's independence or its newly formed government, casting doubts at an international level on the Regency's legitimacy. Further doubts were then cast over who essentially represented the new country when, on 24 February 1822, during the opening session of Mexico's First Constituent Congress, the deputies unanimously voted in favor of becoming the sole depositaries of the Mexican nation's sovereignty, in contention with Iturbide's view that this was shared between the executive (i.e., himself, acting as first regent following O'Donojú's premature death) and the legislative power (i.e., congress). Iturbide and congress were to go on a collision course thereafter, disputing each other's authority, from disagreeing over ceremonial arrangements (such as where Iturbide was allowed/expected to sit in the chamber of congress) to far heftier considerations, including who had the right to demand and authorize the creation of taxes or to propose and approve decrees that affected the new nation's army, commerce, education, etc.[45] The coup of the early hours of 19 May 1822 initially appeared to favor Iturbide in his power struggle with congress, since it resulted in him being crowned emperor, with the army's forceful intervention succeeding in intimidating sixty-seven of the eighty-two deputies who turned up in congress that morning to vote in favor of him becoming Agustín the First.

However, much to Iturbide's annoyance, regardless of his new title, congress remained hostile and defiant toward him. As a result he imprisoned nineteen deputies on 26 August, together with forty-seven other persons accused of plotting against him, and ultimately lost patience completely with the legislature, closing it down on 31 October. It was during these months of heightened conflict between Iturbide and congress that Garza plotted and launched his pronunciamiento in present-day Tamaulipas.[46]

Having dissolved congress, Iturbide hand-picked forty-seven of its deputies he considered supportive of his actions and installed a new legislature by the name of Junta Instituyente (Instituting Junta) on 2 November. Much to his chagrin, as deputy José María Bocanegra would recall in his memoirs, the Junta Instituyente proved as stubborn as the former congress in opposing Iturbide's despotic tendencies.[47]

Embattled in Mexico City with his own government, Iturbide also faced a parallel power struggle with the Empire's regional governments, which like congress believed sovereignty lay with the elected provincial deputations and not with Iturbide. To quote Jaime E. Rodríguez O., "the provinces held that they themselves possessed sovereignty and that they were relinquishing a portion of that sovereignty to create a national government."[48] Following the restoration of the Cádiz Constitution in 1820, the provinces were governed once more by the provincial deputations that had been in place in 1813–14 (Guadalajara, Interior Eastern Provinces, Interior Western Provinces, Mexico, San Luis Potosí, Yucatán, Puebla, and Chiapas). Furthermore, as decreed by the Spanish government on 8 May 1821, the intendancies of Arizpe, Guanajuato, Michoacán, Oaxaca, Veracruz, and Zacatecas were granted permission to establish their own provincial deputations, which they did, bringing the number of these Cádiz-inspired regional governments to fourteen on the eve of independence. With Iturbide's Regency in place, the number of provincial deputations went on growing as different regional elites vied for greater control over their regions. By November 1822 there were eighteen established provincial deputations.[49] All were highly sensitive to any attempt on the part of Iturbide to interfere in their domestic affairs.[50]

Iturbide was concerned that the geopolitically important province of Veracruz was slipping out of his control. Having been informed that the regional chieftain and provincial deputation champion Santa Anna was beginning to exert more influence there than he was prepared to allow, Iturbide decided to visit Santa Anna in Jalapa in November and take the preventative action of transferring him to Mexico City, far away from his regional power base.[51] It was a decision that would cost him dearly, since it triggered the Veracruz–Casa Mata cycle of pronunciamientos that ultimately resulted in his abdication on 19 March 1823 and departure to Europe on 11 May.[52]

By December 1822, on the eve of the pronunciamiento of Veracruz, fourteen months since Mexico had become independent, the prospects of Iturbide's Mexican Empire staying intact were looking increasingly gloomy. In part, Iturbide's growing problems were the result of his having been unable to satisfy the many, varied, and arguably unrealistic high hopes and expectations that had been pinned on him. The broad and vague tenets of the Plan of Iguala, so effective in bringing about the necessary consensus to achieve independence, proved divisive thereafter. In a sense Iturbide was the victim of his success. Having seen him bring about the independence of Mexico in a matter of months, many people were confident that he could as quickly bring back the idealized prosperity of prewar New Spain. In a country that had seen most of its silver mines and commerce devastated by eleven years of war, this was not possible. Having depleted the government's funds by abolishing a wide range of colonial taxes, Iturbide had little choice but to impose new and equally unpopular ones. Similarly, having committed himself to covering the expenses of the triumphant Army of the Three Guarantees, showering its officers with promotions, he failed to raise enough resources to cover their pay. He offended the Bourbonists by having himself proclaimed emperor. He offended the constitutionalists by closing down congress, replacing it with a hand-picked junta that was perceived as having no legitimacy—and that also opposed him. The "redeemer of the mother-country," to quote José María Tornel, became overnight "and by magic [*encanto*] its despot and oppressor."[53]

Iturbide also pursued a centralist agenda that collided with the powerful federalist impulses of the regions. For Timothy Anna it would be this particular aspect of his reign that would ultimately result in his unmaking: "The urge for provincial or regional control was universal in Mexico, and Iturbide had imposed upon it for a brief time a central political system founded on the consensus of Iguala and modeled on Bourbon Spain. He was unable, however, to overcome the forces of regionalism."[54] On 2 December 1822 Santa Anna, who after their interview in Jalapa went to Veracruz instead of accompanying Iturbide back to Mexico City as instructed, initiated the Veracruz–Casa Mata pronunciamiento constellation in collusion with former insurgent commander General Guadalupe Victoria, calling for the end of the empire and the establishment of a republic.[55] With the assistance of Colombian political envoy Miguel de Santa María, he modified his demands in the subsequent Plan of Veracruz of 6 December, circulated four days later, in the hope of broadening its appeal. Despite it being clear that the pronunciados remained opposed to Iturbide, the declared republicanism of the 2 December address was dropped. Instead, the call for the restoration of the closed-down congress became the more salient demand.[56]

It was this second plan that the pronunciamiento of Chilapa of 13 January, launched in the present-day state of Guerrero by former insurgents Vicente Guerrero and Nicolás Bravo, came out in support of the demands made in Veracruz, albeit further modifying these. They made a point of stating that they were prepared to obey Iturbide as long as congress supported his continuation at the head of the country's executive branch, and they offered the emperor the chance of bringing the crisis to an end were he to listen to their demands and restore congress.[57]

Iturbide's initial reaction was to quell the pronunciamientos by force. Former royalist commander Brigadier José Gabriel de Armijo, who had been humiliatingly defeated during the War of Independence by Guerrero in the battle of Cerro de Barrabás of 30 September 1818, was sent to crush his old adversary, which he did at the battle of Almolonga of 25 January, leaving Guerrero badly wounded. In the meantime, in Veracruz, generals José Antonio Echávarri, Luis de Cortázar, and José María Lobato placed Santa

Voice of the Provinces

Anna and Victoria under siege. However, after two long months in which the besieging imperial forces were unable to force the pronunciados to capitulate, and started to suffer from the "insalubrious climate" of Veracruz with its deadly *vómito* (yellow fever), Echávarri chose to change sides and launched the pronunciamiento of Casa Mata of 1 February 1823.

The reasons for Echávarri's change of heart remain uncertain. It is possible that he realized he could not take the port, following his failed attempt to enter Veracruz on 2 January 1823. There was also the rumor at the time that he had recently joined the Scottish rite of Masons, and given that their lodges opted to use Santa Anna's Plan of Veracruz (2 December 1822) to further their own project, Echávarri had little choice but to turn against Iturbide. Yet the Plan of Casa Mata was conciliatory toward the emperor and did not advocate the creation of a republic. Critical to its success, as already noted, was article 9, which empowered the provincial deputation. Its defense of the powers of the Veracruz Provincial Deputation inspired all the other provincial deputations in Mexico to pronounce in favor of it with a sonorous cloud of actas de adhesión that spread across the young nation, starting in Veracruz on 1 February and reaching all the way to Texas (15 April).[58] Although these did not actually call for the establishment of a republic, with the emphasis being on summoning a new congress, the emperor, in view of the support the Acta de Casa Mata received, opted to abdicate on 19 March 1823. Following the series of pronunciamientos of allegiance Casa Mata received, the "liberating army" entered Mexico City on 27 March 1823, and the restored congress was reconvened two days later.

As was to be expected, the emperor's abdication generated a whole new wave of constitutional and institutional uncertainties.

Who was to govern the country now that he was gone? Should the restored congress—originally established to forge a constitutional monarchy and elected through an unrepresentative process—act as the republic's legislature? Or should a new constituent congress be elected by the triumphant provincial deputations as proposed in Casa Mata? On being reconvened on 29 March, congress decreed that there no longer existed a recognized executive power. And in a bid to prevent another ambitious high-ranking officer from attempting to follow Iturbide's example and step on congress's toes, it created a deliberately weak triumvirate named the Supreme Executive Power (Supremo Poder Ejecutivo), in which the provisional executive power was shared among three individuals. Initially congress appointed generals Nicolás Bravo, Guadalupe Victoria, and Pedro Celestino Negrete as Mexico's new triumvirs. However, given that they were elsewhere leading their troops, José Mariano Michelena, José Miguel Domínguez, and Vicente Guerrero were subsequently named substitute members of the triumvirate. With Guerrero serving in the field as well, and sixty-seven-year-old Domínguez's health being somewhat fragile, it was former insurgent conspirator and wartime political prisoner Michelena who played the leading role in the triumvirate, albeit at congress's behest, while his four-man cabinet, led by minister of interior and exterior relations Lucas Alamán, pursued a centralist agenda that clashed with Michelena's own sympathies and the growing federalism of the provinces. As noted by Timothy Anna: "The creation of a weak executive whose members operated almost independently from each other, combined with the existence of a Congress that lacked credibility in the minds of many people, meant that in the contest for provincial power the central authority was unusually frail."[59]

Proof that the legislature lacked credibility came on 12 April 1823, when it voted in favor of staying put, in defiance of Casa Mata's call for the election of a new congress, conveniently accepting its own commission's recommendation. The result was the vociferous dissent of the provinces, first expressed by the provincial commissioners who had gone to the capital to represent their deputations' views and ensure the terms of Casa Mata were implemented, and subsequently in a new series of pronunciamientos. On 9 May 1823 the Provincial Deputation of Guadalajara together with Captain General Luis Quintanar decided they would not recognize the authority of congress until a new legislature was convened. On 12 May the provincial deputation, now in collusion with the town council of Guadalajara, went one step further and pronounced in favor of the creation of a federal republic, stating that they were no longer going to obey congress or the Supreme Executive Power and would stop remitting funds to Mexico City. The central government's response was twofold. Congress agreed on 20 May to convene a new congress at some point in the near future. But it also ordered Quintanar's replacement as jefe político of Nueva Galicia (Jalisco) by General José Joaquín de Herrera on 26 May. However, Herrera was prevented from reaching Guadalajara by the pronounced local militias of the city and was unable to impose the central government's authority in Jalisco.[60]

The events following Iturbide's abdication serve to highlight Mexico's confused and confusing context, in which constitutional institutions such as the provincial deputations and insurrectionary forces coexisted alongside and mirrored each other. Political measures were informed and influenced using both lawful (constitutional) and unlawful (extra-constitutional) methods. It was unclear where authority truly lay. Not surprisingly, the following months witnessed a battery of arguably legal and unlawful representations and pronouncements aimed at ensuring that the voices of the provinces were heard loud and clear, that a new constituent congress was summoned, and that it forged a federal republican constitution. Santa Anna pronounced in San Luis Potosí on 5 June 1823 in support of the Guadalajara pronunciamiento and the creation of a federal constitution. Provincial deputations voiced their federalism in several ways: by declaring their separation from the national government (e.g., Oaxaca on 1 June, Chiapas on 9 June, Zacatecas on 18 June); by formally calling for the formation of a federal republic (e.g., Interior Eastern Provinces on 5 June, Querétaro on 11 June, Veracruz on 20 June); by voting for such a form of government (e.g., Nuevo Santander on 19 July); or by pronouncing (e.g., Guadalajara on 12 May and 16 June). It was in the midst of this generalized movement for autonomous provincial self-government that the United Provinces of Central America proclaimed their absolute independence from Mexico on 1 July. In response to these regional representations and gestures of rebellion, congress voted on 12 June in favor of the principle of a federated republic, approved on 17 June the electoral law for the new constituent congress (whereby reelected provincial deputations would elect the deputies), and on 16 August offered a general amnesty to all the provinces in revolt, in a desperate attempt to put a stop to the mimetic insurrectionism of provincial Mexico. After a long summer of turmoil Mexico's Second Constituent Congress was inaugurated on 7 November.[61]

It was this congress of 1823–24 that over a period of fourteen months drafted the initial Constitutive Act of 31 January 1824, which established that Mexico would be a "popular, federal representative republic," and eventually composed the Constitution of 1824.[62] The deliberations, debates, and votes that led to the final approval of the 1824 charter were fraught with tension, entailing fifty roll-call votes on matters ranging from prohibiting the reform of the Constitution to approving words such as "free and independent states" to describe the provinces. According to David M. Quinlan, the most divisive issue was how much power should devolve from the center to the periphery.[63] And while the Second Constituent Congress heatedly thrashed out Mexico's first constitution, pronunciamientos went on occurring. José María Lobato, at the head of the Mexico City garrison, pronounced calling for Michelena and Domínguez to be removed and to leave the executive in the hands of Guerrero, demanding as well that the Spanish population be expelled from Mexico (23 January 1824).[64] Brothers Antonio and Manuel León reiterated Lobato's call for the expulsion of Spaniards at the head of the Oaxaca garrison several months later in the summer of 1824.[65]

Although the Constitutive Act of 31 January 1824 was openly federalist, subsequent measures by the government and debates in congress generated further discontent by appearing to confirm the federalists' fears that the centralists were gaining the upper hand in the corridors of power. They suspected, with reason, that the centralists would water down the federalist character of the constitution to such an extent that the political system that would eventually be enshrined would be centralist in all but name. As a result a number of federalist conspiracies were hatched in order to stage pronunciamientos that might ensure the Constituent Congress in Mexico City did not betray the provinces, with one of them simultaneously appearing to back the idea of the return of Iturbide.[66] The pronunciamiento of Jalisco or Guadalajara of 8 June 1824 certainly represented one of the most forceful federalist expressions of the time, with its call to obey the Constitutive Act and disobey the executive. However, the so-called conspiracy of Celaya Street was uncovered, and the pronunciamiento of Jalisco was forcefully quelled by General Nicolás Bravo, who succeeded on 11 June in occupying Guadalajara on behalf of the government, just three days after the pronunciamiento had been launched. The federalist and iturbidista authors and leaders of the plan, Luis Quintanar and Anastasio Bustamante, were both arrested and sent to Acapulco to await exile to South America. It was also during the stormy summer of 1824 that Iturbide returned to Mexico, disembarking in Soto la Marina (Tamaulipas), where none other than former pronunciado Felipe de la Garza, having succeeded in regaining power at a state level as commander-general of the Eastern Interior Provinces, had the former emperor arrested and executed in Padilla on 19 July 1824.

Undeterred, however, the Second Constituent Congress continued in session, creating the conditions for the presidential elections to get under way.[67] As specified in the as yet unratified constitution, after a round of primary elections each state legislature voted for two candidates on 1 September 1824. He who gained the most votes was to become president, and whoever came second would serve as vice president. Thus on 2 October congress opened the ballots. Insurgent hero and diehard republican pronunciado Guadalupe Victoria was elected Mexico's first constitutional president, having won by eleven votes to six.[68] The former insurgent commander Nicolás Bravo, who also had experience as a pronunciado, was runner-up, taking the consolation prize of the vice presidency.[69] On 4 October the 1824 Constitution was finally sworn in, in a three-and-a-half-hour ceremony, and on 9 October President-Elect Victoria took office at midday.

The 1824 Constitution was to last for eleven years (1824–35), and twenty-two years after it was sworn in for the first time it would be resurrected in the early stages of the Mexican-U.S. War (1846–48), lasting from then until 1853. It forged in its fifth article nineteen states and four territories (which would include the Federal District and the territory of Tlaxcala soon afterward, as decreed on 18 and 24 November 1824, respectively).[70] Together with the constitutions that each state went on to draft thereafter between 1824 and 1826, the 1824 charter created a particularly weak executive, placing most of the government's power in the hands of a bicameral congress (it was congress that could pass laws, impose taxes, declare war, form an army, etc.), with the non-reelectable president being solely responsible for executing congress's dispositions (although he was allowed to propose reforms to the chamber of deputies for its consideration; see articles 47–50 and 77, 110–112). The new charter retained the indirect electoral system forged in the 1812 Cádiz Constitution, which left the final vote in the hands of the state legislatures although guaranteeing universal male suffrage at a primary level (arts. 79–94). The control of the civic militias and the town councils was delegated to the state governments, with the ayuntamientos having far-reaching powers at a local level (arts. 157–62). It established a separate judiciary in the form of the Supreme Court of Justice (arts. 123–44), albeit allowing the military and ecclesiastical fueros to remain in place (art. 154). It also officially stated that the Roman Apostolic Catholic faith was the state's religion with tolerance of none other (art. 3), giving the government the right of the *Patronato* (Patronage) to make senior ecclesiastical appointments (art. 50:XII).[71]

In the same way that the consummation of independence was

seen as the dawn of a new era of peace, order, and prosperity, the inauguration of Guadalupe Victoria's term in office witnessed a reprise of the celebrations and intense hope that had characterized the early days of Iturbide's Mexican Empire. The achievement of having forged a liberal, federal, constitutional order in which the states' sovereignty was respected, where the people could enjoy the freedom of the press (art. 50:III), and where Mexico's finances appeared to be on a sound footing following the successful negotiation of four substantial loans from several British banking houses, gave Victoria's government a promising beginning. As Alamán recalled: "President Victoria found himself . . . in the most prosperous of circumstances: the republic was enjoying a period of peace, the factions had been repressed, and the hope of a happy future burned in everybody's hearts."[72]

Sadly, the country's rediscovered hope and confidence was not to last. Just over a year into Victoria's presidency it became startlingly clear that Mexico's economy was on the verge of collapse. By January 1826, notwithstanding the British loans that had amounted to 17 million pesos in cash, there were only 2.7 million pesos left in the national coffers, and Mexico's debt had rocketed to 28 million pesos. A year on from that and not only had Mexico's credit dried up entirely, but it was obliged to repay a total of 32 million pesos in loans plus interest.[73] Matters were not made better by a federal constitution that enabled the state legislatures to hold back from paying their stipulated tax revenue to the center. As Stanley C. Green comments, "The failures of government finance contributed in large measure to the decline in public optimism and the slowing of the Republic's momentum. Lack of government money caused the derailment of all sorts of public and semipublic projects."[74] It also played a not insignificant part in provoking the bitter polarization of politics that came to characterize the second half of Victoria's four-year presidential term.

As the economic crisis made itself felt with salaries going unpaid and jobs proving sparse, Masonic rivalries arose in a contest that Zavala blamed on *empleomanía* (employment-mania) over securing public posts for each lodge's members.[75] The two Masonic factions that dominated the politics of the Mexican Federal Republic between 1825 and 1827 were the more traditional *escoceses* (established in Mexico since 1813 by defenders of the 1812 Constitution) and the trendy *yorkinos* (formally consolidated in Mexico in 1825 with the assistance of interfering, flower-loving, U.S. Minister Plenipotentiary Joel Poinsett—of poinsettia fame).[76] The *yorkino* Masons' need to find "jobs for our boys" and Ferdinand VII's refusal to recognize Mexico's independence were behind a growing tide of Hispanophobia that found expression in increasing calls for Spaniards to be kicked out of those cushy posts that the Plan of Iguala had allowed them to retain.

The power struggle between the escoceses and the yorkinos spilled into the political arena as both Masonic rites developed into loosely formed political parties or factions and fought against each other in the 1826 congressional elections. Although their political programs were far from homogeneous or coherent—given that they were in essence secret societies and not political parties in the modern sense of the word, and that the increasing power and popularity of the yorkinos also resulted in entire lodges belonging to the Scottish rite transferring their allegiance to that of York—in broad terms they did come to be seen to represent conflicting ideological tendencies.[77] On the one hand, the remaining escoceses became associated with a more traditionalist outlook, more elitist, arguably more centralist leaning, pro-British rather than pro-American, and with a Hispanophile undercurrent, even when their grand master, Vice President Bravo, had been an insurgent in the War of Independence. The yorkinos, in contrast, tended to espouse a more radical form of liberalism, harbored populist impulses, were generally federalists, and identified more with Poinsett's modern republican U.S. government than with the British counterpart, Henry George Ward's London-based centuries-long parliamentary monarchy. And following the January 1827 discovery of a conspiracy to stage a pronunciamiento to bring back Spanish rule, the yorkinos came to champion aggressively the expulsion of the Spanish population from Mexico.[78]

Following the uncovering on 19 January 1827 of reactionary Spanish priest Joaquín Arenas's plot, with the assistance of a secret envoy dispatched by Ferdinand VII, to mobilize the Spanish residents and pro-Spanish Mexican officers in the republic into staging a pronunciamiento that would result in Mexico becoming a Spanish dominion once more, the more radical yorkino deputies did not hold back in demanding the approval of expulsion laws like those Lobato and the León brothers had been calling for since 1824. In Tlaxcala a pronunciamiento was launched on 27 March 1827 precisely to lobby the government and put pressure on congress to listen to the "will of the nation" and expel the ungrateful Spanish population from Mexico.[79] With the yorkinos dominating congress after the 1826 elections, the first expulsion laws (forcing Spaniards to leave their jobs in Mexico) were approved on 10 May 1827. Seven months later, on 20 December 1827, against a backdrop of repeated pronunciamientos and acts of disobedience launched to pressure national and state legislatures to *descoyotar* the *gachupines* (pejorative terms for removing

Spaniards), the second and more radical set of expulsion laws was passed, actually forcing Spaniards to leave the country.

Many escoceses supported these laws. However, displaying very poor timing, a number of them launched a pronunciamiento on 23 December from Otumba in the state of Mexico. Although they did not demand a reversal of the expulsion laws, their pronunciamiento was immediately depicted in the yorkino press as a pro-Spanish revolt. By the end of 1827 the factional party disputes between the yorkinos and the escoceses had reached breaking point. With the yorkinos having won the congressional elections of 1826, controlling a number of key ministerial posts in the national government, and dominating most of the state legislatures, the escoceses finally resorted on 23 December 1827 to pronouncing to challenge their political enemies. The demands in Manuel Montaño's pronunciamiento were deliberately moderate and vague. His plan called for the end of all secret societies, although everybody knew at the time that it was mainly aimed at the dominant yorkinos. It called for a change of cabinet without specifically stating who had to go and why. In between the lines, it was again commonly known that it was the prominent yorkinos in President Victoria's government that Montaño was hoping to see replaced by escoceses (or, as he put it: "by men of renowned probity, virtue, and merit").[80] In article 3 he called for the expulsion of meddlesome Joel Poinsett, without naming him or mentioning that the reason the escoceses wanted him to leave the country was because he had been instrumental in founding the Rite of York in Mexico. Last but not least, in a gesture of negotiation, the plan stressed that it defended the constitution and the law. Days after the pronunciamiento was launched, the escocés grand master, Vice President Nicolás Bravo, joined Montaño and the pronunciados in Tulancingo. Unfortunately for them, the Plan of Montaño was only seconded in Veracruz by Miguel Barragán and his escocés state legislature. On 7 January 1828 Vicente Guerrero and Santa Anna, at the head of the government troops that were dispatched to quell the pronunciamiento, routed Bravo and Montaño's men in the battle of Tulancingo. The "earthquake of Tulancingo," as it became known, marked the end of the Scottish Rite Masons as a credible or viable political force in Mexico.

Following the battle of Tulancingo, to quote Enrique González Pedrero, "as is usually the case following such an outright victory, perhaps because this brought an excess of confidence, the yorkinos became divided at the height of their strength, and as occurs with overflowing rivers, the events which followed came like a flood of disasters."[81] However, there was more to those divisions than just an "excess of confidence." The yorkinos, having based their entire propaganda between 1826 and 1827 on an anti-escocés/anti-Spanish platform, found themselves without an enemy, in serious need of replacing their offensive politics with beliefs that consolidated their hegemony. This need to define the politics of *yorkismo* once the escoceses had been defeated brought to light the evident divisions that existed within what until then had been a loosely defined liberal Masonic faction with radical/populist tendencies. In other words, as long as there had been a common enemy, whether reactionary pro-royalist Spaniards or members of the Scottish rite of Masons, moderate and radical yorkinos had been able to overlook their differences and rally together behind the same cause. The absence of a common enemy meant that the yorkinos lost the one thing that had previously united them.

By April 1828, the country's economy was further battered by the departure of large numbers of Spaniards who took with them an estimated 12 million pesos' worth of capital.[82] The in-fighting that surfaced within the yorkino lodges started to make news in the press.[83] The key event that brought these growing divisions to light was the 1828 presidential elections, which became hotly contested between former insurgent mulatto leader and radical yorkino Vicente Guerrero and former royalist well-to-do commander and minister of war Manuel Gómez Pedraza. Following the demise of the escoceses, the dominant faction within the yorkino lodges became increasingly radical and backed Guerrero as their presidential candidate. Gómez Pedraza, on the other hand, acquired the support of the defeated escoceses, those moderate yorkinos who had become concerned with the radicalization of their party, and a coalition that dated from 1826 called the *imparciales* that opposed all Masonic-based political parties.[84] By mid-September, after six months of vitriolic campaigning, it became clear that Gómez Pedraza was going to win. The realization must be qualified. Gómez Pedraza was going to win only because the outcome of the elections was based on an indirect system that left it up to the creole representatives of each state legislature to determine the winner. Each of the nineteen state legislatures (except Durango) cast two votes, one for president, and one for vice president. Manuel Gómez Pedraza, with eleven, beat Guerrero by three votes. As was noted by radical politician Lorenzo de Zavala, "had the elections [been based] on individual suffrage, [Guerrero] would have received an immense majority of votes in his favor."[85] This view was shared by many, including Santa Anna, who was to initiate the ultimately successful Perote–Oaxaca–La Acordada pronunciamiento cycle.

The Plan of Perote of 16 September 1828 was therefore launched in an attempt to force the government to annul the election of

Manuel Gómez Pedraza and have Guerrero invested instead, since "the people everywhere have made their intentions sufficiently clear." He also called for the expulsion of *all* Spaniards, appealing to all those Mexicans who still felt that the laws of 20 December 1827 had not been comprehensive enough.[86] Initially Santa Anna's Plan of Perote did not inspire the wave of plans of allegiance he was hoping for. He found himself placed under siege by the government forces sent to Perote under the command of Manuel Rincón. Although he succeeded in escaping past his besiegers on 19 October, they followed him from Perote to Oaxaca, where Santa Anna became involved in a two-month-long standoff, surrounded first by Rincón and later by José María Calderón's government forces. During his time in Oaxaca, Santa Anna issued two more pronunciamientos (the Modificaciones al Plan de Perote, 5 November 1828, and the Pronunciamiento de Oaxaca, 20 November 1828) in hope of negotiating his way out of Oaxaca while still lobbying the government to annul the election of Gómez Pedraza.[87] In the end it was a separate pronunciamiento or barracks revolt in the capital, the Rebellion of La Acordada, that forcefully brought the conflict to an end and in Santa Anna's favor, albeit unleashing the Parián riot in the capital that resulted in four days of looting and mayhem.[88] Gómez Pedraza fled the country and resigned the presidency, and Guerrero went on to become president. Much to Calderón's displeasure, following Gómez Pedraza's resignation Santa Anna went from being a pronunciado and an outlaw to a defender of the government.

The most obvious result of the success of the Perote–Oaxaca–La Acordada pronunciamiento cycle (apart from demonstrating, once more, that pronunciamientos could result in meaningful political change) was that it raised more questions than it answered regarding the government's legality and legitimacy. A select committee was set up in January 1829, as Guadalupe Victoria completed his term in office—(he would be the only president to succeed in doing this until José Joaquín de Herrera emulated his achievement in 1848–51)—to attempt to resolve constitutionally the conundrum with which they had been left in the wake of Gómez Pedraza's departure and resignation. If they accepted Gómez Pedraza's resignation, they would in effect be confirming that he had won the elections, was the legitimate constitutional president, and had been forced to abandon the capital as a result of an unlawful pronunciamiento cycle. But how else could they explain that Guerrero was to be Mexico's second constitutional president when it was clear for everybody to see that he had not won the elections (however unfair or unrepresentative they may have been), and that his rise to power had been brought about, in essence, by force, following the Acordada barracks uprising of 30 November? For all intents and purposes, by allowing Guerrero to succeed Victoria, the government was condoning pronunciamiento pressure over electoral results. With an illegitimate and illegal government in place the moment Guerrero was sworn in as president on 1 April 1829, what was there to stand in the way of others using pronunciamiento methods to overthrow him and restore the broken constitutional order? The committee was unable to resolve this conundrum satisfactorily. On 9 January they presented their report to the chamber of deputies in which they ultimately argued that the pronunciamientos launched from September onward against the election of General Gómez Pedraza represented the general will, and this had been sadly ignored by the nation's representatives, who had betrayed the trust placed in them by the electorate by not having listened to it. The committee therefore recommended that Gómez Pedraza's victory was declared null and void, that all other votes were considered valid, and that following on from this, congress should elect the next president from the candidates who had come second and third. As a result Guerrero was confirmed to be president, with runner-up Anastasio Bustamante (who had come third, in reality) becoming vice president, winning the in-house election that was held in the chamber of deputies the same day by thirteen votes to two.[89]

Guerrero's nine-month presidency was to be tainted by another constitutional anomaly: his adoption of emergency powers on 25 August 1829. By not including a constitutional clause that could have enabled congress to grant the president emergency powers in a time of crisis, the authors of Mexico's first constitutions (1824, 1836, and 1843) tied the hands of government and forced it to adopt extra-constitutional (even anti-constitutional) authoritarian measures to survive. In so doing, the governments of the 1820s, '30s, and '40s, seriously undermined the prestige of their respective constitutions, showed them up to be impractical and unworkable, and in turn inspired their opponents to challenge and/or overthrow them employing extra-constitutional means such as the ubiquitous pronunciamiento.[90]

The crisis that justified congress's decision to confer on Guerrero emergency powers was news of the landing in Tampico on 27 July 1829 of a three-thousand-strong Spanish expedition led by Brigadier Isidro Barradas. Thus, while Santa Anna and General Manuel de Mier y Terán led the Mexican response to Barradas's attempt at reconquest, succeeding in forcing the Spanish forces to surrender following the dramatic battle of Tampico of 11 September, Guerrero used his newly acquired (and unlawful) emergency powers to bypass congress in the capital and pass a series of radical laws, including the abolition of slavery on 16 September 1829. Bearing in mind how Guerrero had come to power in the first place, and given that he refused to renounce his (unconstitutional) powers after the Spaniards had been defeated, it was not long before rumors started to abound that a plot to overthrow him was under way.

The first pronunciamiento to be launched under Guerrero's presidency was orchestrated by the Campeche garrison in remote Yucatán on 6 November 1829. On paper it was a regional response to Barradas's expedition. From the perspective of pro-Mexico Campeche the Spanish incursion had demonstrated that the federal system was not well-equipped to counter foreign interventions and/or national emergencies of this sort, especially when neighboring Mérida was notoriously pro-Spanish, Cuba was so near, and it had been feared that Barradas would land in Yucatán rather than Tamaulipas. This was to become the first centralist pronunciamiento in Mexican history. However, as can be gathered from articles 5 and 7, local issues and disputes were also behind this act of insubordination. Article 5 called for the removal of the members of the state congress as well as the state governor for opposing the system proposed in the pronunciamiento. Article 7 gave the commander general of Yucatán, Segundo Carvajal, the right to name a provisional provincial government in lieu of the dissolved state authorities.[91] Typical of a pronunciamiento, there was the predisposition to recognize the existing national government as long as it acquiesced to the pronunciados' demands. The remoteness of Yucatán and the problems the national government was forced to face following the success of the pronunciamiento of Jalapa of 4 December 1829 would result in Yucatán becoming a pseudo-independent state for the next two years as a consequence of this pronunciamiento.[92]

Meanwhile, in central Mexico, for a significant sector of the Mexican Army and political class, and in particular for those former royalists, escoceses, imparciales, and *novenarios* who had backed Manuel Gómez Pedraza's candidacy in the 1828 presidential elections, Vicente Guerrero's 1829 government was considered to be illegitimate, dictatorial, and worryingly radical. Guerrero had come to power on the back of the 1828 Perote–Oaxaca–La Acordada pronunciamiento cycle. He was a mulatto, moreover, and a former insurgent leader. According to his radical Yucatecan minister of finance Lorenzo de Zavala, because of the color of his skin and his revolutionary past, Guerrero was despised and perceived as a threat by the racist white criollo elites who had stood by the royalist "causa buena" during the greater part of the 1810–21 civil war.[93] The fact that Guerrero had used the Spanish attempt to reconquer Mexico in the summer of 1829 to have himself awarded emergency powers and had then refused to relinquish these once Isidro Barradas's Spanish expeditionary army was defeated was interpreted as evidence of his dictatorial tendencies. The radical economic policies pursued by his minister of finance, Zavala, had also given rise to concern. What is unquestionable is that the 1828 Perote–Oaxaca–La Acordada pronunciamiento cycle had created a particularly resonant precedent. In forcing the annulment of Gómez Pedraza's election and the successful and forceful imposition of Guerrero, it had demonstrated that pronunciamientos could be used to force a change in government. Although the Plan of Jalapa did not explicitly call for the overthrow of Guerrero's government, the authors were intent on bringing it down, as would become obvious once the Jalapa pronunciamiento cycle got under way.

The plan itself, launched by the reserve army that had been mobilized to Jalapa to support the campaign against Barradas and which remained in the region despite the Spanish expedition having been repulsed, disguised its true intentions by avoiding a specific call for an end to Guerrero's government. Article 1 professed that it was the duty of the army to defend the federal pact. Article 2 asserted that all laws should be strictly abided by. Article 3, making use of the "right to petition," demanded that the president renounce his emergency powers and that congress be reinstated. Article 4 claimed that all those government officials whom public opinion rejected should be removed from office. Article 5 stressed, somewhat paradoxically, that the army obeyed and respected the constituted authorities. Article 6, in a similar vein, stressed that the army would ensure peace and order were guaranteed. Article 7 invited Bustamante and Santa Anna to lead the pronunciamiento (but not the government, since, as can be seen in article 3, the president was being asked to listen and acquiesce to the petitioners' demands by renouncing his emergency powers and reopening congress). Article 8 provided a contingency plan in case Bustamante and/or Santa Anna refused to lead the pronunciamiento, and article 9 invited the centralist pronunciados of Campeche to give up their demands and join this pronunciamiento cycle.[94]

For anyone who was not aware of the pronunciados' undeclared commitment to overthrow Guerrero's government and bring Anastasio Bustamante and the "party of order" to power, the plan's demands were not obviously reactionary. They deliberately appealed to a wide range of political actors, since the majority continued to back the 1824 Federal Constitution, believed in the need to guarantee the rule of law, and knew Guerrero's use of emergency powers was unlawful and unconstitutional. Article 4 was beautifully vague as well, since it did not actually specify who those "rejected" government officials were. It would be article 4 that would be used, unsurprisingly, once Guerrero's government was overthrown by the end of the month, to remove its supporters from all positions of power, at both national and regional levels.

In response to the Plan of Jalapa of 4 December, Guerrero opted to leave the capital to lead the military defense of his government and left José María Bocanegra behind as acting president, given that Vice President Bustamante had endorsed the pronunciamiento. While a number of pronunciamientos de adhesión started to circulate (e.g., Tehuantepec, 17 December; San Luis Potosí, 19 December), it was the Acta del pronunciamiento de México of 23 December, launched by significant numbers of officers stationed in Mexico City, that paved the way for the overthrow of Guerrero's government. It backed the Plan of 4 December but went on to add a number of important demands, including the refusal to accept Bocanegra's legitimacy or authority as interim president.[95] These demands were followed by action. Luis Quintanar, at the head of his troops, stormed the national palace and established a provisional government with Lucas Alamán, while Bustamante made his way to the capital from Jalapa, arriving there on 31 December.

Almost exactly a year after the constitutionally elected president, Manuel Gómez Pedraza, had fled the country in response to a pronunciamiento cycle, a fresh round of pronunciamientos brought a new president to power. In the manifesto Bustamante circulated on 4 January 1830 to account for his actions he was at pains to demonstrate that Guerrero's government was unconstitutional: (1) Guerrero had not been elected; and (2) he had behaved like an "absolutist monarch," using emergency powers to "give free rein to his desires."[96] However, rather than invite Gómez Pedraza to serve as the constitutionally elected president, and rewind the situation back to how it was (and should have been) following the 1828 elections, or even convoke new elections, Bustamante—who sought to give himself airs of legality by insisting on calling himself vice president rather than president—opted to legitimize his government with the claim that the pronunciamiento of Jalapa had represented the "general will" and the "opinion of the people." As argued by Catherine Andrews, in choosing this route Bustamante undermined any rightful claim he might have made to acting legitimately, and exposed his government to the same accusations of unconstitutionality that had weighed on Guerrero's presidency.[97] Faced with the formation of two successive unconstitutional governments, it is unsurprising that the pronunciamiento flourished, paradoxically representing to some a means to salvage the constitutional order first interrupted in 1828, when the elected president, Gómez Pedraza, was unable to take office as a result of the Perote–Oaxaca–La Acordada pronunciamiento series.

The pronunciamientos of Mexico's first independent decade clearly highlight the extent to which the context was one of contested and unclear legitimacies, where not even the constitutional governments were the result of elections, and where they did not always behave constitutionally or lawfully (especially when the president made use of emergency powers that quite simply did not exist). They also show the extent to which mimetic insurrectionism spread across the region, as the provinces came to adopt the pronunciamiento as their preferred means of preserving their relative independence vis-à-vis the center, enabling them to express their regional desires and aspirations forcefully as well as to address local concerns and grievances. The success of the Veracruz–Casa Mata (1822–23), Perote–Oaxaca–La Acordada (1828), and Jalapa–Mexico City (1829) constellations at a national level, of the Plan of Campeche in Yucatán (1829), and of those plans that called for the approval of expulsion laws that were eventually implemented in 1827–29, on the back of the successful pronunciamientos of Cabezas de San Juan (1820) and Iguala (1821), gave substance to the view that this relatively peaceful insurrectionary practice, part lobbying, part intimidating—with its acts of disobedience, circulation of petitioning plans, and reliance on waves of aggressive copycat statements of support purported to represent the voice of the national/popular will—was the most effective way of bringing about meaningful political change.

An analysis of the pronunciamientos of Mexico's first independent decade also allows us to appreciate a number of key points concerning the incipient political culture of early republican Mexico. It shows the determining role the army and the regional authorities (provincial deputations, town councils, state legislatures) had in early Mexican politics. It also highlights which political issues mattered most at the time (e.g., republicanism, the defense of regional sovereignty and federalism, the Spanish question, the quest for meaningful political representation). In order to understand the pronunciamientos of 1821–31 we need to answer two separate yet intimately inter-related questions: Who pronounced? And why did they pronounce?

Of the pronunciamientos launched between 1821 and 1831, the great majority were initiated by army officers, albeit in dialogue with civilian political actors. Focusing exclusively on start-up pronunciamientos, twelve of them were garrison-led: the plans of Iguala (24 February 1821), Veracruz–Chilapa–Casa Mata (2 December 1822–1 February 1823), San Luis Potosí (5 June 1823), José María Lobato (23 January 1824), Veracruz (31 July 1827), Manuel Montaño (23 December 1827), Perote–Oaxaca–La Acordada (16 September–30 November 1828), Campeche (6 November 1829), Jalapa–Mexico City (4–23 December 1829), Juan José Codallos (11 March 1830), Zamora (15 March 1830), and Mexico City (18 August 1830). Even so, in the cases of the pronunciamientos of Iguala (1821) and Casa Mata (1823), these relied heavily on civilian-led pronunciamientos de adhesión, in particular those circulated by ayuntamientos and provincial deputations.[98] The revolt of La Acordada of 30 November 1828 also counted on the critical support of armed civilians (the civic militias of the Federal District led by tailor and militia captain Lucas Balderas) and the leadership of radical politician Lorenzo de Zavala.[99]

For start-up pronunciamientos that were the fruit of an openly declared collaboration between soldiers and civilians, in which garrisons and local authorities joined forces from the beginning, there were six between 1821 and 1831. Garza's plan of 22 September 1822 was sustained by the "jefe of the province of Nuevo Santander, the town council and inhabitants (vecindario) of Soto la Marina and the officers and troops of the militia companies of the said province." Similarly the plans of Jalisco of 9 and 12 May 1823 were launched by captain general Luis Quintanar, the Guadalajara garrison, and the provincial deputation as well as the town council of Guadalajara. The plan de Guadalajara of 8 June 1824 was again pronounced by a similar civilian-military alliance, on this occasion made up of the "Honorable State Constituent Congress and . . . the military division based here." The plans of Tlaxcala (27 March 1827) and Jalisco (7–24 August 1827) were likewise circulated by a combination of army officers and local politicos.

As for state legislature start-up pronunciamientos, there were only three during this decade. The state congress of San Luis Potosí pronounced twice in 1830 (on 13 January and 13 March) in a bid to prevent article 4 of the plan of Jalapa of 4 December 1829 from being implemented in the province, whereby all those "public officials whom public opinion rejected" would be removed (i.e., the yorkino majority in the state congress). The state congress of Yucatán was also responsible for launching a pronunciamiento on 5 April 1830, following up that of the Campeche garrison of 6 November 1829. The only ayuntamiento we know to have launched a start-up pronunciamiento during these years was that of San Juan Bautista (29 April 1830), concerned with reordering the local political scene. Similarly, there was only one priest-led start-up pronunciamiento: that of Father Joaquín Arenas, which was dismantled before it could be launched on 19 January 1827.[100]

What does this say about Mexico's early pronunciamientos and about the political role of the army and the country's regional authorities? Although civilian participation in the pronunciamientos of the first independent decade should not be downplayed, it remains the case that the driving force behind the great majority of the 1821–31 pronunciamientos was the army; or, to put it differently, a not insignificant number of high-ranking officers within the army. Worthy of note is that the army saw itself, at the time, as responsible for ensuring that the general will was heard, viewing itself as the guarantor of independence and Mexican sovereignty. While Iturbide, congress, and the provincial deputations had each come up with different views on where sovereignty truly lay, the veterans of the 1810–21 War depicted themselves from the very beginning as the worthy authors and guarantors of independence, charged with ensuring that the national will was adhered to by the political class. The Plan of Iguala had made clear from the start that it was Iturbide, at the head of the "brave and resolute army" of the Three Guarantees that proclaimed the independence of Northern America. It was a view that was then confirmed in the Treaty of Córdoba, which stated that it was the army that had sustained the pronunciamiento for independence. As captured in Bravo and Guerrero's Plan of Chilapa of 13 January 1823, "the army that today demands its patria's freedom, is the same army of the Three Guarantees that supported the pronunciamiento of Iguala, and the one that knows how to respect and defend your most treasured rights and properties." It was, moreover, an army that would not "put down its arms until the empire's independence and liberty are guaranteed."[101] This was to become the leitmotiv of so many subsequent garrison-led pronunciamientos; namely, that it was the army's duty to intervene in politics when the country's liberty and independence, and its people's rights (and properties), were alleged to be under threat. As was expressed in Santa Anna's Plan of San Luis Potosí of 5 June 1823, his newly formed pronunciado army, "to be called protector of Mexican liberty" thereafter (art. 1), was to have as its main duty to "sustain the inviolability of the Roman Apostolic Catholic religion" as well as to uphold the other two guarantees sworn in the Plan of Iguala (i.e., independence and union), to "respect the property, security, and equality of every citizen, and to sustain order and public security" (art. 2). It was this army— protector of Mexican liberty—that was to ensure a constituent congress was summoned (art. 3), and whose obligation it was to sustain and guarantee that the "spontaneous will of the provinces could pronounce in favor of a federal republic . . . as long as this was done in an orderly fashion and represented the general vote of the *pueblos* (people or villages (art. 4).[102] The Plan of Perote of 16 September 1828 would reiterate and expand on the view of the army as an institution that somehow acted as the supporting pillar or foundation of the national will and the main role of which was precisely to protect and guarantee the country's independence, rights, and freedom:

> The army, which has always been the support of the people's rights: the army that also freed this precious part of the globe from the hands of the tyrant, and that shook off the nation's domestic yoke [of oppression] to grant it back its freedom . . . pronounces in favor of public opinion as the guarantor of the national will and liberty, because it can distinguish between subordination and servitude; because it is interested in the glories of its *patria* and in preserving unharmed the sacrosanct depositary of its imprescriptible rights.[103]

There is no question—as demonstrated by Christon I. Archer— that the army had become profoundly politicized as a result of the eleven-year war of independence, in which politics and war had become closely intertwined and where commander generals had taken control over their provinces as *jefes políticos*.[104] However, it is also true that the army had the means to make sure officials listened to its views, with the threat of using force not being an idle one.

Specific articles denoting that the pronunciados would not abandon their act of rebellion or would be compelled to fight to the death if their demands were not met would feature prominently in military-led pronunciamientos. Garza's 1822 plan stressed, for example, that his men would not put down their arms until congress's liberty was secured. Santa Anna likewise stated in the eighteenth clarification of his 6 December Plan of Veracruz that were the government's troops to ignore the clamor of the people (and their conscience) and attempt "to fight and destroy their own brothers, who sustain their most precious rights, it will be necessary (albeit regrettable), for us to use our arms and let war determine [the outcome of this pronunciamiento]."[105] With the threat of violence being a common element of the pronunciamiento practice and with soldiers being the ones who could most obviously carry through their violent threats given that they had the troops, weapons, and horses to do so, it is not surprising that the military played such a prominent role in Mexico's pronunciamientos.[106]

However, they did not act alone, needing to have their acts of sedition legitimated through the civilian endorsement of the actas de adhesión by ayuntamientos and provincial deputations. In the cases of the pronunciamientos de adhesión led by the provincial deputation, state congress, or ayuntamiento, what becomes evident is that these civilian institutions viewed themselves as being sovereign, with their voice representing the popular national will, and that by adding their weight behind any given garrison-inspired pronunciamientos, they legitimized these through what amounted to a particularly resonant endorsement. That constitutionally elected and supposedly representative institutions were prepared to act extra-constitutionally, joining a given pronunciamiento cycle with their own copycat acts of defiance and insubordination, eloquently highlights the extent to which the line between what was lawful and unlawful or legitimate and illegitimate was significantly blurred at the time.

In the same way that the military pronunciamientos of the early national period reiterated and developed the view that the army's role was to protect and guarantee the country's independence, rights, and freedom (thus justifying their adoption of insurrectionary methods when it was claimed these were under threat), those that were launched by ayuntamientos, provincial deputations, and state legislatures repeated and projected the notion that they represented the people and that it was consequently their duty to give a voice to the popular will when this had been ignored or trampled (justifying, in turn, their own gestures of rebellion). As expressed by the town council of Morelia in its pro-Plan of Jalapa pronunciamiento de adhesión of 27 December 1829, "this corporation believes that it is one of its most important duties to manifest the grievances of the people whose interests it looks after; it would be a crime if out of fear it hushed its voice and did not dare to demand a remedy to the critical circumstances that engulf us."[107]

In the first independent decade, as already observed, the civilian town councils, deputations, and state legislatures would more often than not issue pronunciamientos de adhesión or counterpronunciamientos rather than start-up pronunciamientos. They saw themselves as sovereign and their act of pronouncing as a legitimate means of ensuring that the voice of the people, the popular will, was heard loud and clear. In those few cases where it was civilian-dominated institutions that attempted to initiate a given pronunciamiento cycle, the onus was more on disobedience than violence. To note one example, the San Luis Potosí state legislature's decree of 13 January 1830 (which was a pronunciamiento in all but name, since it defiantly refused to obey the government that had been formed as a result of the Plan of Jalapa), proclaimed that the state authorities of San Luis Potosí and Guanajuato would defend themselves against any attack from the newly formed *jala-*

pista national government (art. 1); that they would not recognize or abide by any of its unconstitutional reforms (art. 2); and that they would call on all other state legislatures to follow their example (art. 3, eliciting in turn a wave of copycat decrees/actas of allegiance).[108] Having said this, as long as the 1824 Constitution was in place, ayuntamientos and town councils did have civil militias at their disposition, which could be mobilized if needed. As may be seen in the plan of San Juan Bautista (29 April 1830), it was not just the garrisons that accompanied their gestures of rebellion with violent threats. In this strictly regional-based pronunciamiento, the ayuntamiento did not mince words, stating that "all tabasqueños have sworn to defend, even to shed their last drop of blood with pleasure [*gustosísimos*], . . . to obey the fundamental laws of the republic, and exterminate those who attempt to overturn them."[109] As will be seen in the following chapter, civilian- and priest-led pronunciamientos would become far more common and widespread in the 1830s.

Why did Mexico's early pronunciados pronounce? Clearly, there were in all pronunciamientos hidden and personal agendas, forcefully recruited soldiers who did not want to be mobilized to remote and dangerous regions, resentful officers who sought fast-track promotion, even town councilors or state deputies who did not want to lose their jobs. There was no shortage of ambitious men who coveted power and riches and saw the pronunciamiento as a means to acquiring these. It would be naïve to take the grandiloquent altruistic patriotic rhetoric of most pronunciamientos at face value. As late nineteenth-century U.S. consul general David Hunter Strother noted somewhat disdainfully, after reading one drafted by General Miguel Negrete, "It is as empty a piece of Gasconading Stuff as I ever read—the Spanish language being adapted to that style."[110] Nevertheless, the grievances they declared they hoped to address in their pronunciamiento texts were real, and they vividly map out for us what the main political issues of the day were.

Having achieved independence, the big questions as captured in the pronunciamientos of the 1820s display, on the one hand, a determined quest on the part of those who pronounced to find meaningful political representation, whether this was defending a republican system, advocating the need for a federal state where power was devolved to the provinces, supporting congress in its struggle against the emperor, or opposing constitutional abuses, unfair electoral results, and Masonic interfering.[111] On the other hand, they also show that the Plan of Iguala's guarantee of union turned into a major problem once it became obvious that Ferdinand VII's Spain would never recognize Mexico's independence, that there were not enough jobs to go round, and that there were actually Spaniards residing in Mexico who were plotting to restore the mother country's control over the region.

In terms of figures, the majority of pronunciamientos for this decade were launched by the provinces against the center to protect or extend their provincial political authority. Ten pronunciamiento cycles were federalist in one form or another, whether because they empowered the provincial deputations, called for the 1824 Constitution to be federal or more federal than it was, or rejected the implementation of article 4 of the 1829 plan of Jalapa at a regional level (Casa Mata, 1 February 1823; Jalisco, 9 and 12 May 1823; San Luis Potosí, 5 June and 6 September 1823; Guadalajara, 8 June 1824; San Luis Potosí, 13 January and 13 March 1830; Codallos, 11 March 1830; and Zamora, 15 March 1830). Also significant was the number of anti-Spanish plans: six start-up pronunciamientos during these years (Lobato, 23 January 1824; Oaxaca, June 1824; Tlaxcala, 27 March 1827; Jalisco 7–24 August 1827; Perote, 16 September 1828).[112] The Plan of Campeche of 6 November 1829 was the only centralist pronunciamiento of this decade (discounting the Plan of Guadalajara of 27 November 1829, which did not get beyond the conspiracy stage); there would be many more in the 1830s.

If these statistics are anything to go by, and pronunciamiento grievances are deemed to be representative of Independent Mexico's political concerns and urges, the two most pressing issues of the 1820s, once the republic was consolidated, were the regions' need for greater control over their domestic affairs and the Mexicans' drive to expel the supposedly ungrateful, reactionary, and plotting Spanish population from Mexico. Both concerns, of course, were intrinsically tied to the very experience of early independence. They reflected, on the one hand, the regional elites' desire to seize the opportunity independence suddenly afforded them of controlling their own destiny after decades or centuries of centralist rule. On the other, they stemmed from a context where the consensus of Iguala allowed the resident Spanish population to remain in Mexico, hanging onto their wealth and positions of power, despite the fact that Spain itself maintained a stance of open hostility toward the new nation, refusing to acknowledge its independence, bombarding the port of Veracruz from the island fortress of San Juan de Ulúa, and eventually sending a military expedition to Tampico from Cuba.

As discussed in the following chapter, the flaws and weaknesses of the 1824 Constitution would eventually give way to a decade in which, contrastingly, centralist pronunciamientos would become as common as federalist ones, if not more so. As for the 1820s Spanish question, the expulsion laws of 1827–36, paired with Barradas's defeat in 1829, and the eventual Spanish recognition of Mexican independence in 1836, would mean that it ceased to be a burning issue by the mid-1830s. In its place, the popular defense of clerical values, fueros, and institutions would become one of the most striking political impulses of the following decade.

The pronunciamientos of 1821–31 that worked at a national level, with the arguable exception of the 1829 Jalapa–Mexico City series, which was mainly led and backed by military forces, were those that involved collaboration between army officers and civilians (Iguala, 1821; Veracruz–Casa Mata, 1822–23; Perote–Oaxaca–La Acordada, 1828; and the anti-Spanish pronunciamientos of 1824–28). They were also those in which the demands were the vaguest or appeared to reach out to a broader power base, pushing several buttons, both general and concrete, simultaneously. The successful constellations of 1821, 1822–23, 1823–24, 1824–28, 1828, and 1829 most definitely affected the political life, institutions, and laws of the young nation both profoundly and indelibly. They satisfied the pronunciados' demands for independence, a republican system, a federal constitution, the expulsion of the Spanish population, the annulment of Gómez Pedraza's electoral victory, and an end to Guerrero's unlawful presidency, while enabling some of the individuals involved to improve their political and/or economic standing. At a national level Iturbide became an emperor, and both Guerrero and Bustamante became president thanks to pronunciamiento pressure. At a regional level Carvajal became governor of Yucatán. The dramatic manner in which this insurrectional practice spread—with the majority of 1820s pronunciamientos having featured regionalist demands—certainly points to the fact that it catered to provincial concerns and aspirations,

Voice of the Provinces

accounting in no small measure for the evolution of mimetic insurrectionism in peripheral Mexico. Most of the pronunciamientos reviewed so far were orchestrated and led by elite political actors, whether these were high-ranking officers or regional or state authorities. This would change dramatically in the 1830s as subaltern groups took to pronouncing as well, giving way to a decade in which the pronunciamiento was to go viral.

4. When the Pronunciamiento Went Viral

The Popularization of the Pronunciamiento, 1832—1842

One of the critical questions that requires an answer when thinking about the phenomenon of the pronunciamiento in Independent Mexico is the extent to which it involved popular participation. Was the pronunciamiento an exclusively elite-led practice? Was it mainly orchestrated and led by high-ranking officers and elite actors (i.e., wealthy and educated politicians, state governors, town councilors, clergymen, businessmen, and merchants)? Or was it adopted meaningfully by subaltern groups—the disenfranchised, the urban poor, popular indigenous and agrarian political actors?

Common wisdom, based both on a number of contemporary sources and on some studies of the pronunciamiento, would seem to suggest that this was very much a well-to-do *hombres de bien* form of contestation and protest, accounting in no small measure for its controlled nature and its game theory elements.[1] The bureaucratic legalistic language of pronunciamiento texts paired with its instigators' need to be able to read, write, and sign their names at the end of the petitions would certainly appear to confirm such a view. In the mind of José Luis Comellas, writing about the early Spanish pronunciamientos of the nineteenth-century: "These were the work of a minority. The masses did not participate in them, not even a segment of the masses. The people remained always apart, and were mostly hostile toward these maneuvers [*intentos*]."[2] Spanish philosopher José Ortega y Gasset would go one step further in arguing that not only were pronunciamientos the work of a minority, but they were orchestrated by a delusional and deluded few: a handful of "madmen and imbeciles" who actually believed that if they pronounced in their garrison or from the "sparsely attended corner of a coffee-shop gathering [*tertulia*], a gentlemen's club [*casino*], a flag room, or quite simply from [a place in their] imagination," they would be changing the face of the whole wide expanse of Castile.[3]

While not admitting to madness or imbecility, seasoned pronunciado José María Tornel, looking back in 1852 at the first three national decades, nevertheless came to this conclusion: "The people were silent and obeyed, as they have always obeyed and been silent, without there having been a single stimulus that may have brought them out of the cold indifference with which they witness the comings and goings of so many revolutions in which they have never had a part or anything to gain."[4] It is a view with which Fanny Calderón de la Barca, the Scottish wife of the Spanish minister plenipotentiary, concurred when witnessing the apathetic way the popular classes in Mexico City behaved during the 1841 series of pronunciamientos that became known as the Revolución de Jalisco or the Triangular Revolt: "The tranquillity of the sovereign people during all this period is astonishing. In what other city in the world would they not have taken part with one or other side? Shops shut, workmen out of employment, thousands of idle people, subsisting, Heaven only knows how, yet no riot, no confusion, apparently no impatience. Groups of people collect on the streets, or stand talking before their doors, and speculate upon probabilities, but await the decision of their military chiefs, as if it were a judgment from Heaven, from which it were both useless and impious to appeal."[5]

Wherever there is evidence of popular participation the tendency would appear to have been to depict this as the result of coercion or cooption. The people joined whichever was the most recent revolutionary bandwagon either out of fear or because there was fun, money, or booze to be had. The idea that they may have upheld a given ideology, or that they would have supported a pronunciamiento out of their own political conviction, was certainly not noted by contemporary observers such as penniless traveling Prussian scientist Karl Heller or Rose Georgina Kingsley, the daughter of British university professor and writer Reverend Charles Kingsley. Witnessing a pronunciamiento in Veracruz on 23 December 1845, Heller stated: "One made what is here called a *pronunciamiento*, namely, a procession in the street, which proclaims the change of administration and to which, as everywhere, a mob of the lowest rabble attaches itself."[6] He was to make a similar observation in Toluca several months later, on 5 August 1846, when he described how the pronounced dignitaries and military band were "followed by a mob of poor folk, who incessantly broke out with the cry, 'Viva Santa Anna y la Federación, muera Paredes!'"[7] In the cynical words of a Mexican officer Kingsley met in the early 1870s: "I have only to go out on market or fiesta day, and call the people round me, and say, 'Now you shall have as much *pulque* as you like and I will give you your four reals a day if you will pronounce for me'; and then I give them *pulque*, and they all get drunk, and then I draw my sword and I make them a speech about '*la Patria*' and '*Libertad*,' and they all pronounce, and then there is a revolution."[8]

When one considers recent scholarship on popular politics

in nineteenth-century Mexico, and pays attention to the sheer number of pronunciamientos that were launched in the 1830s, it is difficult to accept that the great majority of Mexicans looked on with passive indifference as one cycle of insurrections followed another. As demonstrated by both John Tutino and Juan Ortiz Escamilla, much of the agrarian political violence of the War of Independence was perpetrated by peasant guerrillas.[9] Women who fought and participated in the revolution did not, as Elsa Chaney once claimed, "return . . . to the silence of their colonial siesta."[10] They were different once the war was over.[11] In the same way, the politicized popular classes did not regress to a state of apolitical stoic passivity.

Florencia Mallon made a strong case back in 1995 for us to "take seriously the intellectual history of peasant action."[12] She demonstrated how any attempted hegemonies were not imposed by the elites on a silent, "innocent, ignorant, or naïve rural folk," but rather were negotiated "between and among popular and elite factions; between and among regional political cultures; within and between rural communities, villages, and towns; between young and old, women and men, rich and poor, and different ethnic groups—help[ing] to make the kind of nation-states that Mexico and Peru brought into the contemporary period."[13] Focusing on the Puebla Sierra during the midcentury reform period, Guy Thomson argued that "Liberalism was not only embraced by *gente de razón*—by an emerging mestizo bourgeoisie—but also accommodated within Indian communities (not necessarily the most acculturated ones)."[14] It is a view that resonated and was further substantiated in Peter Guardino's seminal studies of peasant politics in provincial Guerrero and Oaxaca for the first half of the nineteenth century. In these Guardino showed that popular federalism, as he termed it (i.e., the predecessor of Thomson's mid- to late nineteenth-century popular liberalism), with its inclusive understanding of citizenship, stress on local autonomy, and opposition to the elite minority, was actively endorsed by subaltern indigenous groups, who "adapted to their needs both the discourses of post-independence politics and techniques like the use of plans and proclamations [i.e., pronunciamientos] to seek out potential allies."[15] Karen D. Caplan's research has similarly helped us appreciate how indigenous communities in Oaxaca and Yucatán made national political projects work for them, actively engaging with the political ideas and practices that became prevalent after the consummation of independence. In Caplan's unequivocal words, "indigenous people and peasants were capable of political thought and capable of interpreting and acting on the ideologies at play in national politics."[16] As Jaime E. Rodríguez O. has argued recently: "The evidence indicates that poor people, whether urban or rural, were not only affected by high politics but also understood their interests and took action to defend them; that is, they engaged in politics."[17]

In a sense, for us to appreciate the extent to which this is true, it is necessary to take Thomson's advice and go local: "Historians must shift their focus from the federal and state capitals, to villages and small towns where most people lived."[18] By studying the pueblo-based pronunciamientos *de adhesión* or *rechazo* of the 1830s, it becomes clear that, to go back to Guardino's point, "peasants were actively involved in the formation of Mexico's state."[19] Or as Francie R. Chassen-López has argued with reference to Oaxaca: "*comuneros, rancheros, minifundistas, terrazgueros*, peons, and *jornaleros* made numerous decisions that shaped the way social, economic, and political relationships developed."[20]

When the Pronunciamiento Went Viral

This is particularly evident in the way that villages in Mexico started to make faraway calls for change to address their concrete local needs in the 1830s, as they appropriated and employed pronunciamiento pressure and tactics to serve their own ends. A decade after independence had been consummated as a result of the military-led pronunciamiento cycle of Iguala, a much broader range of people made the pronunciamiento practice their own, using it to address local issues and interests. Among the participants were *vecinos* (neighbors) and *vecinos principales* (leading neighbors), *labradores* (farm laborers), *numeroso pueblo* (numerous villagers), *ciudadanos* (citizens), *empleados* (employees), and even on occasion *multitudes del pueblo*.

As an example, in the case of the pronunciamiento launched by the barely literate villagers of the Purépecha region of Tarecuato in Michoacán, who got together in Tangamandapio on 26 January 1832 to oppose the Plan of Veracruz of 2 January, news of Santa Anna's gesture of rebellion provided them with a chance to gather and forcefully voice their discontent over several local grievances. In this instance, apparently in reaction to the economic activities of a group of unnamed English merchants or landowners based in the area, the villagers of Tarecuato used the opportunity to pronounce in favor of the government and against Santa Anna, "who harms us by stirring things up" (art. 11), so that they could put a stop to the Englishmen's commercial activities and take their lands—forcing them, moreover, as punishment, to "plough *our* [land]" (art. 9).[21]

The opening article—full of spelling mistakes and employing a strikingly ungrammatical structure—declared: "These villages are free of dependence, and are sovereign, and neither regal patrimony, nor the English [*ingleso*], nor Santa Anna [*santano*]. We live as God commands." From this we can infer that they considered themselves to be sovereign, God-fearing, and opposed to monarchists, English people, and Santa Anna. Article 5 made it clear that they were against "foreign commerce," and articles 9 and 11 attacked the English, whose lands they planned to confiscate, calling for giving them and Santa Anna a good thrashing (*cuero con inglés y con Santa Anna*). Interestingly, to those members of other states who came to Tarecuato to join their pronunciamiento, they offered a field in which to camp as well as water, wood, and stubble but noted that they would expect payment for any hay or maize (art. 4). Tellingly, following their professed defense of the Roman Apostolic Catholic faith, article 7 randomly noted that "the poor will be entitled to get married."[22] Such socially conscious demands together with the spelling and grammatical mistakes that feature prominently throughout the text certainly point to the fact that this pronunciamiento's authors were barely literate and did not belong to the elite. This in turn illustrated how by the early 1830s the pronunciamiento as a practice had started to be adopted by different subaltern groups who were neither members of the military nor hombres de bien. It also confirms Terry Rugeley's view that "local actors used apparent support for national agendas to mask their real intentions"; he evocatively referred to start-up pronunciamientos from other parts of the country as "Echoes of Distant Thunder."[23] As evidenced in the case of the Tarecuato pronunciamiento de rechazo, it was launched by villagers to protect their agricultural activities from the British presence in the area, while supposedly responding to Santa Anna's plan of Veracruz.

As the 1830s progressed, increasing numbers of villages and rural communities in provincial Mexico, like the Purépecha people of Tarecuato, would use news of faraway pronunciamientos to pronounce over what ultimately were strictly local concerns. Thus one Captain José Antonio Rodríguez used the pronunciamiento of adhesión of Tampico of 10 March 1832 to take over the command of the local garrison.[24] The garrison of San Juan Bautista used theirs of 4 June 1832 to call for the pro-government auxiliary militias from neighboring Chiapas to leave the state, and for unpopular officers Francisco Palomino, Ramón Payán, and Mateo González to be dispatched to Veracruz.[25] The fortress of San Diego in Acapulco in tandem remonstrated on 11 August in support of the 2 January Plan of Veracruz, while also reordering the local political scene by having Juan Álvarez become commander-in-chief of the region and inviting itinerant government commander Francisco Hernández to change sides and join them.[26] And in the north on 26 September 1832 the Culiacán garrison adopted the same strategy—backing Santa Anna while addressing local concerns, in this case ensuring that local councilor Pedro Sánchez and town judge Pedro Bermudes were kicked out of Sinaloa.[27] Concentrating on events in the district of Huejutla (in present-day Hidalgo), Michael Ducey has researched how the major national pronunciamientos of 1830–34 affected rural Mexico reaching down to the "lowest level of politics." He observes: "As pronunciamientos became more frequent, . . . farmers, ranchers, and smalltime merchants who occupied municipal offices were swept up into debates over the fate of the nation," and their local authorities found themselves seeking "to challenge or accommodate national political plans to their own needs."[28]

More often than not this would entail reordering the local political scene, calling for the removal of given local bigwigs—be they district prefects, town councilors, mayors, or political chiefs.

Thus, to note a couple more examples from Michoacán, the villagers of Huetamo pronounced on 19 September 1832 *in favor* of Santa Anna's Plan of Veracruz (unlike those from Tarecuato, who had opposed it), and, while they were at it, invited local commander Anselmo Elisalde to take over the local authorities as leader of the pronunciamiento. Likewise those from Zacapu unpronounced on 24 September (having previously pronounced in favor of Santa Anna's Veracruzan movement) with their corresponding *despronunciamiento* and, in so doing, replaced subprefect José María Cierra with 1831 mayor Antonio Verdusco. The inclusion of additional demands that addressed specific local concerns would become frequent and common thereafter in community-based pronunciamientos as villages and town councils came to use the pronunciamiento de adhesión or rechazo as a means to overcome local problems while appearing to voice their adherence or opposition to a given national movement or "echo of distant thunder."[29] To quote Ducey again, they "became opportunities to rearrange the distribution of power and offered the possibility of dislodging the establishment in favor of upstarts" at a local or village level.[30]

Start-up pronunciamientos like that of Jalapa of 4 December 1829 or of Cuernavaca of 25 May 1834 would prove popular precisely because they included articles that, from the perspective of provincial Mexico, could be exploited by local communities in *legitimately* reordering the local political scene as they saw fit, regardless of whether they believed in the broader goals of the original grito. Article 4 of the Plan of Jalapa, in stating that "all functionaries who have been condemned by public opinion" should be removed, allowed communities across Mexico to remove town councilors, prefects, state deputies, and governors on the grounds that public opinion was allegedly against them.[31] Five years later article 4 of the Plan of Cuernavaca of 24 May 1834 had the same effect, stating not only that those deputies who had sanctioned or supported the anti-constitutional and anti-clerical laws of the 1833–34 Congress should be removed from office but so should "all other functionaries" who had supposedly done the same.[32] As was noted in the second article of the pronunciamiento de adhesión the garrison of San Cristóbal de Colima launched on 3 July 1834 with the support of a "considerable number of neighbors" (*un número considerable de vecinos*): "In virtue of that which is noted in Art. 4 of the mentioned Plan [of Cuernavaca], and the confidence we have in national militia captain don Manuel Ceballos, we name him acting political chief of the territory."[33]

Communal indigenous practices and traditional popular corporate forms of organization and association found expression, moreover, in ayuntamiento-led pronunciamientos, in the manner in which this liberal insurrectionary practice contained within it a noteworthy traditional corporate form of politicking. As was noted by François-Xavier Guerra, "those who act and speak [in pronunciamientos] are men grouped together in [corporate] bodies, a characteristic that is underlined by the [use of] terms such as 'unanimously' or 'by common consent' [*mancomunadamente*] which manifest the collective nature of their action."[34] There are even instances in some village pronunciamientos de adhesión of individuals signing the pronunciamiento text at the end on behalf of their respective communities rather than as individuals, as in that of the town council, farm laborers (*labradores*), and neighbors of the municipality of Coronanco (Puebla) of 4 June 1834 in support of that of Cholula. Thus a group of predominantly indigenous representatives signed the pronunciamiento text of

Coronanco on behalf of their respective villages—with Luciano de Guadalupe Yxehual doing so for the village of San Gabriel, Manuel Cipriano Tepalí for that of San Mateo, Miguel Antonio Xochileuila for San Lucas, José Leandro Ramires for Tlaltenango, Feliz Martín Mendoza for Xoxtla, José Marcos Hernández for San Antonio, Lucas Antonio Titlán for Ocotlán and its haciendas, Antonio Flores for San Lorenzo and its haciendas, and José María Pérez for San Martín Zoquiapan and its hacienda.[35]

The discourse of representativeness may have been questionable, yet for the communities who gathered to discuss their response to the latest pronunciamiento text to arrive and be read out in the community, there must have been a ring of truth or a disposition to believe that by pronouncing in favor of or against whichever plan was doing the rounds, they were exercising their own form of sovereignty, giving voice to the aggrieved general, national, or popular will. As noted in the first chapter, just as the members of the 2011 Occupy movement saw themselves representing and belonging to the "99 percent," the pronunciados of Independent Mexico viewed themselves very much as representatives and spokespeople of the general, national, or popular will (*voluntad general, voluntad nacional/de la nación, voluntad del pueblo/de los pueblos*), stating as much in their pronunciamiento texts.

According to Elspeth Gillespie, between 1821 and 1855 between 26 and 29 percent of pronunciamiento texts actually made explicit reference to the "will of the nation," with military pronunciados making use of the expression only marginally more than civilian ones–3 percent more. Having said this, she also noted an evolution in the use of the concept, so that while 25 percent of pronunciamientos in 1834 invoked the "national will," by 1842, after the pronunciamiento had gone viral in the mid-1830s, 43 percent of the texts that circulated that year did so. Gillespie also found that the concept was used far more commonly to oppose existing constitutions, laws, and government policies and personnel, and to call for reform (63 percent), than to support a given existing constitution or administration (12 percent). In this sense it is telling that the "popular will" was more often than not at odds with the prevailing order—or at least, that was how the pronunciados saw it and, in turn, legitimized their insubordination on the grounds that this will had been ignored or trampled on by those in power. Among Gillespie's findings and equally worthy of note is that the "will of the nation" proved to be a concept that was more popular in centralist pronunciamientos (with 39 percent of centralist pronunciamientos alluding to it) than in federalist ones (22 percent). In terms of regional patterns, the pronunciamientos that made mention of the "will of the nation" tended to be launched from the more central provinces, with the remarkable exception of Campeche (where 47 percent of the pronunciamientos employed this terminology, far outstripping neighboring Yucatán, 8 percent). This last statistic would appear to reflect the animosity that existed between Campeche and Mérida, the former traditionally pro-Mexico and thus concerned with the "national will," the latter notoriously independent and thus comparatively indifferent to it.[36]

There is evidence, moreover, that popular participation took place in town council meetings and fiestas. There are numerous instances where the pronunciamiento text noted the involvement of the "people" in the discussions that led to a given community's decision to pronounce one way or another. References to neighbors turning up en masse would become widespread and many as the 1830s unfolded, such as the crowd of neighbors (*en masa el vecindario*) who gathered with the members of the town council of Ayotzingo (present-day state of Mexico) on 7 June 1834 to support the plan of Cuernavaca, or the "copious number of inhabitants" (*un muy copioso número del resto de habitantes*) who joined the prefect, town council, priest, judge, federal and state employees, and Taxco's principal neighbors on 1 June 1835 to pronounce in favor of the centralist pronunciamiento of Toluca.[37]

Although most pronunciamiento texts are unfortunately brief in their account of the discussions that led to a given community pronouncing, with the elected secretaries having preferred to gloss over what was said and by whom before a decision was reached, those who did minute the discussions in greater detail allow us to appreciate that pronunciamientos were not necessarily *faits accomplis*, dictated from above through coercion or the patronizing offer of *pulque*, and that communities across Mexico actually did engage in heated discussions before endorsing insurrectionary action. The following cases offer fascinating insights into the extent to which the gatherings that preceded the launching of a given village pronunciamiento, whether it was *de adhesión* or *de rechazo*, involved discussion, dissension, persuasion, and in some instances meaningful consultation.

As may be evidenced in the Acta of the pronunciamiento de rechazo of the community of Mineral de Nieves in Zacatecas, of 17 June 1833, following the arrival of news of the pronunciamiento of Ignacio Escalada of 26 May that year, an extraordinary meeting was called at nine in the evening. The *jefe político*, mayor, village priest, judge, infantry and cavalry captains, officers, sergeants, corporals, and soldiers stationed there, together with several neighbors (*varios vecinos*) all gathered in the town hall to discuss what their response should be. Initially, to ensure that their decision was well informed, the jefe político read out loud the letter the state governor had sent to inform him of the pronunciamiento cycle, the governor's decree opposing the pronunciamiento, the state congress's response, that of the vice president of the republic, Valentín Gómez Farías, and ten further related documents, all reproduced in the press, including the text of the pronunciamiento itself. Thereafter the jefe político let his views be known, expressing outright opposition to Escalada and Mariano Arista, the latter having pronounced on the back of Escalada's movement on 8 June from Huejotzingo, Puebla. The parish priest spoke afterward, arguing that it was their sacred duty to "obey, respect, and make [others] obey and respect all of the legally constituted authorities," and concluded by supporting the jefe político's proposal to reject Escalada's movement and stand by the government. The town judge went next and agreed with the jefe político and the priest. He added that he would pursue those who conspired or employed subversive words "forever [*hasta lo infinito*]." Thereafter, one after another, different captains, officers, sergeants, corporals, and even soldiers had their say, as did nameless individuals who were present ("*demás particulares*"). By the end of the night the people gathered in the town hall of Mineral de Nieves agreed unanimously to inform the governor and the state congress that they were "prepared to sacrifice their very existence to defend the patria, and the actual form of government, upholding at all costs the legally constituted supreme authorities, and resolutely avenge the insults committed on the person of the first magistrate of the nation" (at that point Santa Anna, who had been kidnapped by the pronunciados).[38]

The pronunciamiento of Mineral de Nieves affords us an example of an occasion when the entire community was in agreement about how to proceed. Even then, a lengthy discussion in which all those present were allowed—even expected—to express their views was held before the decision to pronounce was actually taken. In other detailed pronunciamiento minutes, such as that of the Acta of the village of Teotihuacán of 3 June 1834 in the present-day state of Mexico, what becomes clear is that such discussions did not always go as smoothly as in the preceding example of the unanimously agreed Mineral de Nieves pronunciamiento de rechazo. In Teotihuacán, on receiving news of the Plan of Cuernavaca of 25 May 1834, it turned out that not everyone present was in favor of pronouncing for it. In fact, town councilors Rafael de Aldana, Simón Tena, Francisco Rosales, and Jacinto Álvarez made a point of stating that they did not want to be associated with any pronunciamiento de adhesión launched from their community, and they wanted this recorded explicitly in the pronunciamiento's corresponding Acta. Interestingly, rather than being browbeaten into falling in line with the majority of those gathered, the four government-loyal, pronunciamiento-shy councilors were allowed to differ from the rest. The pronunciamiento thus went ahead despite the councilors' opposition, and the text duly acknowledged that this was not the result of a unanimous vote. Teotihuacán was pronouncing in favor of the Plan of Cuernavaca because "the majority" supported such a move.[39] There are, in fact, numerous examples of individuals who made a point of having their opposition to a given proposal to pronounce noted in the relevant pronunciamiento Acta, which in turn says something about the representative nature of certain pronunciamientos. Some definitely appear to have been genuinely consultative, and the context in which the discussions were held was not necessarily characterized by intimidation. It was possible for members of a given community to dissent and disagree with the majority of their neighbors, and even to ensure that their opposition to the will of that majority was noted, without their suffering as a result.

In the case of the pronunciamiento launched by the town council, priest, and judge of Mineral de Cimapán of 8 June 1834 in the present-day state of Hidalgo, although all those present were unanimous in supporting the Plan of Toluca of 31 May, interestingly, there were opposed views (*"diversos pareceres"*) over whether their community should express adherence to the Toluca movement via a peaceful representation or by launching a pronunciamiento. This question—to pronounce or not as a means to convey their support for the Plan of Toluca—gave way to a particularly lengthy discussion (*"habiéndose discutido largamente el punto"*), which was only resolved by having those present conduct a formal secret ballot, in which two councilors, Juan Manuel Terán and José María Lugo, acted as returning officers. As it turned out, two thirds of those gathered voted in favor of voicing their support with a pronunciamiento, while one third voted for doing so via a "simple representation (*manifestación*)." Of particular interest is that the town councilors and villagers of Mineral de Cimapán had a clear idea of and strong views about the difference between launching a pronunciamiento and issuing a statement or representation. It can be confidently noted that the pronunciamiento was perceived at the time as the more forceful means of airing a community's political views and standpoint. Equally or more revealing was the manner in which the practice itself could entail not just consultation but the carrying out of a vote to determine a given community's final resolution. In this instance, notwithstanding significant opposition to the act of pronouncing, the majority—that is, two thirds of those present—

carried the vote, with the result that Mineral de Cimapán joined the 1834 Cuernavaca–Toluca cycle with its very own pronunciamiento de adhesión.[40]

The inclusion of ballots and voting as part of the decision-making process whereby given communities resolved to pronounce or not in 1830s Mexico was actually fairly widespread and, as can be seen in the Acta of the ayuntamiento of Atlixco (Puebla) of 9 June 1834, was inextricably linked to the noted concept of the popular/national/general will. In this instance the town council chose to postpone any decision over whether they should pronounce (in favor of the 31 May Plan of Toluca) until the entire local community was present to discuss the matter. In the words of one councilor who considered it a difficult choice (he used the term *obscure*), it was imperative to summon the entire town council and all the village neighbors in order to hear everybody's opinion, because whatever was their final resolution this needed to "emanate directly from the will of the people."[41]

Corroborating the earlier description of the arguably representative nature of certain pronunciamientos, and that some appear to have been genuinely consultative, following the town council president's invitation to all present to express their views with utmost frankness, Captain Atenógenes Projano, who had arrived in Atlixco with news of the Toluca wave of pronunciamientos, made a point of stating that people should make their opinions known without fear of any reprisals. The point would be reiterated as an article in the final wording of the pronunciamiento, where article 5 stated: "Nobody will be harmed [*molestado*] for their opinions whatever they may be"; that is, provided they did not *take action* against the pronunciamiento.[42]

The minutes of the Atlixco pronunciamiento de adhesión offer

When the Pronunciamiento Went Viral

as well as a detailed account of the interventions of those present—
señores Projano, José María Fonseca, Cayetano Gaviño, José Antonio Serrano, Manuel Boleaga, etc.—evidence of the commitment
by the assembled dignitaries to consult their community as widely
as possible before making a decision. When one José María Pro-
diles argued that they need not delay their decision further by
waiting to summon the entire village, since the town council had
been voted in by the people and thus already represented them,
councilor Francisco Sánchez Boleaga retorted that they could not
"go without hearing the voice of the people from whom the town
council has received its power." As a result, the meeting was indeed
suspended until enough people from Atlixco could be consulted.
The outcome of the pronunciados' extensive consultation was to
pronounce in favor of the Plan of Toluca, adding an article ensuring that those public officials of their municipality who did not
act according to this plan would be replaced by "individuals who
deserve the public confidence of this very municipality" (art. 4).[43]

Further evidence of the fact that the pronunciamiento was
not exclusively an elite-led practice is that by the mid-1830s disenfranchised groups such as women and Indian tribes started
to adopt pronunciamiento tactics to engage with the politics of
the period and address their particular grievances. On 29 July
1833, there appears to have been a group of women in Zacatlán
de las Manzanas, in Puebla, who pronounced and took up arms
in defense of the government, in defiance of the threat posed by
the arrival of a bandit supporter of Arista's 8 June 1833 pronunciamiento of Huejotzingo. As can be seen in the pronunciamiento
text—subsequently circulated as a pamphlet by an anonymous
author who made a point of praising these "patriotic *zacatlanque-
ñas*" who not only embraced the just cause of the government but

defended it with their "beautiful arms"—the women of Zacatlán gathered in one María Candia's house to resolve how they should respond to the arrival of the "ungrateful Ponce" and his band of pronunciados in the area. They were very conscious of the fact that Zacatlán was to be left unprotected the moment the soldiers and men of the village set off to track down and confront Ponce's forces. As a result, following the customary discussion, Juana Cano, María Candia, Nicolasa Martínez, and the "principal patriotic women of the community" (*las principales patriotas de esta población*) resolved to take up arms and die before succumbing to tyranny and Arista's "Bourbonist plan" (art. 1), and to inform the commander general of their resolution in the hope that he would approve of it, furnishing them with two hundred rifles and the necessary ammunition (arts. 2, 3). This pronunciamiento de rechazo of itself highlights the extent to which the pronunciamiento, as a practice, had started to be taken up by all kinds of groups of people, including disenfranchised and subaltern sectors of society such as women. Likewise, it demonstrates how the norms and rituals that governed the practice had become so common and widespread that even a group of politically marginalized women such as these knew the form and style a pronunciamiento text should take.[44]

In a similar vein, by the mid-1830s there were several indigenous groups, such as the Opata Indians in Sonora, who adopted pronunciamiento tactics to lobby the president to address their grievances over land ownership. As an example, on 2 July 1836, thirty-six Opata villages or communities came together in Arizpe to force the president to listen to their grievances and intercede on their behalf. They felt compelled to address the president as the result of a dispute over land ownership between the Opata

tribe and a number of men who had sold and bought their ances-
tral land. The fact that the Opata people opted to use pronunciamiento tactics and rhetoric to pressure the government into
addressing their grievances provides further evidence that the
pronunciamiento went viral in the 1830s, being adopted by people from all walks of life.[45]

Perhaps the most striking evidence I have found substantiat-
ing the point that subaltern groups took to pronouncing is José
Urrea's 1842 response to the Yaqui Indian pronunciamientos of
Sonora. Urrea was a seasoned pronunciado in his own right who
had either led or been involved in numerous pronunciamientos,
including the 1821 Plan of Iguala, the 1823 Acta de Casa Mata,
the 1827–28 Plan of Montaño, that of Jalapa in 1829, Veracruz in
1832, Arizpe in 1837, Tuxpan in 1839, and Mexico City in 1840.
Having become the respectable governor of Sonora in 1842, he
did not take kindly to others pronouncing. To be precise, Urrea
could not stomach the idea that subaltern groups such as Yaqui
Indians could have the gall to adopt a form of insurrectionary
action he clearly saw as belonging to an hombres de bien repertoire of forceful negotiation. His decree of 12 July 1842, issued to
bring an end to the Yaquis' adoption of pronunciamiento tactics,
eloquently shows how for a gentleman pronunciado like Urrea,
the very notion that Indians could be pronouncing was entirely
unacceptable.

In it Urrea made a point of stating that while pronunciamientos
could cause much harm to society, never was this more obvious
than when these were instigated by "those classes whose ignorance makes them easy prey to seduction and the influence of
perverse people." It was to put a stop to indigenous pronunciamientos that Urrea decreed that all Indians who took part in a

revolution against the government, either by rising up in arms or aiding the revolutionaries, would have their land confiscated by the state government (art. 1). All confiscated land would then be redistributed to loyal and landless Indians by the state government's judges of the peace (art. 2). In those vicinities where there were no loyal and landless Indians, the judges of the peace would rent out the confiscated land to whoever was best placed to rent it from the state government (art. 3). To those Indians who had participated in a pronunciamiento and who did not surrender within fifteen days of the publication of this decree, Urrea warned that they would not only lose their land but would suffer the many and severe penalties established by the law for insurrectionary criminal activity (art. 4). Moreover, anyone who was deemed to have seduced the Indian population to pronounce was to be imprisoned with immediate effect (art. 5).[46]

It is not insignificant that Urrea chose to stop the Yaquis from pronouncing by attacking them where it hurt most; namely, by confiscating their land. Unlike earlier "gentlemanly" responses to pronunciamientos, such as the Convenio de Zavaleta of 23 December 1832, in which a general amnesty was typically offered to all and sundry regardless of which side they had supported, Urrea was not prepared to let off the hook those Yaqui Indians who had dared to pronounce. As Shara Ali noted recently—in studying how the Yucatecan elite did everything possible to hijack Santiago Imán's popular pronunciamiento of 1836–40 and minimize his importance, especially once he mobilized the Maya—for the elites, "No pronunciamiento in their minds had any business empowering the lower classes . . . ; that was too dangerous. A . . . pronunciamiento was to them simply an excuse and a justification from them to gain power in the capital and implement the decrees they favored."[47] The discomfort that elite actors such as Urrea and the Yucatecan elite showed toward indigenous pronunciamientos demonstrates in itself that after a decade of pronunciamiento frenzy, the pronunciamiento had gone from being the 1820s domain of the elite-military few to a genuinely popular political practice.

Pronunciamientos may have started along the lines conceived by Comellas and Ortega y Gasset, with a delusional and deluded minority of army officers and hombres de bien convinced that if they pronounced, following in Riego's steps, they could meaningfully and relatively peacefully change the prevailing political situation. However, by the mid-1830s everyone was pronouncing. As I have noted elsewhere, the pronunciamiento, which originated in the barracks, spearheaded by Masonic conspiracies in opposition to Ferdinand VII's absolutism and initially used to negotiate political change forcefully, became part of everyday life, accepted, used, and endorsed by almost everybody regardless of the fact that it was outside the law.[48]

By 1837 even the demands being made in some pronunciamientos in rural Mexico started to develop a singularly popular and agrarian agenda. It was not just that the dangerous classes took to pronouncing: they pronounced to address social grievances that affected and mattered to them. Gordiano Guzmán's federalist Pronunciamiento of Aguililla of 1 December 1837, and the agrarian revolutionary movement he went on to lead in Jalisco and Michoacán (which lasted until 1842) provides a perfect example of the extent to which this insurrectionary practice became popular; popular in terms of its content and popular in terms of the very people who adopted the pronunciamiento as part of their political repertoire. The pronunciados in this instance were mainly former civic militiamen who had fought for the insurgency during the War of Independence, and joining them were small landholders. They were federalists, radicals, and had a degree of popular support, including from Purépecha Indian communities. As a result they received significant backing from most rural authorities in Michoacán, gaining some adherents in neighboring Jalisco.

The social demands Guzmán made in letters and addresses he circulated alongside the actual pronunciamiento (which called for a return to a federal constitution) did not escape the attention of the local elites, who immediately set out to crush the pronunciamiento employing brutal force. As can be seen in the letter Guzmán addressed to the governor of Michoacán, General Isidro Reyes, on 1 March 1838, beyond his ardent federalism was a strong commitment to improving the lives of Mexico's dispossessed:

> Can you not hear the tearful voices of those men and women who have been cast into poverty because they have had their few assets [*cortos patrimonios*] confiscated? In what way does the republic support its indigent classes, who do not even have the freedom to enjoy the few emoluments they have earned at the cost of so much suffering? Who else other than the government is to be blamed for the wrongs, tangible and moral, that have left [so many] families in such a state of confusion? Some [families] have lost their brothers and husbands, recruited to fill the army; others, without resources, in debt, have had their few belongings taken from them by immoral and idle guards; others despair looking for work and, as a result, find themselves if not forced into a life of crime, condemned to a reprehensible inactivity; none of this can be denied because it is there for all to see. Can Guzmán—as long as he is alive—do nothing about this [*permanecer inerte*]?[49]

Guzmán's movement gained significant support from the rural communities of Michoacán and Jalisco. Unsurprisingly, the civil and military authorities in Zamora were dismayed that "rabble of the area" (*la plebe del lugar*) joined Guzmán's pronunciados, while those of Coyuca made a point of stressing that "the respectable people and authorities" (*las autoridades y las gentes respetables*) were forced to flee from Tetela del Río out of fear of what these revolutionary hordes would do to them.[50] By the late 1830s, as illustrated by Gordiano Guzmán's insurrectionary movement, there were pronunciamientos in provincial Mexico that were launched and/or supported by subaltern and agrarian political actors to address social injustice and wealth disparity. Although most *national* pronunciamientos were elite-led, at a local level, where popular political participation was real, the pronunciamiento was adopted by just about everyone, regardless of class, ethnicity, education, or social status, to address grievances. The popular classes pronounced not just because they were told to do so, but also because politics mattered to them, and because the pronunciamiento became *the* way of influencing politics in nineteenth-century Mexico.

Thus following the success of the 1829 Plan of Jalapa it did not take long for the insurrectionary model of the pronunciamiento to be adopted by subaltern actors. Between 1832 and 1842 more than eight hundred individual pronunciamientos were launched (start-ups, pronunciamientos de adhesión, and counter- and despronunciamientos). These years saw more than fifteen constellations or groups, which I distinguish here in terms of five types of pronunciamiento clusters.

First, there were five particularly forceful constellations that engaged with national concerns, spread across several states or regions, and were ultimately successful in achieving their aims—whether these were explicitly stated or not. These were the Veracruz–Lerma–Zacatecas 1832 series that resulted, after a year of conflict, in the demise of Anastasio Bustamante's government and the return from exile of Manuel Gómez Pedraza to complete his interrupted term in office; the Cuernavaca–Toluca series of 1834 that led to the closure of the radical 1833–34 congress and the repeal of most of its anti-clerical laws and reforms; the Orizaba–Toluca series of 1835 that brought an end to the First Federal Republic and ushered in the Central Republic (1835–46); the 1841 Guadalajara–Ciudadela–Perote series, otherwise known as the Triangular Revolt, that gave way to the overthrow of Bustamante's second government and Santa Anna's return to power; and the 1842 San Luis Potosí–Huejotzingo series that gave acting -president General Nicolás Bravo the justification he needed—claiming he was listening to the voice of the "national will"—not to allow the draft 1842 federal constitution to be approved and to close down the Constituent Congress on 19 December that year.[51]

Second, there were three distinct pronunciamiento cycles that engaged with national concerns and spread across several states or regions but failed to achieve their aims. The Escalada–Durán–Arista series of 1833, calling initially for the protection of the church and its ecclesiastical *fueros* from the anti-clerical reforms that were starting to be discussed in congress, and which culminated with the demand that Santa Anna be proclaimed dictator; lasted six months; and spread across the present-day states of Michoacán, Mexico, Puebla, and Guanajuato but was personally quelled by Santa Anna in October that year. The Sonora–Sinaloa–Tamaulipas cycle of federalist pronunciamientos of 1837–40, initially started by the authorities of Arizpe, Sonora, and which

When the Pronunciamiento Went Viral

would be led by José Urrea for a significant period of time, lasted over three years, and spilled into San Luis Potosí and Puebla at different junctures, but was brought to an end on 8 November 1840 following General Mariano Arista's successful pacification of the north of the country, with the signing of the armistice of Los Olmitos, Tamaulipas, by government general Isidro Reyes and the last remaining pronunciado, Antonio Canales. Last but not least, there was Gordiano Guzmán's Aguililla pronunciamiento cycle of 1837–42, noted earlier, which rumbled along for five years, spreading across the countryside of provincial Michoacán and Jalisco, until Guzmán handed himself in on 24 February 1842, making the most of a general amnesty Santa Anna's government offered him.[52]

Third, there were a number of pronunciamiento clusters that engaged with national concerns but that, unlike the three constellations noted in the previous paragraph, failed to spread beyond their region of origin. The most striking of these were Nicolás Bravo's misleadingly named Plan of Reconciliation of Chichihualco (Guerrero) of 2 December 1833, calling for the creation of a new government and constituent assembly; State Governor Manuel Cosío's Zacatecan federalist pronunciamiento of 30 March 1835, launched in an attempt to preempt the government's visible shift toward centralism; José Ramón García Ugarte's federalist pronunciamiento of San Luis Potosí of 14 April 1837; and the pronunciamiento of 15 July 1840 in which Urrea seized the National Palace in Mexico City, temporarily taking President Anastasio Bustamante prisoner. Having said this, there were numerous other start-up pronunciamientos during these years that did not prosper. Most of these were launched following the change to centralism in 1835, in a desperate bid to turn back the clock and restore the abolished 1824 Federal Constitution. To note but a sample of individual start-up federalist pronunciamientos that failed to inspire meaningful waves of actas de adhesión beyond their region, there was the Californian pronunciamiento of 6 November 1836 (Monterey, California), Colonel Mariano Olarte's Plan of 20 December 1836 (Papantla, Veracruz), the military pronunciamiento of Monte Alto of 1 June 1838 (State of Mexico), Longinos Montenegro's pronunciamiento of 7 October 1838 (Tampico, Tamaulipas), the pronunciamiento of Ciudad Victoria of 12 December 1838 (Tamaulipas), that of Mier (Tamaulipas) of 17 May 1840, and that of Capula (Querétaro) of 30 July 1841. They were all characterized by their calls to restore the Federal Constitution and their inability to muster enough support to have an impact on national politics beyond adding their voice to what amounted to an extensive but uncoordinated chorus of federalist disapproval to the centralist governments of 1835–46.[53]

Fourth, there were two pronunciamiento cycles that engaged with national concerns, failed to spread beyond their region, but succeeded in significantly reordering the local political scene. The Texan federalist pronunciamiento of 22 June 1835 did not spread beyond Texas but eventually resulted in the independence of the province from Mexico after it triggered the Texan Revolution of 1835–36. Similarly, Santiago Imán's federalist pronunciamiento of Valladolid (Yucatán) of 12 February 1840, launched after several years of insurrectionary activity—once it was hijacked by the pronunciamiento of Mérida (Yucatán) of 18 February 1840 with its additional demand that Yucatán become independent from Mexico—as with Texas also resulted in the independence of the province from Mexico (albeit temporary in this instance).[54]

The fifth and last category involves pronunciamientos that were engaged with strictly regional concerns. These did not intend to influence national politics and did not seek to elicit support from elsewhere. They were launched by local political actors with the sole purpose of reordering the local political scene or addressing very specific regional grievances. It is impossible to list all of them here, but the following examples serve to provide a representative notion of the kind of demands they made. In the plan of Arizpe of 12 August 1833 the town council and neighbors of Arizpe used the pronunciamiento format and process to call for disobeying the state legislature and to recognize Manuel Escalante y Arvizu as the new state governor, with an array of related regional demands. The pronunciamiento of Chiapas of 27 November of the same year, which aggressively called for the armed defense of the country's ecclesiastical fueros and privileges, echoing some of the Escalada–Durán–Arista cycle's demands, went on to demand the overthrow of the current state legislature, the return of the previous incumbents, a ban on all yorkinos from positions of political power, and the appointment of Lieutenant Colonel José Anselmo de Lara as commander general of Chiapas, in an attempt to reorder the local political scene. The regional plan of Opodepe (Sonora) of 28 November 1838 again was one concerned with strictly regional concerns and was not intended to influence politics beyond the confines of its state. In this instance the community of Opodepe used their right of petition to demand that Manuel Gándara, who had been involved in the 1837–38 Sonoran cycle of federalist pronunciamientos, was removed as provincial governor and political chief.[55]

Apart from these five clearly defined categories of pronunciamientos, Mexico witnessed during its second decade as an independent country a number of pronunciamiento conspiracies that were intended to engage with national concerns but that were uncovered before they could be launched, such as that of José de Jesús Velázquez, a certain Fiz, and José María Quijano; their particularly aggressive federalist pronunciamiento of 13 September 1837 (Tampico) called to have all those who opposed them beheaded (art. 2). Arguably the most intriguing of these failed pronunciamientos that did not go further than the initial drafting of a plan was the plan of priests Carlos Tepsteco Abad and Epigmenio de la Piedra's of 2 February 1834 (Ecatzingo, Puebla) to forge an Indian monarchy with a descendant of Moctezuma's on the throne. Among its elaborate and farfetched proposals was an early form of eugenics, captured in its article 7, which stated that the emperor was to marry a white woman if he were an Indian or a "pure Indian" if he were white, six months after having been crowned. Unsurprisingly, nothing came of this pronunciamiento.[56]

Among those pronunciamiento conspiracies that did not prosper and that deserve a mention there was also Valentín Gómez Farías, Lorenzo de Zavala, and José Antonio Mejía's federalist "Plan de la Junta Antifictiónica de Nueva Orleans" of 6 September 1835, which they launched from their exile in New Orleans in the hope that it would serve as a rallying cry in Mexico to the overthrown federalist authorities of 1833–34.[57] At the time, all three men were under the impression that the Texan rebels were sincere in their call to safeguard the 1824 Constitution. However, once it became apparent that the Texan rebels were actually intent on seceding from Mexico, Gómez Farías and Mejía withdrew their support for the Texan movement. Zavala, on the other hand, would end up participating in the drafting of the Texan Constitution and succeeded in being elected vice president of the Lone Star Republic once Texan independence was achieved in 1836. Zavala would not live long enough to see the consolidation of Texas' independence, since he died of pneumonia on 15 November 1836. Before I analyze these pronunciamientos, it is worth summarizing the main events of the years 1832–42, so as to appreciate the extent to which pronunciamiento pressure determined the political evolution of 1830s Mexico.

General Anastasio Bustamante's government, formed in 1830 as a result of the Jalapa–Mexico City 1829 series discussed in the previous chapter, represented a return to power of several prominent veterans of the War of Independence who had fought with the royalists prior to the launch of the 1821 Plan of Iguala. Thus from 1830 to 1832 the party of order, as it became known, moved into the National Palace. Under the guidance of Lucas Alamán, General Bustamante's government curtailed the power of the federal states and limited the universality of male suffrage to more clearly defined property-owning citizens. The traditionalist politicians who had been ostracized since the 1826 congressional elections, former royalists, escoceses, and centralists, made an important comeback. It was an administration determined to protect church and army, empower the national government, and put in their place the radical liberals who had dominated politics under Victoria and Guerrero's presidencies. It was also committed to ensure Texas was not lost by forbidding U.S. citizens from being able to settle in the province (6 April 1830). Several attempts were made, moreover, to inject new life into the Mexican economy through the creation of a bank, the Banco de Avío (16 October 1830), assisting Mexico's dormant industry with protectionist policies. The initial economic success of the administration's policies was fairly impressive. However, Bustamante's government soon became characterized by its repression.[58]

The tide of opinion turned against the government when it authorized the execution of Vicente Guerrero (14 February 1831)— who had led a year-and-a-half-long rebellion against the *jalapista* government from his home province in the south, following his escape from Mexico City in December 1829. The execution of a high-ranking officer who was also an ex-mandatory of the republic, an action that had not been carried out since Emperor Agustín I's execution in Padilla (19 July 1824), served to turn against Bustamante's government the majority of those moderates who had initially supported the party of order. Consequently, when the Plan of Veracruz of 2 January 1832 was launched, it unleashed a year-long cycle of pronunciamientos and a particularly sanguinary civil war. Between the launching of this plan and the signing of the Treaty of Zavaleta that brought the conflict to an end, on 23 December 1832, four major pitched battles were fought between Bustamante's government forces and Santa Anna's pronunciados (Tolome, 3 March; El Gallinero, 18 September; El Palmar, 29 September; and Rancho de Posadas, 6 December). The 1832 Civil War would become the bloodiest civil conflict to take place in Mexico between the War of Independence (1810–21) and the Revolution of Ayutla (1854–55).[59]

The Veracruz–Lerma–Zacatecas cycle of pronunciamientos began with the Plan of Veracruz of 2 January 1832. Worthy of note and characteristic of a pronunciamiento (as opposed to a *golpe de estado*), it did not actually state that the pronunciados' intentions were to overthrow the government. Instead they limited themselves to stating that the rebels supported the federal constitution (art. 1); that Bustamante should renew his cabinet, since it was dominated by centralists responsible for tolerating unforgivable crimes against the country's civil liberty and individuals' rights (art. 2); that Santa Anna would be offered the leadership of the pronunciamiento (art. 3); and that they awaited his orders once he took over the pronunciamiento (art. 4). As can be seen by reading the following one hundred or so pronunciamientos that the Veracruzan start-up pronunciamiento inspired, these original demands would change and develop as the pronunciamiento cycle got under way and different actors and factions added their own particular grievances and aspirations to the movement.[60]

For the first three months following the launch of the Veracruzan plan, few were the garrisons and communities that came out in support of the pronunciamiento, and Santa Anna and his men found themselves besieged in the port of Veracruz. Neither Bustamante's government nor the pronunciados appeared to have the upper hand. Santa Anna had lost the first major engagement of the conflict in Tolome on 3 March and was cornered in Veracruz. However, by holding onto the port with its custom house, and with other pronunciados having taken Tampico on 10 March, he could still hold the government to ransom. The besieging government commander José María Calderón, on the other hand, lost up to a thousand men to yellow fever just by being outside the walls of Veracruz and could not see an easy way of defeating Santa Anna. It was at this point that a different pronunciamiento, launched by General Ignacio Inclán in Lerma, in the State of Mexico, added a new twist to the situation. In the Plan of Lerma of 27 April 1832, Inclán blamed the republic's problems on the illegal overthrow of Gómez Pedraza in 1828. The subsequent Plan of Jalapa of 4 December 1829, the forceful rise to power of Bustamante, and the War of the South that ensued (1830–31), were, in his mind, all the consequence of Mexico having abandoned the constitutional path. It was a matter of turning back the clock to

1828 and restoring the constitutionally elected government that had been overthrown as a result of the Perote–La Acordada pronunciamiento cycle. Inclán then turned to Santa Anna, rather than the "illegal" government, and called on him, "if the caudillo of Veracruz is sincere in his protests," to strive to give Mexico a legitimate government and back his pronunciamiento. Inclán added that if Santa Anna's motives for pronouncing were purely personal, as his enemies claimed they were, he would not support the Plan of Lerma. This entailed ratifying their commitment to obey the 1824 Constitution (art. 1), not to recognize any government but that elected in 1828 (art. 2), and to combat both government and Santa Anna if they did not endorse it (art. 3). Inclán's military division was to remain neutral until a decision was reached in response to his plan (art. 4).[61]

As had been the case with the Plan of Casa Mata in 1823, it was this subsequent pronunciamiento that inspired the wave of actas de adhesión Santa Anna had been hoping for, rather than his cronies' original plan of 2 January 1832. As may be seen in the subsequent pronunciamientos of Veracruz and San Juan de Ulúa (5 July) and Zacatecas (10 July), Santa Anna and his fellow pronunciados were quick to seize the opportunity. Following the Plan of Lerma of 27 April 1832, Santa Anna set about organizing the return of Manuel Gómez Pedraza from exile. On 5 July 1832 Ciriaco Vázquez and the garrisons of Veracruz and San Juan de Ulúa issued a follow-up pronunciamiento, reiterating the demands of 2 January but also endorsing the Plan of Lerma's demand for Anastasio Bustamante to stand down and for the "legitimate president" to take up his position. While this pronunciamiento did not mention Gómez Pedraza by name, the Plan of Zacatecas of 10 July did. By endorsing the return of Gómez Pedraza this pronunciamiento cycle finally started gaining more adherents every day.[62] Thereafter the pronunciamiento cycle that had started in Veracruz on 2 January 1832 calling for the removal of certain centralist ministers in Bustamante's cabinet—who in fact did stand down on 17 May to appease the pronunciados (Alamán resigned as minister of relations and José Antonio Facio resigned as minister of war)—became a generalized call for the restoration of the 1828 government, overthrown as a result of the Perote–La Acordada cycle.[63]

After nearly a year of conflict and pronunciamiento pressure, Bustamante gave in and signed the peace treaty of Zavaleta of 23 December 1832 that brought the 1832 Civil War to an end. In a nutshell, the treaty guaranteed Mexico's 1824 Federal Constitution (art. 1); restored the authorities that had been in place on 1 September 1828, before the Plan of Perote led to the pronunciamiento cycle that annulled the electoral results (art. 2); allowed President Manuel Gómez Pedraza to complete his term in office (which was to end on 1 April 1833; art. 6); called for elections to be held (arts. 3, 4, 5); and offered a general amnesty to all involved, regardless of which side they had fought for, noting that nobody could be tried for any opinions they may have held during the revolution (arts. 9, 10).[64]

In the end the Treaty of Zavaleta led to Bustamante standing down, and Gómez Pedraza serving as president until 1 April 1833. By making Gómez Pedraza president, Santa Anna and the Zacatecan federalists succeeded in giving constitutional legitimacy to their revolt and created the right circumstances for a new round of elections. Not surprisingly, the two favored candidates were Santa Anna and Dr. Valentín Gómez Farías, both of whom had played a major part in leading the 1832 revolution.

Indicative of Santa Anna's popularity at the time is that sixteen of the eighteen state legislatures voted for him; only Chihuahua and Guanajuato did not. However, Santa Anna claimed he was unwell and was unable to be in Mexico City for the start of his term in office on 1 April 1833. He left it to elected vice president Gómez Farías to lead the nation. Some contemporary observers suspected he already knew he was going to have a hard time presiding over a newly elected radical congress with which he did not entirely sympathize.

With Santa Anna allegedly convalescing in Manga de Clavo and Gómez Farías serving as acting president, it took only one month for congress to provoke a major political crisis. In a chaotic series of proposals congress put Bustamante's cabinet on trial for the execution of Guerrero (contravening the agreements made in the Treaty of Zavaleta), nationalized the properties of Spanish conquistador Hernán Cortés's descendant, the duke of Monteleone, and decreed that the Mexican government could appoint all ecclesiastical posts (thus exercising the *patronato*).[65] The press exacerbated the increasing tension by either advocating truly radical measures, such as the abolition of military and church privileges (proposing an end to the fueros), or embracing an aggressive reactionary agenda, inviting the regular army to close down congress in the name of their sacred religion. Less than two months after the new government had been formed, on 26 May 1833, Ignacio Escalada, at the head of the garrison in Morelia, issued the plan that carried his name, demanding that the church and army fueros be protected and that Santa Anna act as the protector of his cause. Escalada also used the pronunciamiento to attack local former and current state governors Mariano Amezcua and José Salgado.[66] Both had replaced jalapista governor Diego Moreno as a result of the Treaty of Zavaleta, with Amezcua having served as acting governor while elections were held and Salgado having become the elected governor of Michoacán on 1 March 1833.[67]

Escalada's pronunciamiento was to be the first of three that year that called upon Santa Anna to defend the military and ecclesiastical fueros. On 1 June another similar plan, launched in Tlalpan to the south of Mexico City by General Gabriel Durán, took the pronunciados' demands further, including a local attack on radical state governor Lorenzo de Zavala.[68] And on 8 June 1833, in the town of Huejotzingo, Puebla, Mariano Arista espoused Durán's cause and issued his own plan promising to defend the privileges of both army and church and to make Santa Anna "Supreme Dictator . . . to cure all the ills that the nation suffers today."[69] Santa Anna refused to back this pronunciamiento series. Although he was taken captive by the pronunciados in June when he went to parlay with them in a particularly colorful and conspiracy-theory-inspiring incident that led those with suspicious minds to believe the president had initially been in on the plan, he managed to escape and spent the next three months, from June to October 1833, quelling the revolt.[70]

In the meantime, the radical congress of 1833–34 became increasingly confident in the pursuit of its marked anti-clerical agenda. Between 12 June and 6 November 1833 it proposed and passed a whole array of highly controversial laws. The staff of Mexico City town council (which was still composed of politicians who had been named by Bustamante) was replaced with its 1829 predecessors on 12 June. The *Ley del Caso* was then approved on 23 June, expelling from the republic fifty-one politicians whose views were considered to be unpatriotic (including General Bustamante). The missions in California were secularized on 17 August. Church property belonging to the missionaries from the Philippines was expropriated on the 31st of the same month, and the ecclesiastical Colegio de Santa María de Todos los Santos was then shut down on 14 October. On the 18th the properties of the Philippine and San Camilo missionaries were offered at auction to the general public. On the 19th the Catholic and church-dominated University of Mexico was shut down, and on the 21st the closed university was replaced by a (secular) Dirección General de Instrucción Pública. On the 24th it was determined that the closed Colegio de Santa María de Todos los Santos was to become a national library and that the Dirección General de Instrucción Pública was to be financed through the expropriation of church properties, which included the Monastery and Church of San Camilo, the Hospital and Church of Jesús, the Hospital de Belén, the Asylum of the Poor of Santo Tomás, the Old Inquisition building, and the Monastery and Church of the Espíritu Santo. The civil obligation to pay *diezmos* (tithes to the church) was then abolished on 27 October. The 16 May 1831 law that granted the church the right to nominate its priests, bishops, and archbishops was abolished on 3 November, and three days later, on the 6th, the civil obligation to take ecclesiastical vows was abolished.[71]

The 1833 Escalada–Durán–Arista pronunciamiento cycle had already shown that there were high-ranking officers who were virulently opposed to congress's measures and believed in defending church and military privileges. Nicolás Bravo's isolated Plan of Reconciliation of Chichihualco of 2 December 1833 called for the summoning of a new congress precisely as a reaction to congress's antics. These early reactions to congress's heady reformism were soon to proliferate into an increasingly aggressive wave of pro-clerical pronunciamientos, especially after the plans of Cuernavaca (25 May 1834) and Toluca (31 May 1834) were launched. These plans and the more than three hundred pronunciamientos that they inspired provide ample evidence that congress's anticlericalism proved intensely unpopular, provoking the largest number of recorded pronunciamientos until then. The fact that in the first months of 1834 congress directed its attention to reforming the regular army—seeking to reduce it to just six battalions and two regiments, replacing its forces where possible with civic militias, and bringing its number of division generals down to six and brigadier generals to ten—inevitably inspired most army officers to join the Cuernavaca–Toluca cycle.[72]

The Plan of Cuernavaca called for "Religion, the *fueros*, and Santa Anna" and demanded a reversal of congress's policies. According to the plan's five articles, in response to the "atrocious chaos, confusion and disorder" the country was in as a direct result of the legislature's behavior, its advocates wanted to ensure that (1) all decrees issued against individuals (the *Ley del Caso*) and the church and in favor of Masonic sects were abolished; (2) all laws that violated the constitution and the general will were reversed; (3) Santa Anna be given the authority to execute these demands; (4) all deputies who favored these deeply unpopular reforms were removed from office and replaced by others following the corresponding procedures specified in the 1824 Constitution; and (5) Santa Anna would have those forces who defended the plan at his service to ensure that it was executed accordingly. The demands in the Plan of Cuernavaca were to prove immensely popular, pointing toward a broad consensus of rejection of congress's anti-clerical reformism. Large sections of the population as well as the army were clearly not yet ready to embrace congress's radical attack on church and army. There was no instance of a garrison that opposed the plan, and the more than three hundred plans of allegiance it received between May and August 1834 included a high proportion of civilian-led groupings (such as town councils, municipalities, and regional councils).[73]

The Plan of Toluca of 31 May, which was pronounced six days later, represented an attempt to give leadership and direction to the numerous pronunciamientos that were launched in the spring of 1834 calling for congress's anti-clerical reforms to be overturned. Its author, Colonel José Vicente González, believed that although "the simultaneous pronunciamientos that are being launched in different parts of the state" were "praiseworthy," "in lacking unity" he thought they could prove counterproductive. His hope was that this pronunciamiento would become the one to which all subsequent pronunciamientos would adhere. In it he called for the annulment of the *Ley del Caso* and of all the anti-clerical laws congress had passed (art. 1); he called upon Santa Anna to protect his pronunciamiento's aims (art. 2); he demanded that at a national and a regional level, all those deputies and state representatives who had backed congress's reforms be removed from office (art. 3); he offered Santa Anna the military support of Toluca to implement the pronunciamiento's aims (art. 4); he noted that the Plan of Toluca would be circulated throughout the state to bring about its unifying mission (art. 5). He also "decreed" that all public officials (e.g., prefects) who did not uphold the pronunciamiento would be removed from office (art. 6) and that nobody would be condemned for political opinions (although those who opposed the plan would be punished).[74]

The Plan of Toluca, in tandem with the Plan of Cuernavaca, would succeed in garnering significant support and would serve to unify the pro-clerical demands that featured in the waves of pronunciamientos that spread across the republic throughout the summer of 1834 rejecting congress's radical reforms. The hundreds of pro-clerical and anti-congress pronunciamientos that were launched around and as part of the Cuernavaca–Toluca cycle would provide Santa Anna with the justification he needed to close down congress and reverse its anti-clerical and anti-military legislation, which was exactly what he did.[75]

Thus the constellation of pronunciamientos that were inspired by the Plans of Cuernavaca and Toluca resulted in the demise of the 1833–34 radical administration. In January 1835, with the resulting return of the men of 1830–32 to the corridors of power, Santa Anna opted to retire to his hacienda in Veracruz, leaving Miguel Barragán in charge as acting president. In accordance with these deputies' traditionalist agenda, the newly formed 1835 congress was determined to strengthen the regular army. It also harbored centralist ambitions which, albeit unspoken, were a so-called *secreto a voces* (literally a "voiced secret"; a secret everyone knew even if it was not expressed publicly). On 31 March 1835 congress passed a bill ordering the discharge of local militias in the country with a view to disarming the state civil authorities of the republic. The government in Zacatecas interpreted the law as confirmation that the centralists in congress were on their way to overturning the 1824 Constitution, given that by demobilizing the civic militias, they believed, the central government was effectively seeking to leave the state legislatures without a force with which they could resist Mexico City's assault on their regional power.

On 30 March, preempting the government's resolution, Manuel González Cosío, governor of Zacatecas, raised the standard of revolt by decreeing that "the [state] government is awarded the faculty to make use of its civic militia to repulse any aggression that may be attempted against it."[76] Having returned to Manga de Clavo only three months earlier, Santa Anna nonetheless made his way back to the capital on 9 April on hearing the news of this pronunciamiento. He did not, however, return to Mexico City in order to preside over the republic but to acquire permission to quell the rebellion in person. On 18 April 1835 Santa Anna left Mexico City to force Zacatecas into submission. Using the cover of night to launch his assault on Guadalupe, outside Zacatecas, Santa Anna and his government forces attacked the pronunciados' positions at 2.00 a.m. on 11 May 1835. After two hours of combat, Guadalupe and Zacatecas were taken.[77] The troops' plunder of Zacatecas was brutal, leaving a deep-seated hatred of Santa Anna in the region that would last for the rest of his lifetime.

By the spring of 1835 it had become obvious to many that the experience of the First Federal Republic had been a failure. Since 1828 revolution had followed revolution, and it had become clear that the 1824 Constitution had failed to establish a stable, long-lasting political system suited to the needs and customs of the Mexican people. To quote historian Michael Costeloe, "Pronunciamientos became commonplace, the representative process was discredited and constitutional rule collapsed as the first two vice-presidents [Bravo and Bustamante] led rebellions against the governments of which they were members."[78] Santanistas like José María Tornel and José María Bocanegra arrived at the conclusion that the reality of their country demanded that they change its political system. Mexico needed a new constitution that did not go against the general will, did not create a context in which political upheavals were commonplace, and took into account "the habits, customs, and even preoccupations of the people." As was professed in the pronunciamiento of Orizaba (19 May 1835),

When the Pronunciamiento Went Viral

it was essential that they terminate the federal system, "adopting [instead] another form of government more in tune with the people's needs, demands, and customs, and which can better guarantee our independence, internal peace and the Catholic religion we believe in."[79]

Orizaba-born and minister of war at the time (1835–37), Tornel had become a committed centralist. For him the experience of the First Federal Republic demonstrated that federalism weakened the nation. By 1835 many were of the same view, and the change to centralism did indeed reflect Mexican public opinion at a time when federalism had lost its charm. Following the launch of the pronunciamiento of Orizaba of 19 May 1835, more than four hundred petitions would be written between then and October 1835. A particularly influential plan was that of Toluca, launched ten days later on 29 May. Albeit not making reference to the start-up plan by name, it complemented the call for constitutional change, demanding alongside the Orizaba plan that Mexico adopt a centralist constitution in which the Roman Catholic faith was the sole religion of the state. After a summer of heated deliberations, congress, listening again to the will of the nation as expressed in wave after wave of pronunciamientos, pushed forward the resolution whereby on 23 October 1835, the federalist constitution was abolished, a constituent congress was called for, and a centralist constitution was eventually drafted and approved a year later.[80]

The end of the Federal Republic gave way to the Texan Revolution in the north of the country and a number of federalist pronunciamientos that failed to reverse the consolidation of the Central Republic with the implementation of the 1836 Constitution on 29 December 1836–the *Siete Leyes* (Seven Laws).[81] In early 1836 Santa Anna took it upon himself to crush the Texan

Revolution in person. But following the victory at the Alamo (6 March 1836) and the mass execution of Texan prisoners at Goliad (27 March), he was taken prisoner the day after his forces were defeated at the battle of San Jacinto (21 April 1836). With Santa Anna out of the way—having lost the Texan campaign, been made prisoner, and been returned to Mexico in 1837 to lead a secluded life on his hacienda Manga de Clavo with his prestige and popularity at an all-time low—Anastasio Bustamante came back from exile to occupy the National Palace, elected on this occasion in April 1837.[82]

During his second term in office, 1837–41, Bustamante's government confronted numerous unsuccessful federalist pronunciamientos (e.g., José Ramón García Ugarte's federalist pronunciamiento of San Luis Potosí of 14 April 1837, the Sonora–Sinaloa–Tamaulipas cycle of federalist pronunciamientos of 1837–40, and Gordiano Guzmán's Aguililla pronunciamiento cycle of 1837–42), while also having to fight the French Pastry War (1838–39). That war was provoked by the French government's demand for 600,000 pesos in compensation for harm done to French subjects—including a baker—in the Parián Riot of 1828, and in the conflict Santa Anna redeemed himself (and lost a leg) by defending the port of Veracruz in the action of 5 December 1838. Bustamante's government confronted a not inconsiderable number of problems, including a major rebellion in Yucatán, the impossibility of reconquering Texas, and a constitution that made effective or speedy governmental decision making extremely difficult because of having created a fourth moderating power—the Supremo Poder Conservador or Supreme Conservative Power—that was meant to arbitrate between the executive (the president), the legislative branch (congress), and the judiciary (the Supreme Court). Bustamante nevertheless hung onto power for nearly five years, overcoming in the process what was probably the most dramatic pronunciamiento to affect the capital, namely that of 15 July 1840, in which the pronunciados had the audacity to storm the National Palace and take him prisoner.[83] *Bustamante*

In the early hours of 15 July 1840, José Urrea, who had been moved from Perote to the jail in the Old Inquisition building in Mexico City as punishment for his leadership of the 1837–39 Sonora–Sinaloa–Tamaulipas cycle of federalist pronunciamientos, was freed by a rebel infantry battalion from the local garrison, and together they stormed the National Palace, taking President Anastasio Bustamante prisoner. Urrea then invited Valentín Gómez Farías—back from exile since 1838—to join him, which the well-known liberal politician did immediately. However, despite having taken the National Palace with the president inside, Minister of War Juan Nepomuceno Almonte refused to negotiate with the pronunciados. More important, General Gabriel Valencia, at the head of Mexico City's forces, chose to stand by Bustamante. Therefore after the cannons of the arsenal based in the Ciudadela garrison were moved to outside the National Palace, Valencia's troops opened fire on the pronunciados at 2:00 p.m. on 15 July. Eyewitness Fanny Calderón de la Barca vividly captured the moment when violence broke out in the city center in her classic *Life in Mexico*: "The firing has begun! People come running up the street. The Indians are hurrying back to their villages in double-quick trot. . . . The cannon are roaring now. All along the street people are standing on the balconies, looking anxiously in the direction of the palace, or collected in groups before the doors, and the *azoteas* [terrace roofs], which are out of the line of fire, are covered with men. They are ringing the tocsin—things seem to be getting serious."[84]

Urrea hoped that Almonte would call an end to the bombardment of the pronunciados' positions, and in a pamphlet he circulated on 16 July went on to claim he had not threatened Bustamante in any way and that the president actually backed his call for a return to federalism. Bustamante, however, managed to escape on the 16th and publicly condemned the pronunciamiento.[85] Besieged in the National Palace, Urrea and Gómez Farías tried to muster support by issuing a detailed federalist plan on the 19th. But the support they were hoping to obtain never materialized, and on hearing that Santa Anna was on his way to Mexico City from Veracruz, the pronunciados surrendered at 6:30 a.m. on 27 July.[86]

Although Bustamante's government survived the pronunciamiento of 15 July 1840, it did not overcome the Triangular Revolt that erupted a year later. The first player to move into action on this occasion was the profoundly reactionary, elitist, and hard-drinking General Mariano Paredes y Arrillaga, who on 8 August 1841 launched the pronunciamiento of Guadalajara. In his plan Paredes y Arrillaga called for the creation of a new congress, the sole purpose of which would be to reform the 1836 Charter. He also demanded that the Supreme Conservative Power name one individual who would be given extraordinary powers to oversee the peaceful transition from the current government to the new one.[87]

Much to President Anastasio Bustamante's horror, his faithful aide General Valencia, who had played such an important role in quelling José Urrea and Valentín Gómez Farías's federalist pronunciamiento the previous summer, took the Ciudadela barracks in the capital on 31 August and launched his own pronunciamiento of 4 September. Valencia stated that his aims were to obey the will of the people and that this had been eloquently expressed in the pronunciamiento of Guadalajara. Valencia proclaimed that the people did not want a tyrant, and he went on to stress the need to forge a new constituent congress. Unlike Paredes y Arrillaga, who believed the Supreme Conservative Power should name a provisional president, Valencia believed such an individual should be chosen by a popular junta. In response to Valencia's pronunciamiento, the Supreme Conservative Power gave Bustamante emergency powers, and he immediately set about organizing the defense of the government, declaring the capital to be in a state of siege.[88]

On 9 September, from the Fortress of San Carlos in Perote, Veracruz, Santa Anna made his own revolutionary plan known and started his march toward the capital. In the open letter he addressed to Bustamante in the form of a published pamphlet on 13 September, including a copy of his Plan of Perote of the 9th, Santa Anna justified his decision to take up arms against the government. He claimed that the 1836 Constitution had never been in accordance with his principles or those inspiring the plans that brought about the end of the radical government of 1833. By wresting all power away from the executive, the new constitution made governing Mexico at a time of conflict a near impossibility. The urgent responses required to organize an army, tackle the country's significant diplomatic problems with France, and reform the country's financial and judicial systems were simply not possible under the Seven Laws. With adventurers still running amok in Texas, and with Tabasco and Yucatán in flames, it was about time the government became "strong and vigorous." Texas was waiting to be reconquered. The constitution needed to be reformed. Tabasco and Yucatán had to be brought back into the fold. Santa Anna reminded Bustamante that he had offered to mediate between the president and the rebels. He criticized the president for ignoring his letters. He had been given no choice but to join the revolutionary movement. Proving his point that the 1836 Constitution did not work, he accused the Supreme Conservative Power, of all institutions, of being in breach of article 18 of the 1836 Charter for having given Bustamante emergency powers. As was expressed in the actual Plan of Perote of 9 September, Santa Anna was demanding the removal of Bustamante as the head of the executive, that General Valencia's Plan of 4 September be endorsed, and that all Mexicans should leave aside their factional differences and join in a "conciliatory embrace." Despite Bustamante's attempts to resist what was beginning to emerge as a concerted coup rather than a forceful negotiation, it became evident that he was alone as the forces of Paredes y Arrillaga and Santa Anna made their way to the capital to join Valencia.[89]

By 27 September the three rebel forces converged in the Archbishop's Palace in Tacubaya, on the outskirts of Mexico City. Having succeeded in forcing Bustamante to accept a truce, Paredes y Arrillaga, Valencia, and Santa Anna thrashed out what was to become the Bases de Tacubaya. With this plan, promulgated on 29 September, a temporary dictatorship was established with the objective of calling a new congress to devise a new constitution. Despite Paredes y Arrillaga and Valencia's ambitions, Santa Anna managed to persuade them to let him take the lead once more. In a final and desperate bid to rally support for his cause, on 30 September Bustamante proclaimed the restoration of the federalist charter. Hoping this would inspire the moderate and radical federalists to come to his aid, Bustamante reorganized his defenses, and between 2 and 4 October the capital was exposed once more to the horrors of war. Cannons once again pounded

When the Pronunciamiento Went Viral

the city center and there were bloody street fights. In the end, Bustamante was forced to face the inevitable. He finally met with Santa Anna at Punta del Río on 5 October, outside Mexico City, and they formally agreed the following day to end all hostilities, with Bustamante accepting the Bases de Tacubaya and agreeing to be replaced by Santa Anna as provisional president. On 7 October Santa Anna marched into a battered, tired, and distrustful Mexico City and, following his investiture ceremony on 10 October 1841, initiated what would be his longest and most successful term in office (1841–43, 1843–44).

The result of the Triangular Revolt (August–October 1841) was the creation of a temporary dictatorship with Santa Anna as president that was intended to restore order and stability in the republic while a new constituent congress was formed to deliver a new constitution. Santa Anna, for once, opted to stay in the capital to ensure that his government fulfilled what it had set out to achieve. For an entire year, from 10 October 1841 to 26 October 1842, Santa Anna led his government. It was the longest spell he had spent in the capital until then, serving as president. Initially he kept his word as well. Congressional elections were held at the beginning of the year, and on 6 March 1842 Mexico's new Constituent Congress got to work on drafting a new constitution for the republic. For the centralists who had backed the 1841 cycle of pronunciamientos it was important that the new constitution avoided the mistakes of the Federal Constitution of 1824 as well as those that had made the centralist Constitution of 1836 unworkable. In a nutshell, they wanted a centralist constitution that dispensed with the Supreme Conservative Power and strengthened the powers of the executive. However, renowned federalists made up the majority of deputies who were elected to the Constituent

Congress of 1842, and not surprisingly, they ended up proposing a new federalist constitution.[90] Aware that the centralist factions that had backed the Bases de Tacubaya of 28 September 1841 would not accept it, Santa Anna retreated to his hacienda in Veracruz on 26 October 1842 and left behind the acting president, General Nicolás Bravo, with the unenviable task of finding a way of preventing the Federal Constitution of 1842 from being adopted.

José María Tornel was working frantically behind the scenes. Carlos María de Bustamante was convinced that he penned both the Plan of San Luis Potosí of 9 December and the Plan of Huejotzingo of 11 December 1842.[91] Following the launch of these two plans, December witnessed a veritable bonanza of pronunciamientos, which as a whole called for congress to be closed down, for its federal constitution to be abandoned, and for a new Junta de Notables (Junta of Worthy Men) to be summoned to draft a centralist constitution that was more in line with the so-called general will.[92] After two weeks in which more than one hundred pronunciamientos were launched, Nicolás Bravo, claiming to listen to the voice of the nation, closed down the Constituent Congress of 1842 on 19 December. Set up in January was a hand-picked santanista Junta of Worthy Men who went on to write Mexico's second centralist constitution, the Bases Orgánicas, sworn in on 13 June. This 1843 Constitution would remain in place for just over three years, until a new wave of pronunciamientos in August 1846 resulted in its abolition and the reinstatement of the 1824 Constitution.[93]

The pronunciamientos of Mexico's second independent decade clearly highlight the extent to which the context remained one of contested and unclear legitimacies, where not even the constitutional governments were the result of elections, and where they did not always behave constitutionally or lawfully. As was argued in the 1832 Plan of Lerma, the Perote–Oaxaca–La Acordada cycle of 1828 had resulted in all subsequent governments being constitutionally illegitimate and the result of pronunciamiento pressure. Yet even after the rightful president—Gómez Pedraza—was restored to complete his term in office, pronunciamientos were to remain the way politics were done and proved determining for the country's political shifts and evolution. The closure of the 1833–34 congress and the repeal of most of its reforms in 1834, the end of the Federal Republic and the change to centralism in 1835, the overthrow of Bustamante's 1837–41 government and the abolition of the 1836 Constitution in 1841, and the closure of the 1842 Constituent Congress were all the result of pronunciamiento cycles.

The experience of Mexico's second independent decade also highlights the extent to which mimetic insurrectionism spread not only across the region but beyond the elites, as subaltern groups came to adopt the pronunciamiento as their preferred means of addressing local concerns and grievances. The success of five pronunciamiento constellations at a national level in 1832, 1834, 1835, 1841, and 1842, on the back of the successful pronunciamientos of the 1820s, gave further substance to the view that this relatively peaceful insurrectionary practice—part lobbying, part intimidating, with its acts of disobedience, circulation of petitioning plans, and reliance on waves of aggressive copycat statements of support purporting to represent the voice of the national or popular will—was the most effective way of bringing about meaningful political change.

In this sense the most salient aspect of the pronunciamientos of the 1830s is the extent to which they involved popular participation. They became so frequent, so common, so generalized, that by 1835—as the liberal and civilian politician José Bernardo Couto would observe with bitterness, speaking out against allowing the Orizaba–Toluca constellation of pronunciamientos to bring about the end of the Federal Republic—all decisions were being taken informed by this "turbulent form of democracy." Public officials were being bullied by what he termed "the theory of the general will by pronunciamiento."[94] Indicative of the popularization of the pronunciamiento is that of those launched between 1832 and 1842, at least in terms of pronunciamientos de adhesión, compared to those of the previous decade, the great majority were no longer initiated by army officers. Of the 787 pronunciamientos that at the time of writing are currently held in the St. Andrews pronunciamientos database, and which were circulated between the 1 January 1832 and the 31 December 1842, 571 were civilian-led (with 140 of them having entailed military involvement), launched mainly by town councils but also by state legislatures, villages, and communities. In contrast, 216 were strictly speaking garrison-led. Having said this, it would be misleading to suggest that the military did not continue to play a fundamental role in this insurrectionary practice. Army officers were actually involved in all twelve of the major pronunciamiento constellations that affected the republic during these years, and understandably, given their recourse to armed men and weapons, the officers exerted a determining part.

Nevertheless it remains the case in these twelve nation-spanning cycles, especially in the five successful ones, that they were the result of the open and declared collaboration of a whole range of military *and* civilian actors. Of these twelve major pronunciamiento constellations only three were very evidently led and executed by army officers, namely the 1833 Escalada–Durán–Arista series, Bravo's 1833 plan of Chichihualco, and the Guadalajara–Ciudadela–Perote Triangular Revolt of 1841. The rest were the result of intricate civilian-military alliances and networks. The 1832 Veracruz–Lerma–Zacatecas cycle brought together the garrisons of Veracruz, San Juan de Ulúa, and Lerma as well as Governor Francisco García and the state legislature of Zacatecas. The 1834 Cuernavaca–Toluca series entailed two start-up pronunciamientos, that of the town council of Cuernavaca and the garrison and civilian authorities of Toluca. The same town council–garrison combination was then replicated a year later in the centralist Orizaba–Toluca constellation, with Governor Cosío's Zacatecan decree/pronunciamiento of 30 March 1835 having represented a civilian state-legislature-based act of insubordination. And all three major federalist pronunciamiento cycles—that of García Ugarte in San Luis Potosí in 1837, the Sonora–Sinaloa–Tamaulipas cluster of 1837–40, and Guzmán's 1837 plan of Aguililla—were launched by soldiers and civilians in collusion with one another. As argued recently by Sergio Cañedo Gamboa, liberal civilian intellectuals such as Ponciano Arriaga and Mariano Ávila were behind lieutenant-colonel García Ugarte's pronunciamiento.[95] And General Urrea, similarly, pronounced in Mexico City on 15 July 1840 with physician and politician Valentín Gómez Farías by his side. In contrast to the first independent decade, the majority of start-up pronunciamientos of 1832–42 were the fruit of an openly declared collaboration between soldiers and civilians, in which garrisons and local authorities joined forces from the beginning.

The grievances also changed. Moving into Mexico's second independent decade, the big questions, as captured in the pronunciamientos of the 1830s, expanded beyond the ongoing defense of regional sovereignty and federalism and became noticeably concerned with centralism, church-state relations (and by inference religion), and the need to protect core values and customs that started to be seen as essential aspects of an as yet undefined and incipient Mexican national identity. The flaws and weaknesses of the 1824 Constitution were seen to have given way to a decade in which, contrastingly, centralist pronunciamientos became as common as federalist ones, if not more so. The popular defense of clerical values, fueros, and institutions, moreover, became one of the most impacting political impulses of the decade, and with it came a quest to understand what the new nation's core values and customs involved.

What emerges from an analysis of the plans of 1833–36 is a distinct sense that Roman Apostolic Catholicism was perceived as an essential part of Mexicanness and that the legislators' attempts at curtailing church power and privileges were deemed to be destabilizing and, in a sense, unpatriotic. What also emerges is a widespread view that federalism had failed and that it had done so because it was a *foreign* import. Numerous pronunciamientos echoed the view that the 1824 Charter could never have worked in Mexico because it was a copy of the U.S. 1787 Constitution.[96] Importantly, it did not respect or conform with the customs and the traditions of the Mexican people, who were, by inference, centralist and devoutly religious. As was noted in the plan a group of congregated neighbors from Mexico City circulated on 12 June 1835, "Given that the nation is bound by a solemn oath that its religion will be solely the Roman Apostolic Catholic one, with tolerance of none other, the republican federal system is incompatible with it because by extension it demands the liberty of cults." They could not allow the "the disappearance . . . of the Sacrosanct religion we inherited from our elders" to come to pass.[97]

This reinvigorated traditionalist centralist outlook certainly represented a marked shift from the ideals held in some of the federalist pronunciamientos of the 1820s, and it pointed to a growing sense of despondency among significant elements of society. Representative of what I once defined as the stages of disenchantment (1828–35) and profound disillusion (1836–47), the failure of federalism gave way to increasing calls to hang onto customs, traditions, and beliefs that were associated with a previous and idealized time when order and stability had supposedly prevailed.[98] As yet, constitutionalism remained strong. Although some pronunciamientos, such as Arista's 1833 Plan of Huejotzingo, called for a dictatorship, most supported the defense or creation of representative constitutional models; and in the case of the centralist constellations of the 1830s–40s, constitutional models that were more in tune with the incipient country's historic customs and traditions. As Tornel would have us believe, their "customs and traditions that have long and strong roots [had] been tenaciously undermined; without preparing the ground, we have sown exotic plants that died when they were born."[99]

It was a case of ensuring that those customs and traditions informed the constitutions they drafted. Paradoxically, given its propensity to generate further instability and its potential for violence, the pronunciamiento became the favored insurrectionary practice for countless people, whether they were hombres de bien, reactionary army officers, priests, or God-fearing village folk, to put a stop to what they saw as godless radical demagoguery and to preserve—*conservar*—political and religious values that started to be portrayed as being primordially and essentially Mexican.

The popular participation that characterized the pronunciamientos of the 1830s paired with their defense of traditional values and customs would appear to point toward what I term *popular centralism*. Peter Guardino persuasively proposed in 1996 that "popular federalism" preceded the "popular liberalism" Guy Thomson studied for the midcentury Reform period, and Guardino argued that popular federalism eventually evolved into popular liberalism—"characterized by inclusive definitions of citizenship, an emphasis on local autonomy, and opposition to the wealthy few."[100] Taking into consideration the pro-fueros, pro-clerical, and pro-centralist pronunciamientos of the mid-1830s (there were more than four hundred of them between 1833 and 1835), it could be argued that alongside Guardino's popular federalism, pronounced centralist pro-clerical political ideas gained widespread support in rural Mexico and that Indian communities as well as poor people embraced them to serve their own ends as well as to respond, engage with, and ultimately influence national politics. To put it differently, the 1830s witnessed the emergence of a popular form of centralism that was characterized by corporate values, actions, and institutions; that valued order and central authority and blamed instability on the importation and adoption of foreign anti-clerical federalist institutions that floundered in translation; and that ardently defended the church and the Roman Catholic faith as essentially Mexican. The pronunciamientos of 1833–36 would certainly appear to support such a view.[101]

Interestingly, it was not just the pronunciados' demands that changed and evolved over time—becoming more popular but also more traditionalist. So did the very practice of the pronunciamiento itself. The overt use of the pronunciamiento to overthrow Bustamante's 1837–41 government in the Guadalajara–Ciudadela–Perote series marked, in a sense, the beginning of the end of the pronunciamiento's use as a means to lobby and forcefully negotiate.

From a certain perspective, the 1842 San Luis Potosí–Huejotzingo series would actually be the last of its kind. Subsequent pronunciamientos—as discussed in the next chapter—became less about forceful negotiation, less about lobbying, less about persuading those in power to change their ways through intimidating politics, acts of insubordination, and aggressive petitioning. They ceased to be, as one contemporary noted, "speculations in which one risks nothing and can gain a lot."[102] The pronunciamientos of the 1840s and '50s became much more overtly about overthrowing the government—with explicit calls for the country's different leaders and cabinets to stand down. The polarization of politics that characterized the mid- to late 1840s, paired with the impact the 1846–48 Mexican-U.S. War had on the country, would ultimately blur the distinction between a pronunciamiento and a coup d'état and bring the classic period of the nineteenth-century Mexican pronunciamiento to an end.

5. From Forceful Negotiation to Civil War

The Pronunciamientos, Coups d'État, and Revolutions
of the Mid-Nineteenth Century, 1843–1858

Two decades after Mexico achieved its independence from Spain there was a growing and palpable sense of disillusion. In the speech José María Tornel gave on 27 September 1840 in Mexico City's Alameda Park to mark the thirtieth anniversary of the beginning of Mexico's struggle for independence, on what turned out to be a blustery day marked by heavy rain and thunder, the former insurgent and once idealistic federalist liberal from Orizaba could not help himself from turning what he admitted should have been a piece of jubilant oratory into a particularly dark lament.[1] "Just think about what the country's fortunes have been since it started to exist on the 16th of September of 1810," he told his stunned—and drenched—audience, "and you will find you do not have the stomach to face, or the strength to understand, the sum of all of our misfortunes."[2] As he noted in no uncertain terms: "The Mexican nation, mutilated and ill, is still alive; but its life is torture because even the hope of happiness is nowhere to be seen. I here remember thirty years of constant suffering, thirty years in which we have sailed through a sea of tears and blood, without ever having reached the port. Our pilots have died steering our broken vessel through wind, reefs, and storms."[3] Tragically, he felt that pronunciamientos or "long civil wars" had "exhausted . . . the enthusiasm that accompanies the regeneration of the people."[4]

Tornel was not alone in feeling dispirited with Mexico's political failures, forever hindered by a "despotism that debilitates everything, from an anarchy that consumes everything."[5] Eight years earlier, on 3 July 1832, General Manuel de Mier y Terán, an enlightened and principled high-ranking officer who had accompanied Santa Anna at the battle of Tampico, and who many had predicted would be a great president, had found himself profoundly depressed by "the tumultuous agitation and the terrible bitterness that oppress a society torn asunder by bloody partisanship."[6] He had committed suicide by falling onto his sword on the very spot where liberator Agustín de Iturbide had been executed in 1824.[7] Although Mier's decision to kill himself was undoubtedly a private and personal matter, his suicide, with all its symbolic connotations, taking his life in the exact place where Independent Mexico's first ruler had been shot by his fellow countrymen, embodied in a sense, albeit prematurely, the despair of an entire generation.

For some it was the pronunciamiento, as a phenomenon, that was clearly to be blamed for Mexico's troubled early years of nationhood. As early as 1835, and in the wake of the massive 1834 Cuernavaca–Toluca cycle of pro-clerical pronunciamientos, one group of liberal-sympathizing citizens from Mexico City paradoxically circulated a pronunciamiento to pronounce against the pronunciamiento practice, stressing the importance of the law and arguing: "All the pronunciamientos that have been launched since 1821 and with the exception of that which brought about our independence, have had as their sole aim to remove the people who have occupied the principal posts of our administration, resulting in the backwardness and decadence of our unhappy republic."[8] It was a view Carlos María de Bustamante was to echo in his diary, in an entry written in July 1835: "The pronunciamientos, counter-pronunciamientos [*contrapronunciamientos*], and re-pronunciamientos [*tornapronunciamientos*] of the *minerales*, ayuntamientos and villages just keep coming. . . . This is where our misguided Mexican freedom has landed us."[9] As argued recently by Melissa Boyd, early republican politicians and intellectuals would end up unanimously condemning the practice, even when they may very well have supported a given cycle when it suited them, blaming the military, factional disputes, and an unresolved crisis of legitimacy for the endless proliferation of pronunciamientos.[10] Liberal intellectual and ideologue José María Luis Mora certainly went out of his way to try to demonstrate that for a country to prosper, it needed a national and legitimate government and a population that respected its authority; it needed laws and law-abiding citizens; and it needed to have the institutional mechanisms in place to make the necessary reforms without constantly having to resort to force to implement them. If these principles were not endorsed and accepted, and instead pronunciamientos were interpreted time and again as being somehow representative of the general will, they would be condemned never to see established any meaningful degree of order or stability. It would be impossible to consolidate a long-lasting government or system, because whoever rose to power on the back of a pronunciamiento cycle would always be at risk of being overthrown by another one. The same arguments that were used to justify one conspiracy would serve to legitimate the next. Mora became convinced that pronunciamientos did not bring peace. They engendered more pronunciamientos. Pronunciamiento-formed governments would invariably be challenged by new rounds of pronunciamientos that would make the same allegations of unlawfulness and illegitimacy the current incumbents of the National Palace had made against the previous government when they had pronounced against it. Mora argued that it was imperative for Mexicans to start considering pronunciados as "seditious enemies of order and true delinquents."[11]

Growing up alongside a sense that pronunciamientos had undermined and prevented the Mexican political class's dogged but failed attempts at consolidating a long-lasting constitutional system or government, and were continuing to do so, the distinct view also started to be voiced that they were or with time had become somehow farcical—or theatrical—as well as pointless and detrimental. Disgruntled Chihuahuan army officer, former insurgent, and then governor and commander general of Tamaulipas, José Ignacio Gutiérrez, writing in 1844, came to refer to the pronunciamiento phenomenon evocatively as "a revolutionary circus." He bemoaned the fact that all of them, without fail, were baptized in their inception with flattering names, and typically made the most alluring of promises, only to betray the genuinely patriotic and national objectives they were purported to bring about. Unsurprisingly, he noted, after two long and painful decades of this, the Mexican people were tired of and fed up with suffering and spilling their blood "on the battlefields of our civil wars," only to find that a new bunch of men rose to power and ignored the programs they had once claimed to represent. Whatever the hopes and dreams that fueled the pronunciamiento in question, the outcome was always the same: the people were abandoned to their state of "ignorance, always poor and degraded."

As many Mexicans did by the mid-1840s, Gutiérrez pined for a time when they might have "a stable government that moderates us, corrects us, and makes us just, civilized, and genuinely free."[12]

There was no denying that pronunciamientos had been as much a constant source of instability as the means whereby Mexicans had tried to address their country's unresolved constitutional problems and overcome the shortcomings and arguable or perceived despotic tendencies of different governments. From the perspective of any of the eighty men who were summoned on 23 December 1842 to draft yet another new constitution—following Nicolás Bravo's closure of the elected constituent congress at 4:00 a.m. four days earlier, in the wake of the San Luis Potosí–Huejotzingo constellation of pronunciamientos—it was difficult to think of a time in the new country's history when political decisions and processes had been instigated and implemented abiding by clearly defined, respected, and lawful constitutional means.[13] Pronunciamientos, on the other hand, had been so much more than a striking idiosyncratic feature of the ebb and flow of early Mexican political life: they had in essence defined it, marking the passing of one government to another, becoming by the 1830s almost a daily occurrence in at least some part of the republic. As one foreign traveler put it in 1902, looking back at pre-Porfirian Mexico, albeit arguably overstating her point: "disorder and revolution prevailed from end to end of the land."[14]

In terms of national politics, pronunciamientos were to be blamed or thanked for the consummation of independence in 1821, Iturbide's crowning in 1822 *and* abdication in 1823, the formation of a federalist-inclined constituent congress in 1824, the expulsion of Spaniards in 1827, the annulment of Manuel Gómez Pedraza's electoral victory in 1828, the rise *and* fall of Vicente

Guerrero as well as of Anastasio Bustamante, the reinstatement of Gómez Pedraza as president in 1832, the closure of the 1833–34 congress and the revoking of most of its reforms in 1834, the end of the Federal Republic and the change to centralism in 1835, the overthrow of Bustamante's second presidency and the end of the 1836 Constitution in 1841, and the closure of congress as well as the tearing up of the draft 1842 Constitution before the end of 1842. As I have noted elsewhere, most of the rulers of Independent Mexico had come to power, even if indirectly in some cases, as a result of a wave of pronunciamientos, not elections: Iturbide, 1821–23 (1821 Plan of Iguala and the pronunciamiento of 19 May 1822); the Triumvirate of the Supreme Executive Power, 1823–24 (plans of Veracruz and Casa Mata, 1822–23); Vicente Guerrero, 1829 (1828 plans of Perote, Oaxaca, and the La Acordada revolt); Bustamante, 1830–32 (1829 plans of Jalapa and La Ciudadela); Gómez Pedraza, 1833 (1832 plans of Veracruz, Lerma, and Zacatecas); and Santa Anna, 1841–43 (1841 plans of Guadalajara, Ciudadela, and Perote). It was a pattern that would not change over the next two decades as José Joaquín de Herrera, Mariano Paredes y Arrillaga, Santa Anna, Juan Álvarez, Ignacio Comonfort, and Félix Zuloaga would all come to occupy the presidency on the back of pronunciamientos.[15] From the perspective of the 1843 Junta de Notables, the only government since the consummation of independence that had lasted its full constitutional term in office had been that of Guadalupe Victoria (1824–29), and even then his spell in the National Palace had not been entirely pronunciamiento-free, having been challenged by the 1827–28 pronunciamiento cycle of Montaño and having barely survived the mayhem of the 1828 Perote–Oaxaca–La Acordada constellation with its resulting Parián Riot. As Tornel noted in his 1840 speech, the experience of the first independent decades had been depressingly futile: "We have tried all possible forms of government from the absolute monarchy with its brilliant pomp to the federal republic with its dangerous exaggerations." It had all been for nothing. "A luxury of words, dishonest phrases, vain promises, confused designs, poor means; such has been the fleeting nature of our political systems and governments, which piling up one after another have all disappeared without leaving behind one single and solid memory of any use or profit."[16]

As if the country's situation were not grim enough, twenty years after having achieved its independence from Spain, matters were to take a particularly traumatic turn for the worse in the mid-1840s, as Mexico found itself at war with its northern neighbor, the United States. The war, which would last two long years (1846–48) and would culminate with the star-spangled banner flying over the National Palace in Mexico City, would result in Mexico losing Texas, New Mexico, Arizona, California, Nevada, Colorado, and parts of Utah. In other words, Mexico would lose half of its territory to the United States in the humiliating Treaty of Guadalupe Hidalgo of 2 February 1848. As if the pronunciamiento were in some way an addiction or an irrepressible bad habit, not even the war, with the corresponding advance of U.S. forces in the north and their landing in Veracruz, dissuaded Mexicans from pronouncing against their government.[17]

The defeat would lead Mariano Otero to conclude that "there has not been, nor could there have been, a national spirit, for there is no nation."[18] What would follow, as I argued in 1998, was a pronounced stage of despair that witnessed a marked radicalization and polarization of politics.[19] Politicians who had once been famed for their generous liberal ideals, such as Tornel, came to

From Forceful Negotiation to Civil War

the bitter conclusion that Mexico was not yet ready for representative government; that it needed a dictatorship to survive as a nation. As an editorial of the *santanista* newspaper *La Palanca* put it on 3 May 1849, the Mexican nation was like a sick man in need "not just of a doctor but of a guardian who ensures the prescribed medicine is taken. . . . The people thus need a man who can guide them by the hand along the right path so that they can be cured of their illnesses, diseases caught thanks to the errors of twenty lost years."[20] By 1853 even Lucas Alamán endorsed such a view. In a letter he addressed Santa Anna on 23 March that year, he explicitly noted that his Conservative party, formally constituted in 1849, was "against the federation; against the election-based representative system that has been in place until now, against elected town councils, against anything that may be termed a popular election."[21] José María Luis Mora's friend José María Gutiérrez Estrada, an "*hombre de progreso*," according to the liberal ideologue, went a step further in his despair.[22] Mexico did not need a dictatorship, he thought; it needed to be governed by a monarchy with a European prince on the throne. As he had already noted in 1840 in an open letter addressed to then president Anastasio Bustamante, "We have experimented with all the possible forms a republic can adopt: democratic, oligarchic, military, demagogic, and anarchic; to the extent that all of the parties, and always to the detriment of the nation's honor and happiness, have tried every conceivable republican system [to no avail]."[23] Looking back to Mexico's colonial period and its three hundred years of supposedly stable monarchical rule, Gutiérrez Estrada argued that their customs and habits were essentially monarchical, accounting for the failure of republicanism.[24] It was a view that would be taken up by a group of conspirators linked to General Mariano Paredes y Arrillaga in the mid-1840s.[25] And it would eventually find particularly forceful expression in the Mexican Conservatives' support for the French Intervention (1862–67) with its corresponding imposition of Austrian Habsburg Archduke Ferdinand Maximilian on the Mexican throne (1864–67).[26]

From the perspective of a radicalized younger generation of Mexican liberals who had not come of age until after the War of Independence, and whose memory of the colonial experience was either faint or nonexistent, the problem lay with the way a whole series of antiquated colonial practices and privileges had been allowed to survive well into the early republican period. The pronunciamiento was a symptom of the contradictions that characterized Independent Mexico—republican and constitutionally minded, yet paralyzed by the power of church and army, with their feudal *fueros* and the clergy's parasitic wealth and unused properties. The time had come to take the bull by the horns and drastically reform the country once and for all, bringing an end to all those incongruous colonial legacies. As Benito Juárez stressed in the historical notes he wrote for his children, it was not enough to replace reactionary governments with liberal ones: they had to tackle the fundamental bases upon which an ultimately pro-clerical, unjust, and pronunciamiento-prone Independent Mexico had been forged. Unfortunately, he noted, whenever "a retrograde administration was replaced with a liberal one, the change only involved people, for the constitutions and laws continued to safeguard the ecclesiastical and military fueros, religious intolerance, [and the existence of] a state religion, and [allowed] the Church to continue to own vast quantities of wealth it abused to fund pronunciamientos to cement its disastrous hold on power. This explains why whenever a liberal administration was established,

From Forceful Negotiation to Civil War

it was overthrown and its representatives were persecuted in a matter of months."[27] The reaction to Juárez's generation's aggressive midcentury reforms—with their corresponding assault on the fueros and ecclesiastical power and property—would come, at least in the first instance, in the form of the horrendous three-year Civil War of the Reforma of 1858–60 and the ensuing French Intervention, 1862–67.

In the 1840s national pronunciamientos became even more frequent than before, more violent, more brutal, concerned less with negotiating than with overthrowing whichever was the incumbent government. At one end of the spectrum the plans that were either initiated or backed by army officers no longer disguised the pronunciados' intentions, or focused on lobbying, but instead explicitly called for the end of one government after another. Santa Anna's 1843–44 government was thus brought down by General Paredes y Arrillaga's Guadalajara-based pronunciamiento of 2 November 1844, backed up by the congress-led Revolution of the Three Hours in Mexico City of 6 December, which resulted in General José Joaquín de Herrera becoming president. Herrera's government was then overthrown a year later, as a result of Paredes y Arrillaga's pronunciamiento of San Luis Potosí of 14 December 1845. And not quite eight months later Paredes y Arrillaga's government suffered the same fate as that of Herrera's, when General Mariano Salas pronounced from the Ciudadela barracks in Mexico City on 4 August 1846, five months into the Mexican-U.S. War. With the war still raging on, a further seven months down the line the Polkos' pronunciamientos of 26 February and 8 March 1847 in Mexico City eventually succeeded in having acting president Valentín Gómez Farías replaced by General Pedro María Anaya.

At the other end of the spectrum, as an almost natural result of the pronunciamiento's popularization in the 1830s, increasing numbers of indigenous and peasant groups took to rebelling by using the pronunciamiento petitioning formula to list their demands, while latching onto national gritos to address their very own grievances. The Sierra Gorda region, stretching from the north of the State of Mexico as far north as Tamaulipas, was to witness waves of popular *campesino* rebellions that became confused and overlapped with several national-oriented pronunciamientos.[28] A not dissimilar situation was to be experienced in southeastern Mexico as the Yucatán peninsula erupted in flames, consumed by a particularly brutal Caste War (1847–52). In the same way that the pronunciados of the 1840s and '50s were no longer in the mood for compromise, the peasant and Indigenous rebels of the period proved determined to fight until their lands were duly restored to them, and the large landowners who had abused them for so long were made to pay for all the years they had oppressed and exploited the people.

With the pronunciamiento having become such a common and constant part of everyday life in Mexico, it grimly started to lend itself to parody and ridicule. With marked black humor, one anonymous wag published a mock pronunciamiento in response to Mariano Paredes y Arrillaga's Plan of San Luis Potosí of 14 December 1845: the *Pronunciamiento a la Polka*.[29] In it the anonymous author, in much the same vein as José Ignacio Gutiérrez, quoted earlier, presented the pronunciamiento as a circus-worthy event, in which cowardly yet arbitrary, pompous, and reactionary clownlike army officers postured, rebelled, and bullied the civilian authorities to endorse their acts of sedition. Parodying the bombastic legalistic language of most pronunciamiento texts, the

From Forceful Negotiation to Civil War

Pronunciamiento a la Polka aimed most of its venom at the army: "Art. 1. As long as they are not exposed to hostile fire, the smallest and worst part of the army will gladly support the nation's insane protests against all past, present and future efforts to instill compromise, order or discipline among the troops." It also equated the pronunciamiento and its outcome with a disorganized and inept form of tyranny as well as with backwardness: "Art. 3. As soon as the seditious elements of the army arrive in Mexico City (if they arrive), they will form a junta made up of the worst from all parties, with the pompous title of extraordinary congress, and it will be given ample powers . . . mainly to organize without restriction an energetic government, perhaps like that of Turkey, or that of Russia."[30] Any sense that the pronunciamiento may have been harking back to Rafael del Riego and the 1820s, the "instrument of liberal revolution," as Raymond Carr put it, had certainly vanished by the 1840s.[31] At least in terms of how the pronunciamiento was represented in the *Pronunciamiento a la Polka* parody, this had become a profoundly reactionary form of insurrection: "Art. 5. As soon as it is established, the junta will select, from among the rebellious military, one who most loathes liberal principles." It was also seen to rely heavily on coercion and the existence of a political class more concerned with hanging onto their jobs than with standing up for their principles or legality. Both articles 6 and 8 offered darkly amusing variations on this theme:

> Art. 6. Since not everything can be done at once, and moreover, since there is probably not a shortage of department officials who, in exchange for keeping their jobs, will cooperate in the proposed rebellion, such individuals will remain at their posts, until they can safely be repaid for their treason. . . .

Art. 8. So that some countrymen will join the uprising, the Governor and Departmental Assembly of San Luis will be made to adhere to the proclamation, which they will certainly do because they do not have the strength to resist, and they will not be so foolish as to risk being shot by a firing squad.[32]

One of the funniest portrayals of a Mexican pronunciamiento, if also a bitter one, is to be found in Manuel Payno's vast and masterful panoramic nineteenth-century novel *Los bandidos de Río Frío* (1891). In chapter XV of part II Payno, forgetting his involvement in the 1857 pronunciamiento of Tacubaya, uses the character of Valentín Cruz to depict what he clearly considered to be a typical 1830s pronunciado, narrating Cruz's failed (and ludicrous) pronunciamiento—"Jalisco never loses" (*Jalisco nunca pierde*) with a particularly heavy dose of irony. What becomes obvious, when analyzing Payno's novelistic account of a pronunciamiento, is that by the end of the nineteenth century, like so many of his contemporaries, this famous moderate-liberal-politician-cum-novelist had come to view pronunciamientos as seditious criminal acts of plunder and vandalism that were invariably carried out by thugs, often in collusion with disgruntled politicians, who used the practice's plan and related documents cynically, purporting to stand for grand, yet ultimately false, libertarian ideals. With Valentín Cruz representing your common mid-nineteenth-century Mexican pronunciado, there was no question in Payno's mind that such a political creature was regularly a common criminal, often protected (and used) by friends in high places, who pronounced to avoid arrest and/or for personal gain, and who succeeded in garnering support for his lowly acts of sedition by plying his followers with vast quan-

From Forceful Negotiation to Civil War

tities of cheap alcohol while disguising his true intentions with florid proclamations and plans.[33]

In *Los bandidos de Río Frío* we are told that the character of Cruz was originally a muleteer "of noteworthy fame in Guadalajara, or, more in particular, in the neighborhood of San Pedro." After several years of illicit activities—including having murdered his wife by smashing a bottle full of mescal on her head and his brother-in-law by stabbing him with a knife—he had become rich, "by village standards that is" (*es decir rico de pueblo*). He had taken to "drinking and politics, becoming a form of tribune whom one had to rely on during elections, when staging a pronunciamiento, for absolutely everything." Cruz pronounces in the novel against the governor of Jalisco for no other reason than to avoid going to prison. Amusingly, he turns the local liquor stall of the barrio of San Pedro into his headquarters and succeeds in recruiting three hundred *chinacos*, whom Payno describes as "badly armed but committed, brave, and somewhat drunk," especially after Cruz takes to giving them free booze. In a highly entertaining passage—the night of Cruz's *grito* is actually more akin to a wild party than an act of political justice ("*la noche se pasó en bola y alegría*")—Cruz goes on to award himself the rank of "general," pockets the money and tobacco he finds in the shop he takes over as his headquarters, orders that all men over the age of eighteen pay him twelve pesos a month or suffer forced conscription for the rest of their lives, and issues the gloriously pompous plan of San Pedro—"Jalisco never loses." Probably the most poignant aspect of the novel's treatment of a pronunciamiento is the contrast that Payno draws between some of the elevated ideals proclaimed in Cruz's plan and what the reader knows to be the real causes and individuals behind the insurrection.

Payno ensures that the wording of Cruz's plan resonates with that of so many nineteenth-century pronunciamientos. In a way it is this familiarity, the fact that the style of the text together with its demands are so easily recognizable, so much like those of almost every single pronunciamiento that was circulated in Independent Mexico, that makes Payno's literary representation of the practice all the more humorous *and* painful, especially bearing in mind what actually lies behind Cruz's gesture of rebellion. Payno's tragi-comic interpretation of the pronunciamiento is thus attained through inference. The reader cannot help thinking that all of Mexico's pronunciamientos with their noble demands and claims were nothing other than farcical performances that hid and disguised the criminal machinations and actions of men no different from Valentín Cruz. The preamble to Cruz's plan, unsurprisingly, stresses the extent to which tyranny has become unbearable, that the free people of the republic will tolerate it no further, and that they are impelled to rebel as their only and last recourse to save the country's institutions and its citizens' liberties. The inebriated motley crew of pronunciados we have seen getting drunk on mescal—(there comes a moment when they even have to resort to looting other liquor stores in the vicinity because the one they are in at the beginning of the pronunciamiento runs out of alcohol)—are described in the actual plan as the legitimate forces of the government, an army of "valiant *tapatíos*" (a name given to the people from Jalisco) who "alone will conquer the rest of the republic and subjugate the rebel States." For Payno, the grandiloquent addresses and plans of Mexico's pronunciados were nothing but empty phrases that barely disguised their authors' true and plunder-driven intentions.

The plan's articles, moreover, offer the reader a corrosively sardonic parody of so many pronunciamiento texts. Typically enough, some articles concentrate on reordering the local political scene ("Art. 1. The State authorities cease to carry out their functions"). Others have a recognizable populist flavor, blatantly included to broaden the pronunciamiento's popular support (e.g., article 2 frees all political prisoners—*and* petty criminals; and article 3 cuts taxes by 50 percent). Characteristically, Payno would argue, two articles also serve to legitimize aspects of Cruz's plunder—article 4 authorizes him to take over all tobacco revenue, and article 5 allows him to take over the customs house of San Blas—allegedly on behalf of the state government. The plan, responding to pressure from Cruz's patron in Mexico City, the disgruntled lawyer and politician Crisanto Bedolla, also demands in article 5 the removal of the national government's ministers, and it concludes with an offer to the president along the lines that he will be respected and may continue to serve as the republic's mandatory as long as he supports Cruz's plan. Cruz and his pronunciados are eventually easily defeated since, by the time the governor's forces reach the district of San Pedro and attack Cruz's headquarters ("Valentín's liquor store, that is"), the pronunciados are quite simply too drunk to respond. Notwithstanding Payno's sharp wit, the result of the whole shambolic affair remains one of "streets littered with corpses."[34]

After two long decades of pronunciamiento-filled years, perhaps unsurprisingly, the more prejudicial side effects of insurrectionary people power were apparent, such as instability, lack of continuity at a government level, fiscal disarray, the rise of warlordism (*caudillismo*), repeated Cruz-style acts of plunder, "streets littered with corpses," etc. In the minds of most contemporary writers these aspects started to outweigh the benefits of pronunciamientos, such as expanded political participation, contestation of unjust or unconstitutional measures, and overthrow of unpopular or despotic governments via relatively peaceful means. It is clear, as well, that mimetic insurrectionism had the potential to become chronic. Paradoxically, it was probably because of this that the pronunciamientos of the 1840s and '50s became somehow nastier and more fiercely intransigent. Pronunciados were no longer lobbying or hoping to force their enemies to the negotiating table through aggressive petitioning. They wanted to crush their enemies and, at the same time, forcefully put an end to pronunciamiento politics. In tandem, and as a reaction to the pronunciados' increased virulence, the governments' response also hardened and became more unflinchingly violent. As of 1848 pronunciados began to be executed, something that had generally been avoided until then. This departure was, in many ways, symptomatic of the disillusion and despair of the 1840s and 1850s. There was a definite sense that enough was enough. The days when pronunciados knew they stood a good chance of being pardoned, amnestied, or at worst sent into exile were becoming a thing of the past, as government commanders took to placing their pronunciado prisoners before firing squads. As was noted by none other than Anastasio Bustamante—twice president, and leader as well as beneficiary of the 1829 Jalapa pronunciamiento cycle and the general amnesty conferred on all parties concerned in the Zavaleta Treaty that ended the 1832 Civil War—"The absolute impunity . . . which revolutionaries have enjoyed, one way or another, for such a very long time, has not only allowed for the scandalous repetition of our military pronunciamientos, it has also meant that many . . . have blindly adhered to whichever plan has been proposed to them."[35] It was a view that resonated with President José Joaquín de Herrera's belief that "a firm hand, not leniency, was needed if Mexico was to be spared a continued 'frenzy of factions' and political instability." Herrera's minister of war in the late 1840s, Mariano Arista, was adamant that the summary execution of political offenders had become the only "sure remedy to prevent other revolutions."[36]

Evidence of how pronunciados ceased to be treated with the comparative leniency of the 1820s and 1830s can be seen in the way government forces began to execute the pronunciados of the Sierra Gorda. Building on several months of insurrectionary activity on the part of Paredes y Arrillaga, Father Celedonio Domeco Jarauta pronounced in Guanajuato on 15 June 1848 against the Guadalupe Hidalgo peace treaty with the United States and the Mexican government that had signed it.[37] He was executed on 18 July together with all the other pronunciados who were captured following Anastasio Bustamante's storming of the city.[38] Similarly Eleuterio Quiroz's "eminently social and political pronunciamiento of Río Verde" of 14 March 1849 (San Luis Potosí), called for a range of radical demands.[39] It ended not quite a year later, in 1849, with Quiroz executed and 478 of the rebels deported.[40] By the time Santa Anna returned to power for one last time in 1853, the Law of Conspirators of 1 August went on to give the government the right to court-martial and execute anyone who was found guilty of conspiring against public order. You no longer had to pronounce to be shot. Just planning to pronounce could result in your facing the firing squad.[41]

Each pronunciamiento of the 1840s and '50s was thus, in a sense, meant to be the last; the one that finally put a stop to what Otero termed Mexicans' "baneful habit of [starting] revolutions" (*funesta manía de las revoluciones*).[42] Each one of them was meant to usher in a period of order, peace, and stability, where representative government was based on a solid, respected, and long-lasting constitution. However, the end of compromise—a value that had played a determining role in most of the successful pronunciamiento cycles of the 1820s and '30s—did not bring an end to this insurrectionary practice. Rather it removed negotiating qualities and, in so doing, transformed the pronunciamiento into a disguised coup d'état. The result, as the politics of despair took hold of the republic following the Mexican-U.S. War, was an increasingly acrimonious, violent and polarized context. This, together with the emergence of what became irreconcilable conservative and liberal viewpoints, each determined to avenge the other's preceding pronunciamiento cycle, was eventually to degenerate into the bloodshed of the so-called midcentury Reform period.

Between 1843 and 1858 more than 520 separate individual pronunciamientos were launched, including start-up pronunciamientos, pronunciamientos de adhesión, counterpronunciamientos, or despronunciamientos. In terms of actual national pronunciamiento constellations, cycles, or series there were at least thirteen distinct groups which, for analytical purposes, I distinguish here in terms of five different types of pronunciamiento clusters.[43]

Unlike in the previous two decades, between 1843 and 1858 there were no pronunciamiento cycles that engaged with national concerns, failed to spread beyond their region, but succeeded in significantly reordering the local political scene, as had happened previously both in Texas (1836) and Yucatán (1829 and 1840). What there was, however, was an appallingly violent Caste War in Yucatán, 1847–52, in which race violence and ethnic hatred became entwined in the insurrectionary politics of southeastern Mexico.[44]

Six particularly forceful constellations were experienced during these years that engaged with national concerns, spread across several states or regions, and were ultimately successful in achieving their aims. These were the Guadalajara–Mexico City series of 1844 that brought an end to Santa Anna's 1843–44 government; the Plan of San Luis Potosí of 14 December 1845 that overthrew José Joaquín de Herrera's moderate administration (1844–45); the Plan of the Ciudadela of 4 August 1846 that, in turn, brought down General Paredes y Arrillaga's government (1845–46; receiving a posteriori more than eighty pronunciamientos de adhesión from all over the republic); the 1852 Blancarte series in Jalisco that spread to the capital and eventually resulted in the end of Mariano Arista's government (1851–53) and the return of Santa Anna from his exile in Colombia; the plans of Ayutla, Guerrero, of 1 and 11 March 1854 that brought down Santa Anna's 1853–55 dictatorship after just over a year of civil war; and the plans of Tacubaya and Félix Zuloaga of 17 December 1857 and 11 January 1858, which initially abolished the 1857 Constitution (in certain regions of the republic), resulted in the closure of the national congress, and culminated with the overthrow of President Ignacio Comonfort by Zuloaga and the conservatives, giving way to the three-year-long Civil War of the Reforma (1858–60).

There was also one particular constellation that, without spreading beyond the capital, did result in a significant government change at a national level. Although the plans of the Polkos of February–March 1847—after two months of street fighting in the center of Mexico City—failed to force Santa Anna's resignation, they did succeed in pressurizing him into replacing radical liberal vice president Gómez Farías with a moderado, General Pedro María Anaya, and shelving the decree of 11 January 1847, which had been passed to nationalize and sell 15 million pesos' worth of church property to pay for the war effort against the United States.

There were also four distinct pronunciamiento cycles that engaged with national concerns, spread across several states or regions, but failed to achieve their aims. All these took place in the mountainous region of the Sierra Gorda that rises up through parts of the present-day states of Querétaro, Guanajuato, San Luis Potosí, Hidalgo, Mexico, and Tamaulipas, and all became either subsumed or overtaken by a major large-scale peasant rebellion that lasted from 1847 to 1850. On the one hand, the pronunciados tried to use the discontent of the rural communities of the Sierra Gorda to promote their own political projects, hijacking or co-opting the campesino rebellion to serve their own ends.[45] On the other, agrarian and indigenous rebels made the most of the national-oriented pronunciamientos to address their own local grievances. The Sierra Gorda peasant rebellion thus became intertwined with the pronunciamientos of army officers Tomás Mejía (1848), Mariano Paredes y Arrillaga (1848), Leonardo Márquez (1849), and Eleuterio Quiroz (1849).[46]

As a fourth category, there were a number of pronunciamiento clusters that engaged with national concerns but, unlike the constellations noted in the previous paragraph, failed to spread beyond their region of origin. Pronunciados circulated their respective petitions alongside others without gaining much or any support. One example was the Acta del Ayuntamiento del Pueblo de San Agustín del Palmar, Veracruz, of 30 May 1843, calling for Santa Anna to put an end to any anti-clerical reforms his government may have been considering.[47] Another was the Plan de la guarnición de Guanajuato of 8 January 1851, which demanded an end to Herrera's cabinet's reforms of the regular army and removal of his ministers.[48]

From Forceful Negotiation to Civil War

However, one particularly dramatic pronunciamiento that was brought to an end on the very same day it was launched was Ramón Othón and Joaquín Rangel's "Proclama y plan de la guardia nacional" of 7 June 1845, in which they called for the restitution of the 1824 Constitution (art. 1), the replacement of Herrera as president with the president of the Supreme Court of Justice (art. 2), the election of a new congress (art. 3), the reorganization of the government (arts. 4–7) and the creation of an army to reconquer Texas (art. 8).[49] Like the pronunciamiento of 15 July 1840, that of 7 June 1845 also entailed the seizure of the National Palace by the pronunciados and the temporary capture of the incumbent president, this time José Joaquín de Herrera. Perhaps unsurprisingly, Valentín Gómez Farías was again one of the conspirators behind this botched pronunciamiento/palace coup, although on this occasion he chose not to join the pronunciados in situ as he had done with Urrea five years earlier. According to Michael Costeloe, the event itself involved "considerable firing along the corridors and in the courtyards, resulting in twenty-three dead, including Othón, and a number of wounded." The action was brought to end as a result of Herrera's apparent show of integrity and remarkable gift with words, since he "refused to be intimidated and managed to persuade his captors of the error of their ways so successfully that they switched sides and released him." Free from captivity, Herrera set about walking the corridors of the palace complex and convincing the pronunciados to give up. By 5:00 p.m., only two hours after the pronunciados had stormed the palace, the pronunciamiento was all over.[50]

Another notorious cycle to have engaged with national concerns, which unfolded in only one region and which failed, was that of the plans of Zacapoaxtla–Puebla, 1855–56. Making this constellation worthy of note are its duration and the escalation of violence it entailed, including a large-scale battle at Ocotlán on 8 March 1856, three notably destructive sieges of Puebla (17–23 January, 4–22 March, and 30 October–4 December 1856), and the involvement of the president himself, Ignacio Comonfort, in leading the campaign of March 1856 (Tomás Moreno would lead the government's siege of October–December 1856) against the conservative forces that seized the state capital on two separate occasions. The conservative pronunciados involved in the different plans of Zacapoaxtla, 12 December 1855, and Puebla, 20 October 1856, were none other than Antonio Haro y Tamariz, who led the capture of Puebla in January–March, and Miguel Miramón and Francisco Orihuela, who followed in Haro y Tamariz's steps in October–December 1856. Haro y Tamariz was a respected politician, a former minister of finance (1844, 1846, and 1853), whose political trajectory, like that of so many of his disillusioned contemporaries, took him from being a liberal to becoming a conservative and eventually a monarchist as time went by. Miramón at the time was an eager twenty-five-year-old officer who had fought as a cadet in the Mexican-U.S. War and was soon to become one of the main leading conservative generals and president during the Civil War of the Reforma. The Plan of Zacapoaxtla called for the national government to stand down for having betrayed the aims of the Ayutla Revolution (arts. 1, 2), and proposed bringing back the centralist 1843 Bases Orgánicas constitution (art. 3). The Puebla plan was in favor of the "religion of Jesus Christ, our social guarantees and the decorum of the army."[51] It resulted in Orihuela demanding an end to the Ley Juárez and the Ley Lerdo.[52] These pronunciamientos ultimately failed to impact the national government, even though Puebla was held by these conservative

From Forceful Negotiation to Civil War

pronunciados for a combined period of more than five months. Both Haro y Tamariz and Miramón would make a comeback as *imperialistas* and supporters of the French Intervention (1862– 67) and the imposition of Archduke Maximilian on the Mexican throne (1864–67).

The fifth and last category involves pronunciamientos that were engaged with strictly regional concerns. These did not intend to influence national politics and did not seek to elicit support from elsewhere. They were launched by local political actors with the sole purpose of reordering the local political scene or addressing very specific regional grievances. A book focused mainly on national pronunciamientos is not the place for a comprehensive overview of the many pronunciamientos that took place simultaneously across the republic, as different regional political actors attempted to reorder the local political scene via pronunciamiento pressure. The following are but a sample, noted here to give a sense of what most regional pronunciamientos were intent on achieving between 1843 and 1858; namely, to remove whoever was the current state governor. Thus the Plan of the Mineral of Temascaltepec of 2 January 1849 was solely concerned with overthrowing the governor of the State of Mexico, Mariano Arizcorreta.[53] Similarly that of Comitán in Chiapas, of 21 May 1851, was exclusively intent on reordering the local political scene by overthrowing state governor Nicolás Maldonado.[54] In Tabasco the pronunciamiento de San Juan de Tierra Adentro, of 26 July 1851, was likewise focused on replacing the current governor, in this case with José Julián Dueñas, who had been deposed in a preceding pronunciamiento on 15 October 1850.[55] Reflecting a shift in national politics, although these and most other regional pronunciamientos for this period employed pronunciamiento tactics, outlining the pronunciados' demands through the circulation of petitioning texts, they were no longer so much intent on negotiation as concerned with removing their respective regional political leaders—by threats, intimidation, and if need be, by force.

Apart from these five clearly defined categories of pronunciamientos, Mexico witnessed during its third and fourth decades as an independent country a number of pronunciamiento conspiracies that were intended to engage with national concerns but were uncovered before they could be launched. One such plot, aimed at bringing Santa Anna back from exile to make him dictator, was the Plan of Guanajuato of 9 July 1851.[56] Antonio Haro y Tamariz was also supposedly involved in a monarchist conspiracy that was uncovered in late 1855, when a search of his house in Mexico City revealed him to be in possession of an as yet unpronounced pronunciamiento text—"El Plan del Llano del Rodeo," which aimed to revive the Three Guarantees of the Plan of Iguala and present the crown to Iturbide's son.[57] Regardless of whether Haro y Tamariz had drafted this plan or it had been deliberately planted in his home by his enemies, as argued by his biographer Jan Bazant, he was arrested on 2 January 1856 and dispatched to Veracruz.[58] From there he managed to escape, temporarily getting to take over Puebla at the head of the Plan of Zacapoaxtla, mentioned earlier, which did not call for the imposition of a monarchy with an Iturbide descendant on the throne.[59]

In order to appreciate how the practice of the pronunciamiento evolved during the mid-nineteenth century, shedding its original consultative qualities, it is essential to grasp the chronology of the main events of these years, 1843–58. A study of the national pronunciamiento constellations of this period highlights, on the one hand, the overwhelming extent to which pronunciamiento pressure determined the political shifts and conflicts of mid-nineteenth-century Mexico and how the pronunciamiento, as a practice, changed visibly and dramatically from being a forceful form of negotiation to becoming a barely disguised form of coup d'état or revolution.

Following the December 1842 San Luis Potosí–Huejotzingo cycle that gave acting president Nicolás Bravo the justification to close down congress and avoid adopting the federalist 1842 Constitution, he had the closed constituent congress of 1842 replaced with a handpicked *santanista*-traditionalist-centralist Junta de Notables. Bravo, who had been serving as acting president since October 1842 while Santa Anna was allegedly convalescing at his haciendas in Veracruz, then handed in his resignation toward the end of February 1843, forcing Santa Anna to return to the capital to resume his role as the country's executive on 4 March.

With Santa Anna staying put in Mexico City for seven months (4 March–4 October 1843), the Veracruzan caudillo was able to oversee the drafting of what was to be the 1843 Constitution—the Bases Orgánicas—by the newly formed Junta de Notables.[60] However, he did not wait for the electoral results and returned to Veracruz on 5 October, this time leaving a close friend, General Valentín Canalizo, as acting president. Santa Anna was therefore at his hacienda El Encero when he heard that he had won the presidential elections by a landslide victory.[61] Although the Bases Orgánicas specified that he was to begin his five-year term as constitutional president on 1 February 1844, Santa Anna did not return to the capital until June that year. By then the santanistas had become profoundly divided, crippled by in-fighting, faced with the impossibility of governing Mexico as they had hoped. Between February and September 1844 Santa Anna lost the favor of his cabinet, in part out of personal disagreements and petty jealousies and in part because he refused to listen to his ministers' advice. In a matter of months he lost his ministers of war, relations, and finance. Congress found ways, moreover, of undermining his manipulation of the composition of the senate and became increasingly hostile toward him.

The merchant class and lobbies that had backed him in 1841 were no longer behind him. The fact that the santanistas had been responsible for imposing an extraordinary number of taxes during the years they had been in office without exempting either the church or the wealthier landowning families meant that they had lost the support of the more traditional factions by the middle of 1844. The corruption that became associated with Santa Anna and his most loyal followers had become particularly galling in the face of ever-increasing taxes. The federalists had not forgiven the santanistas, either, for the 1842 dissolution of congress and were ready to fight the government. Santa Anna's return to the capital in June 1844 did not extend to more than three months. Aware that he was losing his grip on the situation, he retreated to El Encero following the death of his first wife, *doña* Inés de la Paz García, on 12 September. His marriage by proxy to fifteen-year-old Dolores Tosta on 3 October, barely a month after his previous wife had been buried, did not endear him to the population.[62]

In the meantime General Paredes y Arrillaga had grown increasingly restless. Having initiated the Triangular Revolt in 1841, he had ended up serving as a stepping-stone for Santa Anna. His frustration was paired with humiliation he had suffered at the hands of Santa Anna over a drinking incident in 1843.[63] Together these factors led him to start a pronunciamiento in Guadalajara (2 November 1844), in which he called for congress to place Santa

Anna on trial for having violated the 1841 Bases de Tacubaya and the 1843 Bases Orgánicas and for having misgoverned the republic from 10 October 1841 to 31 December 1843.[64] On hearing the news of Paredes's pronunciamiento, Santa Anna returned to Mexico City on 18 November and set off three days later to quell the revolt in person. While Santa Anna was away his acting president, Canalizo, tried to prevent congress from supporting the pronunciamiento by attempting to dissolve congress on 29 November. Just over a week later, on 6 December 1844, Canalizo's anti-congress antics were met with a liberal-led coup known as the Revolution of the Three Hours, which forced Canalizo's resignation and put an end to Santa Anna's fourth term in office without a gunshot being fired.[65]

Much to Paredes y Arrillaga's frustration, events in the capital resulted in General José Joaquín de Herrera becoming interim president rather than himself. Santa Anna did try to fight back, wreaking havoc in Querétaro and Puebla along the way, but was eventually arrested in Xico, Veracruz, as he attempted to leave the country. Although many expected Santa Anna to be placed on trial, Herrera opted to send him into exile instead, after he had spent four months in prison. This was to be one of many unpopular decisions Herrera was to make during the twelve months he served as president. His moderate-led cabinet hesitated over replacing the centralist 1843 Constitution with the federalist 1824 Charter. The fear of a war with the United States was strong enough for the moderates to believe it preferable to retain the 1843 Charter, despite their federalist ideals.[66] The *puros* believed, in contrast, that only bringing back the 1824 Constitution would cause the people to rally behind the government against the United States. They soon became incensed, as well, with Herrera's reluctance to replace the large regular army with civic militias. Herrera's inner circle also started to consider the controversial possibility of recognizing the independence of Texas.

Extraordinary as it may seem, a number of radicals, disgruntled with the moderate government Herrera formed in the wake of the Revolution of the Three Hours, started to look into the possibility of getting Santa Anna to support their cause even before he went into exile on 2 June 1845. The fact that radical liberals and santanistas had started to conspire together became evident to Herrera's government following the dramatic events of 7 June 1845, when Joaquín Rangel, Ramón Othón, and their men took the National Palace by force and arrested President Herrera together with the ministers of relations and justice. As noted earlier, the pronunciamiento failed, but it highlighted that santanistas and puros were plotting together to bring down Herrera's government.[67]

In the end it would be third-time-lucky Paredes y Arrillaga who would succeed in overthrowing Herrera's government with his Plan of San Luis Potosí of 14 December 1845. With Herrera's government's reputation damaged by its disposition to consider recognizing the independence of Texas—a disposition that was foiled by the Texan government's decision to join the United States on 15 July 1845 (the formal U.S. annexation of Texas was officially ratified on 29 December 1845)—they had nobody to rally to their defense when Paredes y Arrillaga finally pronounced. Puros, centralists, santanistas, and an emerging faction of monarchists were all opposed to Herrera. They accused the government of being weak and clamored for war.[68]

Thus on 14 December 1845 the commander general of San Luis Potosí, Manuel Romero, following Paredes y Arrillaga's instruc-

From Forceful Negotiation to Civil War

tions, launched the pronunciamiento of San Luis Potosí at the head of the army that had been formed and equipped to reconquer Texas. As may be evidenced by studying the plan's articles and demands, the pronunciados' aims were aggressively blunt and uncompromising. Nothing the current government decreed would be taken for valid (art. 1). Both chambers of congress as well as the president were to stand down with immediate effect (art. 2). The moment the army took over the capital a new congress would be summoned (art. 3), made up of representatives from different sectors of society (art. 4).[69] Unsurprisingly, Paredes y Arrillaga was called upon to lead this movement (art. 7).[70] Despite Herrera's government's initial determination to resist, it became obvious by the end of the month, as Paredes y Arrillaga advanced toward the capital and news of pronunciamientos de adhesión came thick and fast from all over the republic, that the government's days were numbered. Following the pronunciamiento de adhesión of the Mexico City garrison on 30 December 1845, Herrera chose to resign.[71] General Gabriel Valencia, who had also been a leading pronunciado in the Triangular Revolt of 1841, and who like Paredes y Arrillaga until that point had never made it to the presidency, tried to impose himself as the country's ruler by becoming leader of the Mexico City pronunciamiento. However, he failed to muster any significant support and opted in the end to stand aside, allowing Paredes to take over the government on his arrival in the capital on 2 January 1846.[72]

However, General Paredes y Arrillaga's government was not to last long either. Faced with the imminence of war, a growing faction of monarchists, encouraged by the Spanish minister plenipotentiary, Salvador Bermúdez de Castro, tried to persuade Paredes to prepare the ground for the crowning of a European prince in

Mexico.[73] There was the fact that Gutiérrez Estrada's views, first publicized in 1840, had gained significant support in some quarters. Experience, the monarchist conspirators adduced, demonstrated that Mexicans were unable to govern themselves, and a monarchy was perceived as a system that suited Mexico's political customs and traditions. There was, however, the more pragmatic fact that if Mexico's destiny could be linked to that of a European power, there was every hope that the country would have a strong enough ally to fend off any U.S. aggression. Notwithstanding the persuasiveness of such an argument at a time when desperate measures were called for, the majority's republicanism thwarted the monarchist plot of 1846. Once news got out of Paredes y Arrillaga's perceived monarchist sympathies he lost the support of most of the factions almost overnight. A number of anti-Paredes federalist santanista-republican pronunciamientos were staged from April through to May, such as that of Mazatlán (7 May).[74] They grew increasingly aggressive, such as that of Guadalajara (20 May).[75] As Paredes y Arrillaga divided his army to quell the uprisings and defend the northern border, war broke out with the United States on 25 April 1846.

Viscerally opposed to Paredes y Arrillaga's dictatorship, puros and *moderados*, federalists alike, remarkably started to overcome their virulent differences so as to bring down the government. Both groups saw as well the logic of including Santa Anna in their plans.[76] As for Santa Anna, exiled in Cuba since June 1845, he was itching to return to Mexico and lead the defense of the country, happy to leave it to Gómez Farías to run the government.[77] Aware that santanistas and puros were plotting against him, Paredes had a number of their prominent politicians arrested between 17 and 20 May, including former minister of finance Ignacio Trigueros, pronunciado Rangel, and Gómez Farías himself.[78] It was not enough to prevent him from being overthrown.

On 4 August 1846, regardless of the fact that the war with the United States was in full swing by now, with Mariano Arista's forces having suffered the major defeats of Palo Alto and Resaca de Palma (8 and 9 May 1846) in the north of the country, General Mariano Salas woke up the capital with the sound of roaring cannon fire at 5:30 in the morning. Seizing on Paredes having vacated Mexico City a week earlier at the head of three thousand men, he marched his troops from the Ciudadela garrison to the center of Mexico City, surrounding the National Palace. In the plan of the Ciudadela of 4 August 1846, attributed to Gómez Farías and accompanying this show of force, Salas called for the dissolution of the current government and the reintroduction of the 1824 Constitution (art. 1), for Santa Anna to join their movement (art. 2), and for elections to be held so that within four months of the liberation of the capital a new congress was in place (art. 4).[79] With Salas having cunningly removed most of the ammunition stored in the National Palace ahead of the pronunciamiento, acting president Nicolás Bravo realized early on that it would be impossible for him to resist. Bravo therefore capitulated on 6 August, and Salas was able to move into the National Palace and take over the presidency, as a temporary measure, while elections were called following the 1823 guidelines that informed the 1824 federal charter. Paredes, returning to the capital at the head of a small escort, was arrested on the same day, bringing a very definite end to his brief stint in power.[80]

Worthy of note is that what was for all intents and purposes a palace coup—albeit with a petitioned plan to legitimize it—was welcomed by more than eighty pronunciamientos de adhesión. Some were launched from as nearby as Toluca in the state of Mexico (5 August 1846).[81] Others were as far afield as the village of Ochuc, in remote southern Chiapas (26 August 1846).[82] Rather than rely on the customary constellation of plans to force the incumbent government to listen or stand down, with Salas having successfully taken over the National Palace on 6 August, the 1846 plans of allegiance that were inspired by the pronunciamiento of La Ciudadela served more as a legitimating round of applause, resembling, as Barbara Tenenbaum put it, "an audience shouting bravo after a concert."[83]

With the return on 16 August of Santa Anna, controversially allowed through the U.S. blockade of Veracruz by a deceived or deluded President Polk, the 1824 Federal Constitution was formally reintroduced on 22 August, bringing an end to the Central Republic (1836–46). Valentín Gómez Farías became the president of the Council of State set up under the provisional presidency of General Salas, and Santa Anna set off to San Luis Potosí on 28 September 1846 to prepare an expeditionary army with which to fight the Northern Campaign against Zachary Taylor's forces.[84]

It was while Santa Anna was in San Luis Potosí that elections were held. Santa Anna and Gómez Farías, in a repeat of the 1833 elections, were elected president and vice president, respectively, on 23 December 1846. Santa Anna, however, did not return to Mexico City to take up his post as president and allowed Gómez Farías to lead the country as vice president. Santa Anna's sole concern was to organize an army that could confront Taylor's forces.

As it became increasingly obvious to Santa Anna that the army desperately needed funds to defend the country, he fully backed Gómez Farías's drive to finance the much needed resurrection of Mexico's armed forces with church funds.[85] Santa Anna authorized the Executive Power to confiscate up to 15 million pesos by mortgaging or selling unused church properties, as was stipulated in the congressional decree of 11 January 1847.[86] What neither Santa Anna nor Gómez Farías expected was the reaction such a decree would provoke: moderates and priests now took to pronouncing against the government, regardless of the fact that Mexico was at war.

Only days after Santa Anna attacked General Taylor's invading army at the battle of La Angostura–Buena Vista (23 February 1847), and while General Winfield Scott was preparing for an imminent landing in Veracruz, the moderados, funded by the clergy, pronounced against the government on 27 February 1847.[87] The Revolt of the Polkos, as it became known, proved extremely disruptive (it was thus named, according to some, because the well-to-do moderates who backed it were known to dance the trendy polkas of the day; and according to others because the revolt favored Mr. Polk's war effort). In the original plan, made up of thirteen articles, General Matías de la Peña Barragán demanded the resignation of Santa Anna and Gómez Farías as well as the dissolution of congress (art. 1; although he recognized Santa Anna as general in chief of the Mexican Army, art. 13), and he called for new federal and state elections (arts. 3, 6, 7). Article 12, critically important, demanded the abolition of the law of 11 January concerning the confiscation of church properties.[88]

Initially Santa Anna sent a number of letters from San Luis Potosí, on his way back from the Northern Campaign, supporting Gómez Farías's government. He urged the acting president to be tough on the pronunciados, to crush them with "firmness and energy."[89] However, neither side seemed able to gain the upper hand in the capital. With it becoming apparent that public opinion was beginning to turn against the rebels, on 8 March, the Polkos took back their original plan of 27 February and replaced it with a single-article follow-up pronunciamiento limited to demanding Gómez Farías's removal from office.[90] The leading luminaries of the moderado party now saw in Santa Anna, just as the puros had only six months earlier, the providential leader who could and would bring an end to the nation's crises and triumph over the U.S. expeditionary armies. On 10 March 1847, forty-one prominent moderates signed a petition begging Santa Anna to return to the capital to take over the presidency: by "calling on him" (*invocando su nombre*) they hoped to save their country.[91]

Despite the changes in the moderates' demands, hostilities continued in the capital between the warring liberal factions, with street fighting becoming more intense as time went by. When Santa Anna finally reached the outskirts of the capital on 21 March he was forced to arbitrate once more between Mexico's feuding parties. In the light of almost a month of violent clashes in the capital, Santa Anna, who had fully supported and celebrated the 11 January decree, as Costeloe notes, "now abandoned it and Gómez Farías, both because of political expediency and to some extent because of his government's desperate need for money to prosecute the war."[92] A compromise was reached. The church agreed to lend the government between 1.5 and 2 million pesos in cash. Santa Anna agreed, as president, to remove Gómez Farías and the post of vice president; to name as acting president a moderado, General Pedro María Anaya, while he set off to organize the Mexican defense of Xalapa, Córdoba, and Orizaba; and to nullify the 11 January anti-clerical legislation.

The following eleven months would be among the darkest and most traumatic of Mexico's history. At the same time as indigenous communities took to rebelling in the Sierra Gorda and a horrendously violent Caste War got under way in Yucatán at the end of July 1847, Santa Anna's forces fought and lost the battles of Cerro Gordo in April; Padierna, Contreras, and Churubusco in August; and Casa Mata, Molino del Rey, and Chapultepec in September. An estimated 25,000 Mexicans died in the conflict. Moreover, although Mexico City fell to the U.S. expeditionary forces on 15 September, peace was not ratified until the Treaty of Guadalupe Hidalgo was signed on 2 February 1848, and the months that unfolded between the occupation of the capital and the end of the war witnessed further skirmishes and killings. As if this were not depressing enough, the treaty resulted in Mexico losing more than 500,000 square miles of territory to the United States.[93]

The moderate liberal–dominated Mexican government, which had moved to Querétaro in September as the U.S. forces closed in on the capital, alternately presided over on an interim basis by Pedro María Anaya and Manuel de la Peña y Peña while Santa Anna initially tried to continue the struggle from Puebla before going into exile, eventually ratified the Treaty of Guadalupe Hidalgo on 30 May 1848. On the same day General William Orlando Butler ordered the evacuation of the U.S. forces from Mexico City, and the national congress based in Querétaro elected José Joaquín de Herrera president. Notwithstanding his initial reluctance to accept the post, on 3 June Herrera became Mexico's supreme executive for a second time. On the 12th the remaining U.S. forces left Mexico City, and on the 15th the Mexican government returned to direct the republic's affairs from the capital.[94]

Herrera was to have the merit, unheard of since Guadalupe Victoria's day, of completing his term in office as president, governing

Mexico from 3 June 1848 to 15 January 1851. However, although it might be assumed from the fact that he was not actually overthrown by a pronunciamiento cycle that his time in power was marked by peace, order, and stability, the events in the Sierra Gorda and Yucatán instead attest to his government having had to confront particularly virulent waves of political and agrarian violence. It is true that President Herrera's administration benefited from the 15 million pesos received from the United States as part of the indemnity agreed in the Guadalupe Hidalgo treaty and was temporarily able to "put its public finances in order," according to Jan Bazant.[95] But U.S. military historian Roswell S. Ripley's view, as expressed in 1849, was overstated, to say the least: he claimed that the effect of the war upon Mexico had been "beneficial" because the prestige of the army had been "entirely swept away," resulting in "the comparative quietude which has existed in Mexico since the conclusion of peace, and the at least apparent stability of a government administered upon republican principles."[96]

According to Herrera's biographer, Thomas Ewing Cotner, the 15-million-dollar indemnity "was dissipated in an effort to meet the immediate expenses of the government."[97] A significant part of it was spent repaying the *agiotistas* who had lent the government money in the past, both in the build-up to and during the Mexican-U.S. War.[98] Evidence that Mexico's dire straits were in no way resolved is that under Herrera, and over a period of not more than two and a half years, eleven different individuals served as minister of finance, with the post changing hands sixteen times, most incumbents having resigned when they realized the enormity of the task that sorting out Mexico's economy entailed. The author of the *Los bandidos de Río Frío*, a then forty-

From Forceful Negotiation to Civil War

year-old Manuel Payno, would be one of them, lasting a record six months and nine days in the post (4 July 1850–13 January 1851).[99]

Herrera's government was certainly characterized by its good intentions and succeeded in introducing some major reforms— such as the drastic reduction of the regular army to 273 officers and 9,999 enlisted men.[100] But it was ultimately plagued by an array of issues—agrarian and indigenous discontent, uprisings, and raids; clerical resistance to reform; aggressive party factionalism; and a very noticeable polarization of politics; and all of these encompassed in a context of profound postwar despair and fiscal disarray—which spilt unresolved into Mariano Arista's presidency, culminating in the 1852 Blancarte series of pronunciamientos that eventually resulted in the return of none other than Santa Anna.

The Blancarte series of pronunciamientos started off with the regional-based pronunciamiento of Colonel José María Blancarte of 26 July 1852, in which an unlikely alliance of Guadalajara-based radical liberals and conservatives set out to remove moderado Governor Jesús López Portillo.[101] It was met with pronunciamientos de rechazo, such as that of the town council of Colotlán of 3 August.[102] But there were also pronunciamientos de adhesión.[103] However, more important, López Portillo was forced to vacate Guadalajara and retreat to San Juan de los Lagos while Gregorio Dávila was named interim governor by Blancarte and his mixed group of pronunciados. With the pronunciamiento having thus resulted in the fall of the moderate state government of Jalisco, a number of politicians and officers, intent on bringing down Arista's moderate government in Mexico City, converged in Guadalajara in mid- to late August with a view to using the Plan of Blancarte and events in Jalisco to launch their own follow-up national-oriented pronunciamiento. Among the conspirators who arrived in Guadalajara in August were santanista generals José María Yáñez and Juan Suárez y Navarro. Yet although they were determined to pronounce against the national government and call for the return of Santa Anna, they found that pronunciado and new interim Governor Dávila was staunchly opposed to such a move.

It was in an attempt to unite the increasingly disparate political factions gathered in Guadalajara that Blancarte's own follow-up pronunciamiento of 13 September called upon Dávila, in article 11, to back his call for the removal of the national president and all those officials who had lost the people's confidence (art. 2), while defending the 1824 federal constitution (art. 1). The Second Plan of Blancarte, as it became known, did call for the return of Santa Anna, but it did not ask for him to become president—just to "cooperate with the defense of the federal system and the restoration of peace and order" (art. 8), and it named Blancarte leader of the movement (art. 10).[104] Dávila was not prepared to compromise and was consequently forcefully removed by Blancarte, who went on to serve as interim governor for ten days. Blancarte, in turn, was replaced by santanista general José María Yáñez. As noted by Rosie Doyle, "the support base of [the original pronunciamiento now] broadened to include santanistas, conservatives, federalists, anti-federalists, and crucially, the clergy and merchants."[105] It was this new coalition, led by santanistas, that launched the Plan del Hospicio of 20 October, which reiterated the defense of the 1824 Constitution (art. 1) and the call for Arista and anyone who had lost the people's confidence to stand down (art. 2), but went on to propose the erection of a temporary dictatorship (art. 3), emphatically demanded the return of Santa Anna—"worthy of the nation's gratitude" (art. 11), and

From Forceful Negotiation to Civil War

called upon General José López Uraga to lead their movement (art. 12), with Yáñez remaining governor of Jalisco (art. 13).[106] The Plan del Hospicio, alongside the Second Plan of Blancarte, went on to inspire pronunciamientos de adhesión across the republic, ultimately persuading Arista that the time had come for him to resign, which he did on 5 January 1853, in disgust and feeling betrayed, after congress refused to give him emergency powers.

Arista was replaced by Juan Bautista Ceballos, who in turn resigned a month later, on 8 February, unwilling to be part of the so-called Agreements of Arroyo Zarco, ratified by the rebels in the first week of February, whereby it was agreed that the temporary president would be awarded extraordinary powers for a year. Thereafter a constituent congress would be summoned and a republican, representative, and popular *magna carta* would be drafted. In the immediate future, the governors of the republic were asked to elect the man who should lead this one-year dictatorship, and it was agreed that this man would then name the twenty-one individuals who would form his State Council.[107]

General Manuel María Lombardini, a die-hard santanista who had accompanied the caudillo during the Northern Campaign and participated in the Battle of Angostura–Buena Vista, stepped in following Ceballos's resignation with the sole objective of preparing the ground for Santa Anna's return. He proved remarkably adept at his job. Under his supervision, when the votes of all twenty-three states were counted on 17 March 1853, Santa Anna secured a comfortable majority with eighteen ballots cast in his favor.[108]

Santa Anna therefore returned to Mexico from his exile in Colombia in 1853 on the back of a santanista-conservative-puro alliance and established an extravagant and repressive centralist dictatorship. It was during this government that Santa Anna allowed himself to become a monarch of sorts. He became the grand master of the Order of Guadalupe and was addressed as "His Serene Highness" (*Su Alteza Serenísima*). It was during this government that Santa Anna controversially sold the valley of La Mesilla in present-day Arizona and New Mexico to the United States for 10 million pesos in the Gadsden Purchase, and that he dispatched José María Gutiérrez Estrada to Europe to find a European prince willing to take the Mexican throne. It would be Santa Anna's last government.[109]

The movement that ultimately resulted in his downfall got under way in the present-day state of Guerrero and was initiated with a start-up pronunciamiento from the town of Ayutla on 1 March 1854 and a follow-up pronunciamiento from Acapulco ten days later. The original Plan of Ayutla was drafted in late February at Juan Álvarez's hacienda of La Providencia by the liberal cacique of the south, his son Diego, Tomás Moreno, Trinidad Gómez, Eligio Romero, and *moderado poblano* retired militia colonel Ignacio Comonfort and was then pronounced by Colonel Florencio Villarreal from Ayutla on 1 March at the head of four hundred troops.[110] In it the pronunciados called for the removal of Santa Anna and his government from power (art. 1); demanded that representatives from each state should be summoned to elect a temporary president—and in using the term *state* inferred that Mexico would be governed by a federal system (art. 2); gave emergency powers to the temporary president mentioned (art. 3); ordered the leader of the Ayutla movement, together with seven individuals chosen by him, to produce a temporary statute that could be applied in governing the states that backed the pronunciamiento (art. 4); and stressed that fifteen days after the interim president was in place, a constituent congress would be elected, following the 1841 regulations that had given rise to the 1842 federalist-inclined congress (art. 5). The customary pronunciamiento threat was included in article 8, which stated that those who opposed the plan would be treated as enemies of Mexico's national independence. And the pronunciamiento ended by inviting Nicolás Bravo, Juán Álvarez, and Tomás Moreno to lead the movement (art. 9).[111]

As noted by Silvestre Villegas, sensing that in committing themselves to federalism, the pronunciados ran the risk of not garnering the kind of broad base of support they considered necessary to bring down Santa Anna, Comonfort opted to tinker with the original plan of Ayutla in the follow-up reformed Plan de Ayutla he launched from Acapulco on 11 March 1854.[112] In the Acapulco-based pronunciamiento's preamble, Comonfort was credited with having stressed that "the plan they were about to second needed a few minor changes, with the object of demonstrating clearly to the nation that . . . they had not the least intention of imposing any conditions upon the sovereign will of the nation, [by] reestablishing the federal system by force of arms, or returning things to how they were when the [1852] plan of Jalisco [was pronounced]." It was up to the constituent congress, once it was elected, to determine the kind of political system and constitution Mexico needed. As a result, in the reformed Plan de Ayutla of 11 March, all references to "states" were replaced with "departments and territories." Otherwise, little was actually modified. In the revised version, article 4 stated that the pronunciamiento's leader would appoint five rather than seven individuals to help draft a provisional statute, and article 5 gave a time limit of four months for how long it should take for the constituent congress to be formed following its summoning. A new article

10 was included, which allowed the pronunciados and others to make further modifications to the plan should the majority of the nation deem it desirable.[113]

It proved to be the beginning of the end for Santa Anna's last government. By 1854 his dictatorship had succeeded in alienating just about everyone. Many conservatives felt betrayed by the fact that Santa Anna was doing little to pacify the increasing popular discontent, which was threatening to destroy their property. An extraordinary rise in taxes had proven profoundly unpopular with all sectors of society. The moderates and the radicals despised everything about the regime: its constitutional illegality, its repressive measures, and the government's preposterous levels of corruption. The sale of La Mesilla, paired with the realization that the funds it was meant to generate had been squandered by the spring of 1854, turned even some of Santa Anna's most loyal supporters, such as Antonio Haro y Tamariz, into his enemies. The government's repression had also become intolerable, even for many of those *hombres de bien* who had initially welcomed the arrival of a strong regime.

Santa Anna led three failed expeditions against the Ayutla pronunciados, the first to Acapulco in March–May 1854, the second to Iguala in February 1855, and the third and last to Morelia and Zamora in April–June 1855.[114] At the same time, as it became increasingly obvious to him that it was only a matter of time before his government was overthrown, other pronunciamientos were staged in different parts of the republic, which although responding to the Ayutla goal of bringing down the dictatorship did not necessarily share or support Álvarez or Comonfort's liberal aspirations. As Brian Hamnett reminds us, the "Revolution of Ayutla encompassed a broad coalition of contradictory forces,"

From Forceful Negotiation to Civil War

including what he terms the "Ayutla Conservatives," men such as Chihuahuan landholding general Félix Zuloaga, who joined the insurrection in Michoacán on 18 January 1855.[115]

Further evidence of this is that on 13 May 1855 Santiago Vidaurri, governor of Nuevo León, rose up in arms in Lampazos, and ten days later took over Monterrey, from where he issued the Plan of Monterrey of 24 May. As was noted by Luis Medina Peña, Vidaurri's plan adhered in a roundabout way to the Plan of Ayutla but was ultimately aimed at ensuring his regional dominance over Nuevo León, Coahuila, and Tamaulipas: his plan invited the governments of Tamaulipas and Coahuila to adhere to his cause and, if they believed it appropriate to come together "to form under a sole government a united political body to be respected and feared both by foreigner and Indian."[116] In reaction to Vidaurri's pronunciamiento, the governor of Tamaulipas, Juan José de la Garza, staged his own pronunciamiento, on 13 July 1855, resulting in the violent siege of Ciudad Victoria.[117]

The moment it became known that Santa Anna had left Mexico City in the early hours of 9 August 1855 with a view to abdicating, which he did in a letter written at El Encero three days later, going into exile on 16 August, a further series of pronunciamientos was staged as various political actors and groups vied to take control of the situation. On 13 August Mexico City governor and commander general Rómulo Díaz de la Vega staged the pronunciamiento of the Mexico City garrison, calling on paper to uphold the reformed Plan of Ayutla.[118] He went on to summon a moderado-heavy junta the following day that named former santanista General Martín Carrera provisional president. With the moderates in control of the capital—and Carrera intent on exploiting the situation to secure his own hold on power and prevent Juan

Álvarez and the puros from taking over the government—two further different and simultaneous counterrevolutionary movements found expression.[119] One pronunciamiento constellation was initiated by Haro y Tamariz in San Luis Potosí on 13 August and the other by Manuel Doblado in Piedra Gorda, Guanajuato, on 17 August 1855.[120]

In the pronunciamiento of San Luis Potosí, Haro y Tamariz, together with General Anastasio Parrodi and governor and commander general Francisco Güitian, ceased to recognize Santa Anna as president (art. 1), called for an ad hoc congress to be summoned (art. 2), vowed to defend property, church, and army (art. 3), and invited generals, pronounced forces, departments, and governors to support their cause (arts. 4, 5).[121] The pronunciamiento de Piedra Gorda of the former geography and law teacher-cum-liberal congressional deputy Manuel Doblado, proclaimed four days later, was much more ambiguous in its terms, with a view to taking over the governorship of Guanajuato, which he did on 23 August, overthrowing conservative governor Francisco Pacheco. Doblado opposed Santa Anna and Carrera, inferring that the latter was a product of the fallen dictatorship; and with no mention of the Plan of Ayutla or Juan Álvarez, vaguely called for "honest men whatever their political beliefs or the political party they may have supported, [to] come together with their intelligence [*luces*] and influence to give the republic the kind of government most suited to its circumstances and the opinion and interests of the majority of its inhabitants."[122]

In the end it would come down to Comonfort, who had declared from Guadalajara on 22 August that Juan Álvarez was the rightful interim president of the republic who would succeed in bringing the Ayutla Revolution to an end. Thanks to Comonfort's mili-

tary maneuvers and negotiation skills, Haro, Doblado, and Vidaurri eventually agreed (at least temporarily in the case of Haro)
to put down their arms and accept the Ayutla-inspired government in Mexico City. Carrera, in turn, resigned as president on
11 September and was briefly replaced by Díaz de la Vega, and
on 14 November Álvarez finally marched into the capital, moving into the National Palace.

The liberal government that was formed—presided over briefly
by Álvarez, and then by Comonfort after Álvarez on 11 December 1855 used his emergency powers to name Comonfort as his
successor—was over a period of two years to instigate and implement courageously but also divisively a series of dramatic reforms
that would result in the Mexican midcentury becoming popu-
larly known as the period of the Reforma. Two laws in particular stand out as emblematic of the Ayutlan government's resolve
to bring an end, once and for all, to those elements of society
that dated back to the colonial period and had lingered on into
the independent era: the Juárez Law of 23 November 1855 and
the Lerdo Law of 25 June 1856. The first essentially abolished the
ecclesiastical and military fueros and restricted corporate privileges, aiming to make everyone equal before the law.[123] The second, controversially, made it possible for church properties and
corporate lands to be expropriated and put up for auction.[124] Lerdo's aim was to incentivize the land property market by removing
clerical landownership, turn community peasants into responsible small-property owners, and raise funds for the state with
taxes stemming from the process of expropriation and auction of
communal lands.[125] Equally representative of the puros' reformist agenda if not more so was the constitution that was finally
approved in February 1857, which created a federal political sys-

tem; espoused universal male suffrage; did away with the senate to speed up the pace of reform; and not only ceased to recognize the Roman Catholic faith as Mexico's state religion, with tolerance of none other, but actually granted civil powers the right to intervene in matters of ecclesiastic discipline.[126]

When summarizing the most salient reforms of Álvarez and Comonfort's presidencies (1855–57) one could be forgiven for thinking that their governments were united by their ostensible radical liberal determination to bring about a genuinely transformative change in Mexico's society and political institutions. However, behind the scenes, the in-fighting that went on between radicals and moderates, even within the president's own cabinet, was particularly acute. Comonfort was a moderate president struggling, and failing, to rein in both his more radical ministers' proposals as well as those of the puro-dominated constituent congress. And while the radical liberals clashed with Comonfort, it did not take long for a wide-ranging and varied alliance of conservative forces made up of affronted reactionary army officers, devout Catholic indigenous communities, indignant priests, centralists, monarchists, and nostalgic santanistas to resort to pronouncing against the divided liberal government in Mexico City.

Tomás Mejía pronounced in the Sierra Gorda on 2 December 1855. From Tolimán he called for the restoration of the 1824 Constitution, free state elections, and the defense of clergy and army, abandoned and antagonized by Juan Álvarez's government, which he accused of betraying the aims of the Ayutla Revolution. He invited General José López Uraga to lead his movement.[127] His pronunciamiento was followed by priest Francisco Ortega's plan of Zacapoaxtla, initiated in the Puebla Sierra on 12 December and refusing to recognize the current government on the grounds that it had "falsified the object of the [Ayutla] revolution."[128] As noted earlier, Puebla would go on to witness a year of particularly violent clashes, being subjected to three lengthy sieges in 1856, as first Haro and then Orihuela and Miramón led two major albeit contained conservative rebellions against the national government.[129]

Although moderado government commander Tomás Moreno succeeded in retaking Puebla and forcing the pronunciados to capitulate on 3 December 1856, other conservative pronunciamientos ensued, if anything becoming even more virulent once the 1857 Constitution was inaugurated in February of that year.[130] By the time Comonfort was sworn in as constitutional president in September 1857, having convincingly defeated radical liberal candidate Miguel Lerdo de Tejada in the presidential elections, the number of conservative rebellions was fast proliferating in Mexico's central regions. Four days after inaugurating the constitutional congress on 8 October 1857, Comonfort found himself asking to be awarded emergency powers so that he could deal effectively with the conservative challenges to the national government. With the Cuernavaca garrison up in arms following their pronunciamiento of 16 October 1857 and Mejía succeeding in taking over Querétaro on 2 November, the constitution was shown to be flawed. Not even nine months since it had been approved, congress found itself suspending several of the new charter's articles until 30 April 1858 so that Comonfort could deal speedily with the escalation of conservative uprisings.[131]

That Comonfort disliked the 1857 Constitution was no secret. He believed the country needed a stronger executive that did not have its hands tied by congress. He wanted the president to have the power to veto congressional action when he saw fit.

And he opposed both congressional interference in fiscal affairs as well as the danger of demagoguery that he considered a one-chamber congress to invite. As he would note in retrospect as he attempted to justify his actions of December 1857 from his exile in New York:

> The constitution that was meant to be a rainbow of peace and a fountain of good health . . . was to provoke one of the worst political storms ever to have struck Mexico. With it power was disarmed before its enemies, . . . to abide by it was impossible, its lack of popularity a palpable fact; whichever government tied its fortune to it was a lost government.[132]

Manuel Payno shared Comonfort's misgivings. When asked in October by Comonfort what he thought of the constitution, Payno replied: "I believe that you cannot govern according to its provisions, because the head of an office has perhaps more powers than the Head of the Executive."[133]

The puro-moderado divisions of 1857, between the radical congress and the country's moderate president, in a context in which the conservative reaction to the national government's reforms was escalating across the republic and becoming increasingly aggressive, ultimately led Comonfort to allow himself to be persuaded to take the unprecedented decision of endorsing a pronunciamiento from the National Palace against his own administration. Ironically, this *autogolpe* of sorts was not intended to facilitate the return of the conservatives to power. Quite the opposite: Comonfort and the moderate liberals who orchestrated the pronunciamiento of Tacubaya of 17 December 1857 chose to close down congress and abandon the 1857 Constitution precisely so as to prevent the escalating conservative backlash from triumphing. From where they

From Forceful Negotiation to Civil War

were standing, the constitution made it quite simply impossible for the president to preside.

Therefore on 17 December—following the occupation of the capital by Félix Zuloaga's troops, their closure of congress, and the arrest of both the president of congress and the president of the Supreme Court of Justice, then none other than Benito Juárez—the plan of Tacubaya was circulated, stating that the 1857 Constitution was thereby abolished (art. 1); that Comonfort would remain in place as president (art. 2); that he would summon a new constituent congress in three months' time, whose responsibility it would be to draft a new constitution that would be put to a general vote before being adopted (art. 3); that once the constitution was approved, presidential elections would be held (art. 4); that while this constituent congress was summoned, Comonfort would have the authority to form a temporary council with a representative and substitute for each state (art. 5); and last but not least, that all authorities who opposed this plan would be deposed.[134] As argued by Brian Hamnett, "This was a coup by the moderate Liberals against the radicals of their own movement."[135] And it backfired. Badly.[136]

It quickly became evident that Comonfort's gamble had not inspired the waves of pronunciamientos de adhesión he had hoped it would. If anything, it turned most liberals against him while emboldening the conservative movement. Zuloaga, who had always harbored conservative tendencies anyway, notwithstanding supposedly being a friend of Comonfort's, turned against the isolated president and supported General Juan de la Parra's follow-up pronunciamiento of 11 January 1858, which modified the second article of the Plan of Tacubaya, calling for Zuloaga rather than Comonfort to serve as president.[137] Unable to muster sufficient support to quell the pronunciamiento, despite several days of street fighting in the capital, Comonfort realized the game was up. He negotiated his departure from power and into exile on 21 January, having had the foresight to order the release of Juárez from prison beforehand. As Zuloaga and the conservative forces converged on Mexico City and Comonfort left the country for the United States, Juárez escaped to Guanajuato. There, as the legitimate president of Mexico—given that the constitutional president had stood down, and according to the 1857 Constitution it fell upon the president of the Supreme Court of Justice to step in as acting president—Juárez set up a liberal administration intent on challenging and overcoming the conservative pronunciado-government in Mexico City.[138] It was the beginning of the Civil War of the Reforma (1858–60).

The three-year bloodbath that ensued and tore Mexico apart, with the conservatives in control of the national government in Mexico City and the liberals eventually based in the port of Veracruz, resulted in eight thousand dead and crippling debts. Benito Juárez's legitimate liberal government enjoyed initial victory, and returned to the capital in January 1860, but was then undermined two years later as retaliatory Mexican conservative forces now backed by Napoleon III's French Expeditionary Army restarted the war, resulting in the imposition on the Mexican throne of a woefully deluded Austrian archduke who believed the Mexican people wanted him for their emperor. Juárez would once more be a legitimate president on the run, while conservatives, moderados, and French military forces took the capital. Following five more years of civil conflict in which liberal guerrillas clashed with the imperialist army, Juárez would eventually have Maximilian, Miramón, and Mejía executed on 19 June 1867, applying the law of 25 January 1862, and would see the liberal republic restored in the summer of 1867.[139]

After what amounted to ten years of heightened political violence, what Miguel Galindo y Galindo was to term the Great National Decade (1857–67), Mexico had changed significantly, if not beyond recognition.[140] The mid-nineteenth-century Mexican conservatives, finally and truly defeated, either retreated to the margins of political life or reinvented themselves as Porfirian liberals. Liberalism triumphed and became hegemonic, albeit having assimilated certain traits—such as a defense of order as well as of progress—from its former conservative adversaries. In terms of public institutions, education, and civil society, Mexico became for all intents and purposes a much-proclaimed secular state in which civil marriage and divorce were legal. This did not mean that in the private sphere the proud anti-clerical liberals of Benito Juárez's generation ceased to be devout churchgoing Roman Catholics. Universal male suffrage was guaranteed, moreover—even though elections could quite often be rigged, as would become evident under General Porfirio Díaz (1876–1910). Freedom of the press was safeguarded. Church and communal lands were expropriated and auctioned. Although the hope was that *campesinos* would seize on the opportunity to become small landholders and join a growing responsible liberal middle class, this never quite materialized, as it was the wealthy *hacendados* who made the most of the liberals' land reforms and bought up whatever seized land was made available. The army was professionalized. The visceral political divisions of the early national period faded away at a government level, at least comparatively, in a regime that prided itself on its philosophy of "plenty of administration, no politics." Antiquated traditional political norms and customs, the notorious fueros, were finally put to rest. Material progress, in contrast, advocated zealously from a positivist ideological standpoint, became the be all and end all of the triumphant liberal governments of the last decades of the nineteenth century. Train tracks were laid down at a breathtaking pace, fast uniting the nation. Silver mining thrived again. Mexico was even able to pay off, in 1884, the debts it owed British investors dating back to 1824. After Porfirio Díaz rose to power in 1876 and managed, at least for a couple of decades, to give the country a degree of stability unlike anything that had been experienced before, allowing his propagandists to claim that Mexico came to enjoy the benefits of a so-called *pax porfiriana*, pronunciamientos became few and far between, a thing of the past.[141]

In many ways the Plan of Tacubaya, with the ensuing bloodshed of the War of the Reforma and the French Intervention, marked the end of the era of the pronunciamiento. In part it could be argued that Mexicans came to suffer, understandably, from pronunciamiento-fatigue. In part the way violence spiraled out of control after 1857 also resulted in any potential pronunciado of the 1870s or 1880s thinking twice before gathering the local garrison, town council, and community and calling for the government to listen to him "or else." The days of negotiating forcefully were gone. Pronunciados now got shot. However, also important, as persuasively argued by Erika Pani, was the manner in which the 1857 Constitution, "in the heat of [the war of the French Intervention], was transformed from a controversial, often unpopular document into the flag of Liberalism and patriotic resistance. This certainly contributed to its consolidation as the framework for political contention until 1917."[142]

As seen in this chapter, the demise of the pronunciamiento was also due in part to the way this insurrectionary practice changed in the 1840s–1850s. On the one hand, pronunciamientos clearly ceased to be about negotiation. They were, in their great majority, openly committed to overthrowing the government. The pronunciamiento of Guadalajara of 2 November 1844 that brought an end to Santa Anna's 1843–44 government called for the president to be removed from office and brought to justice. Joaquín Rangel's plan of 7 June 1845, which he issued as he stormed the National Palace and took Herrera prisoner, demanded that the president be replaced by the president of the Supreme Court of Justice. The Plan of San Luis Potosí of 14 December 1845 that succeeded in overthrowing José Joaquín de Herrera's moderate administration (1844–45) six months later protested against the president and congress and stated—not demanded but *stated*—that they ceased to be recognized in post. The Plan of the Ciudadela of 4 August 1846, which in turn brought down General Paredes y Arrillaga's government (1845–46), likewise ceased to recognize the incumbent president and congress as being legitimate. The first plan of the Polkos of 27 February 1847, in identical fashion, claimed in its first article that "the Legislative and Executive cease most certainly in their general functions for being unworthy of the nation's trust." The 1852 Plan del Hospicio that eventually resulted in the end of Mariano Arista's government (1851–53) mirrored the demands of the preceding plans of San Luis Potosí (1845), Ciudadela (1846), and Polkos (1847) in claiming in its second article that "all the political powers that are deemed unworthy of the nation's trust cease to exercise their respective functions." The plans of Ayutla of 1 and 11 March 1854 claimed that Santa Anna was to cease to serve as president with immediate effect, again for having proven himself unworthy of the nation. And although the plan of Tacubaya of 17 December 1857 initially avoided calling for the removal of the president, its follow-up pronunciamiento of 11 January 1858 did so. The only aspect about the national pronunciamientos of the 1840s–50s that differentiated them from a straightforward unashamed coup d'état was their recourse to seek in the elicited waves or constellations of pronunciamientos de adhesión a supposed legitimacy they would otherwise not have had. In this sense, they continued to cling to the notion that they represented the will of the people or the general will.

As social theorist Norbert Elias was to note when discussing the perpetuation of collective violence in Germany, "the use of violence by a particular group against another gives rise with a high degree of probability to the use of violence by the other group against the former, as soon as there is the slightest chance to do so. The violence of the second group then in many cases triggers off increased violence from the first group. If such a process, a double-bind process, is once set in motion, then it is exceedingly difficult to halt; it often gains a momentum of its own."[143] Thinking of the retaliatory nature of the pronunciamientos of the 1840s–50s, and the insurrectionary mimeticism that characterized them, it can be confidently asserted that this proved determining in leading the country to civil war while wresting from the pronunciamiento practice itself those negotiating qualities that had characterized it in the 1820s and '30s. After over a decade of barely disguised coups, escalating violence, and a tit-for-tat vicious circle in which moderados, puros, conservatives, and santanistas avenged one another's preceding pronunciamiento cycle with a pronunciamiento of their own, there was no going back to a time when governments occasionally listened to pronounced garrisons and communities without being overthrown,

From Forceful Negotiation to Civil War

and when pronunciados could actually be forgiven for their insurrectionary indiscretions.[144]

On the other hand and at the other end of the spectrum, in rural Mexico the pronunciamientos of the 1840s–50s became less about addressing the concerns of the hombres de bien, or those of ambitious disgruntled army officers, and more about addressing acute social grievances, injustices, and inequality. In the Sierra Gorda and Yucatán, pronunciamiento politics were overtaken or enveloped by aggressive agrarian, peasant, and indigenous revolutionary movements. These popular revolts retained the petitioning format of the pronunciamiento in some of the protests and calls to arms that they generated, but again negotiation was no longer an aim. The agrarian and indigenous rebels of the 1840s–50s wanted justice, and they wanted it now. As Shara Ali has argued, in the case of Yucatán the pronunciamientos of the 1830s and early 1840s provided a school of sorts for insurrectionists, giving the Maya the revolutionary language, practices, and strategies they would go on to appropriate and make their own when they finally rose up against the white elites of the peninsula in the Caste War of 1847–52.[145] However, by the time they revolted, as noted by Terry Rugeley, what characterized those "among the long oppressed" who took up arms was not so much an appetite for dialogue but a mood of revolutionary "euphoria born of cathartic violence."[146]

After the Liberal Restoration of 1867 Mexico would witness only one successful national pronunciamiento: that of Tuxtepec of 10 January 1876, in which Porfirio Díaz, claiming to defend the ignored 1857 Constitution (art. 1), demanded in much the same way that the pronunciamientos of the 1840s and '50s had done that the president, Sebastián Lerdo de Tejada, and his government stand down (art. 3), because of their illegal and unconstitutional reelection (art. 2). Following eleven months of conflict, the rebellion of Tuxtepec culminated with the exile of Lerdo de Tejada, Díaz's entrance into Mexico City on 23 November, and the beginning of his remarkably long stint in power (1876–1910).

Francisco I. Madero's Plan of San Luis Potosí of 5 October 1910, which would call in its seventh article for Mexicans to rise up in arms against Díaz's government on 20 November at 6:00 p.m., initiating what would become the Mexican Revolution (1910–20), albeit written in petitioned form echoing the nineteenth-century pronunciamiento format, unambiguously called for armed revolution, not forceful negotiation. The same could be said for Emiliano Zapata's Plan of Ayala of 25 November 1911. It was written like a pronunciamiento, but it offered no space for compromise. It demanded that Madero "and the other dictatorial individuals of the current and old regime" be removed from office (arts. 2, 14) alongside calls for the redistribution of land (arts. 6–9).[147] There is no doubt that the memory of pronunciamiento politics informed Madero and Zapata's drafting of their respective plans and has remained intriguingly a part of Mexico's insurrectionary political tradition. As recently as 1994 the Zapatista uprising in Chiapas witnessed the circulation of a pronunciamiento-styled Plan of the Lacandón Jungle, which Subcomandante Marcos circulated using the Internet, calling for the removal of the "dictator" Carlos Salinas de Gortari.[148]

However, the pronunciamiento, as an originally liberal political practice that evolved from Riego's successful pronunciamiento of 1 January 1820 and was adopted in Mexico following the success of the Plan of Iguala, ceased to be employed after 1858 to lobby, address and rectify constitutional failings, call despotic govern-

From Forceful Negotiation to Civil War

ments to order, replace unworkable political systems, or revoke unjust or unrepresentative laws and arbitrary measures. It was no longer used to remove unpopular ministers, state governors, and politicians; to summon a new constituent congress, call new elections, or restore the interrupted constitutional order; or to give voice to an ignored, misrepresented, and mistreated general will, allowing the disenfranchised a means to participate in national politics. At least it was no longer used in that way, by those actors, for those reasons. As seen in this chapter, in great measure this was as a result of the way the pronunciamiento evolved into little else than a disguised coup d'etat. Beyond the bloodshed of the midcentury Reform period and following the consolidation of a stable government, founded on a resilient albeit reformed 1857 Constitution, there was no longer the appetite or the need for pronunciamiento politics. Thereafter Mexicans would engage in the political life of the republic either by constitutional means or through outright rebellion, at least until the failings of the last years of the Porfirian regime provoked the full-scale revolution of 1910, giving way to yet another cycle of horrendous violence.

Conclusion

Mimetic Insurrectionism, the Pronunciamiento,
and Independent Mexico

F ollowing the success of the pronunciamiento of Cabezas de
San Juan in Spain of 1 January 1820 and that of Iguala of 24
February 1821, the insurrectionary model of the pronunciamiento went on to be adopted in Mexico by high-ranking officers,
civilian politicians, regional and state authorities, town councils,
and eventually a whole array of individuals, groups, and communities as the new country's incipient political class struggled to
find a constitutional model that was long-lasting. With a government that lacked authority and legitimacy, the pronunciamiento,
as a practice, method, or course of action, became without question the most common and widespread means of bringing about
meaningful political change in Independent Mexico. It emerged
and developed alongside the incipient country's early constitutions, at times even becoming confused with as well as entan-
gled in the supposed lawful processes of the new nation-state.
Mexicans pronounced as much to save the constitution from a
government's abuses as because the constitution did not work. It
almost goes without saying that at one point or another, everybody who was somebody pronounced. It is difficult to think of
any major politician or high-ranking officer from Independent
Mexico who did not participate at some point in a given pronunciamiento cycle, even though of course there were a princi-

pled few who did not.[1] What can be stated unequivocally is that at one point or another absolutely everyone benefited, suffered, or was affected, on an individual or communal level, by a given pronunciamiento cycle. There was no escaping the phenomenon.

Between 1821 and 1858 more than 1,350 separate individual pronunciamientos were launched, whether these were what I have here defined as start-up pronunciamientos, follow-up pronunciamientos, pronunciamientos de adhesión, counterpronunciamientos, or despronunciamientos (out of the 1,500 in the AHRC–St. Andrews database for 1821–76). The figures in themselves are staggering. There were no less than *fifteen* pronunciamiento constellations that engaged with national concerns, spread across several states or regions, and were actually successful, dramatically impacting Mexican politics four times in the 1820s, three times in the 1830s, five in the 1840s, and three more in the 1850s.[2] In terms of pronunciamiento cycles that engaged with national concerns, spread across several states or regions, but failed to achieve their aims, there was a not insignificant total of *eight*, which, failure notwithstanding, still affected the communities where they took place once in the 1820s, three times in the 1830s, and four times in the 1840s.[3] For pronunciamientos that engaged with national concerns, did not spread beyond the region from where they were launched, but were still successful, there were *two* particularly dramatic cycles, which understandably took place in Mexico City, in 1822 and 1847.[4] As for pronunciamiento clusters that engaged with national concerns, failed to spread beyond their region of origin, and were quelled, there were *ten* that, again despite failure, inevitably shook their respective provinces or cities three times each in the 1820s and 1830s and twice each in the 1840s and 1850s.[5] And there were *three* notorious pronunciamiento cycles that engaged with national concerns, failed to spread beyond their region, but succeeded in reordering the local political scene in Texas in 1835–36, and in Yucatán in 1829 and 1840.[6] In the case of Texas there would be no looking back.

In a book concerned with national pronunciamientos there has not been the time or space to dwell in equal measure or with comparable detail and attention to the numerous pronunciamientos that were engaged with strictly regional concerns. Although to date research has been undertaken by scholars such as Shara Ali, Rosie Doyle, and Kerry McDonald on the pronunciamientos of given regions, resulting in entire studies being dedicated to the experience of the pronunciamiento in Yucatán, Jalisco, and San Luis Potosí, we are still awaiting the study of pronunciamiento-prone states such as Puebla, Tamaulipas, and Veracruz as well as of pronunciamiento-shy states like Durango, Guanajuato, and Querétaro. I cannot therefore provide an accurate number for the pronunciamientos that were launched between 1821 and 1858 by local political actors with the sole purpose of reordering the local political scene or addressing very specific regional grievances.[7] A superficial glance at the regional pronunciamientos of the period would appear to confirm there were indeed many. The pronunciamiento, whether it was adopted to negotiate forcefully with the national government or with the local authorities (and quite often it was with both), was as much a prominent feature of political life in the capital as it was in provincial Mexico.

In bringing together in these concluding pages all the types of pronunciamiento clusters Mexico witnessed during these years, it becomes overwhelmingly evident that the pronunciamiento was the most salient, dominant, and important political practice of Independent Mexico. Its frequency is certainly striking.

Between 1821 and 1858, not a year passed in which a pronunciamiento was not recorded in some part of the republic. To put it differently, between 1821 and 1858, in a period spanning less than four decades, thirty-seven years to be precise, there were only four years in which the Mexican national government was not actually challenged or lobbied by a given pronunciamiento cycle: 1825, 1826, 1831, and 1850. One can almost forgive an outsider like Kentucky volunteer and prisoner of war William W. Carpenter for thinking that Mexicans were "incapable of governing themselves," as "their past history plainly shows," with "these frequent pronunciamientos" and "annual revolution[s]."[8]

The dynamic of the pronunciamiento, moreover, was clearly one that engendered more pronunciamientos. It very obviously became *the* way to do politics, *the* way to address constitutional failings and contest arbitrary policies; to inspire new laws, policies, and reforms; to remove unpopular politicians; and in the long run to promote and support the rise *and* fall of a plethora of ambitious officers. Once one pronunciamiento worked, others took to pronouncing. There was no turning the clock back.

The context that gave rise to the pronunciamiento, as discussed in chapters 1 and 2, was definitely one of acute instability, contested authority, and blurred legitimacies. The constitutional vacuum that resulted from Mexico's separation from Spain, paired with the inability of the political class to forge a long-lasting constitutional order, gave way to four decades of pronounced political vigilantism. Paradoxically, although most pronunciamientos were launched with a view to addressing and correcting Mexico's constitutional failures, they in turn made the establishment of any long-term constitutional system near impossible. Having been seen to be the most effective way of bringing about swift and meaningful political change, both at a national and at a regional level, the pronunciamiento as a practice went on to be adopted by just about everyone at some point or other. It became unquestionably the preferred option, despite the regular laments Mexicans proffered about their country's repeated "revolutions." Time and again the pronunciamiento was chosen over waiting for the next round of elections to vote out any allegedly despotic government, or over proposing reforms via established institutional channels using peaceful and constitutionally recognized means.

As argued in chapters 2 and 3, the way the pronunciamiento spread as a practice in the 1820s and '30s is an eloquent example of what I have termed mimetic insurrectionism. In the first instance it spread because it worked. Presented with an example of *successful* insurrectionary activity, first in Cabezas de San Juan, and then in Iguala, Mexicans took to mimicking it by applying its methods and model to their own particular and local contexts. But mimetic insurrectionism, as a phenomenon, also occurred and spread in Mexico because of the very nature and dynamics of the pronunciamiento, in part because the practice itself, with its required pronunciamientos de adhesión, relied on and encouraged the launch and circulation of copycat pronunciamientos. However, it also spread because, with a number of important exceptions, it was understood to be a relatively peaceful, albeit intimidating, form of aggressive petitioning. Unlike a full-blown bloody revolution or even a straightforward armed rebellion, the pronunciamiento was more about insurrectionary posturing, issuing revolutionary threats, and waiting for outcomes, rather than violently attacking and harming the members of a given government or community. It entailed listening too, reaching compromises, changing one's original demands in the light of however many pronunciamientos de adhesión a given pronunciado or group of pronunciados received or did not receive, as evidenced in the emergence of subsequent follow-up pronunciamientos as well as despronunciamientos. As seen in chapter 3, the fact that the pronunciamiento served the interests of the regional elites in renegotiating their political position vis-à-vis the center was also critical in its early proliferation in 1820s provincial Mexico. A decade later, as explored in chapter 4, the pronunciamiento had gone viral, coming to be adopted by a whole range of subaltern political actors and turning into the favored means of engaging with politics not just for soldiers and civilians and *hombres de bien* but also for the disenfranchised.

Linked to mimetic insurrectionism and the popularization of the pronunciamiento, what this monograph has also shown is that as a practice, the pronunciamiento evolved. On the one hand, it evolved in terms of who pronounced; what could be controversially described as the democratization of the pronunciamiento. From being very much an elite-led practice in the 1820s, instigated and promoted by senior army officers in collusion with well-to-do-politicians, priests, and businessmen, with its game theory dynamics and gentlemanly agreements whereby pronunciados and fallen governments were generally amnestied or forgiven, the pronunciamiento went on to be adopted in the 1830s by aggrieved *campesinos*, indigenous groups, and even, in one instance, a group of defiant *zacatlanqueña* women. On the other hand, this particular insurrectionary practice evolved in terms of how it was employed. In the 1820s and 1830s it very evidently served pronunciados to negotiate forcefully with those in power. There was a definite lobbying dimension to the pronunciamiento as it relied on its legitimizing constellation of pronunciamientos de adhesión to force the government to listen. To note four obvious examples where, without the need to overthrow the government, given waves of pronunciamientos succeeded in getting either congress or the president to legislate in favor of the pronunciados' demands: there were those that called for the expulsion of the Spanish population from Mexico in 1827, the annulment of the results of the 1828 presidential elections, a stop to congress's rampant reformism in 1834, and the abolition of the 1824 Constitution in 1835. The pronunciamientos of the 1820s and '30s were not really about regime change, even if many did result in the overthrow of given governments. However, by the 1840s this was no longer the case. From pronunciamientos seldom calling for the country's leading magistrate to stand down (before 1840, only Santa Anna's address of 2 December 1822 had done so), they became almost exclusively about overthrowing the government after the Triangular Revolt of 1841. In fact, it could be argued that it was the retaliatory nature of the 1840s–50s national pronunciamientos that ultimately led to the Civil War of the Reforma. With political violence becoming an increasingly terrifying component of the practice, leaving no room for consensus, compromise, or negotiation, all of which had been integral characteristics of the pronunciamiento practice of the 1820s–30s, it is perhaps not surprising that the original appeal of these "gestures of rebellion" gradually faded away. Although mimetic insurrectionism can still be seen to be a recurrent phenomenon in other countries in the present day, with Mexico, after the pronunciamiento degenerated into the coups, revolutions, and counter-coups and revolutions of the 1840s–50s, culminating in the sanguinary civil war of 1858–60 and the ensuing French Intervention, 1862–67, it ceased to prosper.[9]

The themes of the pronunciamientos—what they were about, the grievances that lay at the heart of them, that they were launched with a view to addressing, resolving, or correcting—also changed and evolved with time, reflecting the evolution of Mexico's political ideas and movements. As explored in chapter 3, the majority of pronunciamientos that were launched between 1821 and 1831 were instigated by the provinces against the center to protect or extend their provincial political authority. Federalism proved a major concern. In Mexico's first independent decade more than nine pronunciamiento cycles were federalist in one form or another. The Plan of Campeche of 6 November 1829 (without counting the Plan of Guadalajara of 27 November 1829, because it did not get beyond the conspiracy stage) was the only centralist pronunciamiento of this decade. The number of anti-Spanish plans was also significant, although these were not as numerous as the federalist ones, with there having been more than six individual start-up pronunciamientos during these years. Therefore, if pronunciamiento demands are anything to go by, the two most pressing issues of the 1820s, once the republic was consolidated, were the regions' need for greater control over their domestic affairs and the Mexicans' drive to expel the supposedly ungrateful, reactionary, and plotting Spanish population from Mexico.

Interestingly, by the 1830s these concerns had changed and expanded beyond the ongoing defense of regional sovereignty and federalism, becoming noticeably concerned with centralism, church-state relations (and by inference religion), and the need to protect core values and customs that started to be seen as essential aspects of an as yet undefined and incipient threatened Mexican national identity. The perceived flaws and weaknesses of the 1824 Constitution thus gave way to a decade in which, contrast-

ingly, centralist pronunciamientos became as common as federalist ones, if not more so. The popular defense of clerical values,
fueros, and institutions in response to the 1833–34 Congress's perceived ungodly anti-clericalism became, moreover, one of the most
impacting political impulses of the decade, and with it came a
quest to understand what the new nation's core values and customs involved. By the 1840s, as evidenced in chapter 5, more than
being about political ideas (although the federalist-centralist divide
remained a burning issue), pronunciamientos proved to be essentially just about overthrowing whoever was in power, with the
moderados determined to bring down their liberal cousins, the
puros, and vice versa, and showing an unexpected disposition to
link up with such unlikely bedfellows as the conservatives and
the *santanistas* at given junctures. By the late 1850s the different
cycles of political violence had come to mirror and exacerbate
what were by then irreconcilable liberal-conservative standpoints.

A study of Mexico's pronunciamientos also highlights how fluid
the different factions' alliances were. Yet certain patterns can be
seen to emerge, with it becoming particularly clear that despite
the shared liberal ideology of moderados and puros, these distinct
liberal parties were profoundly divided. Their opposition was, in
fact, strong enough for them to have allied themselves with either
the santanistas or the conservatives to challenge or overthrow
each other from positions of national or regional power. Puros
thus linked up with santanistas to overthrow Herrera's 1845 government, and with santanistas and conservatives to bring down
Mariano Arista in 1852–53. The moderados proved no different,
being prepared to appeal to Santa Anna to remove Gómez Farías
as acting vice president in 1847 and to join up with the conservatives to abolish the 1857 Constitution and close down the puro-

dominated congress in 1857. Moderados and puros joined forces only twice, against Paredes y Arrillaga in 1846 and against Santa Anna in 1854–55. Even then, during the Revolution of Ayutla, theirs was a particularly fragile alliance in which a moderado such as Martín Carrera tried to hijack the movement against Santa Anna's dictatorship from Mexico City.

Although this book was originally conceived as a study of this particularly intriguing insurrectionary practice, preoccupied with how and why it started, evolved, and became highly contagious, I am very aware that I have inadvertently ended up writing a concise history of Independent Mexico, 1821–58. In analyzing Mexico's pronunciamientos, and in my attempt to provide the historical background behind the hundreds of *gritos* that were experienced during the early national period, I have inevitably concerned myself with the different governments and political movements that came and went between the consummation of independence and the advent of the "Great National Decade." This should not surprise us. It is in itself eloquently indicative of how important the pronunciamiento was during these years, of how most Mexicans pronounced at one stage or another, of how almost every single significant change that took place, both nationally and at a regional level, was informed or determined by pronunciamiento pressure. The pronunciamiento ultimately became indistinguishable from, and intricately as well as integrally part of, Mexico's difficult constitutional and political evolution during its early national period. To study the pronunciamiento has been, in essence, to study the politics of Independent Mexico. The two endeavors have proven meaningfully and intimately interconnected. To think about Independent Mexico is thus to think about the pronunciamiento, and to think about the pronunciamiento is to think about Independent Mexico. What remains yet to be researched is how it spread, evolved, and impacted the politics of provincial Mexico, from a regional perspective, in a number of all-important states. I leave it to others to take up the challenge to do so, hoping this volume assists them with a helpful starting point and a clear sense of how important the pronunciamiento was and how, as a practice and a phenomenon, it determined the course of Mexican politics after independence.

Notes

1. "Soft" Coups, Occupations, and "Gestures of Rebellion"

1. The elected prime minister, Adolfo Suárez, had decided to resign twenty-five days earlier. On 23 February 1981 the Cortes was assembled, for a second time, to vote over whether Leopoldo Calvo Sotelo was the right man to replace Suárez, having failed to give him a majority on 20 February.

2. The extraordinary footage of the first half hour of the coup can be seen on YouTube: http://www.rtve.es/alacarta/videos/programa/archivo-asalto-tejero-congreso-23–1981/392929/.

3. Fowler, "Introduction: Understanding Individual and Collective Insurrectionary Action," in Fowler, *Malcontents*.

4. Carlton, *State against the State*, 2, 5. For a classic study on coups d'état, see Luttwak, *Coup d'état*.

5. Worthy of note is that although the action of 11 September 1973 was clearly a coup d'état, its perpetrators preferred to call it a "pronunciamiento militar." By implication, the term *golpe* was in some form tainted for Augusto Pinochet and his *golpistas*. Calling their coup a pronunciamiento clearly appeared to grant their action a certain gravitas and air of legitimacy in their minds. See the junta's *Libro blanco del cambio de gobierno en Chile*, where it is stressed that theirs was *not* "un típico 'cuartelazo,' desatado por militares ambiciosos" (5).

6. A great many books have been written about the coup of 11 September 1973, and it is not possible for me to attempt to provide a comprehensive bibliography here on the subject. However, thinking of first-time students of Latin American history, the following titles should serve as a helpful starting point when trying to understand the events that led to and that resulted from the overthrow of Salvador Allende's government: Falcoff, *Modern Chile*; Alexander, *The Tragedy of Chile*; Arriagada, *Pinochet*; and MacEoin, *Chile*. For an extraordinary study of how Chileans have subsequently struggled

with the trauma and memory of Pinochet's Chile, see Steve J. Stern's trilogy *The Memory Box of Pinochet's Chile*, which consists of *Remembering Pinochet's Chile, Battling for Hearts and Minds*, and *Reckoning with Pinochet*. For a contemporary visual record of the months leading up to the coup, watch Patricio Guzmán's haunting two-part documentary *La batalla de Chile* (1977–78). With regard to the Honduran coup of 28 June 2009, at the time of writing, it is still too recent for any serious academic study to have been published about it. However, a number of academic events were organized to reflect on its cause and effect, such as the symposium "The Coup in Honduras and the Implications for Latin America," which Barry Cannon, Mo Hume, and Marina Prieto Carrón convened at the 2010 Annual Conference of the Society for Latin American Studies held in Bristol, 9–10 April 2010. The University of St. Andrews had the privilege of being addressed by Honduran women's rights activists Evelyn Cuellar and Mercedes Lainez from the Centro de Estudios de la Mujer—Honduras (CEM-H), accompanied by Katherine Ronderos, program and advocacy coordinator for Central America Women's Network (CAWN), on 8 April 2011, who rendered a highly disturbing account of how women's rights have suffered immensely as a direct result of the coup. Also see Cáceres di Lorio, *The Good Coup*.

7. Cercas, *Anatomía de un instante*, 404.

8. Cercas, *Anatomía de un instante*, 86.

9. See "Bando del General Milans del Bosch en Valencia" and "Manifiesto de Tejero," in Busquets et al., *El Golpe*, 77–78, 89.

10. The text of King Juan Carlos's TV address is included in Busquets et al., *El Golpe*, 71–72.

11. Http://en.wikipedia.org/wiki/Pronunciamiento.

12. Baquer, *El modelo español de pronunciamiento*, 40.

13. For information on the 15-M movement in Spain, see the protestors' online newspaper *15-M News* at http://madrid.tomalaplaza.net/files/2011/06/15m-news.pdf and their e-book *¡Indignados! 15-M* (Madrid: www.MandalaEdiciones.com, 2011).

14. "US 'Occupy' Protests Spread to 70 Cities," *Observer*, 9 October 2011.

15. For a thought-provoking journalistic analytical response to the "new global revolutions" of 2011, see Mason, *Why It's Kicking Off Everywhere*. Interestingly, following a similar line of thought to Javier Cercas, only in Mason's case with reference to the fall of Mubarak on 11 February 2011, he argues that this came about as a result of "a soft coup" (17).

16. Costeloe, "A Pronunciamiento," 245.

17. I discuss this in "Introduction: The Nineteenth-Century Practice," in Fowler, *Forceful Negotiations*, xv–xvi.

18. Article 4 of the Plan of Iguala stated: "4. Fernando VII y en sus casos los de su dinastía o de otra reinante serán los emperadores, para hallarnos con un monarca ya hecho y precaver los atentados de ambición." The Plan of Iguala of 24 February 1821 is located in the Archivo General de la Nación (hereafter cited as AGN): Impresos Oficiales, vol. 60, núm. 62. All pronunciamiento texts cited in this volume can be accessed online at http://arts.st-andrews.ac.uk /pronunciamientos/.

19. Article 3 of the Treaty of Córdoba stated: "3. Será llamado a reinar en el Imperio mexicano (previo el juramento que designa el artículo 4 del Plan) en primer lugar el señor don Fernando VII, rey católico de España, y por su renuncia o no admisión, el serenísimo señor Infante don Francisco de Paula; por su renuncia o no admisión, el serenísimo señor don Carlos Luis, infante de España, antes heredero de Etruria, hoy de Luca y por renuncia o no admisión de éste, el que las Cortes del Imperio designaren." The Treaty of Córdoba of 24 August 1821 is reproduced in De la Torre, *La independencia de México*, 278–81.

20. My emphasis. The "Proclama Iturbidista" of 19 May 1822 can be accessed at http://arts.st-andrews.ac.uk/pronunciamientos/dates.php?f=y&pid =742&m=5&y=1822.

21. The Acta de Tlalmanalco stated that "todos de esos mismos sentimientos declararon libre y espontáneamente que secundan el expresado Plan y Pronunciamiento de la Villa de Cuernavaca, adhiriéndose en un todo a los cinco artículos que contiene sin alterarlo en nada de lo substancial, y solo por cuanto a que no hay en esta municipalidad ninguna guarnición se sustituye al articulo 5° el siguiente: Que para contribuir al sostenimiento de las providencias que dicte el Excmo. señor don Antonio López de Santa-Anna, primer magistrado de la federación de conformidad con las ideas que van expresadas se le ofrece la eficaz cooperación de todos los ciudadanos vecinos de esta municipalidad quienes se prestarán de la mejor manera que les sea posible a dicho sostenimiento."

22. My emphasis. The "Acta de Tlalmanalco" of 6 June 1834 is located in AGN: Gobernación, 1834, s/s, caja 206, f. 26.

23. The "Acta de la guarnición de Veracruz y fortaleza de San Juan de Ulúa" of 12 January 1832 is located in Colección Josefina Z. Vázquez, Planes y Documentos, 1832, Archivo Histórico del Colegio de México, caja 6.

24. *El Censor*, 8 January 1832.

25. The "Plan de Lerma" of 27 April 1832 is reproduced in Vázquez (ed.), *Planes en la nación mexicana*, vol. 2, 120.

26. For studies on the 1832 pronunciamiento cycle, see Rodríguez O. "The Origins of the 1832 Rebellion," and Vázquez, "Los pronunciamientos de 1832," both in Rodríguez O. (ed.), *Patterns of Contention*, 145–62, 163–86, respectively. My "Joseph Welsh: A British *Santanista* (Mexico, 1832)," offers an analysis of how the British consul in Veracruz decided to support the pronunciamiento actively. The 1832 Civil War is clearly and succinctly explained in Costeloe, *La primera república federal*, 327–49. It is also studied from Santa Anna's perspective in my *Santa Anna of Mexico*, 133–43.

27. The "Acta de la fortaleza de San Diego" of 11 August 1832 is located in Colección Josefina Z. Vázquez, Planes y Documentos, 1832, Archivo Histórico del Colegio de México, caja 6.

28. In alphabetical order: Ali, "The Pronunciamiento in Yucatán (1821–1840)"; Doyle, "The Pronunciamiento in Nineteenth-Century Mexico"; and McDonald, "The Experience of the Pronunciamiento in San Luis Potosí, 1821–1849." Also see McDonald, "Los inicios del pronunciamiento en San Luis Potosí," in Mendoza, *12 Ensayos*, and McDonald, "The Origins of the Pronunciamientos of San Luis Potosí," in Fowler, *Forceful Negotiations*, 101–24.

29. As may be seen in the database "The Pronunciamiento in Independent Mexico 1821–1876," for the months of January–March 1832, there are thirty-seven pronunciamientos de rechazo that have been transcribed and digitized and that can be accessed online. Arts and Humanities Research Council (AHRC)–University of St. Andrews web-based database, http://arts.st-andrews.ac.uk/pronunciamientos/.

30. Archivo Histórico de la Secretaría de la Defensa Nacional, Mexico City (hereafter cited as AHSDN): XI/481.3/803, f.118: "Acta de la guarnición de Veracruz y de la fortaleza de Ulúa reiterando el Plan de Veracruz y desconociendo el gobierno de Bustamante, 5 de julio de 1832."

31. AGN: Gobernación, 1832, s/c, caja 17, holds the original pronunciamiento of Tancahuitz of 8 April 1832. The despronunciamiento of 1 June 1832 is located in AHSDN: XI/481.3/781, ff. 29–30.

32. The "Petición de Miguel Barragán" of 17 November 1830 is located in Colección Josefina Z. Vázquez, Planes y Documentos, 1830 y 1831, Archivo Histórico del Colegio de México, caja 5.

33. AHSDN: XI/481.3/839, f. 112: "Acta del ayuntamiento de San Juan Bautista en apoyo al gobierno y denunciando el Plan de Veracruz, 1 de febrero de 1832."

34. *Diario del Gobierno*, 17 October 1838. The document—"Crítica del manifiesto y pronunciamiento de Tampico" (7 October 1838)—can also be accessed at http://arts.st-andrews.ac.uk/pronunciamientos/dates.php?f=y&pid =148&m=10&y=1838.

35. See my "'As Empty a Piece of Gasconading Stuff,'" in Fowler, *Celebrating Insurrection*.

36. Stealey (ed.), *Porte Crayon's Mexico*, 529.

37. Proust, *Remembrance of Things Past*, book 3: *The Guermantes Way*, 2:250.

38. Boyd, "Contemporary Verdicts," in Fowler, *Celebrating Insurrection*, 172.

39. Isabel Allende, "Chile under the Gun," *Independent, Extra*, 12 December 2006.

40. E. Bradford Burns's argument that caudillos, "whether we like it or not and whether the leaders of the central governments of the day liked or not, were the legitimate and perhaps natural leaders—the voices—of their home provinces," is suggestively taken up by Timothy E. Anna in *Forging Mexico 1821–1835*, 22.

41. For two recent volumes that engage with the extent to which the 1812 Cádiz Constitution impacted upon Mexico during and after the War of Independence through the creation of ayuntamientos, see Ortiz Escamilla and Serrano Ortega (eds.), *Ayuntamientos y liberalismo gaditano en México*, and Salinas Sandoval et al., *Poder y gobierno local en México*. For a study on how and why ayuntamientos adopted the pronunciamiento model from the regional perspective of Tlaxcala, see Buve, "Ayuntamientos and Pronunciamientos," in Fowler, *Malcontents*.

42. Caplan, *Indigenous Citizens*, 50.

43. For a study that shows how Brigadier de la Cruz, as military comandante general of Nueva Galicia and president of the Audiencia from 1811 to 1821, became "something of a prototype for the provincial caudillo," see Archer, "Politicization of the Army of New Spain."

44. For two studies that show how Joaquín de Arredondo became a force unto himself in Nuevo Santander and the Provincias Internas de Oriente, see Andrews and Hernández Jaimes, "La lucha por la supervivencia," and Jáuregui, "Las tareas y tribulaciones de Joaquín de Arredondo," both in Ibarra (ed.), *La independencia en el septentrión de la Nueva España*.

45. *El Aguila Mexicana*, 9 September 1828.

46. The "Plan de Perote" of 16 September 1828 is reproduced in Jiménez Codinach (ed.), *Planes en la Nación Mexicana*, 1:209–10.

47. *El Regulador Yucateco*, 16 June 1832.

48. See Ducey, "Municipalities, Prefects, and Pronunciamientos: Power and Political Mobilizations in the Huasteca during the First Federal Republic," in Fowler, *Forceful Negotiations*, for a study that shows how national pronunciamientos could have entirely unintended consequences at a local level and how these, in turn, could be extremely violent.

49. I argued as much in my essay "Civil Conflict in Independent Mexico, 1821–57: An Overview."

50. Pérez Galdós, *Tormento* (originally published in 1884), 49: "una voz puramente española, como el vocablo *pronunciamiento*, que está dando la vuelta al mundo y anda ya por los antípodas."

51. Pérez Galdós, *Fortunata y Jacinta*, 2:736: "Los disparates que aquel hombre dijo acerca del *Pronunciamiento* de Francia hicieron reír mucho a todos, particularmente al portero de la Academia de la Historia."

52. Calderón de la Barca, *Life in Mexico*, 412.

53. Of particular note are the following titles: Reina, *Las rebeliones campesinas en México*(1980); Tutino, *From Insurrection to Revolution* (1986); Katz (ed.), *Riot, Rebellion, and Revolution* (1988); Mallon, *Peasant and Nation* (1994); Rugeley, *Yucatán's Maya Peasantry and the Origins of the Caste War* (1996); Ducey, *A Nation of Villages* (2004); Rangel Silva and Ruiz Medrano, *Discursos públicos, negociaciones y estrategias de lucha colectiva* (2006); and Servín et al. (eds.), *Cycles of Conflict* (2007).

54. Timothy E. Anna listed alongside the "chaos school" of scholarship, "the 'disintegration school,' and the 'caudillo school,' (we will not mention the 'Mexicans were congenitally incapable of self government school')," as well as "the 'regionalism makes things too murky for words school,'" as proof of the fact that historians found it hard to understand the imperfect process of "defining, creating, building nationhood." See Anna, "Demystifying Early Nineteenth-Century Mexico," 122.

55. Taken from Edmundo O'Gorman, "Precedentes y Sentido de la Revolución de Ayutla," in *Seis estudios históricos de tema mexicano*, 133, quoted and translated into English in Stevens, *Origins of Instability*, 1–2.

56. These were Comellas, *Los primeros pronunciamientos en España*; Payne, *Politics and the Military in Modern Spain*; Busquets, *Pronunciamientos y golpes*; and Baquer, *El modelo español de pronunciamiento*.

57. The view that the pronunciamiento was an essentially liberal practice, born out of the 1812 Cádiz Constitution's expectation that it was the people's obligation to rebel if the government did not abide by its liberal laws, is shared by Raymond Carr, who noted that "the pronunciamiento was the instrument of liberal revolution in the nineteenth century," in his *Spain 1808–1939*, 124.

58. Comellas, *Los primeros pronunciamientos en España*, 26, 357–61.

59. Payne, *Politics and the Military in Modern Spain*, 15.

60. Busquets, *Pronunciamientos y golpes*, 13–14.

61. These were the pronunciamientos and coups of Francisco Javier Elío (1814), Rafael del Riego (1820), General Quesada (1834), Sergeant García (1836), the Coalicionistas (1843), the Vicalvarada (1854), Francisco Serrano and Juan Prim (1868), Manuel Pavía (1874), Arsenio Martínez Campos (1874), Miguel Primo de Rivera (1923), and Francisco Franco (1936). See Busquets, *Pronunciamientos y golpes*, 28.

62. Baquer, *El modelo español de pronunciamiento*, 40.

63. Baquer, *El modelo español de pronunciamiento*, 10, 15, 17, 20, 30.

64. Baquer, *El modelo español de pronunciamiento*, 15–20, 28–34, 39, 40, 52, 72

65. Baquer, *El modelo español de pronunciamiento*, 41–42, 77.

66. These include Cepeda Gómez, *El ejército español en la política española* and *Los pronunciamientos en la España del siglo XIX*.

67. I am referring here, in chronological order, to the following volumes: Fontana, *La quiebra de la monarquía absoluta* (1971); Blanco Valdés, *Rey, cortes y fuerza armada* (1988); Castells, *La utopía insurrecional del liberalismo* (1989); Castells, "El liberalismo insurreccional español" (2008); and Blanco Valdés, "Paisanos y soldados en los orígenes de la España liberal" (2008).

68. Josefina Zoraida Vázquez's 1980s "Planes" project resulted in the following anthologies, three of which she edited herself, providing particularly useful and detailed introductory chapters: Jiménez Codinach (ed.), *Planes en la Nación Mexicana*; Vázquez (ed.). *Planes en la nación mexicana*, vols. 2, 3, and 4 (1987); and De la Torre Villar (ed.), *Planes en la nación mexicana* (1987). Subsequently Román Iglesias González produced a shorter anthology, yet which spanned until 1940: Iglesias González (ed.). *Planes políticos, proclamas, manifiestos* (1998).

Our own research project, building on the findings made in these anthologies, produced the online relational database "The Pronunciamiento in Independent Mexico, 1821–1876," http://arts.st-andrews.ac.uk/pronunciamientos/. For a collection of documents that includes translations of pronunciamientos in English, see Thomas B. David and Amado Ricon Virulegio (eds.), *The Political Plans of Mexico.*

69. See Vázquez, "Political Plans and Collaboration"; and Vázquez, "El modelo de pronunciamiento mexicano."

70. Vázquez, "Political Plans and Collaboration," 20.

71. Those of Veracruz, 2 December 1822; Casa Mata, 1 February 1823; Montaño or Otumba, 23 December 1827; Perote, 16 September 1828; Jalapa, 4 December 1829; Veracruz, 2 January 1832; Convenios de Zavaleta, 23 December 1832; Huejotzingo, 8 June 1833; Cuernavaca, 25 May 1834; Toluca, 31 May 1834; Orizaba, 19 May 1835; Tampico, 7 October 1838; Guadalajara, 8 August 1841; Bases de Tacubaya, 28 September 1841; Huejotzingo, 11 December 1842; Guadalajara, 2 November 1844; San Luis Potosí, 14 December 1845; and Ciudadela, 4 August 1846. See Vázquez, "Political Plans and Collaboration," note 10, 36.

72. See Vázquez, "El modelo de pronunciamiento mexicano," 31, 46–49.

73. Tenenbaum, "'They Went Thataway'"; Guerra, "El pronunciamiento en México"; Guerra, "Mexico from Independence to Revolution."

74. Tenenbaum, "'They Went Thataway,'" 187, 199.

75. Guerra, "El pronunciamiento en México," 15, 18, 21–22, 24.

76. In addition to those studies that feature in my three edited volumes on the pronunciamiento phenomenon, see Ali, "Yucatecan-Mexican Relations at the Time of Independence"; Fowler and Ortiz Escamilla, "La revuelta del 2 de diciembre de 1822"; Fowler, "Santa Anna y el Plan de San Luis Potosí, 1823"; Ortiz Escamilla, "El pronunciamiento federalista de Gordiano Guzmán"; Costeloe, "A Pronunciamiento"; and Costeloe, "Triangular Revolt."

77. Beyond the period covered by this project, a recent study on pronunciamientos and banditry in Porfirian Mexico worthy of note is Gantús, "La inconformidad subversiva."

78. A chapter in this volume that has not already been referred to in this introduction is Germán Martínez Martínez's study of the practice from a cultural perspective: "Inventing the Nation," in Fowler, *Forceful Negotiations.*

79. Chapters in this volume that have not already been referred to in this introduction include Rugeley, "Compass Points of Unrest"; Ortiz Esca-

milla, "Veracruz: The Determining Region"; Staples, "The Clergy and How It Responded to Calls for Rebellion Before the Mid-Nineteenth Century"; Thomson, "The End of the 'Catholic Nation'"; Vázquez, "In Search of Power"; Pani, "Intervention and Empire: Politics as Usual?"; and Flores Clair, "A Socialist Pronunciamiento: Julio López Chávez's Uprising of 1868."

80. Chapters in this volume that have not already been referred to in this introduction include Doyle, "Refrescos, Iluminaciones and Te Deums"; McDonald, "The Political Life of Executed Pronunciados"; Santoni, "Salvas, Cañonazos y Repiques"; Pi-Suñer Llorens, "The Crumbling of a 'Hero'"; Zárate Toscano, "Porfirio Díaz and the Representations of the Second of April"; and Salazar Mendoza, "Juan Bustamante's Pronunciamiento and the Civic Speeches that Condemned It."

81. Fowler, "El pronunciamiento mexicano del siglo XIX." Previous studies that have noted the extent to which pronunciamientos were the result of military and civilian groups working together include Hamnett, "Partidos políticos mexicanos e intervención militar"; and Jaime E. Rodríguez O., "Los caudillos y los historiadores."

82. On origins see Fowler, "Introduction: The Nineteenth-Century Practice," in Fowler, *Forceful Negotiations*; and Fowler, "Rafael del Riego." A separate study that has also looked at the impact Riego's pronunciamiento had in Mexico between 1820 and 1821 is Moreno Gutiérrez, "The Memory and Representation of Rafael del Riego's Pronunciamiento," in Fowler, *Celebrating Insurrection*. On dynamics see Fowler, "Introduction: The Nineteenth-Century Practice"; and Fowler, "Los pronunciamientos mexicanos de las primeras décadas nacionales, 1821–1855," *20/10 México: Nación y Modernidad, 1821–1910*, in press.

83. Fowler, "'I Pronounce Thus I Exist,'" in Fowler, *Forceful Negotiations*.

84. Fowler, "Introduction: Understanding Individual and Collective Insurrectionary Action," in Fowler, *Malcontents*.

85. Fowler, "The Pronunciamientos of Antonio López de Santa Anna, 1821–1867," in Fowler, *Malcontents*.

86. Fowler, "Entre la legalidad y la legitimidad."

87. Will Fowler, "El discurso de la legitimidad insurreccional en los pronunciamientos del México independiente, 1821–1858," paper delivered at the international conference "Consenso, legitimidad y negociaciones formales e informales en la primera mitad del siglo XIX mexicano," held at the Colegio de Michoacán in Zamora, Mexico, in May 2012.

88. Fowler, "The Damned and the Venerated."

89. Fowler, "'As Empty a Piece of Gasconading Stuff.'"

2. Origins of Mexico's Mimetic Insurrectionism

1. Quoted in Kimball (ed.), *To Reason Why*, 31.

2. Karnow, *Vietnam*, 24.

3. DeGroot, *A Noble Cause?* 59.

4. Lenin, "'Left-wing' Communism, an infantile disorder," in *Selected Works*, 2:430.

5. Lenin, "'Left-wing' Communism," 2:412.

6. Lenin, "The Proletarian Revolution and the Renegade Kautsky," in *Selected Works*, 2:106.

7. Lenin, "'Left-wing' Communism," 430–31.

8. Lenin, "The Proletarian Revolution," 2:16.

9. For studies on the Left, with reference to Marxism-Leninism and the Spanish and Greek civil wars, see Bolloten, *The Spanish Revolution*; and Close (ed.), *The Greek Civil War*.

10. Rapport, *1848: Year of Revolution*, ix.

11. In a nutshell, Guevara's idea was that a *foco* (insurrectionary center), made up of a handful of committed revolutionaries, based in the jungle or in the mountains, employing guerrilla warfare, could generate the conditions necessary for a revolution to take place. To quote Régis Debray, who analyzed the Cuban revolutionary model: "It is the 'small motor' that sets the 'big motor' of the masses in motion and precipitates the formation of a front, as the victories won by the small motor increase" (Debray, *Revolution in the Revolution?* 83).

12. To name but some of the revolutionary guerrilla armies formed or inspired by Guevara's *foco revolucionario* model: FARC (Armed Revolutionary Forces of Colombia), FMLN (Farabundo Martí National Liberation Front, El Salvador), FSLN (National Sandinista Liberation Front, Nicaragua), the *Montoneros* (Argentina), *Sendero Luminoso* (Shining Path, Peru), the *Tupamaros* (Uruguay), and URNG (National Revolutionary Guerrilla Unity, Guatemala). See Fowler, *Latin America since 1780*, 139–40.

13. Quoted in Gott, *Guerrilla Movements*, xxvii.

14. Quoted in Gott, *Guerrilla Movements*, xxvii.

15. For a recent collection of thought-provoking essays on the 1968 revolutions, see Tismaneanu (ed.), *Promises of 1968*.

16. For the 1989 revolutions see *The Revolutions of 1989*, also edited by Vladimir Tismaneanu.

17. For an engaging journalists' analysis of the Arab Spring, see Manhire (ed.), *The Arab Spring*. Also see Filiu's combative *The Arab Revolution*.

18. Although my concept of mimetic insurrectionism does not entail a faithful application of René Girard's notion of "mimetic desire," as developed in his seminal study on collective violence, *The Scapegoat* (1982), it is undoubtedly informed and influenced by his thinking. According to Girard, we do not just copy each other instinctively (something which is an essential part of the way we learn to walk, talk, and grow to behave like those around us). We are also caught up in a mimetic space in which we cannot help having the same desires, even when the objects of those desires would not necessarily have aroused our interest if they had not aroused that of the one we find ourselves compelled to imitate. In other words, at its most primeval, mimetic desire can be seen to occur when two children fight over the same toy and do so only because they are essentially mirroring the other's desire for the toy (if the toy was of no interest to the one child, the other would show no interest in it either). With collective violence Girard saw, therefore, a tragic example of how our mimetic tendencies prevent us from finding peaceful solutions to violent problems. To put it differently, we desire the same as the Other because we mimic the Other's desire, and we hurt the Other because we mimic the Other hurting us. For a discussion on collective political violence and the construction of national identity in Latin America that takes on board Girard's theory of mimetic desire, see Fowler, "The Children of the Chingada."

19. See Geggus (ed.), *The Impact of the Haitian Revolution*.

20. Lynch, *The Spanish American Revolutions*, 295.

21. Rodríguez O., *The Independence of Spanish America*, 1.

22. See Stein and Stein, *Apogee of Empire*. For a compilation of writings by and about the Bourbon reformers and translated into English, see Floyd, *The Bourbon Reformers*.

23. Fowler, *Latin America since 1780*, 9. Also see Burkholder and Johnson, *Colonial Latin America*, 324–27. Two noteworthy studies on Bourbon bureaucracy are Deans-Smith, *Bureaucrats, Planters, and Workers*, and Arnold, *Bureaucracy and Bureaucrats in Mexico City*.

24. For Lucas Alamán, José Valadés's 1938 biographical study *Alamán: Estadista e historiador* remains an essential point of reference. A succinct but

noteworthy study is Lira, *Lucas Alamán*. We await the publication of Eric Van Young's new biography, but a preview of his findings may be sampled in his article "Vidas privadas y mitos públicos."

25. Alamán, *Historia de México* (1938 edition; originally published as *Historia de Méjico* in 1849), 1:54, 57.

26. See Fisher, *Commercial Relations between Spain and Spanish America*.

27. Lynch, *The Spanish American Revolutions*, 12.

28. Brading, *Miners and Merchants*, in particular 129–207. For a seminal study on silver mining in colonial Mexico under the Habsburgs, see Bakewell, *Silver Mining and Society in Colonial Mexico*.

29. Chowning, *Wealth and Power in Provincial Mexico*, 93.

30. For Mora see Hale, *Mexican Liberalism in the Age of Mora*.

31. Mora, *Méjico y sus revoluciones* (first published in 1836), 2:300.

32. Taylor, *Magistrates of the Sacred*, 472. For the Bourbon ecclesiastical reforms and their impact in New Spain, also see Brading, *Church and State in Bourbon Mexico*, and O'Hara, *A Flock Divided*, in particular 93–184.

33. As argued by Eric Van Young, "The conjunction of a local tradition of popular piety (or perhaps better said, crypto-paganism) stretching back to the pre-Columbian period, criticism or outright attempted suppression of elements of that tradition by the Church, and the outbreak of the independence struggle is particularly well documented." See Van Young, "In the Gloomy Caverns of Paganism," 52.

34. Taylor, *Magistrates of the Sacred*, 472.

35. John Lynch, "Introduction," in Lynch (ed.), *Latin American Revolutions*, 27.

36. To note two obvious examples: Francisco de Miranda and Simón Bolívar. Discussions of how the ideas of the Enlightenment figured in their own writings can be found, respectively, in Racine, *Francisco de Miranda*, and Lynch, *Simón Bolívar*, in particular 24–39. For a study that focuses on the ideological origins of the Mexican War of Independence, offering a qualified view of how the ideals of the Enlightenment influenced events, see Villoro, *El proceso ideológico de la revolución de independencia*, in particular 50–51. For a study that, in contrast, highlights the extent to which the writings of Montesquieu, Rousseau, Voltaire, and Raynal circulated in Spanish America influencing creole political thought, see Madariaga, *The Fall of the Spanish American Empire*, in particular the chapter "The Four Philosophers," 221–44.

37. Liss, *Atlantic Empires*, 143.

38. Rousseau, *Discours sur l'origine et les fondements de l'inégalité* (first published 1755).

39. Jaime E. Rodríguez O. made this point in the question and answer round that was held at the end of the session on "Los referentes doctrinales de la cultura política," at the International Conference "Los procesos de independencia en la América española: Crisis, guerra y disolución de la monarquía hispana," Universidad Veracruzana, Veracruz, 25–28 November 2008.

40. In French: "Article 35. Quand le gouvernement viole les droits du peuple, l'insurrection est, pour le peuple et pour chaque portion du peuple, le plus sacré des droits et le plus indispensable des devoirs." The English translation included here is taken from Anderson (ed.), *The Constitutions and Other Select Documents*, 174.

41. Clavigero, *Historia antigua de México* (first published in Italian as *Storia antica del Messico* in 1780–81), xvii.

42. See by D. A. Brading both *The Origins of Mexican Nationalism* and *The First America*. Also see my encyclopaedic essay on "Mexico," in Herb and Kaplan (eds.), *Nations and Nationalism*, 344–57.

43. Although technically speaking and for all intents and purposes, Ferdinand VII was made prisoner by Napoleon on 10 May 1808—when, having been enticed to Bayonne across the border in France, he was forced to abdicate in favor of Napoleon's brother Joseph—the reality of the Spanish king's captivity was far from grueling. His time in "captivity" was actually spent in the sumptuous château de Valençay (1808–13). See the château's official website to appreciate the luxurious castle Ferdinand VII lived in during his years as Napoleon's captive monarch: http://loire-chateaux.co.uk/19-Chateaux/Chateau -Of-Valencay.html.

44. For a recent study on the 1808 coup in Mexico City, see Eissa Barroso, "Political Culture in the Spanish Crisis of 1808." Also see Warren, *Vagrants and Citizens*, 24–31.

45. Hidalgo did not explicitly call for independence. He remained, at least on paper, outspokenly loyal to the captive Spanish monarch—*el deseado* (desired) Ferdinand VII—even though for most people it was obvious that the insurgent movement of Dolores was intent on bringing about independence. As scrutinized in Marco Antonio Landavazo's study *La mascara de Fernando VII*, both insurgents and royalists used their alleged loyalty to the captive monarch to further their own agendas in a bid to broaden their support base and

give legitimacy to their respective causes. For a recent biography of Hidalgo, see Herrejón Peredo, *Hidalgo*.

46. Hamnett, *Roots of Insurgency*, 204.

47. Mora, *México y sus revoluciones*, 3:21.

48. Van Young, *The Other Rebellion*, 3.

49. For two examples of Hidalgo's early addresses, see "Proclama del cura Hidalgo a la nación americana (1810)," in De la Torre, *La independencia de México*, 213–15, and "Proclama de don Miguel Hidalgo en la que se refiere vagamente a un plan (octubre de 1810)," in Jiménez Codinach (ed.), *Planes en la nación mexicana*, 1:103–4.

50. Van Young, "Of Tempests and Teapots," 27.

51. For the counterinsurgency, see Archer, "'La Causa Buena.'" Also see Hamnett, *Revolución y contrarevolución*.

52. For a study that shows how the criollo elite's initial support for Hidalgo's movement quickly dried up as news of its acts of violence became widely known, see Ortiz Escamilla, "Las élites novohispanas."

53. For Morelos see Lemoine Villicaña, *Morelos*, and Herrejón Peredo, *Los procesos de Morelos*.

54. These were José Ignacio Beye Cisneros (Mexico City), José Eduardo Cárdenas (Tabasco), José María Couto (Puebla), Francisco Fernández Munilla and José Cayetano Foncerrada y Uribarri (Valladolid), Miguel González Lastiri (Mérida), José Miguel Gordoa y Barrios (Zacatecas), Juan José Guereña y Garayo (Durango), José Miguel Guridi y Alcocer (Tlaxcala), José Gutiérrez de Terán, Máximo Maldonado (Guadalajara), Joaquín Maniau (Veracruz), Mariano Mendiola Velarde (Querétaro), Manuel María Moreno (Sonora), Octaviano Obregón (Querétaro), Antonio Joaquín Pérez y Martínez Robles (Puebla), Pedro Bautista Pino (New Mexico), José Miguel Ramos Arizpe (Coahuila), Andrés Sabariego, Salvador Samartín (Guadalajara), and José Simeón Uría (Guadalajara). See Suárez, *Las Cortes de Cádiz*, 43–44.

55. The 1812 Constitution is reprinted in Tena Ramírez, *Leyes fundamentales*, 60–104.

56. Nettie Lee Benson, "Introduction," in Benson (ed.), *Mexico and the Spanish Cortes*, 8.

57. For Zavala's criticism of Hidalgo's theocratic fanaticism, see Zavala, *Ensayo histórico de la revoluciones* (first published in 1831), 1:54. Zavala, of course, went on to act as elected deputy for Yucatán in the Spanish Cortes when the

constitution was restored in 1820. For Zavala see Parcero, *Lorenzo de Zavala*; Trejo, *Los límites de un discurso*; and Henson, *Lorenzo de Zavala*.

58. For the 1814 Constitution of Apatzingán, see Tena Ramírez, *Leyes fundamentales*, 32–58.

59. Numerous studies have been written about the War of Independence in recent years. A good starting point for students of the period is the comprehensive historiographical review Antonio Annino and Rafael Rojas provide, with the collaboration of Francisco A. Eissa-Barroso, in their *La independencia*.

60. Viceroy Apodaca to Ministry of War, document no. 30, Mexico City, 31 October 1816, in Apodaca, *Apuntes biográficos del excmo. Señor D. Juan Ruiz de Apodaca y Eliza*, 114–20.

61. Coatsworth, "Los límites del absolutismo colonial," 53–54.

62. Taylor, *Drinking, Homicide, and Rebellion*, 115.

63. Ducey, *A Nation of Villages*, 171.

64. Tutino, *From Insurrection to Revolution*, 212.

65. Holden, *Armies without Nations*, 13.

66. Guardino, *Peasants, Politics*, 75.

67. For a concise encyclopaedic essay on the Spanish American Revolutions of Independence, see Fowler, "Spanish American Revolutions of Independence."

68. Zavala, *Ensayo histórico*, 1:85–86.

69. Alcalá Galiano, *Apuntes para servir a la historia del origen y alzamiento del ejército*, 13–15.

70. According to conspirator Antonio María Alcalá Galiano, it was an army "al cual no podía oponer otro España" (Spain had none other with which to confront it). See his *Recuerdos de un anciano*, 222–23. In Alcalá Galiano's *Memorias* he reiterated the point, adding that the conspirators were convinced that "conseguido de un modo o de otro el alzamiento del Ejército expedicionario, por seguro debía tenerse que terminaría en su triunfo" (one way or another, were the expeditionary army to turn against the government, it could be taken for granted that it would triumph). See Antonio María Alcalá Galiano, *Memorias*, in Campos (ed.), *Obras escogidas de Antonio Alcalá Galiano* (first published in 1886), 1:475.

71. These were the battalions of Aragón 1st and 2nd, Ligero Canarias, Rey 2nd, Soria 2nd, Valencia 2nd, Princesa 2nd, Málaga 2nd, Cataluña 1st and 2nd, Guías del General, Asturias 2nd, Príncipe, América, Guadalajara, Sevilla, Artillería a pie, and Zapadores; the Escuadrón Artillería; and the regiments

Dragones del Rey, Dragones del General, Farnesio, and Alcántara. See Varo Montilla, "La participación de la tropa," 29.

72. Rafael del Riego, "Proclama a las tropas," Cabezas de San Juan, 1 January 1820, reprinted in Gil Novales (ed.), *Rafael del Riego*. For an account of how news of the pronunciamento was received in Mexico see Alamán, *Historia de Méjico* (1986 edition), 5:18–20.

73. Zavala, *Ensayo histórico*, 1:86.

74. Fondo General Palafox, Archivo-Biblioteca-Hemeroteca del Ayuntamiento de Zaragoza, caja 08174: *Gaceta de Madrid*, 18 March 1820.

75. Alamán, *Historia de Méjico*, 5:18–19.

76. Alamán, *Historia de Méjico*, 5:18.

77. A Coruña (21 February), El Ferrol (23 February), Santiago (28 February), Vigo, Pontevedra, Lugo (1 March), Orense (4 March), Zaragoza (5 March), Madrid (7 March), Barcelona, Tarragona, Girona, Mataró (10–12 March), and Pamplona (11 March).

78. Comellas, *Los primeros pronunciamientos en España*, 336–44.

79. Alamán, *Historia de Méjico*, 5:18–19. Also see Arrangoiz, *México desde 1808 hasta 1867* (first published in 1871–72), 259. In Arrangoiz's account he has Dávila saying these words to a "stupid" freemason from Navarre.

80. Zavala, *Ensayo histórico*, 1:86.

81. Cunniff, "Mexican Municipal Electoral Reform," 82.

82. Hamnett, *Revolución y contrarevolución*, 298–99.

83. Alcalá Galiano, *Apuntes para servir a la historia del origen y alzamiento del ejército*, 8, 12.

84. Comellas, *Los primeros pronunciamientos en España*, 324.

85. Vázquez, "El modelo del pronunciamiento mexicano," 34.

86. Artola, *La burguesía revolucionaria*, 49.

87. Castells, *La utopia insurreccional del liberalismo*, 28.

88. Tornel, *Manifiesto del origen, causas, progresos y estado*, 8.

89. *La Abeja Poblana*, 5 April 1821.

90. Quoted in De la Torre, *La independencia de México*, 127.

91. For Iturbide see Anna, *The Mexican Empire of Iturbide*.

92. For la güera Rodríguez see Arrom, *Women of Mexico City*, 24, 127, 223, 248, and the biographical entry in the University of Nottingham's "Gendering Latin America" website: http://www.genderlatam.org.uk/PersonDetails.php ?PeopleID=184.

93. Anna, "Iguala: The Prototype," 3.

94. For studies that outline the conspiratorial stages of the Plan of Iguala and demonstrate the extent to which this was a collective endeavor, bringing together civilian as well as military actors, and Mexican as well as Spanish liberal deputies, see Benson, "Iturbide y los planes de independencia"; Archer, "Where Did All the Royalists Go?"; Rodríguez O., "The Transition from Colony to Nation; Ávila, *En nombre de la nación*, in particular 196–201; Rodríguez O. "Los caudillos y los historiadores"; Frasquet, *Las caras del águila*, in particular 29–88; Frasquet and Chust, "Agustín de Iturbide."

95. For Iturbide and Guerrero's correspondence in the build-up to the launch of the Plan of Iguala, see *Cartas de los señores generales D. Agustín de Iturbide y D. Vicente Guerrero*.

96. Nettie Lee Benson Latin American Collection, University of Texas at Austin (hereafter cited as BLAC), Genaro García Collection: Vicente Guerrero, "Manifiesto patriótico que hizo siendo comandante general de la primera división del Ejército de las Tres Garantías," Mexico City, 1821.

97. Quote taken from Plan of Iguala. The version consulted here is: "Plan de la independencia de México proclamada en el pueblo de Iguala en los días 1 y 2 de marzo de 1821," held in AGN: Impresos oficiales, vol. 60, no. 62.

98. See Anna, *The Fall of the Royal Government in Mexico City*.

99. Anna, "Agustín de Iturbide and the Process of Consensus," 191.

100. Where it would differ would be in the emergence of the Acta, which, albeit including a justificatory preamble following the Plan of Iguala's template, also had the minutes (*actas*) of the meeting in which the given pronounced community (e.g., garrison and/or town council) had deliberated and then decided to pronounce.

101. "Plan de la independencia de México proclamada en el pueblo de Iguala en los días 1 y 2 de marzo de 1821."

102. "Plan de la independencia . . . 1 y 2 de marzo de 1821."

103. "Plan de la independencia . . . 1 y 2 de marzo de 1821."

104. BLAC, Hernández y Dávalos Collection: Agustín de Iturbide, "Memoria de Livorno," 27 September 1823. The translation belongs to Michael Joseph Quinn, 1823.

105. Worthy of note is that the word *union* does not actually figure in the plan. However, it was evidently being bandied about at the time, given that the pronunciados had agreed on calling their liberating army that of the "Three

Guarantees." There is mention of "union" in the postscript to the original published plan, where the final exhortation ends with Iturbide saying: "Long live the union that makes our happiness."

106. Although the plural term for court—Cortes—had been used in medieval Spain to refer to the different gatherings of the nobles, clergymen, and principal burghers of the Spanish kingdoms of Castilla y León, Aragón, Cataluña, Valencia, and Navarra, its modern usage—that is, as meaning the Spanish Constitutional Parliament—was first employed to describe the besieged Cortes of Cádiz. See *El Congreso de los Diputados*, 9.

107. Iturbide, *A Statement of Some of the Principal Events*, 16–17.

108. For Santa Anna's campaign in Veracruz, see Fowler, *Santa Anna of Mexico*, 43–56.

109. Zavala, *Ensayo histórico*, 1:92.

110. The Treaty of Córdoba is reproduced in De la Torre, *La independencia de México*, 278–81.

111. De la Torre, *La independencia de México*, 278–81.

112. Anna, *The Fall of the Royal Government*, 221–23.

113. The triumphal procession was due to go from Tlaxpana via San Cosme, passing by the viceroy's palace, but instead went along the Calle de la Profesa where la güera Rodríguez lived. Valle Arizpe, *La güera Rodríguez*.

114. Santa Anna went on to liberate Perote on 7 October, and the port of Veracruz was liberated on 28 October. The island fortress of San Juan de Ulúa, sitting in Veracruz harbor, remained Spanish, however, until 17 November 1825.

115. The Acta de Independencia is reproduced in De la Torre, *La independencia de México*, 281–82.

116. Anna, "Iguala: The Prototype," 19.

3. Voice of the Provinces

1. Ocampo, *Las ideas de un día*. I developed the idea that Mexico went from a stage of hope in 1821 to one of despair after 1847 in my *Mexico in the Age of Proposals, 1821–1853*. Indicative of the sense of disillusion that characterized the early national period following the way the high hopes of independence never quite materialized is the title of Josefina Zoraida Vázquez's recent reworking of the introductions she wrote for her *Planes en la nación mexicana*, vols. 2–4: *Dos décadas de desilusiones: En busca de una formula adecuada de gobierno (1832–1854)*.

2. Translated quote taken from Humboldt, *Political Essay on the Kingdom of New Spain: The John Black Translation*, 233. The Special Collections Depart-

ment of the Main Library of the University of St. Andrews holds a copy of the first edition of Humboldt, *Essai politique sur le Royaume de la Nouvelle-Espagne*. For Humboldt's influence in Mexico, see Ortega y Medina, *Humboldt desde México*, and Ita Rubio and Sánchez Díaz (eds.), *Humboldt y otros viajeros*.

3. Humboldt, *Political Essay*, 240.

4. Tenenbaum, *The Politics of Penury*, 13. For a lengthy discussion of the destruction the War of Independence caused in the mining sector, see Ward, *México en 1827* (first published in English in 1828), 344–69; also see Staples, *Bonanzas y borrascas mineras*.

5. Tenenbaum, *The Politics of Penury*, 13–14.

6. Tenenbaum, *The Politics of Penury*, 13. For a contemporary attempt at collating Mexico's key statistics following the consummation of Independence, see Tadeo Ortiz de Ayala, *Resumen de estadística del imperio mexicano 1822* (originally published in 1822).

7. Bazant, *Historia de la deuda exterior de México*, 16.

8. For other studies that address Mexico's debt and economy during this period, see Chowning, *Wealth and Power in Provincial Mexico*; Costeloe, *Bonds and Bondholder*; Costeloe, *Bubbles and Bonanzas*; Hernández Jaimes, "El diseño de las políticas fiscales y comerciales en México, 1821–1855"; Herrera Canales, *El comercio exterior de México*; Ludlow (ed.), *Los secretarios de hacienda y sus proyectos*; Ludlow and Marichal (eds.), *La banca en México*; Ludlow and Marichal (eds.), *Un siglo de deuda pública en México*; Olveda (ed.), *Inversiones y empresarios*; Villegas Revueltas, *Deuda y diplomacia*; and Zaragoza, *Historia de la deuda externa*.

9. Of the thirty-one men who served between 1821 and 1858 as Mexico's president (emperor in the case of Iturbide), some on more than one occasion, twenty-two were army officers, and of these nineteen fought in the War of Independence. Five were insurgents—Juan Álvarez, Nicolás Bravo, Vicente Guerrero, Melchor Múzquiz, and Guadalupe Victoria; and the other fourteen were royalists prior to the Plan of Iguala—Pedro María Anaya, Mariano Arista, Miguel Barragán, Anastasio Bustamante, Valentín Canalizo, Martín Carrera, Pedro Celestino Negrete, Manuel Gómez Pedraza, José Joaquín de Herrera, Agustín de Iturbide, Manuel María Lombardini, Antonio López de Santa Anna, Mariano Paredes y Arrillaga, and Mariano Salas. For essays on a number of these generals' presidential terms in office, see Fowler, *Gobernantes mexicanos*.

10. For creole patriotism see by David Brading *The First America*, and *The Origins of Mexican Nationalism*. For the army's nationalist rhetoric see my *Military Political Identity and Reformism* and *Tornel and Santa Anna*, 213–15.

11. Buve, "Ayuntamientos and Pronunciamientos," 129.

12. Humboldt, *Political Essay*, 45.

13. We still do not have concrete literacy figures for the period, although the studies by Dorothy Tanck de Estrada and Anne Staples in *Historia de la alfabetización y de la educación de adultos en México* offer some figures; for example, 8 out 32 schoolgirls were able to sign with their names (Tanck de Estrada, "Reformas borbónicas y educación utilitaria 1700–1821," 98). The fact that 90 percent of the population lived in the countryside (Staples, "Leer y escribir en los estados del México independiente," 135) certainly places into context any urban figure; for instance, 20.6 prisoners capable of reading and writing between 1828 and 1835 (Tanck de Estrada, "La alfabetización: Medio para formar ciudadanos de una democracia 1821–1840," 132). Also see Tanck de Estrada, *La educación ilustrada 1786–1836*, and Staples, *Recuento de una batalla inconclusa*.

14. See Title III, articles 11–24, in 1836 Constitution; Tena Ramírez, *Leyes fundamentales*, 408–10.

15. See by Vázquez both *Mexicanos y norteamericanos ante la guerra del 47*, 27–49, and *La intervención norteamericana 1846–1848*, 131–32. For other studies arguing that the 1846–48 War served as a watershed in the awakening of a clear national consciousness in Mexico, see Reséndez Fuentes, "Guerra e identidad nacional," 413; Velasco Martínez and Benjamin, "La guerra entre México y Estados Unidos, 1846–1848," 113; and Delgadillo Sánchez, *San Luis Potosí durante la guerra*. The concept of "imagined community" is taken from Anderson, *Imagined Communities*.

16. Knight, *The Mexican Revolution*, 1:2.

17. For a vivid depiction of the noise and salespeople's calls that could be heard "desde la mañana á la noche" in Mexico City at the time, see Arróniz, *Manual del viajero* (first published in 1858), 130–34.

18. Quoted in Gregory, *Brute New World*, 136. For a biographical study of William Bullock, see Costeloe, *William Bullock*.

19. Almonte, *Guía de forasteros y repertorio de conocimientos útiles*, 430–31; Arróniz, *Manual del viajero*, 47; Olivera and Crété, *Life in Mexico under Santa Anna*, 69–88.

20. Poinsett, *Notes on Mexico*, 95–96.

21. For the minutes of the congressional meetings that unfolded between 1821 and 1824, see Mateos, *Historia parlamentaria de los congresos mexicanos*, vols. 1 and 2.

22. An example of the titles Santa Anna started to award himself in September 1821 can be found in his "Circular," Cuartel general del Molino sobre Perote, 9 September 1821, held in the Archivo Histórico Municipal de Xalapa (hereafter cited as AHMX): "Libro de acuerdos del ilustre ayuntamiento constitucional de la villa de Xalapa, para el año de 1821," vol. 32, ff. 269–70.

23. AHMX: "Libro de acuerdos del ilustre ayuntamiento constitucional de la villa de Xalapa, para el año de 1821," vol. 32, ff. 118–20 y ff. 121–22: Town Council minutes of 28 and 29 September 1821.

24. AHMX: "Libro de acuerdos del ilustre ayuntamiento constitucional de la villa de Xalapa, para el año de 1821," vol. 32, ff. 121–22: Town Council minutes of 29 September 1821.

25. AHSDN: XI/481.3/230, "Parte del coronel Ramón de Soto, dando cuenta del pronunciamiento del general brigadier Antonio López de Santa Anna, a favor de la república," December 1822, f. 2, notes that Santa Anna's regiment was made up of more than eight hundred men.

26. For a recent study on Mariano Otero, see Boyd, "The Career and Ideology of Mariano Otero."

27. Otero, *Ensayo sobre el verdadero estado*, 80.

28. The military and ecclesiastical fueros still need to be studied in depth. However, the following two essays by Linda Arnold have made an important contribution toward our understanding of how the military fuero was applied and protected and how it affected both those concerned and Mexico's early liberal institutions: see Arnold, "Justicia militar en el México republican," and "Virtual Legality." With regard to ecclesiastical fueros, we are still waiting for them to be studied in detail. There are surprisingly few works on the church between independence in 1821 and the midcentury reform period in 1856, with plenty having been written about it before and after these years. The books that do address church-state relations include Connaughton, *Clerical Ideology in a Revolutionary Age*; Connaughton, *Entre la voz de Dios y el llamado de la patria*; Costeloe, *Church Wealth in Mexico*; Costeloe, *Church and State in Independent Mexico*; O'Hara, *A Flock Divided*; and Staples, *La iglesia en la primera república federal*. A seminal text that engages with the ecclesiastical wealth and privileges after 1856 is Bazant, *Los bienes de la Iglesia en México*.

29. For a study that shows how Indians and their communities retained their lands for the greater part of the colonial period (and beyond), see Taylor, *Landlord and Peasant*.

30. For a study on the Mexican legal system(s) during this period, see Arnold, *Política y justicia*. For all the listed constitutions see Tena Ramírez, *Leyes fundamentales*.

31. Carl Schmitt, writing in the context of early 1930s Germany, would add to this the possibility that more than faith or trust, legitimacy requires "compliance" with authority; that is, a "choice not to resist such authority." See Schmitt, *Legality and Legitimacy* (originally published in 1932).

32. Weber, *The Theory of Social and Economic Organization*, 382; and Runciman (ed.), *Weber*, 235–36.

33. Lipset, *Political Man*, 64. Rosie Doyle provides a noteworthy discussion of the legitimacy of the pronunciamiento from the perspective of Jalisco in chapter 3 of her thesis, "The Pronunciamiento in Nineteenth-Century Mexico," 78–107.

34. Lipset, *Political Man*, 68. The concept of "site of memory" was first propounded by Pierre Nora in his edited *Lieux de memoire*.

35. For further reading on theories of legitimacy, see Peter, *Democratic Legitimacy*, in particular chapter 4, 56–74; Schatzberg, *Political Legitimacy in Middle Africa*, in particular chapter 7, 201–21; and Simmons, *Justification and Legitimacy*.

36. *Descoyotar* is a verb that was used repeatedly in 1827–28, in documents that set out to demand the expulsion of the Spanish population in Mexico, literally meaning to "free of coyotes." According to Lucas Alamán, Spaniards were called either "coyotes" or "gallicoyotes" at the time, finding themselves equated with a kind of "wolf peculiar to Mexico, that hunted the Mexicans who were represented as chickens." See Alamán, *Historia de Méjico*, 5:477, footnote 26.

37. Copies of the "Plan de descoyotar en el Estado de Jalisco, por convenir así la Nación Americana," Guadalajara, 7 August 1827; the "Verdadero decreto del Congreso de Jalisco para la salida de los españoles," Guadalajara, 24 August 1827; and the Decreto No. 101 del Gobierno del Estado de Jalisco, Guadalajara, 3 September 1827, can all be found in the British Library: Mexico, Collection of Broadsides, News-sheets etc. 1850.a.26. I thank Dr. Rosie Doyle for locating and transcribing them for the St. Andrews pronunciamientos database.

38. The expulsion laws of 10 May 1827 are reproduced in Tornel y Mendívil, *Breve reseña histórica*, 167. For studies of the expulsion of Spaniards between

1821 and 1836, see Sims, *La expulsion de los españoles de México*; Sims, *The Expulsion of Mexico's Spaniards*; and Blázquez Domínguez, "La expulsion de los españoles en Xalapa y Veracruz."

39. See Fowler, "Fiestas santanistas"; Fowler, *Celebrating Insurrection*.

40. Zavala, *Ensayo histórico*, 1:96.

41. The "Representación del brigadier don Felipe de la Garza al emperador, 22 de septiembre de 1822," is reproduced in Jiménez Codinach (ed.), *Planes en la nación mexicana*, 1:137–38.

42. Andrews, "The Rise and Fall," 22.

43. For the Acta de Casa Mata and the numerous actas de adhesión it inspired, see AHSDN: XI/481.3/258, exp. "Disposiciones gubernativas con motivo del triunfo del movimiento encabezado en Veracruz por don Antonio López de Santa Anna, y salida fuera del país de don Agustín de Iturbide, bajo la custodia del general don Nicolás Bravo. Adhesiones al plan de Casa Mata. Año de 1823. 140 fojas."

44. Ocampo, *Las ideas de un día*, 13–45.

45. For the clashes between Iturbide and the First Constituent Congress, see *Actas del Congreso Constituyente Mexicano*. Also see Rodríguez O., "The Struggle for Dominance."

46. For Iturbide's empire see Anna, *The Mexican Empire of Iturbide*; Ávila, *En nombre de la nación*; Ávila, *Para la libertad*; Ávila, "El gobierno imperial de Agustín de Iturbide," in Fowler, *Gobernantes mexicanos*; Frasquet, *Las caras del águila*, 121–283; and Frasquet and Chust, "Agustín de Iturbide."

47. Bocanegra, *Memorias* (originally published in 1892), 1: 106–8.

48. Rodríguez O., "The Constitution of 1824," 76.

49. These were (1) Sonora and Sinaloa; (2) Chihuahua and Durango; (3) Coahuila, Nuevo León, and Texas; (4) Nuevo Santander; (5) San Luis Potosí; (6) Zacatecas; (7) Guadalajara; (8) Guanajuato; (9) Querétaro; (10) Michoacán; (11) México; (12) Tlaxcala; (13) Puebla; (14) Oaxaca; (15) Veracruz; (16) Chiapas; (17) Yucatán; (18) Nuevo México.

50. For the provincial deputations, see Nettie Lee Benson, *La diputación provincial*.

51. Little is known of Santa Anna's actions as president of the Provincial Deputation of Veracruz, except that he collided with the iturbidista ayuntamientos during his time there. See the minutes of the Ayuntamiento of Xalapa, AHMX: "Libro de acuerdos del ilustre ayuntamiento constitucional de la villa

de Xalapa, para el año de 1822," vol. 33, ff. 79–83: Town Council minutes of 25 October 1822; AHMX: "Libro de acuerdos del ilustre ayuntamiento constitucional de la villa de Xalapa, para el año de 1823," vol. 34, ff. 4–6, 34–35, 39–40: Town Council minutes of 7 January, 21 March, 11 April 1823; f. 181: "Impreso de la Diputación Provincial de Veracruz al Ayuntamiento Constitucional de Jalapa. Fdo. por Santa Anna, Veracruz, 18 de marzo de 1823."

52. See Fowler and Ortiz Escamilla, "La revuelta del 2 de diciembre de 1822," and Fowler, *Santa Anna of Mexico*, 56–67.

53. Tornel y Mendívil, *Breve reseña histórica*, 9.

54. Anna, *The Mexican Empire of Iturbide*, 204.

55. The "Proclama del general Santa Anna," of 2 December 1822, is reproduced in Bustamante, *Diario histórico*, 1:74–75, entry for Thursday 19 December 1822.

56. The "Plan de Veracruz," of 6 December 1822, is reproduced in Bustamante, *Diario histórico*, 1:102–3, entry for Tuesday 14 January 1823.

57. The "Plan de Chilapa," of 13 January 1823, is reproduced in Bustamante, *Diario histórico*, 1:131, entry for Friday 7 February 1823.

58. In between the Veracruzan and Texan pronunciamientos de adhesión, there were acts of allegiance launched in Oaxaca (7 February), Puebla (8 February), Toluca (18 February), and Guanajuato (between 23 and 26 February 1823); Guadalajara, Querétaro, and Mexico City (26 February 1823), Michoacán and the garrison in Valladolid (present-day Morelia, 1 March 1823); Zacatecas and San Luis Potosí (2 March 1823); Yucatán and Campeche (4 March 1823); and Durango (5 March 1823), Saltillo (14 March 1823), Nuevo Santander (9 April 1823), and the Interior Eastern Provinces (9 April 1823). Benson, *La diputación provincial*, 122–37. Also see Benson, "The Plan of Casa Mata."

59. Anna, *Forging Mexico 1821–1835*, 112.

60. See Centro de Estudios de Historia de México CONDUMEX, Mexico City, Miscelánea Varios Autores, núm. 9, doc. 13: *Proclama del Sr. Quintanar a los habitantes de Nueva Galicia sobre la separación del congreso mexicano* (Mexico City: Reimp. en la Of. liberal del C. Juan Cabrera, 1823); *Voto general de los pueblos de la provincia libre de Xalisco denominada hasta ahora de Guadalajara sobre constituir su forma de gobierno en república federada* (Guadalajara: Poderes de Jalisco, 1973 [originally published in 1823]); and "Manifiesto que hace la diputación provincial del estado libre de Xalisco del derecho y conveniencia de su pronunciamiento en república federada," in *Colección de los decretos, circulares y órdenes de los poderes legislativo y ejecutivo del estado de Jalisco,*

vol. 1 (Guadalajara: Tip. De M. Pérez Lete, 1874), 1:5–22. For a book chapter on this Guadalajara series of pronunciamientos, see Olveda, "Jalisco: El pronunciamiento federalista de Guadalajara."

61. For a very useful "Chronology of Provincial Action" for these months, see Anna, *Forging Mexico 1821–1835*, 118–20. For Guerrero, Domínguez, and Michelena's hopeful and celebratory Manifesto written to mark the opening of the Second Constituent Congress, after "the immense accumulation of difficulties that preceded it," see *El Sol*, 8 November 1823.

62. Both documents can be found in Tena Ramírez, *Leyes fundamentales*, 154–61, and 167–95, respectively.

63. Quinlan, "Issues and Factions in the Constituent Congress"; Rodríguez O., "The Constitution of 1824."

64. The Plan de José María Lobato of 23 January 1824 is reproduced in Jiménez Codinach (ed.), *Planes en la nación mexicana*, 1:195.

65. Although I have yet to locate this pronunciamiento, it is discussed in Tornel y Mendívil, *Breve reseña histórica*, 22–23; he and Victoria set off from Mexico City on 8 August to parlay with the pronunciados.

66. Andrews, "The Defence of Iturbide."

67. For electoral practices in Mexico at the time, see Warren, *Vagrants and Citizens*; and Aguilar Rivera (ed.), *Las elecciones y el gobierno representativo*.

68. For Guadalupe Victoria, see Flaccus, "Guadalupe Victoria, Mexican Revolutionary"; Victoria Gómez, *Guadalupe Victoria*; Briseño Senosiain et al., *Guadalupe Victoria, primer presidente*; and Anna, "Guadalupe Victoria," in Fowler, *Gobernantes mexicanos*.

69. For Nicolás Bravo, see Miranda Arrieta, *Nicolás Bravo*.

70. States: (1) Chiapas; (2) Chihuahua; (3) Coahuila and Texas; (4) Durango; (5) Eastern State—Sonora and Sinaloa; (6) Guanajuato; (7) Mexico; (8) Michoacán; (9) Nuevo León; (10) Oaxaca; (11) Puebla; (12) Querétaro; (13) San Luis Potosí; (14) Tabasco; (15) Tamaulipas; (16) Veracruz; (17) Xalisco; (18) Yucatán; and (19) Zacatecas. Territories: (1) Alta California; (2) Baja California; (3) Colima; (4) Santa Fe de Nuevo México.

71. For the 1824 Constitution, see Tena Ramírez, *Leyes fundamentales*, 167–95. Also see Barragán Barragán, *Principios sobre el federalismo*; Ferrer Muñoz, *La formación de un estado nacional*; Vázquez, "El establecimiento del federalismo en México"; and Vázquez and Ortega (eds.), *Práctica y fracaso del primer federalismo mexicano*.

72. Alamán, *Historia de Méjico*, 5:468.

73. Tenenbaum, *The Politics of Penury*, 21–22.

74. Green, *The Mexican Republic*, 154.

75. Zavala, *Ensayo crítico de la revoluciones de México desde 1808 hasta 1830*, in Zavala, *Obras: El historiador y el representante popular*, 264.

76. For Poinsett, see Fuentes Mares, *Poinsett*.

77. Tornel y Mendívil, *Breve reseña histórica*, 46: "Varias logias escocesas y bastantes individuos de otras fueron á engrosar las filas de la nueva secta, que brillaba con el esplendor de un sol que nace y con toda la popularidad que otorga el poder cuando proteje [sic]."

78. For the yorkino-escocés divide, see Costeloe, *La primera república federal* (first published in 1975); Di Tella, *National Popular Politics* 155–218; Solís Vicarte, *Las sociedades secretas*; Vázquez Semadeni, *La formación de una cultura política republicana*; and Romero Valderrama, "The Pedracista Alliance."

79. *Plan formado en Tlaxcala para nuestra total independencia y pacífico establecimiento en los Estados Unidos Mexicanos* (Puebla: Oficina de Moreno Hermanos, 1827).

80. The Plan of Montaño is reproduced in Bocanegra, *Memorias*, 1:56–57.

81. González Pedrero, *País de un solo hombre*, 1:388–89.

82. Tornel y Mendívil, *Breve reseña histórica*, 171.

83. See Fowler, *The Mexican Press*. Also see Rojas, *La escritura de la independencia*.

84. For the imparciales, see Romero Valderrama, "La mirada imparcial."

85. Lorenzo de Zavala, *Viaje a los Estados Unidos del Norte de América* (originally published in Paris in 1834), in Zavala, *Obras: Viaje a los Estados Unidos del Norte de América*, 11.

86. The Plan of Perote of 16 September 1828 is reproduced in Jiménez Codinach (ed.), *Planes en la nación mexicana*, 1:209–10.

87. See Fowler, *Santa Anna of Mexico*, 109–16; and Fowler, "The Pronunciamientos of Antonio López de Santa Anna," 218–22.

88. See Arrom, "Popular Politics in Mexico City."

89. Costeloe, *La primera república federal*, 209–10.

90. Aguilar Rivera, *El manto liberal*.

91. The Plan of Campeche of 6 November 1829 is reproduced in Jiménez Codinach (ed.), *Planes en la nación mexicana*, 1:225–27.

92. See Vázquez, "Two Reactions," and Ali, "The Pronunciamiento in Yucatán (1821–1840)," 143–57.

93. Zavala, *Ensayo crítico*, in Zavala, *Obras: El historiador*, 353.

94. The Plan of Jalapa of 4 December 1829 is reproduced in Bocanegra, *Memorias*, 2:55–56.

95. The Acta del pronunciamiento de México of 23 December 1829 is located in British Library: catalogue num. 600 I. 23 (18).

96. Bustamante, *Manifiesto que el vice-presidente*, 2.

97. Andrews, *Entre la espada y la constitución*, 138.

98. In contrast the Jalapa–Mexico City-inspired pronunciamientos de adhesión and counterpronunciamientos of 4 December 1829–18 August 1830 were all garrison-led, with the exception of that of adhesión of the town council of Morelia (27 December 1829).

99. Tornel y Mendívil, *Breve reseña histórica*, 383–394.

100. All the pronunciamientos noted can be accessed at the AHRC-University of St. Andrews web-based pronunciamiento database, http://arts.st-andrews.ac.uk /pronunciamientos/.

101. Plan of Chilapa, included in Bustamante, *Diario histórico*, 1:131, entry for Friday 7 February 1823.

102. *Plan de San Luis Potosí* (San Luis Potosí: Imp. de Estrada, 5 de junio de 1823); located in Archivo Histórico Municipal de Veracruz: caja 144, vol. 189, ff. 279–81.

103. "Plan de Perote," 16 September 1828.

104. Archer, "Politicization of the Army of New Spain."

105. "Plan de Veracruz," 6 December 1822, included in Bustamante, *Diario histórico*, 1:102–3, entry for Tuesday 14 January 1823.

106. All the following similar explicit threats are from garrison-led pronunciamientos:

> Cúmplase lo ofrecido en el Plan de Iguala y Tratados de Córdoba, que nos prometieron una representación nacional libre y sin trabas, y no pediremos otra cosa. No queremos guerra; pero la haremos a los que quieran subyugarnos. Nos declaramos libres e independientes del gobierno de D. Agustín de Iturbide, y no le faltaremos a las consideraciones que exige el derecho de gentes, y nuestro carácter agradecido y sincero. En su mano está evitar las desgracias y males que son consiguientes a las guerras civiles. (Plan of Chilapa, 13 January 1823)

Art. 6°. El ejército se situará donde mejor convenga a su objeto, y sin mezclarse para nada en ninguna operación hostil; sólo le será lícito, como es de derecho natural, repeler la fuerza con la fuerza, en caso de ser atacado, u osen atentar contra la sagrada libertad de los pueblos. (Plan of San Luis Potosí, 5 June 1823)

Vuelvo a asegurar a V. Soberanía que nada quiere esta guarnición con violencia, pues que siempre obedecerá sus augustos decretos. (Plan of José María Lobato, 23 January 1824)

Movidos a sentimientos patrióticos de los buenos mexicanos, es llegado el caso de presentarse con las armas en la mano, para sostener un deber que les imponen las leyes, el bien general de la república y nuestra justa libertad. (Plan of Veracruz, 31 July 1827)

5°. El ejército libertador lleva el fin de que no se derrame sangre mexicana en el presente pronunciamiento, sino es que se vea comprometido a su defensa. (Plan of Perote, 16 September 1828)

9°. A todos los empleados se les exigirá el juramento de sostenerla, y conservarla a toda costa, y él que así no lo hiciere, cesará en él ejercicio de sus funciones; protestando los cuerpos que lo han verificado, no dejar las armas de la mano, hasta haber conseguido el objeto que se propusieron. (Plan of Campeche, 6 November 1829)

2°. El ejército protesta no dejar las armas de la mano hasta ver restablecido el orden constitucional con la exacta observancia de las leyes fundamentals. (Plan of Jalapa, 4 December 1829)

Convencidos íntimamente de que bajo este orden de cosas la nación se encuentra en el momento crítico de perder su existencia política, que tantos y tan grandes sacrificios ha costado a los mexicanos; nos hemos resuelto decididamente a sacrificarnos en las aras de la patria, sosteniendo a todo trance el siguiente Plan. (Plan of Juan José Codallos, 11 March 1830)

Las que continúen haciendo la guerra a los michoacanos, ultrajando su constitución y soberanía, y consumiendo sus recursos, serán expelidos de su territorio a fuerza de armas. (Plan of Zamora, 15 March 1830)

107. The pronunciamiento of Morelia of 27 December 1829 is located in Colección Josefina Z. Vázquez, Planes y Documentos, 1830 y 1831, Archivo Histórico del Colegio de México, caja 5.

108. The San Luis Potosí state legislature decree (pronunciamiento) of 13 January 1830 is located in Colección Josefina Z. Vázquez, Planes y Documentos, 1830 y 1831, Archivo Histórico del Colegio de México, caja 5.

109. The plan of San Juan Bautista of 29 April 1830 is located in Colección Josefina Z. Vázquez, Planes y Documentos, 1830 y 1831, Archivo Histórico del Colegio de México, caja 5.

110. Stealey (ed.), *Porte Crayon's Mexico*, 70.

111. Republicanism: there were two republican pronunciamiento cycles (Garza, 22 September 1822; Veracruz, 2 December 1822). Congress and the federal state: the Veracruz–Chilapa–Casa Mata 1822–23 constellation was also pro-congress (whether it was to restore the congress Iturbide had dissolved in October 1822 or to summon a new constituent one). Constitutional abuse: the Jalapa–Mexico City 1829 series was, in part, a response to Guerrero's constitutional abuses—namely his misuse of unconstitutional emergency powers. Unfair elections: the 1828 Perote–Oaxaca–La Acordada cycle was a reaction against what was presented as an unfair or unrepresentative electoral result. Masonic interference: the 1827 plan of Montaño sought to end the inordinate power the Masons had come to wield behind the scenes at both a local and national level.

112. For two other anti-Spanish pronunciamientos of 1828, see AHSDN: XI/481.3/450: exp. "Pronunciamiento del teniente coronel Manuel Reyes Veramendi en el pueblo de Monte Alto, Mex., a favor de la expulsión de de los españoles y secundado en Zempoala, Hgo., por el teniente coronel Pero José de Espinoza. Año de 1828. 43 fojas." I thank Dr. Ev Meade for locating these and drawing them to my attention.

4. When the Pronunciamiento Went Viral

1. For an interpretation of what constituted an *hombre de bien*, see Costeloe, *Central Republic*, 16–30.

2. Comellas, *Los primeros pronunciamientos en España*, 357.

3. Ortega y Gasset, *España invertebrada* (originally published in 1921), 80, 83–84.

4. Tornel y Mendívil, *Breve reseña histórica*, 12.

5. Calderón de la Barca, *Life in Mexico*, 246.

6. Heller, *Alone in Mexico*, 57.

7. Heller, *Alone in Mexico*, 121.

8. Kingsley, *South by West*, 243.

9. Tutino, *From Insurrection to Revolution*, in particular 193–258; and Ortiz Escamilla, *Guerra y gobierno*, 101–56.

10. Chaney, "Old and New Feminists," 332.

11. I argued as much in a paper I gave titled "Las soldaderas de Santa Anna: Women and the Mexican Army, 1821–1855," at the international colloquium "Gender Conflict and Post-Conflict 200 Years On" held at the University of Nottingham, 17–19 November 2006. Peter F. Guardino provides numerous examples of female political activism in Oaxaca during the early national period—intimidating male voters outside polling stations during elections, participating in riots, drafting petitions, etc.; see Guardino, in *The Time of Liberty*, 173–76, 248–49, 268–69. Also see Davies et al., *South American Independence*, and Conway, "Sisters at War."

12. Mallon, *Peasant and Nation*, 10.

13. Mallon, *Peasant and Nation*, 329–30.

14. Thomson, "Popular Aspects of Liberalism," 281. Also see Thomson with LaFrance, *Patriotism, Politics, and Popular Liberalism*.

15. Guardino, *Peasants, Politics*, 216. Also see Guardino, *The Time of Liberty*.

16. Caplan, *Indigenous Citizens*, 11. For a parallel study that concentrates on the second half of the nineteenth century, see Chassen-López, *From Liberal to Revolutionary Oaxaca*.

17. Rodríguez O., *"We are now the True Spaniards,"* 3.

18. Thomson, "Popular Aspects of Liberalism," 288.

19. Guardino, *Peasants, Politics*, 211.

20. Chassen-López, *From Liberal to Revolutionary Oaxaca*, 343.

21. I have been unable to track down who these British landowners were. However, for studies on British activities in Mexico at the time, see by Costeloe, *William Bullock*, in particular chapter 6, "The Mexican Adventure" 126–66, and his *Bubbles and Bonanzas*; also see Villalobos Velázquez, *British Immigrants in the Mining District*.

22. The "Plan reformador de Tarecuato," 26 January 1832, is located in AGN: Gobernación, 1832, without classification, caja 4.

23. Rugeley, "Compass Points of Unrest," 5–6.

24. "Acta de la oficialidad de Tampico," 10 March 1832, is located in AHSDN: XI/481.3/784, f. 237.

25. "Pronunciamiento de Tabasco," 4 June 1832, is located AHSDN: XI/481.3/839, f. 74.

26. "Acta de la Fortaleza de San Diego," 11 August 1832, is located in Colección Josefina Z. Vázquez, Planes y Documentos, 1832, Archivo Histórico del Colegio de México, caja 6.

27. "Pronunciamiento de Culiacán," 26 September 1832, is located in AHSDN: XI/481.3/816, ff. 38–19.

28. Ducey, "Municipalities, Prefects, and Pronunciamientos," 75.

29. The "Plan de Huetamo," 9 September 1832, is located in AGN: Gobernación, 1832, unclassified, caja 12, f. 17; the "Despronunciamiento de Zacapu," is located in AGN: Gobernación, 1832, unclassified, caja 10, f. 15.

30. Ducey, "Municipalities, Prefects, and Pronunciamientos," 75.

31. The Plan of Jalapa of 4 December 1829 is reproduced in Bocanegra, *Memorias*, 2:55–56.

32. The Plan of Cuernavaca of 24 May 1834 is reproduced in Bocanegra, *Memorias*, 2:573–74.

33. The "Acta de adhesión de la ciudad de Colima al Plan de Cuernavaca y manifestación de cambio de autoridades" of 3 July 1834 is located in AHSDN: XI/481.3/1030, f. 3.

34. Guerra, "El pronunciamiento en México," 18.

35. The "Acta del ayuntamiento, labradores y vecinos de la municipalidad de Coronanco" of 4 June 1834 is located in AGN: Gobernación, 1834, s/s, caja 203, f. 27.

36. Elspeth Gillespie was the recipient of a St. Andrews University Research Internship Programme (URIP) award and spent the summer of 2010 working with the St. Andrews web-based pronunciamientos database (http://arts.st-andrews.ac.uk/pronunciamientos), presenting her findings in the URIP poster event held in Parliament Hall, University of St. Andrews, on 6 October 2010.

37. The "Acta del ayuntamiento de Ayotzingo para adherirse al Plan de Cuernavaca" of 7 June 1834 is located in AGN: Gobernación, 1834, s/s, caja 206, exp. 26; and the "Acta del pronunciamiento del Mineral de Taxco en favor del centralismo" of 1 June 1835 is located in AHSDN: XI.481.3/1120, f. 12.

38. The "Acta del Mineral de Nieves" of 17 June 1833 is located in AGN: Gobernación, 1833, s/s, caja 8. See Fowler, *Santa Anna of Mexico*, 146–52; and Costeloe, "The British and an Early Pronunciamiento, 1833–1834."

39. The "Acta del pueblo de Teotihuacán" of 3 June 1834 is located in AGN: Gobernación, 1834, s/s, caja 206, f. 26.

40. The "Acta del ayuntamiento, cura y juez de Mineral de Cimapán" of 8 June 1834 is located in AGN: Gobernación, 1834, s/s, caja 206, exp. 19.

41. The "Acta de ayuntamiento de la villa de Atlixco" of 9 June 1834 is located in AGN, Gobernación, 1834, s/s, caja 206, exp. 26.

42. "Acta de ayuntamiento de la villa de Atlixco," 9 June 1834.

43. "Acta de ayuntamiento de la villa de Atlixco," 9 June 1834.

44. The "Pronunciamiento de las mujeres de Zacatlán" of 29 July 1833 was discovered by Dr. Rosie Doyle in the British Library.

45. The "La tribu ópata se dirige al presidente para presentarle sus agravios" of 2 July 1836 is located in AGN: Gobernación, 1836, s/s.

46. The "Decreto del gobernador y comandante de Sonora, 12 de julio de 1842," is located in AHSDN: XI/481.3/1711, f. 372.

47. Ali, "Memory and Manipulation," 101–2.

48. Fowler, "'I Pronounce Thus I Exist,'" 262–63.

49. Gordiano Guzmán to Isidro Reyes, Tepalcatepec, 1 March 1838. Reproduced in Jiménez Camberos (ed.), *Gordiano Guzmán*, 105–6.

50. See Olveda, *Gordiano Guzmán*, and Ortiz Escamilla, "El pronunciamiento federalista de Gordian Guzmán." The outcome of this pronunciamiento was four years of civil conflict and acute instability in the region, with Guzmán conducting a campaign of guerrilla warfare and hit and run operations from the Sierra. This particular pronunciamiento cycle—which degenerated into a long-drawn-out agrarian revolt of sorts—did not end until 24 February 1842, when Guzmán finally handed himself in, making the most of a general amnesty Santa Anna's government offered him.

51. The texts for all of these pronunciamientos can be accessed at the AHRC–University of St. Andrews web-based pronunciamientos database, http://arts.st-andrews.ac.uk/pronunciamientos/.

52. See http://arts.st-andrews.ac.uk/pronunciamientos/.

53. http://arts.st-andrews.ac.uk/pronunciamientos/.

54. http://arts.st-andrews.ac.uk/pronunciamientos/.

55. http://arts.st-andrews.ac.uk/pronunciamientos/.

56. http://arts.st-andrews.ac.uk/pronunciamientos/.

57. The "Plan de la Junta Antifictiónica de Nueva Orleans" of 6 September 1835 was reproduced in *El Mosquito Mexicano*, 6 December 1835.

58. See Costeloe, *La primera república federal*, 275–306, and Andrews, *Entre la espada y la constitución*, 137–220.

59. Costeloe, *La primera república federal*, 307–49; Fowler, *Santa Anna of Mexico*, 133–42.

60. The Plan of Veracruz of 2 January 1832 is reprinted in Bocanegra, *Memorias*, 2:265–68.

61. The "Plan de Lerma" is reproduced in Vázquez (ed.), *Planes en la nación mexicana*, vol. 2, 120.

62. The "Acta de la guarnición de Veracruz y de la fortaleza de Ulúa reiterando el Plan de Veracruz y desconociendo el gobierno de Bustamante, 5 de julio de 1832," is located in AHSDN: XI/481.3/803, f.118; the "Plan de Zacatecas" of 10 July 1832 is reproduced in Vázquez (ed.), *Planes en la nación mexicana*, vol. 2, 131.

63. For accounts of the events see Anna, *Forging Mexico*, 246–58; Costeloe, *La primera república federal*, 327–46; Fowler, *Santa Anna of Mexico*, 133–42; Fowler, "The Pronunciamientos of Antonio López de Santa Anna," 223–28; and Fowler "Joseph Welsh."

64. Treaty of Zavaleta (Puebla) of 23 December 1832 is located in AHSDN: XI/481.3/945, ff. 77–79.

65. For the patronato debate see Costeloe, *Church and State in Independent Mexico*, and Staples, *La iglesia en la primera república federal*, 35–93.

66. The Plan of Escalada is reproduced in Vázquez (ed.), *Planes en la nación mexicana*, vol. 2, 178.

67. Aguilar Ferreira, *Los gobernadores de Michoacán*, 18–20. I thank Marco Antonio Landavazo for providing me with this source.

68. Durán, *Carta y plan del señor General Don Gabriel Durán.*

69. Plan of Huejotzingo of 8 June 1833 is reproduced in Vázquez (ed.), *Planes en la nación mexicana*, vol. 2, 184–85.

70. Costeloe, *La primera república federal*, 385–91; Costeloe, "The British and an Early Pronunciamiento, 1833–1834"; and Fowler, *Santa Anna of Mexico*, 146–54. Three key primary sources on this pronunciamiento are Arista, *Reseña histórica de la revolución*(1835); *Cartas dirigidas al Exmo. Sr. General Presidente* (1833); and Gerónimo Cardona, "Relación de lo ocurrido al Escmo. Sr. Presidente de la República desde su salida de la ciudad federal, hasta su entrada en ésta, por el teniente coronel ciudadano Gerónimo," held in Archivo Histórico del Instituto Nacional de Antropología e Historia, 3era serie, leg. 365, reg. 138, doc. 144 (Mexico, 1833). For an analysis of Arista's *Reseña histórica de la revolución*, see Irwin, "Mariano Arista's *Plan de Huejotzingo.*"

71. Costeloe, *La primera república federal*, 396–98.

72. *El Fénix de la Libertad*, 1 December 1833.

73. The Plan of Cuernavaca of 25 May 1834 is reproduced in Bocanegra, *Memorias*, 2:573–74.

74. The Plan of Toluca of 31 May 1834 is located in AGN: Gobernación, 1835, s/c caja 203, f. 3.

75. For a detailed account of how Santa Anna responded to the Plan of Cuernavaca and gradually, over the next few months, reversed the actions of the 1833–34 Congress, see Sordo Cedeño, *El congreso en la primera república centralista*, 61–106.

76. "Manuel G. Cosío, gobernador del Estado libre de Zacatecas a sus habitantes, 30 de marzo de 1835," is located in AGN: Gobernación, 1835, s/c, caja 5, f.179.

77. For account of the battle of Guadalupe, see Santa Anna's dispatch of 24 May 1835 (Cuartel General de Zacatecas), "Detalle de la gloriosa acción del 11 de mayo de 1835 en Zacatecas y documentos relativos," printed in *Diario del Gobierno*, 31 May 1835.

78. Costeloe, *Central Republic*, 29.

79. The Plan of Orizaba of 19 May 1835 is located in AGN: Historia, v. 559, cuaderno 21.

80. The Plan of Toluca of 29 May 1835 is located in AGN: Historia, v. 283. For the change to centralism see Costeloe, "Federalism to Centralism"; Vázquez, "Iglesia, ejército y centralismo"; and Sordo Cedeño, "El congreso en la crisis del primer federalismo (1831–1835)."

81. The 1836 Constitution is reproduced in Tena Ramírez, *Leyes fundamentales*, 204–48. Also see Pantoja Morán, *El Supremo Poder Conservador*; Costeloe, *Central Republic*, 93–120; and Sordo Cedeño, *El congreso en la primera república centralista*, 199–261.

82. Costeloe, *Central Republic*, 121–48.

83. Costeloe, *Central Republic*, 149–83; Andrews, *Entre la espada y la constitución*, 221–305.

84. Calderón de la Barca, *Life in Mexico*, 226.

85. José Urrea, "Aclaración de José Urrea de 16 de julio," *Boletín de Gobierno*, 22 July 1840.

86. Costeloe, "A Pronunciamiento."

87. The Plan of Guadalajara of 8 August 1841 is reproduced in *Colección de decretos, circulares y órdenes* (originally published in 1874).

88. The Plan of the Ciudadela of 4 September 1841 is reproduced in the *Boletín Oficial*, 6 September 1841.

89. The Plan of Perote of 9 September 1841 is reproduced in the *Boletín Oficial*, 14 September 1841. For the Triangular Revolt see Costeloe, "Triangular Revolt."

90. See Noriega Elío, *El Constituyente de 1842*.

91. Bustamante, *Diario histórico de México, 1822–1848*, CD-2, entry for Wednesday 14 December 1842.

92. "Pronunciamiento de San Luis Potosí," 9 December 1842, is located in AHSDN: XI/481.3/1716, f. 63; and "Pronunciamiento de Huejotzingo," 11 December 1842, is located in AGN, Gobernación, leg. 168, caja 254, exp. 3.

93. Costeloe, *Central Republic*, 206–12.

94. Quoted in Fowler, "The Damned and the Venerated," xxvii.

95. Cañedo Gamboa, "Ponciano Arriaga and Mariano Ávila's Intellectual Backing."

96. José Antonio Aguilar Rivera has convincingly argued that the 1824 Constitution was not a replica of the 1787 U.S. Constitution. Yet the reality did not stop 1830s Mexicans from persuading themselves that this had been the case, thus explaining Mexico's early constitutional failures. See Aguilar Rivera, *En pos de la quimera*.

97. "Plan de varios vecinos de la ciudad de México para declarar que su apoyo a la religión es incompatible con el sistema republicano federal, 12 de junio de 1835," reproduced in Vázquez (ed.), *Planes en la nación mexicana*, vol. 3, 44.

98. Fowler, *Mexico in the Age of Proposals*, 5.

99. Tornel, *Discurso que pronunció el Ecsmo. Sr. General D. José María Tornel y Mendívil*, 7.

100. Guardino, *Peasants, Politics*, 217.

101. See Smith, *Roots of Conservatism*.

102. *El Siglo XIX*, 19 August 1845.

5. From Forceful Negotiation to Civil War

1. Bustamante, *Diario histórico de México, 1822–1848*, CD-2, entry for Sunday 27 September 1840, "(Lluvia y truenos)."

2. Tornel, *Discurso . . . aniversario de la independencia*, 4–5.

3. Tornel, *Discurso . . . aniversario de la independencia*, 5.

4. Tornel, *Discurso . . . aniversario de la independencia*, 8.

5. Tornel, *Discurso . . . aniversario de la independencia*, 16. For an analysis of Tornel's 1840 speech, see Fowler, *Tornel and Santa Anna*, 174–79.

6. Mier y Terán, *Texas by Terán*, 139, entry for 16 January 1829.

7. For a vivid account of Mier y Terán's suicide see Krauze, *Siglo de caudillos*, 116–17.

8. *Pronunciamiento en favor de la verdadera opinión general, julio 1835*.

9. Bustamante, *Diario histórico de México, 1822–1848*, CD-2, entry for Tuesday 14 July 1835.

10. Boyd, "Contemporary Verdicts."

11. José María Luis Mora, "Discurso sobre las conspiraciones," in Luis Mora, *El clero, la milicia y las revoluciones*, 126–28. For Mora see Hale, *Mexican Liberalism in the Age of Mora*.

12. "Manifiesto de José Ignacio Gutiérrez, Santa Anna de Tamaulipas, 19 de noviembre de 1844" is located in AHSDN: XI/481.3/2040, f. 47.

13. On Bravo's action see Costeloe, *Central Republic*, 214–15.

14. Tweedie, *Mexico as I Saw It*, 121.

15. Fowler, "Entre la legalidad y la legitimidad," 102–3.

16. Tornel, *Discurso . . . aniversario de la independencia*, 7–8.

17. See Santoni, "Salvas, Cañonazos, y Repiques," and Megas, "The Pronunciamientos of the Mexican-American War."

18. Quoted and translated in Santoni, *Mexicans at Arms*, 232.

19. Fowler, *Mexico in the Age of Proposals*, 5, 29–32.

20. *La Palanca*, 3 May 1849.

21. Lucas Alamán to Santa Anna, 23 March 1853, reproduced in García Cantú (ed.), *El pensamiento de la reacción mexicana*, 315.

22. Costeloe, *Central Republic*, 170.

23. Gutiérrez Estrada, *Carta dirigida al Excelentísimo Señor Presidente*.

24. For a discussion of Gutiérrez Estrada's ideas, see Fowler, *Mexico in the Age of Proposals*, 69–72.

25. Soto, *La conspiración monárquica*.

26. Pani, *Para mexicanizar el Segundo Imperio*.

27. Benito Juárez, "Apuntes para mis hijos," reproduced in Tamayo (ed.), *Epistolario de Benito Juárez*, 29. For Juárez, see Hamnett, *Juárez*.

28. The four main national pronunciamientos that were launched and became confused with the peasant and indigenous rebellions of the Sierra Gorda were Tomás Mejía's Plan of Mineral de San José de los Amoles, 4 June 1848; Paredes y Arrillaga and Father Jarauta's pronunciamiento of Querétaro of 15 June 1848; General Leonardo Márquez's pronunciamiento of Sierra Alta of 11 February 1849; and Eleuterio Quiroz's Río Verde plan of 14 March 1849.

29. *Pronunciamiento a la Polka: Traduccion libre del plan del general Paredes* (Durango: Imp. de Manuel Gonzalez, 1845). The document is held at University of Texas at Arlington Library, Special Collections, and can be accessed online at the Center for Greater Southwestern Studies' website *A Continent Divided: The U.S.-Mexico War,* http://library.uta.edu/usmexicowar/.

30. *Pronunciamiento a la Polka.* Translation is published online at http://library .uta.edu/usmexicowar/translationresult.php?content_id=148.

31. Carr, *Spain 1808–1939,* 124.

32. *Pronunciamiento a la Polka,* http://library.uta.edu/usmexicowar/translation result.php?content_id=148.

33. Cruz, we are told, has Mexico City-based lawyer and politician Crisanto Bedolla—one of the main characters in the novel—as his patrón; Payno, *Los bandidos de Río Frío,* 410.

34. Payno, *Los bandidos de Río Frío,* 408–13.

35. AHSDN: XI/481.3/2803, f. 23, Anastasio Bustamante to Minister of War, Guanajuato, 24 July 1848. Quoted in Andrews, *Entre la espada y la constitución,* 321.

36. Both Herrera's and Arista's views are quoted in Cotner, *The Military and Political Career,* 182–83.

37. "Proclama del general Paredes y Arrillaga, al levantarse en armas contra el gobierno de la república, protestando contra la aprobación de los tratados de paz con los Estados Unidos," 15 June 1848, is reproduced in Vázquez (ed.), *Planes en la nación mexicana,* vol. 4, 388. Also see Cotner, *The Military and Political Career,* 174–86.

38. Andrews, *Entre la espada y la constitución,* 319–22.

39. These included that the permanent army was abolished and replaced with militias (the Guardia Nacional; art. 4), for the clergy to be reformed and moralized (art. 6), for all fueros to be abolished (art. 8), for the redistribution of the land—so that the "working class (*clases menesterosas*) improve their situation" (art. 10; articles 11–15 actually outlined how large hacienda estate own-

ers were to be made to redistribute their land among the peons and peasants who worked for or rented ranches from them), and that Santa Anna should never be allowed to return to Mexico (additional art. 2). The "Plan político y eminentemente social, proclamado en Río Verde, San Luis Potosí por el Ejército Regenerador de Sierra Gorda," 14 March 1849, is reproduced in *El Siglo XIX*, 30 March 1849.

40. AHDSN: XI/481.3/2921, exp. Operaciones Militares. Año de 1849: "Informe a la cámara de diputados de los servicios prestados del capitán Tomás Mejía, en la campaña de la Sierra Gorda, y solicitando su promoción al grado de teniente coronel. Febrero 28 de 1849." Also see McDonald, "The Experience of the Pronunciamiento," in particular chapter 7, "Legitimising a Rebellion: 'El Plan Político Eminentemente Social, proclamado en esta ciudad—Rioverde, San Luis Potosí—por el Ejército Regenerador de la Sierra Gorda' of 14 March 1849," 212–31.

41. Dublán and Lozano (eds.), *Legislación mexicana*, 6: 624.

42. Otero, *Ensayo sobre el verdadero estado*, 86.

43. The thirteen were, in chronological order (1) the Guadalajara–Mexico City series of 1844; (2) Othón and Rangel's pronunciamiento of 7 June 1845; (3) the Plan of San Luis Potosí of 14 December 1845; (4) the Plan of the Ciudadela of 4 August 1846; (5) the pronunciamientos of the Polkos of 1847; (6) Mejía's plan of 1848; (7) Paredes y Arrillaga and the Quéretaro series of 1848; (8) the 1848 plan of Leonardo Márquez; (9) the 1849 pronunciamiento of Quiroz and Verástegui; (10) The 1852 Blancarte series in Jalisco; (11) the plans of Ayutla, Guerrero, of 1 and 11 March 1854, and the whole Revolution of Ayutla series; (12) the Zacapoaxtla-Puebla series of 1855–56; and (13) the plans of Tacubaya and Félix Zuloaga of 17 December 1857 and 11 January 1858.

44. For the Caste War in Yucatán see Rugeley, *Yucatán's Maya Peasantry and the Origins of the Caste War, 1800–1847* and *Rebellion Now and Forever*. Also see Reed, *The Caste War of Yucatán*, and Dumond, *The Machete and the Cross*.

45. Kerry McDonald has argued this was the case with San Luis Potosí disgruntled hacendado Manuel Verástegui when he became involved in Eleuterio Quiroz's radical 1849 pronunciamiento: McDonald, "The Experience of the Pronunciamiento," in particular chapter 7, 212–31.

46. For the Sierra Gorda Rebellion see Vázquez Mantecón, "Espacio social y crisis política." Also see Reina, *Las rebeliones campesinas en México*, 291–324, and "The Sierra Gorda Peasant Rebellion." Mejía's 1848 pronunciamiento, the "Acta de Mineral de San José de los Amoles," 4 June 1848, is located in AHSDN:

exp. XI/481.3/2827. For Mejía, see Hamnett, "Mexican Conservatives, Clericals, and Soldiers." Paredes y Arrillaga's 1848 pronunciamiento, the "Proclama del general Paredes y Arrillaga, al levantarse en armas contra el gobierno de la república, protestando contra la aprobación de los tratados de paz con los Estados Unidos," 15 June 1848, is reproduced in Vázquez (ed.), *Planes en la nación mexicana*, vol. 4, 388. Also see Cotner, *The Military and Political Career*, 174–86. Leonardo Márquez's 1849 pronunciamiento, the "Pronunciamiento de Sierra Alta," 11 February 1849, is reproduced in Vázquez (ed.), *Planes en la nación mexicana*, vol. 4, 393. Eleuterio Quiroz's 1849 pronunciamiento, the "Plan político y eminentemente social, proclamado en Río Verde, San Luis Potosí por el Ejercito Regenerador de Sierra Gorda," 14 March 1849, is reproduced in *El Siglo XIX*, 30 March 1849.

47. "Acta del Ayuntamiento del pueblo de San Agustín del Palmar," 30 May 1843, is located in AGN: Gobernación, 1843, s/s, caja 206, exp. 26.

48. "Plan de la guarnición de Guanajuato," 8 January 1851, is located in AHSDN: XI/481.3/3293, ff. 73–77.

49. "Proclama y plan del pronunciamiento de la Guardia Nacional," 7 June 1845, is reproduced in *La Voz del Pueblo*, 19 July 1845.

50. Costeloe, *Central Republic*, 270–73; quotation is from 271. Also see Santoni, *Mexicans at Arms*, 78–87; and Cotner, *The Military and Political Career*, 130–31.

51. I have, as yet, to find the actual pronunciamiento text for the Puebla plan of 20 October 1856. The extensive 900-page-long "expediente" dedicated to this pronunciamiento cycle and Tomás Moreno's siege of Puebla, held in AHSDN: exp. XI/481.3/10124, does not hold the plan itself. The call to defend religion, social guarantees, and the army is taken from Miguel Miramón's address of 10 November 1856, reproduced in the *Periódico Oficial del Departamento de Puebla*, 12 November 1856.

52. *Periódico Oficial del Departamento de Puebla*, 25 October 1856.

53. "Plan del Mineral de Temascaltepec," 2 January 1849, is reproduced in Vázquez (ed.), *Planes en la nación mexicana*, vol. 4, 392. Also see Costeloe, "Mariano Arizcorreta and Peasant Unrest."

54. "Plan de Comitán," 21 May 1851, is located in BLAC: Cuestiones de Chiapas, Mexico 1836–1902, Documentos relativos al pronunciamiento verificado en la ciudad de Comitán el día 21 de mayo del corriente año de 1851, 20032875.

55. "Pronunciamiento de San Juan de Tierra Adentro," 26 July 1851, is located in AGN: Gobernación, 1851, 2/s, caja 394, exp. 13, f. 1.

56. "Intentona de Guanajuato," 9 July 1851, is located in Colección Josefina Zoraida Vázquez, Planes y documentos 1851, Archivo Histórico de El Colegio de México, caja 30.

57. "Plan definitivamente regenerador, proclamado en el Llano del Rodeo," December 1855, is located in Colección Josefina Zoraida Vázquez, Planes y documentos 1855–1858, Archivo Histórico de El Colegio de México, caja 34.

58. Bazant, *Antonio Haro y Tamariz*, 109–10.

59. Thomson, "The End of the 'Catholic Nation,'" 160–61.

60. Costeloe, *Central Republic*, 230–33.

61. Fowler, *Santa Anna of Mexico*, 214.

62. Fowler, *Santa Anna of Mexico*, 232–37.

63. Costeloe, "Los generals Santa Anna y Paredes y Arrillaga." Also see Vázquez, "In Search of Power," 187–91.

64. "Manifiesto del general Paredes y Arrillaga a la nación," 2 November 1844, is reproduced in Bustamante, *Apuntes*, 321–28. Also see Vázquez, "In Search of Power."

65. Sordo Cedeño, "Constitution and Congress." Also see Costeloe, *Central Republic*, 255–56.

66. Vázquez, "A manera de introducción," in Vázquez (ed.), *México al tiempo de su guerra*, 13.

67. Costeloe, *Central Republic*, 272–73.

68. Santoni, *Mexicans at Arms*, 39–40.

69. As would become apparent on 27 January 1846, Paredes y Arrillaga was thinking in terms of having 160 deputies who represented and were elected by the following groups: Urban and rural property owners, 38; commerce, 20; mining, 14; manufacturers, 14; literary professions, 14; judiciary, 10; public administration, 10; clergy, 20; and army, 20. See "Enero 27 de 1846.—Decreto del gobierno.—Sobre convocatoria para un congreso extraordinario, a consecuencia del movimiento iniciado en San Luis Potosí, el 14 de diciembre de 1845," in Dublán and Lozano (eds.), *Legislación mexicana*, 5:105–19.

70. "Manifiesto y plan de San Luis," 14 December 1845, is reproduced in *La Voz del Pueblo*, 20 December 1845.

71. "Acta del pronunciamiento de la guarnición de México," 30 December 1845, is reproduced in *La Voz del Pueblo*, 31 December 1845.

72. Costeloe, *Central Republic*, 281–83.

73. Vázquez, "México y la guerra con Estados Unidos," in Vázquez (ed.), *México al tiempo de su guerra*, 33; also see Soto, *La conspiración monárquica*.

74. "Pronunciamiento de la guarnición y autoridades de Mazatlán," 7 May 1846, is reproduced in Vázquez (ed.), *Planes en la nación mexicana*, vol. 4, 315–16.

75. "Pronunciamiento de la guarnición de Guadalajara," 20 May 1846 is reproduced in Vázquez (ed.), *Planes en la nación mexicana*, vol. 4, 317–18.

76. Santoni, *Mexicans at Arms*, 118.

77. Manuel Crescencio Rejón to Gómez Farías, Havana, 13 February 1845, and Rejón to Gómez Farías, Havana, 7 July 1845, BLAC, Valentín Gómez Farías Papers, nos. 1069, 1225.

78. Costeloe, *Central Republic*, 295.

79. "Plan de la Ciudadela," 4 August 1846, is reproduced in Vázquez (ed.), *Planes en la nación mexicana*, vol. 4, 321–22.

80. Costeloe, *Central Republic*, 296.

81. "Acta firmada en Toluca," 5 August 1846, is reproduced in Vázquez (ed.), *Planes en la nación mexicana*, vol. 4, 323–25.

82. "Acta firmada en el pueblo de Ochuc," 26 August 1846, is reproduced in the *Diario del Gobierno*, 19 October 1846.

83. Tenenbaum, "'They Went Thataway,'" 197.

84. Callcott, *Santa Anna*, 243.

85. See letters by Santa Anna to Minister of War, San Luis Potosi, 14 October, 16, 19 November, and 17 December 1846, in Smith (ed.), *Letters of General Antonio López de Santa Anna*, 372, 383–84, 385–86, 393–96. Also see BLAC, Valentín Gómez Farías Papers, no. 2231: Santa Anna to Rejón, San Luis Potosí, 2 January 1847.

86. AHSDN: exp. XI/481.3/2308, f. 1: Santa Anna to Minister of War, San Luis Potosí, 13 January 1847.

87. Costeloe, "The Mexican Church and the Rebellion of the Polkos."

88. The Plan of 27 February 1847 is reprinted in *Planes de la nación mexicana*, vol. 4, 377–378.

89. BLAC, Valentín Gómez Farías Papers, nos. 2717 and 2722: both by Santa Anna to Gómez Farías, San Luis Potosí, 9 March 1847.

90. Costeloe, "The Mexican Church and the Rebellion of the Polkos," 172.

91. *Los diputados que suscriben, a sus comitentes.*

92. Costeloe, "The Mexican Church and the Rebellion of the Polkos," 173.

93. For the Mexican-American War, in alphabetical order, see Conway (ed.), *The U.S.-Mexican War*; Frazier (ed.), *The United States and Mexico at War*; McCaffrey, *Army of Manifest Destiny*; Richmond (ed.), *Essays on the Mexican War*; Santoni, *Mexicans at Arms*; Vázquez, *Mexicanos y norteamericanos ante la guerra del 47*; Vázquez, *La intervención norteamericana 1846–1848*; Vázquez (ed.), *México al tiempo de su guerra*; Velasco Márquez, *La guerra del 47*; Wheelan, *Invading Mexico*.

94. Cotner, *The Military and Political Career*, 168–71.

95. Bazant, "From Independence to the Liberal Republic, 1821–1867," 26.

96. Ripley, *The War with Mexico*, 2:645.

97. Cotner, *The Military and Political Career*, 202.

98. Tenenbaum, "'Neither a borrower nor a lender be.'"

99. Herrera's ministers of finance, in chronological order, were: Mariano Riva Palacio, José Luis Huici, Antonio Icaza, José Luis Huici, Manuel Piña y Cuevas, José Luis Huici, Francisco Arrangoiz, José María de Lacunza, Bonifacio Gutiérrez, Francisco Yturbe, Francisco Elorriaga, Melchor Ocampo, Bonifacio Gutiérrez, José María de Lacunza, Manuel Payno, and José Luis Huici.

100. Cotner, *The Military and Political Career*, 205. Also see DePalo, *The Mexican National Army*, 147–50.

101. "Plan de Blancarte," 26 July 1852, is reproduced in Vázquez (ed.), *Planes en la nación mexicana*, vol. 4, 398–99.

102. "Pronunciamiento del Ayuntamiento de Colotlán," 3 August 1852, is reproduced in Vázquez (ed.), *Planes en la nación mexicana*, vol. 4, 399–400.

103. Doyle, "'The Curious Manner,'" 206.

104. "Segundo Plan de Blancarte," 13 September 1852 is reproduced in Vázquez (ed.), *Planes en la nación mexicana*, vol. 4, 400–1.

105. Doyle, "'The Curious Manner,'" 207.

106. "Plan del Hospicio," 20 October 1852 is reproduced in Vázquez (ed.), *Planes en la nación mexicana*, vol. 4, 401–2.

107. Vázquez Mantecón, *Santa Anna y la encrucijada del Estado*, 30–31.

108. AHSDN: exp. XI/III/1–116 [1–15], vol. VI, ff. 1440–1447 contain Lombardini's dispositions; also see Johnson, *The Mexican Revolution of Ayutla*, 11; and Vázquez Mantecón, *Santa Anna y la encrucijada del Estado*, 33.

109. See Vázquez Mantecón, *Santa Anna y la encrucijada del Estado*, and Fowler, *Santa Anna of Mexico*, 289–316.

110. Portilla, *Historia de la revolución* (first published in 1856), 51. Also Hamnett, "The Comonfort Presidency," 84

111. "Plan de Ayutla," 1 March 1854, is reprinted as an appendix in Portilla, *Historia de la revolución*, xv–xix.

112. Villegas, *Ignacio Comonfort*, 47.

113. The "Plan de Ayutla, reformado en Acapulco," 11 March 1854, is reproduced as an appendix in Portilla, *Historia de la revolución*, xix–xxvii; also see Johnson, *The Mexican Revolution of Ayutla*, 43.

114. Fowler, *Santa Anna of Mexico*, 311–15.

115. Hamnett, "The Comonfort Presidency," 86–87.

116. Luis Medina Peña, "El Plan de Monterrey de 1855: Un pronunciamiento regionalista en México," paper given at the international conference "Forceful Negotiations: The Origins of the Pronunciamiento in Nineteenth-Century Mexico," University of St. Andrews, 20–22 June 2008. The "Plan de Santiago Vidaurri" of 25 May is reproduced in McGowan, *Prensa y poder*, 305–6.

117. Portilla, *Historia de la revolución*, 124–26.

118. "Acta del pronunciamiento de la guarnición de México," 13 August 1855, is reproduced in McGowan, *Prensa y poder*, 301–2.

119. McGowan, *Prensa y poder*, 83–87.

120. Johnson, *The Mexican Revolution of Ayutla*, 100–12. Also see Villegas Revueltas, *El liberalismo moderado en México*, 71.

121. *Acta levantada por Exmo. Sr. Gobernador y Comandante general del Departamento de San Luis Potosí, Sr. General D. Francisco Güitian, la brigada de su nombre, e invitado por S. E. el Sr. D. Antonio Haro y Tamariz, y la guarnición de la capital para subvenir las exigencias públicas* (n.p: Imp. del Gobierno a cargo de Abraham A. Exiga, 13 de agosto de 1855) is located in AHSDN: exp. XI/481.3/4909, ff. 2–3. Also see Bazant, *Antonio Haro y Tamariz*, 82–86.

122. The "Plan de San Pedro Piedra Gorda," is reproduced in *El Omnibus*, 3 September 1855. Also see McGowan, *Prensa y poder*, 89, 303–4.

123. Dublán and Lozano (eds.), *Legislación mexicana*, vol. 8, law number 4572.

124. Dublán and Lozano (eds.), *Legislación mexicana*, vol. 8, law number 4715.

125. Hamnett, "The Comonfort Presidency," 90.

126. The 1857 Constitution is reproduced in Tena Ramírez, *Leyes fundamentales*, 606–29.

127. The "Plan de Tolimán" of 2 December 1855 is reproduced in García (ed.), *Documentos inéditos o muy raros*, 435–36.

128. The "Plan de Zacapoaxtla" of 12 December 1855 is reproduced in *El Siglo XIX*, 22 December 1855. Also see Bazant, *Antonio Haro y Tamariz*, 106–9.

129. There were nevertheless conservative pronunciamientos launched elsewhere that resonated with the poblano pronunciados' demands, including some pronunciamientos de adhesión in neighboring Veracruz and remote Matamoros.

130. AHSDN: exp. XI/481.3/10124 is dedicated to Miramón and Orihuela's pronunciamiento of September 1856 and the siege to which Tomás Moreno subjected Puebla. The printed "Capitulación" is f. 342.

131. Hamnett, "The Comonfort Presidency," 93.

132. Ignacio Comonfort, "Política del general Ignacio Comonfort," in Portilla, *México en 1856 y 1857*, 375.

133. Payno, *Memoria sobre la revolución* (first published in 1860), 42, 45.

134. The "Plan de Tacubaya" of 17 December 1857 is reproduced in Iglesias González (ed.), *Planes políticos*, 328–329.

135. Hamnett, "The Comonfort Presidency," 95.

136. See Pi-Suñer Llorens, "The Crumbling of a 'Hero,'" for an essay on how the historiography has generally condemned Comonfort for his endorsement of the Plan de Tacubaya.

137. "Modificaciones al Plan de Tacubaya," 11 January 1858, is reproduced in Boletín de la Secretaría de Gobernación, *Leyes fundamentales de los Estados Unidos Mexicanos*, 538.

138. According to Art. 79 of the 1857 Constitution, in case of the incumbent president being unable to serve, it fell upon the president of the Supreme Court of Justice to take over as the legitimate acting president of the republic: "En las faltas temporales del presidente de la República, y en la absoluta mientras se presenta el nuevamente electo entrará a ejercer el poder, el presidente de la Suprema Corte de Justicia."

139. For the Civil War of the Reforma and the French Intervention, see, in alphabetical order, Covo, *Las ideas de la Reforma*; Dabbs, *The French Army in Mexico*; Hamnett, *Juárez*; Lecaillon, *Napoleon III et le Mexique*; Pani, *Para mexicanizar el Segundo Imperio*; Ridley, *Maximilian and Juárez*; Roeder, *Juárez and His Mexico*; Sinkin, *The Mexican Reform*; Thomson with LaFrance, *Patriotism, Politics, and Popular Liberalism*.

140. Galindo y Galindo, *La gran década nacional* (originally published in 1904).

141. For the latter half of the nineteenth century, and in particular the governments of Benito Juárez (1867–72), Sebastián Lerdo de Tejada (1872–76), and Porfirio Díaz (1876–1910), see, in alphabetical order, Garner, *Porfirio Díaz*; Garner, "Porfirio Díaz," in Fowler, *Gobernantes mexicanos*; Hamnett, *Juárez*; Hamnett, "Benito Juárez," in Fowler, *Gobernantes mexicanos*; Knapp, *The Life of Sebastián Lerdo de Tejada*; Lloyd et al. (eds.), *Visiones del Porfiriato*; Pi-Suñer Llorens, "Sebastián Lerdo de Tejada," in Fowler, *Gobernantes mexicanos*; Raat, *El positivismo durante el porfiriato*; Villegas Revueltas, "Compromiso político e inversión," in Fowler, *Gobernantes mexicanos*; Zea, *Positivism in Mexico*.

142. Pani, "Intervention and Empire," 251.

143. Elias, *The Germans*, 216. For a concise and clear introduction to prevalent theories of collective violence, see Conteh-Morgan, *Collective Political Violence*.

144. There is not the time or space here to study the fluidity of the political alliances that were behind the pronunciamientos of the 1840s–50s, but it certainly is a subject worthy of research. On the one hand, it is striking how profoundly divided the moderados and the puros were, regardless of the fact that they were all liberals and federalists and shared many political ideals. The pronunciamientos of 1847 and 1857 highlight the extent to which the moderados were willing to use pronunciamientos to oust their radical cousins from positions of power. The same can be said for the puros, who were prepared to gang up with santanistas and conservatives in both 1845 and 1852.

145. Ali, "The Pronunciamiento in Yucatán (1821–1840)," 249–50.

146. Rugeley, *Rebellion Now and Forever*, 63.

147. The "Plan de San Luis Potosí" and the "Plan de Ayala" are both reproduced in Silva Herzog, *Breve historia de la revolución mexicana* 1:157–68 and 286–93, respectively.

148. "Declaración de la selva lacandona," Comandancia General del EZLN, año de 1993, Selva Lacandona, Chiapas, is reproduced in Rovira, *¡Zapata vive!*, 77–80. For the Chiapas rebellion, see Harvey, *The Chiapas Rebellion*.

Conclusion

1. Even the rabidly law-abiding, law-defending lawyer Benito Juárez, as a young man, added his signature to a *representación* that, albeit not a pronunciamiento in the strictest sense, was launched to make publicly known the federalist views of its signatories in the context of the fast-spreading centralist pronunciamiento cycle of 1835. Juárez and 120 other signatories were hop-

ing to prevent the centralist waves of pronunciamientos from influencing the president by means of the circulation of what amounted to a forceful representation of their own. See the *Representación de los ciudadanos de Oaxaca, 23 de agosto de 1835* (Mexico City: Imp. Francisco Cay Torres, 1835).

2. These were the plan of Iguala of 24 February 1821 that resulted in Mexico's independence from Spain; the Veracruz–Casa Mata series of 2 December 1822–1 February 1823 that brought an end to Agustín de Iturbide's Mexican Empire; the Perote–Oaxaca–La Acordada series of September–November 1828 that overturned General Manuel Gómez Pedraza's victory in the presidential elections in favor of *yorkino* candidate Vicente Guerrero; the Jalapa–Mexico City constellation (December 1829) that gave way to the overthrow of Guerrero and the rise to power of General Anastasio Bustamante (inspiring, in turn, a cluster of counter-Jalapa pronunciamientos as well as the sixteen-month-long War of the South in the present state of Guerrero); the Veracruz–Lerma–Zacatecas 1832 series that resulted, after a year of conflict, in the demise of Anastasio Bustamante's government and the return from exile of Manuel Gómez Pedraza to complete his interrupted term in office; the Cuernavaca–Toluca series of 1834 that led to the closure of the radical 1833–34 Congress and the repeal of most of its anti-clerical laws and reforms; the Orizaba–Toluca series of 1835 that brought an end to the First Federal Republic and ushered in the Central Republic (1835–46); the 1841 Guadalajara–Ciudadela–Perote series, otherwise known as the Triangular Revolt, that gave way to the overthrow of Bustamante's second government and Santa Anna's return to power; the 1842 San Luis Potosí–Huejotzingo series that gave acting president General Nicolás Bravo the justification he needed not to allow the draft 1842 federal constitution to be approved and to close down the Constituent Congress on 19 December that year; the Guadalajara–Mexico City series of 1844 that brought an end to Santa Anna's 1843–44 government; the Plan of San Luis Potosí of 14 December 1845 that overthrew José Joaquín de Herrera's moderate administration (1844–45); the Plan of the Ciudadela of 4 August 1846 that, in turn, brought down General Paredes y Arrillaga's government (1845–46); the 1852 Blancarte series in Jalisco that eventually resulted in the end of Mariano Arista's government (1851–53) and the return of Santa Anna from his exile in Colombia; the plans of Ayutla and Acapulco of 1 and 11 March 1854 that, after just over a year of civil war, brought down Santa Anna's 1853–55 dictatorship; and the plans of Tacubaya and Félix Zuloaga of 17 December 1857 and

11 January 1858, that initially abolished the 1857 Constitution, resulted in the closure of the national congress, and culminated with the overthrow of President Ignacio Comonfort by Zuloaga and the conservatives, giving way to the three-year-long Civil War of the Reforma (1858–60).

3. These included the pronunciamiento cycle of Manuel Montaño or Otumba (23 December 1827), which called for the end of all secret societies, a change of cabinet, and the expulsion of interfering U.S. Minister Plenipotentiary Joel Poinsett, while upholding the 1824 Constitution and the law; the Escalada–Durán–Arista series of 1833, which called initially for the protection of the Church and its ecclesiastical *fueros* from the anticlerical reforms that were starting to be discussed in congress, and which culminated with the demand that Santa Anna be proclaimed dictator; the Sonora–Sinaloa–Tamaulipas cycle of federalist pronunciamientos of 1837–40; Gordiano Guzmán's federalist-agrarian Aguililla pronunciamiento cycle of 1837–42; Tomás Mejía's pronunciamiento of Mineral de San José de los Amoles of 4 June 1848 to bring down the traitors in the government who had signed the peace treaty of Guadalupe Hidalgo and to continue fighting the war against the United States, while upholding some of the agrarian demands of the *campesinos* of the Sierra Gorda; General Paredes y Arrillaga and Father Celedonio Domeco Jarauta's pronunciamiento of Guanajuato of 15 June 1848 against the Guadalupe Hidalgo peace treaty with the United States and the Mexican government that had signed it; Eleuterio Quiroz and Manuel Verástegui's radical "Eminently social and political plan of Río Verde" of 14 March 1849 (San Luis Potosí); and Leonardo Márquez's plan of 11 February 1849, which called for the demise of Herrera's government and the return of Santa Anna.

4. These were the pronunciamiento-coup of 19 May 1822 that resulted in Iturbide becoming emperor and the plans of the Polkos of February–March 1847, which—after two months of street fighting in the center of Mexico City—succeeded in pressurizing Santa Anna into replacing radical liberal vice president Gómez Farías with a *moderado*, General Pedro María Anaya, and shelving the decree of 11 January 1847 that had been passed with a view to nationalize and sell 15 million pesos' worth of church property to pay for the war effort against the United States.

5. The pronunciamiento of Felipe de la Garza in Tamaulipas of 22 September 1822 in defense of congress and its arrested deputies; the plans of Guadalajara and San Luis Potosí (May to June 1823) that were launched to lobby the

authorities in Mexico City to convoke a federalist constituent congress; José María Lobato's anti-Spanish pronunciamiento of 23 January 1824 calling for the removal of all Spanish nationals from posts in the government bureaucracy; the radical federalist plan of Guadalajara (8 June 1824) that defended the Acta Constitutiva of January that year against the watered-down version that was adopted in the form of the 1824 Constitution; Nicolás Bravo's misleadingly named Plan of Reconciliation of Chichihualco (Guerrero) of 2 December 1833, calling for the creation of a new government and constituent assembly; state governor Manuel Cosío's Zacatecan federalist pronunciamiento of 30 March 1835, launched in an attempt to preempt the government's visible shift toward centralism; José Ramón García Ugarte's federalist pronunciamiento of San Luis Potosí of 14 April 1837; the pronunciamiento of 15 July 1840 in which Urrea seized the National Palace in Mexico City, temporarily taking President Anastasio Bustamante prisoner; Ramón Othón and Joaquín Rangel's "Proclama y plan de la guardia nacional" of 7 June 1845, which also entailed the seizure of the national palace by the pronunciados and the temporary capture of the incumbent president, on this occasion José Joaquín de Herrera; and the conservative plans of Zacapoaxtla–Puebla 1855–56, which entailed three notably destructive sieges of Puebla (17–23 January, 4–22 March, and 30 October–4 December 1856).

6. These were the pronunciamiento of Campeche (6 November 1829), which did not spread beyond Yucatán and failed to bring about its national demand to abolish the 1824 Federal Constitution and replace it with a new centralist charter, but which succeeded, arguably unwittingly, in Yucatán becoming a pseudo-independent state for the next two years; the Texan federalist pronunciamiento of 22 June 1835, which did not spread beyond Texas but eventually resulted in the independence of the province from Mexico after it triggered the Texan Revolution of 1835–36; and Santiago Imán's federalist pronunciamiento of Valladolid (Yucatán) of 12 February 1840, launched after several years of insurrectionary activity, which, after it was hijacked by the pronunciamiento of Mérida (Yucatán) of 18 February 1840 with its additional demand that Yucatán become independent from Mexico, as with Texas, also resulted in the independence of the province from Mexico (albeit temporary in this instance).

7. The following eight are but a sample of the ones that, to a greater or a lesser degree, have been noted, at some point, in this study: the plan of Veracruz of 31 July 1827 to remove state governor Miguel Barragán; that of San Juan

Bautista of 29 April 1830 to overthrow the commander general of Tabasco, Francisco Palomino; the plan of Arizpe of 12 August 1833 to recognize Manuel Escalante y Arvizu as the new state governor; the pronunciamiento of Chiapas of 27 November of the same year, calling for the overthrow of the current state legislature, the return of the previous incumbents, a ban on all *yorkinos* from positions of political power, and the appointment of Lieutenant Colonel José Anselmo de Lara as commander general of Chiapas; the plan of Opodepe (Sonora) of 28 November 1838, to remove Manuel Gándara as provincial governor/political chief; the Plan of the Mineral of Temascaltepec of 2 January 1849, to overthrow the governor of the State of Mexico, Mariano Arizcorreta; that of Comitán, in Chiapas, of 21 May 1851, to overthrow state governor Nicolás Maldonado; and the pronunciamiento of San Juan de Tierra Adentro of 26 July 1851, focused on replacing the current governor with José Julián Dueñas, deposed in a preceding pronunciamiento that had taken place on 15 October 1850.

8. Carpenter, *Travels and Adventures in Mexico*, 253.

9. Recent events in Egypt and Ukraine provide contemporary examples of how the pronunciamiento-like actions that initially resulted in the downfall of Hosni Mubarak, on 11 February 2011, and Viktor Yanukovych, on 21 February 2014, respectively, have since gone on to engender mirror insurrections that, in turn, resulted in the overthrow of elected president Mohamed Morsi on 3 July 2013 and the separation of Crimea and Donetsk from Ukraine.

Bibliography

Abbreviations

AGN   Archivo General de la Nación, Mexico City
AHSDN   Archivo Histórico de la Secretaría de la Defensa Nacional,
          Mexico City
AHESLP   Archivo Histórico del Estado de San Luis Potosí
AHMX   Archivo Histórico Municipal de Xalapa
AHRC   Arts and Humanities Research Council
CIDE   Centro de Investigación y Docencia Económicas
BLAC   Nettie Lee Benson Latin American Collection,
          University of Texas at Austin
FCE   Fondo de Cultura Económica
INAH   Instituto Nacional de Antropología e Historia
INEA   Instituto Nacional para la Educación de los Adultos
INEHRM   Instituto Nacional de Estudios Históricos de las Revolución
          Mexicana
SEP   Secretaría de Educación Pública
UASLP   Universidad Autónoma de San Luis Potosí
UNAM   Universidad Nacional Autónoma de México

Libraries, Archives, and Collections

Britain

British Library, London
Public Record Office, British Foreign Office Papers, Kew Gardens

Mexico

Archivo del Ayuntamiento de Puebla, Puebla
Archivo del Ayuntamiento de San Luis Potosí, San Luis Potosí
Archivo del Congreso del Estado de Jalisco, Guadalajara

Archivo General de la Nación, Mexico City
Archivo General del Estado de Yucatán, Mérida
Archivo Histórico de la Secretaría de la Defensa Nacional, Mexico City
Archivo Histórico del Colegio de México, Colección Josefina Z. Vázquez,
    Mexico City
Archivo Histórico del Estado de San Luis Potosí, San Luis Potosí
Archivo Histórico del Instituto Nacional de Antropología e Historia, Mex-
    ico City
Archivo Histórico Municipal de Veracruz, Veracruz
Archivo Histórico Municipal de Xalapa, Xalapa
Archivo Municipal de Guadalajara, Guadalajara
Biblioteca de la Universidad Autónoma de Puebla, Puebla
Biblioteca Nacional de México, Colección José María Lafragua, Mexico City
Biblioteca Nacional, Hemeroteca, Mexico City
Biblioteca Pública del Estado de Jalisco, Guadalajara
Centro de Apoyo a la Investigación Histórica de Yucatán, Mérida
Centro de Estudios de Historia de México CONDUMEX, Mexico City

Spain
Fondo General Palafox, Archivo-Biblioteca-Hemeroteca del Ayuntamiento
    de Zaragoza

United States
Nettie Lee Benson Latin American Collection, University of Texas at Austin
    Cuestiones de Chiapas, Mexico 1836–1902
    Genaro García Collection
    Hernández y Dávalos Collection
    Mariano Paredes y Arrillaga Archive
    Valentín Gómez Farías Papers
University of Texas at Arlington Library, Special Collections
University of California at Berkeley, Bancroft Library

Published Sources
Acle Aguirre, Andrea. "Ideas políticas de José Bernardo Couto y José Joaquín
    Pesado, 1801–1862." BA hons. thesis, El Colegio de México, 2006.
Actas del Congreso Constituyente Mexicano. 3 vols. Mexico City: Imprenta de
    Alejandro Valdés, 1823.

Aguilar Ferreira, Melesio. *Los gobernadores de Michoacán*. Morelia: Talleres gráficos del Gobierno del Estado, 1974.

Aguilar Rivera, José Antonio. *El manto liberal: Los poderes de emergencia en México 1821–1876*. Mexico City: UNAM, 2001.

———. *En pos de la quimera: Reflexiones sobre el experimento constitucional atlántico*. Mexico City: FCE, CIDE, 2000.

Aguilar Rivera, José Antonio (ed.). *Las elecciones y el gobierno representativo en México (1810–1910)*. Mexico City: FCE, Consejo Nacional de Ciencia y Tecnología, 2010.

AHRC–University of St. Andrews. "The Pronunciamiento in Independent Mexico 1821–1876." Web-based database. http://arts.st-andrews.ac.uk /pronunciamientos/.

Alamán, Lucas. *Historia de México*. 5 vols. Mexico City: Publicaciones Herrerías, S.A., 1938.

Alamán, Lucas. *Historia de Méjico*. 5 vols. Mexico City: Libros del Bachiller Sansón Carrasco, 1986.

Alcalá Galiano, Antonio María. *Apuntes para servir a la historia del origen y alzamiento del ejército destinado a ultramar en 1 de enero de 1820*. Madrid: Imp. De Aguado y Compañía, 1821.

———. *Recuerdos de un anciano*. Madrid: Imp. Central a cargo de Víctor Saiz, 1878.

Alexander, Robert J. *The Tragedy of Chile*. Westport CT: Greenwood Press, 1978.

Ali, Shara. "Memory and Manipulation: The Lost Cause of the Santiago Imán Pronunciamiento." In Will Fowler (ed.), *Celebrating Insurrection: The Commemoration and Representation of the Nineteenth-Century Mexican Pronunciamiento*. Lincoln: University of Nebraska Press, 2012. 93–113.

———. "The Origins of the Santiago Imán Revolt, 1838–1840: A Reassessment." In Will Fowler (ed.), *Forceful Negotiations: The Origins of the Pronunciamiento in Nineteenth-Century Mexico*. Lincoln: University of Nebraska Press, 2010. 143–61.

———. "The Pronunciamiento in Yucatán (1821–1840): From Independence to Independence." PhD diss., University of St. Andrews, 2011.

———. "Yucatecan-Mexican Relations at the Time of Independence: The Yucatecan Pronunciamiento of 1821." *Bulletin of Latin American Research* 33:2 (2014): 189–202.

Almonte, Juan Nepomuceno. *Guía de forasteros y repertorio de conocimientos útiles*. Mexico City: Instituto Mora, 1997.

Anderson, Benedict. *Imagined Communities: Reflections on the Origin and Spread of Nationalism*. London: Verso, 1983.

Anderson, Frank Maloy (ed.). *The Constitutions and Other Select Documents Illustrative of the History of France 1789–1901*. Minneapolis: H. W. Wilson, 1904.

Andrews, Catherine. "The Defence of Iturbide or the Defence of Federalism? Rebellion in Jalisco and the Conspiracy of the Calle de Celaya, 1824." *Bulletin of Latin American Research* 23:3 (2004): 319–38.

———. "The Rise and Fall of a Regional Strongman: Felipe de la Garza's Pronunciamiento of 1822." In Will Fowler (ed.), *Malcontents, Rebels, and Pronunciados: The Politics of Insurrection in Nineteenth-Century Mexico*. Lincoln: University of Nebraska Press, 2012. 22–41.

———. *Entre la espada y la constitución: El general Anastasio Bustamante 1780–1853*. Ciudad Victoria: Universidad Autónoma de Tamaulipas, 2008.

Andrews, Catherine, and Jesús Hernández Jaimes. "La lucha por la supervivencia: El impacto de la insurgencia en el Nuevo Santander, 1820–1821." In Ana Carolina Ibarra (ed.), *La independencia en el septentrión de la Nueva España: Provincias internas e intendencias norteñas*. Mexico City: UNAM, 2010. 35–78.

Anna, Timothy E. "Agustín de Iturbide and the Process of Consensus." In Christon I. Archer (ed.), *The Birth of Modern Mexico 1780–1824*. Wilmington DE: Scholarly Resources, 2003. 187–204.

———. "Demystifying Early Nineteenth-Century Mexico." *Mexican Studies/Estudios Mexicanos* 9:1 (Winner 1993): 119–37.

———. *The Fall of the Royal Government in Mexico City*. Lincoln: University of Nebraska Press, 1978.

———. *Forging Mexico 1821–1835*. Lincoln: University of Nebraska Press, 1998.

———. "Guadalupe Victoria." In Will Fowler (ed.), *Gobernantes mexicanos, vol. 1: 1821–1910*. Mexico City: FCE, 2008. 51–74.

———. "Iguala: The Prototype." In Will Fowler (ed.), *Forceful Negotiations: The Origins of the Pronunciamiento in Nineteenth-Century Mexico*. Lincoln: University of Nebraska Press, 2010. 1–21.

———. *The Mexican Empire of Iturbide*. Lincoln: University of Nebraska Press, 1990.

Annino, Antonio, and Rafael Rojas, with the collaboration of Francisco A. Eissa-Barroso. *La independencia: Los libros de la patria.* Mexico City: CIDE, FCE, 2008.

Apodaca, Fernando de Gabriel y Ruiz de. *Apuntes biográficos del excmo. Señor D. Juan Ruiz de Apodaca y Eliza, Conde del Venadito, Capitán General de la Real armada.* Burgos: Librería de José Antonio de Azpiazu, 1849.

Archer, Christon I. "'La Causa Buena': The Counterinsurgency Army of New Spain and the Ten Years' War." In Jaime E. Rodríguez O. (ed.), *The Independence of Mexico and the Creation of the New Nation.* Los Angeles: UCLA Latin American Center Publications, 1989. 85–108.

———. "Politicization of the Army of New Spain during the War of Independence, 1810–1821." In Jaime E. Rodríguez O., *The Origins of Mexican National Politics.* Wilmington DE: Scholarly Resources, 1997. 11–37.

———. "Where Did All the Royalists Go? New Light on the Military Collapse of New Spain, 1810–1822." In Jaime E. Rodríguez O. (ed.), *The Mexican and Mexican American Experience in the 19th Century.* Temple AZ: Bilingual Press, 1989. 24–43.

Arista, Mariano. *Reseña histórica de la revolución que desde 6 de junio hasta 8 de octubre tuvo lugar en la república el año de 1833 a favor del sistema central.* Mexico City: Imp. por Mariano Arévalo, 1835.

Arnold, Linda. *Bureaucracy and Bureaucrats in Mexico City, 1742–1835.* Tucson: University of Arizona Press, 1988.

———. "José Ramón García Ugarte: Patriot, Federalist, or Malcontent?" In Will Fowler (ed.), *Malcontents, Rebels, and Pronunciados: The Politics of Insurrection in Nineteenth-Century Mexico.* Lincoln: University of Nebraska Press, 2012. 91–110.

———. "Justicia militar en el México republicano: Las amnistías, visitas y los arrendamientos no pagados." In Luis Jáuregui and José Antonio Serrano Ortega (eds.), *Historia y nación.* Vol. 2: *Política y diplomacia en el siglo XIX mexicano.* Mexico City: El Colegio de México, 1998. 157–69.

———. *Política y justicia: La Suprema Corte Mexicana (1824–1855).* Mexico City: UNAM, 1996.

———. "Virtual Legality: Military Justice and the Fuero Militar, 1821–1832." In Dirección General del Centro de Documentación, Análisis, Archivos y Compilación de Leyes (comp.), *Historia de la justicia en México, siglos*

XIX y XX, tomo I. Mexico City: Suprema Corte de Justicia de la Nación, 2005. 23–54.

Arrangoiz, Francisco de Paula de. *México desde 1808 hasta 1867.* Mexico City: Porrúa, 1996.

Arriagada, Genaro. *Pinochet: The Politics of Power.* Boston: Unwin Hyman, 1988.

Arrom, Silvia Marina. "Popular Politics in Mexico City: The Parián Riot, 1828." *Hispanic American Historical Review* 68:2 (1988): 245–68.

———. *The Women of Mexico City, 1790–1857.* Stanford CA: Stanford University Press, 1985.

Arróniz, Marcos. *Manual del viajero en México.* Mexico City: Instituto Mora, 1991.

Artola, Miguel. *La burguesía revolucionaria (1808–1874).* Madrid: Alianza Universidad, 1983.

Avalos Calderón, Denis, and Flor de María Salazar Mendoza. "El Santa Anna de San Luis Potosí: Pronunciamiento santanista 1823." In *Memoria Electrónica del 10 Verano de la Ciencia de la Región Centro.* San Luis Potosí: UASLP, 2008. 1–5.

Ávila, Alfredo. "El gobierno imperial de Agustín de Iturbide." In Will Fowler (ed.), *Gobernantes mexicanos, vol. 1: 1821–1910.* Mexico City: FCE, 2008. 29–49.

———. *En nombre de la nación: La formación del gobierno representativo en México.* Mexico City: CIDE, Taurus, 2002.

———. *Para la libertad: Los republicanos en tiempos del imperio, 1821–1823.* Mexico City: UNAM, 2004.

Bakewell, P. J. *Silver Mining and Society in Colonial Mexico, Zacatecas 1546–1700.* Cambridge: Cambridge University Press, 1971.

Baquer, Miguel Alonso. *El modelo español de pronunciamiento.* Madrid: Rialp, 1983.

Barragán Barragán, José. *Principios sobre el federalismo mexicano: 1824.* Mexico City: Departamento del Distrito Federal, 1984.9

Bazant, Jan. *Antonio Haro y Tamariz y sus aventuras políticas, 1811–1869.* Mexico City: El Colegio de México, 1985.

———. *Los bienes de la Iglesia en México (1856–1875): Aspectos económicos y sociales de la Revolución liberal.* Mexico City: El Colegio de México, 1971.

———. "From Independence to the Liberal Republic, 1821–1867." In Leslie Bethell (ed.), *Mexico since Independence.* Cambridge: Cambridge University Press, 1991. 1–48.

————. *Historia de la deuda exterior de México (1823–1946)*. Mexico City: El Colegio de México, 1968.

Beezley, William H. *Mexican National Identity: Memory, Innuendo, and Popular Culture*. Tucson: University of Arizona Press, 2008.

Beezley, William H., and David E. Lorey (eds.) *Viva Mexico! Viva La Independencia! Celebrations of September 16*. Wilmington DE: Scholarly Resources, 2001.

Benson, Nettie Lee. *La diputación provincial y el federalismo mexicano*. Mexico City: El Colegio de México–UNAM, 1994.

————. "Iturbide y los planes de independencia." *Historia Mexicana* 2:3 (enero–marzo 1953): 439–46.

————. "The Plan of Casa Mata." *Hispanic American Historical Review* 25:1 (February 1945): 45–56.

————. *The Provincial Deputation in Mexico*. Austin: University of Texas Press, 1992.

Benson, Nettie Lee (ed.). *Mexico and the Spanish Cortes, 1810–1822: Eight Essays*. Austin: University of Texas Press, 1966.

Blanco Valdés, Roberto L. "Paisanos y soldados en los orígenes de la España liberal: Sobre revoluciones sociales, golpes de Estado y pronunciamientos militares." In Jaime E. Rodríguez O. (ed.), *Las nuevas naciones: España y México 1800–1850*. Madrid: Fundación MAPFRE, 2008. 273–92.

————. *Rey, cortes y fuerza armada en los orígenes de la España liberal, 1808–1823*. Madrid: Siglo XXI de España–Institució valenciana d'estudis i investigació, 1988.

Blázquez Domínguez, Carmen. "La expulsión de los españoles en Xalapa y Veracruz (1827–1828)." *Siglo XIX: Cuadernos de Historia* 2:4 (October 1992): 31–58.

————. *Políticos y comerciantes en Veracruz y Xalapa 1827–1829*. Xalapa: Gobierno del Estado de Veracruz, 1992.

Bocanegra, José María. *Memorias para la historia de México independiente, 1822–1846*. 3 vols. Mexico City: FCE–Instituto Cultural Helénico, 1987.

Boletín de la Secretaría de Gobernación, *Leyes fundamentales de los Estados Unidos Mexicanos y planes revolucionarios que han influido en la organización política de la república*. Mexico City: n.p., 1923.

Bolloten, Burnett. *The Spanish Revolution: The Left and the Struggle for Power during the Civil War*. Chapel Hill: University of North Carolina Press, 1978.

Boyd, Melissa. "Contemporary Verdicts on the Pronunciamiento during the Early National Period." In Will Fowler (ed.), *Celebrating Insurrection: The Commemoration and Representation of the Nineteenth-Century Mexican Pronunciamiento*. Lincoln: University of Nebraska Press, 2013. 152–75.

———. "The Career and Ideology of Mariano Otero, Mexican Politician (1817–1850)." PhD diss., University of St. Andrews, 2012.

———. "A Reluctant Advocate: Mariano Otero and the *Revolución de Jalisco*." In Fowler (ed.), *Forceful Negotiations: The Origins of the Pronunciamiento in Nineteenth-Century Mexico*. Lincoln: University of Nebraska Press, 2010. 162–79.

Brading, D. A. *Church and State in Bourbon Mexico: The Diocese of Michoacán 1749–1810*. Cambridge: Cambridge University Press, 1994.

———. *The First America: The Spanish Monarchy, Creole Patriots, and the Liberal State, 1492–1867*. Cambridge: Cambridge University Press, 1991.

———. *Miners and Merchants in Bourbon Mexico 1763–1810*. Cambridge: Cambridge University Press, 1971.

———. *The Origins of Mexican Nationalism*. Cambridge: Centre of Latin American Studies, 1985.

Briseño Senosiain, Lillian, Laura Solares Robles, and Laura Suárez de la Torre. *Guadalupe Victoria, primer presidente de México (1786–1843)*. Mexico City: SEP, Instituto Mora, 1986.

———. *José María Luis Mora: Obras Completas*. 8 vols. Mexico City: Instituto Mora, Consejo Nacional para la Cultura y las Artes, 1986.

———. *Valentín Gómez Farías y su lucha por el federalismo, 1822–1858*. Mexico City: Instituto Mora, Gobierno del Estado de Jalisco, 1991.

Brown, Matthew. *Adventuring through Spanish Colonies: Simón Bolívar, Foreign Mercenaries and the Birth of New Nations*. Liverpool: Liverpool University Press, 2006.

Brunk, Samuel, and Ben Fallaw (eds.) *Heroes and Hero Cults in Latin America*. Austin: University of Texas Press, 2006.

Burkholder, Mark A., and Lyman L. Johnson, *Colonial Latin America*. New York: Oxford University Press, 2010.

Busquets, Julio. *Pronunciamientos y golpes de estado en España*. Barcelona: Planeta, 1982.

Busquets, Julio, Miguel A. Aguilar, and Ignacio Puche, *El Golpe: Anatomía y claves del asalto al congreso*. Barcelona: Ariel, 1981.

Bustamante, Anastasio. *Manifiesto que el vice-presidente de la república Mexicana dirige a la nación.* Mexico City: Imp. A cargo de Tomás Uribe y Alcalde, 1830.

Bustamante, Carlos María de. *Apuntes para la historia del gobierno del general don Antonio López de Santa Anna, desde principios de Octubre de 1841 hasta el 6 de Diciembre de 1844, en que fue depuesto del mando por uniforme voluntad de la nación.* Mexico City: FCE, 1986.

———. *Cuadro histórico de la revolución mexicana.* 8 vols. Mexico City: FCE, 1985.

———. *Diario histórico de México, 1822–1848.* 2 CDS. Edited by Josefina Zoraida Vázquez and Cuauhtémoc Hernández Silva. Mexico City: CIESAS–El Colegio de México, 2003.

———. *Diario histórico de México: Diciembre 1822–Junio 1823.* 2 vols. Mexico City: INAH, 1980.

———. *El nuevo Bernal Díaz del Castillo, o sea, historia de la invasión de los anglo-americanos en México.* 2 vols. Mexico City: INEHRM, 1987.

Buve, Raymond. "Ayuntamientos and Pronunciamientos during the 19th Century: Examples from Tlaxcala between Independence and the Reform War." In Will Fowler (ed.), *Malcontents, Rebels, and Pronunciados: The Politics of Insurrection in Nineteenth-Century Mexico*, 129–47. Lincoln: University of Nebraska Press, 2012.

Cáceres di Lorio, Marco. *The Good Coup: The Overthrow of Manuel Zelaya in Honduras.* London: CCB Publishing, 2010.

Calderón de la Barca, Madame. *Life in Mexico.* London: Century, 1987.

Callcott, Wilfrid Hardy. *Santa Anna: The Story of an Enigma Who Once Was Mexico.* Norman: University of Oklahoma Press, 1936.

Cameron, Charlotte. *Mexico in Revolution: An Account of an English Woman's Experiences and Adventures in the Land of Revolution, With a Description of the People, the Beauties of the Country and the Highly Interesting Remains of Aztec Civilisation.* London: Seeley, Service and Company, 1925.

Campos, Jorge (ed.). *Obras escogidas de Antonio Alcalá Galiano.* 2 vols. Madrid: Atlas, 1955.

Cañedo Gamboa, Sergio Alejandro. "The First Independence Celebrations in San Luis Potosí, 1824–1847." In William H. Beezley and David E. Lorey (eds.) *¡Viva México! ¡Viva la Independencia! Celebrations of September 16.* Wilmington DE: Scholarly Resources, 2001. 77–87.

———. "Ponciano Arriaga and Mariano Ávila's Intellectual Backing of the 14 April 1837 Pronunciamiento of San Luis Potosí." In Will Fowler (ed.), *Malcontents, Rebels, and Pronunciados: The Politics of Insurrection in Nineteenth-Century Mexico*. Lincoln: University of Nebraska Press, 2012. 111–28.

Caplan, Karen D. *Indigenous Citizens: Local Liberalism in Early National Oaxaca and Yucatán*. Stanford CA: Stanford University Press, 2010.

Carlton, Eric. *The State against the State: The Theory and Practice of the Coup d'État*. Aldershot, UK: Scolar Press, 1997.

Carpenter, William W. *Travels and Adventures in Mexico: In the Course of Journeys of Upward of 2500 miles, Performed on Foot: Giving an Account of the Manners and Customs of the People, and the Agricultural and Mineral Resources of the Country*. New York: Harper and Brothers, 1851.

Carr, Raymond. *Spain 1808–1939*. Oxford: Clarendon Press, 1966.

Cartas de los señores generales D. Agustín de Iturbide y D. Vicente Guerrero. Mexico City: Imp. Imperial, 1821.

Cartas dirigidas al Exmo. Sr. General Presidente de la República D. Antonio López de Santa Anna por el General Mariano Arista y sus contestaciones. Mexico City: Imp. del Águila, 1833.

Castells, Irene. "El liberalismo insurreccional español (1815–1833)." In Xosé Ramón Barreiro Fernández (ed.), *O liberalismo nos seus contextos: Un estado da cuestión*. Santiago de Compostela: Universidade de Santiago de Compostela, 2008. 71–87.

———. *La utopía insurreccional del liberalismo: Torrijos y las conspiraciones liberales de la década omniosa*. Barcelona: Editorial Crítica, 1989.

Cepeda Gómez, José. *El ejército español en la política española (1787–1843): Conspiraciones y pronunciamientos en los comienzos de la España Liberal*. Madrid: Fundación Universitaria Española, 1990.

———. *Los pronunciamientos en la España del siglo XIX*. Madrid: Arco, 1999.

Cercas, Javier. *Anatomía de un instante*. Barcelona: Mondadori, 2009.

Chaney, Elsa. "Old and New Feminists in Latin America: The Case of Peru and Chile." *Journal of Marriage and the Family* 35:2 (1973): 331–43.

Chassen-López, Francie R. *From Liberal to Revolutionary Oaxaca: The View from the South, Mexico 1867–1911*. University Park: Pennsylvania State University Press, 2004.

Chowning, Margaret. *Wealth and Power in Provincial Mexico: Michoacán from the Late Colony to the Revolution*. Stanford CA: Stanford University Press, 1999.

Clavigero, Francisco Xavier. *Historia antigua de México*. Mexico City: Porrúa, 2003.

Close, David H. (ed.). *The Greek Civil War, 1943–1950: Studies of polarization*. London: Routledge, 1983.

Coatsworth, John H. "Los límites del absolutismo colonial: Estado y economía en el siglo XVIII." In John Coatsworth (ed.), *Los orígenes del atraso: Nueve ensayos de historia económica de México en los siglos XVIII y XIX*. Mexico City: Alianza–Patria, 1990. 37–56.

———. "Obstacles to Economic Growth in Nineteenth Century Mexico." *American Historical Review* 83 (February 1978): 80–100.

Colección de decretos, circulares y órdenes de los poderes legislativo y ejecutivo del Estado de Jalisco. Guadalajara: Congreso del Estado de Jalisco, Palacio de Gobierno, 1981.

Comellas, José Luis. *Los primeros pronunciamientos en España 1814–1820*. Madrid: Consejo Superior de Investigaciones Científicas, 1958.

Connaughton, Brian. *Clerical Ideology in a Revolutionary Age: The Guadalajara Church and the Idea of the Mexican Nation (1788–1853)*. Calgary: University of Calgary Press, 2003.

———. *Entre la voz de Dios y el llamado de la patria*. Mexico City: FCE, 2010.

Conteh-Morgan, Earl. *Collective Political Violence*. New York: Routledge, 2004.

A Continent Divided: The U.S.-Mexico War. Website, University of Texas at Arlington Library, Special Collections. http://library.uta.edu/usmexico war/.

Conway, Christopher. "Sisters at War: Mexican Women's Poetry and the U.S.-Mexican War." *Latin American Research Review* 47:1 (2012): 3–15.

Conway, Christopher (ed.). *The U.S.-Mexican War: A Binational Reader*. Indianapolis: Hackett Publishing Company, 2010.

Costeloe, Michael P. *Bonds and Bondholders: British Investors and Mexico's Foreign Debt, 1824–1888*. Westport CT: Praeger, 2003.

———. "The British and an Early Pronunciamiento, 1833–1834." In Will Fowler (ed.), *Forceful Negotiations: The Origins of the Pronunciamiento in Nineteenth-Century Mexico*. Lincoln: University of Nebraska Press, 2010. 125–42.

———. *Bubbles and Bonanzas: British Investors and Investments in Mexico, 1821–1860*. Lanham: Lexington Books, 2011.

————. *The Central Republic in Mexico, 1835–1846: Hombres de Bien in the Age of Santa Anna*. Cambridge: Cambridge University Press, 1993.

————. *Church and State in Independent Mexico: A Study of the Patronage Debate, 1821–1857*. London: Royal Historical Society, 1978.

————. "Church-State Financial Negotiations in Mexico during the American War, 1846–1847." *Revista de Historia de América* 60 (July–December 1965): 91–123.

————. *Church Wealth in Mexico: A Study of the Juzgado de Capellanías in the Archbishopric of Mexico, 1800–1856*. Cambridge: Cambridge University Press, 1967.

————. "Federalism to Centralism in Mexico: The Conservative Case for Change, 1834–1835." *Americas* 45 (1988): 173–85.

————. "Los generales Santa Anna y Paredes y Arrillaga en México, 1841–1843: Rivales por el poder o una copa más." *Historia Mexicana* 39:2 (1989): 417–40.

————. "Mariano Arizcorreta and Peasant Unrest in the State of Mexico, 1849." *Bulletin of Latin American Research* 15:1 (January 1996): 63–79.

————. "The Mexican Church and the Rebellion of the Polkos." *Hispanic American Historical Review* XLVI:2 (1966): 170–78.

————. *La primera república federal de México (1824–1835): Un estudio de los partidos políticos en el México independiente*. Mexico City: FCE, 1983.

————. "A Pronunciamiento in Nineteenth-Century Mexico: '15 de julio de 1840." *Mexican Studies/Estudios Mexicanos* 4:2 (Summer 1988): 245–64.

————. "The Triangular Revolt in Mexico and the Fall of Anastasio Bustamante, August–October 1841." *Journal of Latin American Studies* 20 (1988): 337–60.

————. *William Bullock, Connoisseur and Virtuoso of the Egyptian Hall: Picadilly to Mexico (1773–1849)*. Bristol: HiPLAM Bristol, 2008.

Cotner, Thomas Ewing, *The Military and Political Career of José Joaquín de Herrera 1792–1854*. Austin: University of Texas Press, 1949.

Covo, Jacqueline. *Las ideas de la Reforma en México (1855–1861)*. Mexico City: UNAM, 1983.

Cuevas, Luis Gonzaga. *Porvenir de México*. 2. vols. Mexico City: Consejo Nacional para la Cultura y las Artes, 1992.

Cunniff, Roger L. "Mexican Municipal Electoral Reform, 1810–1822." In Nettie Lee Benson (ed.), *Mexico and the Spanish Cortes 1810–1822*. Austin: University of Texas Press, 1966. 59–86.

Bibliography

Dabbs, Jack A. *The French Army in Mexico, 1861–1867: A Study in Military Government*. Hague: Mouton and Company, 1963.

David, Thomas B., and Amado Ricon Virulegio (eds.). *The Political Plans of Mexico*. Lanham MD: University Press of America, 1987.

Davies, Catherine, Claire Brewster, and Hilary Owen. *South American Independence: Gender, Politics, Text*. Liverpool: Liverpool University Press, 2006.

Deans-Smith, Susan. *Bureaucrats, Planters, and Workers: The Making of the Tobacco Monopoly in Bourbon Mexico*. Austin: University of Texas Press, 1992.

Debray, Régis. *Revolution in the Revolution?* Harmondsworth: Penguin, 1968.

Defensa del inmortal D. Rafael Riego. Mexico City: Oficina de J. M. Benavente y Socios, 1820.

DeGroot, Gerard J. *A Noble Cause? America and the Vietnam War*. London: Pearson, 2000.

Delgadillo Sánchez, Andrés. *San Luis Potosí durante la guerra contra Estados Unidos de Norteamérica. Identidad nacional, símbolos y héroes patrios 1846–1848*. San Luis Potosí: Editorial Ponciano Arriaga, 2012.

DePalo, William A. Jr. *The Mexican National Army, 1822–1852*. College Station: Texas A&M University Press, 1997.

Di Tella, Torcuato S. *National Popular Politics in Early Independent Mexico, 1820–1847*. Albuquerque: University of New Mexico Press, 1996.

Diccionario Porrúa: Historia, biografía y geografía de México, 2nd ed. Mexico City: Porrúa, 1964.

Doyle, Rosie. "'The Curious Manner in Which Pronunciamientos Are Got Up in this Country': The Plan of Blancarte of 26 July 1852." In Will Fowler (ed.), *Forceful Negotiations: The Origins of the Pronunciamiento in Nineteenth-Century Mexico*. Lincoln: University of Nebraska Press, 2010. 203–25.

———. "The Pronunciamiento in Nineteenth-Century Mexico: The Experience of Jalisco 1821–1853." PhD diss., University of St. Andrews, 2011.

———. "Refrescos, Iluminaciones and Te Deums: Celebrating Pronunciamientos in Jalisco in 1823 and 1832." In Will Fowler (ed.), *Celebrating Insurrection: The Commemoration and Representation of the Nineteenth-Century Mexican Pronunciamiento*. Lincoln: University of Nebraska Press, 2013. 50–73.

Dublán, Manuel, and José María Lozano. *Legislación mexicana*. 34 vols. Mexico City: Imp. del Comercio, 1876.

Ducey, Michael T. "Municipalities, Prefects, and Pronunciamientos: Power and Political Mobilizations in the Huasteca during the First Federal Republic." In Will Fowler (ed.), *Forceful Negotiations: The Origins of the Pronunciamiento in Nineteenth-Century Mexico*. Lincoln: University of Nebraska Press, 2010. 74–100.

———. *A Nation of Villages: Riot and Rebellion in the Mexican Huasteca, 1750–1850*. Tucson: University of Arizona Press, 2004.

Dumond, Don E. *The Machete and the Cross: Campesino Rebellion in Yucatán*. Lincoln: University of Nebraska Press, 1997.

Durán, Gabriel. *Carta y plan del señor General Don Gabriel Durán, 1 de junio de 1833*. Mexico City: Imp. de Tomás Uribe y Alcalde, 1833.

Eissa Barroso, Francisco A. "Political Culture in the Spanish Crisis of 1808: Mexico City's Experience." MA thesis, Department of History, University of Warwick, Conventry, 2007.

El Congreso de los Diputados. Madrid: Publicaciones del Congreso de los Diputados, 2001.

Elias, Norbert. *The Germans: Power Struggles and the Development of Habitus in the Nineteenth and Twentieth Centuries*. New York: Columbia University Press, 1996.

Falcoff, Mark. *Modern Chile 1970–1989: A Critical History*. New Brunswick NJ: Transaction Publishers, 1991.

Ferrer Muñoz, Manuel. *La formación de un estado nacional en México: El Imperio y la República federal, 1821–1835*. Mexico City: UNAM, 1995.

Filiu, Jean-Pierre. *The Arab Revolution: Ten Lessons from the Democratic Uprising*. London: Hurst and Company, 2011.

Fisher, John. *Commercial Relations between Spain and Spanish America in the Era of Free Trade, 1778–1796*. Liverpool: Institute of Latin American Studies, 1985.

Flaccus, Elmer William. "Guadalupe Victoria, Mexican Revolutionary Patriot and First President, 1786–1843." PhD diss., University of Texas at Austin, 1951.

Flores Clair, Eduardo. "A Socialist Pronunciamiento: Julio López Chávez's Uprising of 1868." In Will Fowler (ed.), *Malcontents, Rebels, and Pronunciados: The Politics of Insurrection in Nineteenth-Century Mexico*. Lincoln: University of Nebraska Press, 2012. 255–76.

Floyd, Troy S. *The Bourbon Reformers and Spanish Civilization*. Boston: D. C. Heath and Company, 1966.

Fontana, Josep. *La quiebra de la monarquía absoluta, 1814–1820*. Madrid: Ariel, 1971.

———. "Prólogo." In Irene Castells, *La utopia insurrecional del liberalismo: Torrijos y las conspiraciones liberales de la década omniosa*. Barcelona: Editorial Crítica, 1989.

Foster, John W. *Diplomatic Memoirs*, vol. 1. London: Constable and Company, 1910.

Fowler, Will. "'As Empty a Piece of Gasconading Stuff as I Have Ever Read.' The Pronunciamiento through Foreign Eyes." In Will Fowler (ed.), *Celebrating Insurrection: The Commemoration and Representation of the Nineteenth-Century Mexican Pronunciamiento*. Lincoln: University of Nebraska Press, 2012. 247–72.

———. "British Perceptions of Mid-Nineteenth Century Mexican Society: The Topos of the Bandit in Madame Calderón de la Barca's *Life in Mexico* (1843)." *Septentrión* 1 (enero–junio 2007): 65–87.

———. "The Children of the Chingada." In Will Fowler and Peter Lambert (eds.), *Political Violence and the Construction of National Identity in Latin America*. Basingstoke: Palgrave Macmillan, 2006. 1–18.

———. "Civil Conflict in Independent Mexico, 1821–57: An Overview." In Rebecca Earle (ed.), *Rumours of Wars: Civil Conflict in Nineteenth-Century Latin America*. London: Institute of Latin American Studies, 2000. 49–86.

———. "The Damned and the Venerated: The Memory, Commemoration and Representation of the Nineteenth-Century Mexican Pronunciamiento." In Will Fowler (ed.), *Celebrating Insurrection: The Commemoration and Representation of the Nineteenth-Century Mexican Pronunciamiento*. Lincoln: University of Nebraska Press, 2012. xvii–xlii.

———. "Entre la legalidad y la legitimidad: Elecciones, pronunciamientos y la voluntad general de la nación, 1821–1857." In José Antonio Aguilar Rivera (ed.), *Las elecciones y el gobierno representative en México (1810–1910)*. Mexico City: FCE, Instituto Federal Electoral, Consejo Nacional de Ciencia y Tecnología, Consejo Nacional para la Cultura y las Artes, 2010. 95–120.

———. "Fiestas santanistas: La celebración de Santa Anna en la villa de Jalapa, 1821–1855." *Historia Mexicana* 52:2 (October–December 2002): 391–447.

———. "Introduction: The Nineteenth-Century Practice of the Pronunciamiento and Its Origins." In Will Fowler (ed.), *Forceful Negotiations: The Origins of the Pronunciamiento in Nineteenth Century Mexico*. Lincoln: University of Nebraska Press, 2010. xv–xxxix.

———. "Introduction: Understanding Individual and Collective Insurrectionary Action in Independent Mexico, 1821–1876." In Will Fowler (ed.), *Malcontents, Rebels, and Pronunciados: The Politics of Insurrection in Nineteenth-Century Mexico*. Lincoln: University of Nebraska Press, 2012. xvii–xxxvi.

———. "'I Pronounce Thus I Exist': Redefining the *Pronunciamiento* in Independent Mexico, 1821–1876." In Will Fowler (ed.), *Forceful Negotiations: The Origins of the Pronunciamiento in Nineteenth Century Mexico*. Lincoln: University of Nebraska Press, 2010. 246–65.

———. "Joseph Welsh: A British *Santanista* (Mexico, 1832)." *Journal of Latin American Studies* 36 (2004): 29–56.

———. *Latin America since 1780*. London: Hodder Education, 2008.

———. *Latin America since 1780*. 3rd ed. London: Routledge, 2016.

———. *The Mexican Press and the Collapse of Representative Government during the Presidential Elections of 1828*. Research Paper 21. Liverpool: Institute of Latin American Studies, 1996.

———. *Mexico in the Age of Proposals, 1821–1853*. Westport CT: Greenwood Press, 1998.

———. "Mexico." In Guntram H. Herb and David H. Kaplan (eds.), *Nations and Nationalism: A Global Historical Overview*, vol. 1: *1770–1880*. Santa Barbara CA: ABC-CLIO, 2008. 344–57.

———. *Military Political Identity and Reformism in Independent Mexico: An Analysis of the Memorias de Guerra (1821–1855)*. London: Institute of Latin American Studies, 1996.

———. "El pronunciamiento mexicano del siglo XIX: Hacia una nueva tipología." *Estudios de Historia Moderna y Contemporánea de México* 38 (julio–diciembre 2009): 5–34.

———. "The Pronunciamientos of Antonio López de Santa Anna, 1821–1867." In Will Fowler (ed.), *Malcontents, Rebels, and Pronunciados: The Politics of Insurrection in Nineteenth-Century Mexico*. Lincoln: University of Nebraska Press, 2012. 205–34.

———. "Los pronunciamientos mexicanos de las primeras décadas nacionales, 1821–1855." *20/10 México: Nación y Modernidad, 1821–1910*, in press.

———. "Rafael del Riego and the Spanish Origins of the Nineteenth-Century Mexican *Pronunciamiento*." In Matthew Brown and Gabriel Paquette (eds.), *Connections after Colonialism: Europe and Latin America in the 1820s*. Tuscaloosa: University of Alabama Press, 2013. 46–63.

———. *Santa Anna of Mexico*. Lincoln: University of Nebraska Press, 2007.

———. "Santa Anna y el Plan de San Luis Potosí, 1823." In Flor de María Salazar Mendoza and Carlos Rubén Ruíz Medrano (coords.), *Capítulos de la Historia de San Luis Potosí siglos XVI al XX*. San Luis Potosí: UASLP–AHESLP, 2009. 137–60.

———. "Spanish American Revolutions of Independence." In James V. DeFronzo (ed.), *Revolutionary Movements in World History: From 1750 to the Present*, vol. 3: R-Z. Santa Barbara CA: ABC-CLIO, 2006. 810–24.

———. *Tornel and Santa Anna: The Writer and the Caudillo, Mexico 1795–1853*. Westport CT: Greenwood Press, 2000.

Fowler, Will (ed.). *Celebrating Insurrection: The Commemoration and Representation of the Nineteenth-Century Mexican Pronunciamiento*. Lincoln: University of Nebraska Press, 2012.

———. *Forceful Negotiations: The Origins of the Pronunciamiento in Nineteenth-Century Mexico*. Lincoln: University of Nebraska Press, 2010.

———. *Gobernantes mexicanos*. 2 vols. Mexico City: FCE, 2008.

———. *Malcontents, Rebels, and Pronunciados: The Politics of Insurrection in Nineteenth-Century Mexico*. Lincoln: University of Nebraska Press, 2012.

Fowler, Will, and Juan Ortiz Escamilla. "La revuelta del 2 de diciembre de 1822: Una perspectiva regional." *Historias* 47 (2000): 19–37.

Frasquet, Ivana. *Las caras del águila: Del liberalismo gaditano a la república federal mexicana (1820–1824)*. Castelló: Publicacions de la Universitat Jaume I, 2008.

Frasquet, Ivana, and Manuel Chust. "Agustín de Iturbide: From the Pronunciamiento of Iguala to the Coup of 1822." In Will Fowler (ed.), *Forceful Negotiations: The Origins of the Pronunciamiento in Nineteenth Century Mexico*. Lincoln: University of Nebraska Press, 2010. 22–46.

Frazier, Donald S. (ed.). *The United States and Mexico at War: Nineteenth-Century Expansionism and Conflict*. New York: Simon and Schuster Macmillan, 1998.

Fuentes Mares, José. *Poinsett: Historia de una gran intriga*. Mexico City: Libro Mex Editores, 1960.

Galindo y Galindo, Miguel. *La gran década nacional o relación histórica de la Guerra de Reforma, intervención extranjera y gobierno del archiduque Maximiliano, 1857–1867*. 3 vols. Mexico City: FCE, 1987.

Gantús, Fausta. "La inconformidad subversiva: Entre el pronunciamiento y el bandidaje. Un acercamiento a los movimientos rebeldes durante el tuxtepecanismo, 1876–1888." *Estudios de Historia Moderna y Contemporánea de México* 35 (enero–junio 2008): 49–74.

García, Genaro (ed.). *Documentos inéditos o muy raros para la historia de México: La Revolución de Ayutla*. Mexico City: Porrúa, 1974.

García Cantú, Gastón (ed.). *El pensamiento de la reacción mexicana: Historia documental. Tomo primero (1810–1859)*. Mexico City: UNAM, 1994.

Garner, Paul. *Porfirio Díaz*. London: Pearson, 2001.

———. "Porfirio Díaz." In Will Fowler (ed.), *Gobernantes mexicanos, vol. 1: 1821–1910*. Mexico City: FCE, 2008. 383–401.

Geggus, David P. (ed.). *The Impact of the Haitian Revolution in the Atlantic World*. Columbia: University of South Carolina Press, 2001.

Gil Novales, Alberto (ed.). *Rafael del Riego, La Revolución de 1820, día a día: Cartas, escritos y discursos*. Madrid: Editorial Tecnos, 1976.

Girard, René. *The Scapegoat*. London: Athlone, 1986.

Godechot, Jacques Léon. *France and the Atlantic Revolution of the Eighteenth Century, 1770–1799*. New York: Free Press, 1965.

González Navarro, Moisés. *Anatomía del poder en Mexico, 1848–1853*. Mexico City: El Colegio de México, 1983.

González Pedrero, Enrique. *País de un solo hombre: El México de Santa Anna*. 2 vols. Mexico City: FCE, 1993, 2003.

Gott, Richard. *Guerrilla Movements in Latin America*. London: Seagull Books, 2008.

Green, Stanley C. *The Mexican Republic: The First Decade 1823–1832*. Pittsburgh: University of Pittsburgh Press, 1987.

Gregory, Desmond. *Brute New World: The Rediscovery of Latin America in the Early Nineteenth Century*. London: British Academic Press, 1992.

Guardino, Peter F. *Peasants, Politics, and the Formation of Mexico's National State: Guerrero, 1800–1857*. Stanford CA: Stanford University Press, 1996.

———. *The Time of Liberty: Popular Political Culture in Oaxaca, 1750–1850*. Durham NC: Duke University Press, 2005.

Guerra, François-Xavier. "Mexico from Independence to Revolution: The Mutations of Liberalism." In Elisa Servín, Leticia Reina, and John Tutino (eds.), *Cycles of Conflict, Centuries of Change: Crisis, Reform and Revolution in Mexico*. Durham NC : Duke University Press, 2007. 129–52.

———. "El pronunciamiento en México: Prácticas e imaginarios." *Travaux et Recherches dans les Ameriques de Centre* 37 (juin 2000): 15–26.

Gurr, T. R. "A Causal Model of Civil Strife: A Comparative Analysis Using New Indices." *American Political Science Review* 62 (1968): 1104–24.

———. *Why Men Rebel*. Princeton NJ: University of Princeton Press, 1970.

Gutiérrez Estrada, José María. *Carta dirigida al Excelentísimo Señor Presidente de la República sobre la necesidad de buscar en una convención el posible remedio de los males que aquejan a la república; y opiniones del autor acerca del mismo asunto*. Mexico City: Imp. de I. Cumplido, 1840.

Hale, Charles A. *Mexican Liberalism in the Age of Mora, 1821–1853*. New Haven: Yale University Press, 1968.

Hamnett, Brian R. "Benito Juárez: Técnicas para permanecer en el poder." In Will Fowler (ed.), *Gobernantes mexicanos, vol. 1: 1821–1910*. Mexico City: FCE, 2008. 303–35.

———. "The Comonfort Presidency, 1855–1857." *Bulletin of Latin American Research* 15:1 (January 1996), 81–100.

———. *Juárez*. London: Longman, 1994.

———. "Liberalism Divided: Regional Politics and the National Project during the Mexican Restored Republic, 1867–1876." *Hispanic American Historical Review*, 76:4 (1996): 659–89.

———. "Mexican Conservatives, Clericals, and Soldiers: The 'Traitor' Tomás Mejía through Reform and Empire, 1855–1867." *Bulletin of Latin American Research* 20:2 (2001): 187–209.

———. "Partidos políticos mexicanos e intervención militar, 1823–1855." In Antonio Annino (ed.), *América Latina: Dallo stato coloniale allo state nazione*, vol. 2. Milan: Franco Angeli, 1987. 573–91.

———. *Revolución y contrarevolución en México y el Perú: Liberalismo, realeza y separatismo (1800–1824)*. Mexico City: FCE, 1978.

———. *Roots of Insurgency: Mexican regions, 1750–1824*. Cambridge: Cambridge University Press, 1986.

Harvey, Neil. *The Chiapas Rebellion: The Struggle for Land and Democracy*. Durham NC: Duke University Press, 1998.

Heller, Karl Bartolomeus. *Alone in Mexico: The Astonishing Travels of Karl Heller, 1845–1848*. Translated and edited by Terry Rugeley. Tuscaloosa: University of Alabama Press, 2007.

Henson, Margaret Swett. *Lorenzo de Zavala: The Pragmatic Idealist*. Fort Worth: Texas Christian University Press, 1996.

Hernández Jaimes, Jesús. "El diseño de las políticas fiscales y comerciales en México, 1821–1855." PhD diss., El Colegio de México, 2010.

Herrejón Peredo, Carlos. *Hidalgo. Maestro, párroco e insurgente*. Mexico City: Fomento Cultural Banamex, 2011.

———. *Los procesos de Morelos*. Zamora: El Colegio de Michoacán, 1985.

Herrera Canales, Inés. *El comercio exterior de México 1821–1875*. Mexico City: El Colegio de México, 1977.

Historia de la alfabetización y de la educación de adultos en México. 3 vols. Mexico City: SEP, INEA, El Colegio de México, n.d.

Holden, Robert H. *Armies without Nations: Public Violence and State Formation in Central America, 1821–1960*. Oxford: Oxford University Press, 2004.

Humboldt, Alexandre von. *Essai politique sur le Royaume de la Nouvelle-Espagne*. 2 vols. Paris: Imp. J. H. Stone, 1811.

———. *Political Essay on the Kingdom of New Spain: The John Black Translation* (abridged). Edited with an introduction by Mary Maples Dunn. Norman: University of Oklahoma Press, 1988.

Iglesias González, Román (ed.). *Planes políticos, proclamas, manifiestos y otros documentos de la independencia al México moderno, 1812–1940*. Mexico City: Instituto de Investigaciones Jurídicas, UNAM, 1998.

Irwin, Jason. "Mariano Arista's *Plan de Huejotzingo*: The Daily Reality of a *Pronunciado* (Mexico, 1833)." MA hons. thesis, University of St. Andrews, 2014.

Ita Rubio, Lourdes de, and Gerardo Sánchez Díaz (eds.), *Humboldt y otros viajeros en América Latina*. Morelia, Mich.: Instituto de Investigaciones Históricas de la Universidad Michoacana de San Nicolás de Hidalgo, 2006.

Iturbide, Agustín de. *A Statement of Some of the Principal Events in the Public Life of Agustín de Iturbide, Written by Himself*. London: J. Murray, 1824.

Jáuregui, Luis. "Las tareas y tribulaciones de Joaquín de Arredondo en las Provincias Internas de Oriente, 1811–1815." In Ana Carolina Ibarra (ed.), *La independencia en el septentrión de la Nueva España: Provincias internas e intendencias norteñas*. Mexico City: UNAM, 2010. 271–302.

Jáuregui, Luis, and José Antonio Serrano Ortega (eds.). *Historia y nación*, vol. 2: *Política y diplomacia en el siglo XIX mexicano*. Mexico City: Colegio de México, 1998.

Jiménez Camberos, Isidoro (ed.). *Gordiano Guzmán. Insurgente y federalista*. Guadalajara: Secretaría de Cultura de Jalisco, 2005.

Jiménez Codinach, Guadalupe (ed.), *Planes en la nación mexicana: 1810–1830*, vol. 1. Mexico City: Senado de la República–El Colegio de México, 1987.

Johnson, Richard A. *The Mexican Revolution of Ayutla, 1854–55: An Analysis of the Evolution and Destruction of Santa Anna's Last Dictatorship*. Westport CT: Greenwood Press, 1974.

Karnow, Stanley. *Vietnam: A History*. London: Pimlico, 1994.

Katz, Friedrich Katz (ed.). *Riot, Rebellion, and Revolution: Rural Social Conflict in Mexico*. Princeton: Princeton University Press, 1988.

Kimball, Jeffrey P. (ed.). *To Reason Why*. New York: McGraw-Hill, 1990.

Kingsley, Rose Georgina. *South by West or Winter in the Rocky Mountains and Spring in Mexico*. London: W. Isbister and Company, 1874.

Knapp, Frank Averill Jr. *The Life of Sebastián Lerdo de Tejada 1823–1889: A Study of Influence and Obscurity*. New York: Greenwood Press, 1968.

Knight, Alan. *The Mexican Revolution*, 2 vols. (Cambridge: Cambridge University Press, 1986).

Krauze, Enrique. *Siglo de caudillos: Biografía política de México (1810–1910)*. Barcelona: Tusquets, 1994.

Landavazo, Marco Antonio. *La máscara de Fernando VII: Discurso e imaginario monárquicos en una época de crisis, Nueva España, 1808–1822*. Mexico City: El Colegio de México, Universidad Michoacana de San Nicolás de Hidalgo, El Colegio de Michoacán, 2001.

Lecaillon, Jean-François. *Napoleon III et le Mexique: Les illusions d'un grand dessein*. Paris: L'Harmattan, 1994.

Leija Irurzo, Edgardo, and Flor de María Salazar Mendoza. "San Luis Potosí a la sombra del general Antonio López de Santa Anna: Avenencias y desavenencias políticas, 1822–1823." In *Memoria Electrónica del 10 Verano de la Ciencia de la Región Centro*. San Luis Potosí: UASLP, 2008. 1–5.

Lemoine Villicaña, Ernesto. *Morelos: Su vida revolucionaria a través de sus escritos y otros testimonios de la época*. Mexico City: UNAM, 1965.

Lenin, V. I. *V. I. Lenin: Selected Works in Two Volumes*. 2 vols. Moscow: Foreign Languages Publishing House, 1951.

Libro blanco del cambio de gobierno en Chile: 11 de septiembre de 1973. Santiago: Editorial Lord Cochrane, n.d.

Lipset, Seymour Martin. *Political Man: The Social Bases of Politics.* London: Heineman, 1983.

Lira, Andrés. *Lucas Alamán.* Mexico City: Cal y Arena, 1997.

Liss, Peggy K. *Atlantic Empires: The Network of Trade and Revolution, 1713–1826.* Baltimore MD: Johns Hopkins University Press, 1983.

Lloyd, Jane-Dale, Eduardo Mijangos Díaz, Marisa Pérez Domínguez, and María Eugenia Ponce Alcocer (eds.). *Visiones del Porfiriato. Visiones de México.* Mexico City: Universidad Iberoamericana, Universidad Michoacana de San Nicolás de Hidalgo, 2004.

Los diputados que suscriben, a sus comitentes. Mexico City: Imp. de Santiago Pérez, 1847.

Ludlow, Leonor (ed.). *Los secretarios de hacienda y sus proyectos, 1821–1933.* Mexico City: UNAM, 2002.

Ludlow, Leonor, and Carlos Marichal (eds.). *La banca en México 1820–1920.* Mexico City: Instituto Mora, 1998.

———. *Un siglo de deuda pública en México.* Mexico City: Instituto Mora, 1998.

Luttwak, Edward. *Coup d'état: A Practical Handbook.* London: Penguin, 1968.

Lynch, John. *Simón Bolívar: A Life.* New Haven: Yale University Press, 2006.

———. *The Spanish American Revolutions 1808–1826.* London: Weidenfeld and Nicolson, 1973.

Lynch, John (ed.). *Latin American Revolutions 1808–1826: Old and New World Origins.* Norman: University of Oklahoma Press, 1994.

MacEoin, Gary. *Chile: The Struggle for Dignity.* London: Coventure, 1975.

Madariaga, Salvador de. *The Fall of the Spanish American Empire.* London: Hollis & Carter, 1947.

Mallon, Florencia E. *Peasant and Nation: The Making of Postcolonial Mexico and Peru.* Berkeley: University of California Press, 1994.

Malo, José Ramón. *Diario de sucesos notables de Don José Ramón Malo (1832–1853).* 2 vols. Mexico City: Editorial Patria, 1948.

Manhire, Toby (ed.). *The Arab Spring: Rebellion, Revolution, and a New World Order.* London: Guardian Books, 2012.

Martínez Martínez, Germán. "Inventing the Nation: The Pronunciamiento and the Construction of Mexican National Identity, 1821–1876." In Will Fowler (ed.), *Forceful Negotiations: The Origins of the Pronunciamiento in Nineteenth-Century Mexico*. Lincoln: University of Nebraska Press, 2010. 226–45.

Mason, Paul. *Why It's Kicking Off Everywhere: The New Global Revolutions*. London: Verso, 2012.

Mateos, Juan A. *Historia parlamentaria de los congresos mexicanos*. 13 vols. Mexico City: Imp. de J. F. Jens, 1878.

Matute, Álvaro. *Antología, México en el siglo XIX: Fuentes e interpretaciones históricas*. Mexico City: UNAM, 1981.

McCaffrey, James M. *Army of Manifest Destiny: The American Soldier in the Mexican War 1846–1848*. New York: New York University Press, 1992.

McDonald, Kerry. "The Experience of the Pronunciamiento in San Luis Potosí, 1821–1849." PhD diss., University of St. Andrews, 2011.

———. "Los inicios del pronunciamiento en San Luis Potosí." In Flor de María Salazar Mendoza (ed.), *12 Ensayos sobre política y sociedad potosina durante la Independencia y la Revolución*. San Luis Potosí: Congreso del Estado de San Luis Potosí–UASLP–AHESLP, 2009. 47–53.

———. "The Origins of the Pronunciamientos of San Luis Potosí: An Overview." In Will Fowler (ed.), *Forceful Negotiations: The Origins of the Pronunciamiento in Nineteenth-Century Mexico*. Lincoln: University of Nebraska Press, 2010. 101–24.

———. "The Political Life of Executed Pronunciados: The Representation and Memory of José Márquez and Joaquín Gárate's 1830 Pronunciamiento of San Luis." In Will Fowler (ed.), *Celebrating Insurrection: The Commemoration and Representation of the Nineteenth-Century Mexican Pronunciamiento*. Lincoln: University of Nebraska Press, 2012. 74–92.

McGowan, Gerald L. *Prensa y poder, 1854–1857, La revolución de Ayutla: El Congreso Constituyente*. Mexico City: El Colegio de México, 1978.

Megas, Leonidas Kymon. "The Pronunciamientos of the Mexican-American War, 1846–48." MA thesis, University of St. Andrews, 2010.

Mier y Terán, Manuel de. *Texas by Terán: The Diary Kept by General Manuel de Mier y Terán on his 1828 Inspection of Texas*. Edited by Jack Jackson, translated by John Wheat, with Botanical Notes by Scooter Cheatham and Lynn Marshall. Austin: University of Texas Press, 2000.

Miranda Arrieta, Eduardo. *Nicolás Bravo: Acción y discurso de un insurgente republicano mexicano, 1810–1854*. Mexico City: Instituto de Investigaciones Históricas, Universidad Michoacana de San Nicolás de Hidalgo, 2010.

Monroy Castillo, María Isabel. *Sueños, tentativas y posibilidades: Extranjeros en San Luis Potosí, 1821–1845*. San Luis Potosí: El Colegio de San Luis–AHESLP, 2004.

Mora, José María Luis. *El clero, la milicia y las revoluciones*. Mexico City: Empresas Editoriales, 1951.

———. *Méjico y sus revoluciones*, 3 vols. Mexico City: Instituto Cultural Helénico, FCE, 1986.

Moreno Gutiérrez, Rodrigo. "The Memory and Representation of Rafael del Riego's Pronunciamiento in Constitutional New Spain and Within the Iturbide Movement, 1820–1821." In Will Fowler (ed.), *Celebrating Insurrection: The Commemoration and Representation of the Nineteenth-Century Mexican Pronunciamiento*. Lincoln: University of Nebraska Press, 2012. 1–27.

Muro, Manuel. *Historia de San Luis Potosí*. 3 vols. San Luis Potosí: Sociedad Potosina de Estudios Históricos, Talleres Bloea de México, S.A., 1973.

Nora, Pierre (ed.). *Lieux de memoire*. 7 vols. Paris: Gallimard, 1992.

———. *Realms of Memory: Rethinking the French Past*. English language edition edited and with a foreword by Lawrence D. Kritzman; translated by Arthur Goldhammer. 3 vols. New York: Columbia University Press, 1996.

Noriega Elío, Cecilia. *El Constituyente de 1842*. Mexico City: UNAM, 1986.

Ocampo, Javier. *Las ideas de un día: El pueblo mexicano ante la consumación de su independencia*. Mexico City: El Colegio de México, 1969.

O'Gorman, Edmundo. *Seis estudios históricos de tema mexicano*. Xalapa: Universidad Veracruzana, 1960.

O'Hara, Matthew D. *A Flock Divided: Race, Religion, and Politics in Mexico, 1749–1857*. Durham NC: Duke University Press, 2010.

Olivera, Ruth R., and Liliane Crété. *Life in Mexico under Santa Anna, 1822–1855*. Norman: University of Oklahoma Press, 1991.

Olveda, Jaime (ed.). *Inversiones y empresarios extranjeros en el noroccidente de México: Siglo XIX*. Zapopan: El Colegio de Jalisco, 1996.

Olveda Legaspi, Jaime. *Gordiano Guzmán: Un cacique del siglo XIX*. Mexico City: SEP, INAH, 1980.

———. "Jalisco: El pronunciamiento federalista de Guadalajara." In Josefina Zoraida Vázquez (ed.), *El establecimiento del federalismo en México (1821–1827)*. Mexico City: El Colegio de México, 2003. 189–213.

———. *La política de Jalisco durante la primera época federal*. Guadalajara: Poderes de Jalisco, 1976.

Ortega y Gasset, José. *España invertebrada*. Madrid: Revista de Occidente, 1963.

Ortega y Medina, Juan A. *Humboldt desde México*. Mexico City: UNAM, 1960.

Ortiz Escamilla, Juan. "Las élites novohispanas ante la guerra civil de 1810." *Historia Mexicana* 46:2 (1996): 325–57.

———. *Guerra y gobierno: Los pueblos y la independencia de México*. Seville: Universidad Internacional de Andalucía, Universidad de Sevilla/Instituto Mora, Colegio de México, 1997.

———. "El pronunciamiento federalista de Gordiano Guzmán, 1837–1842." *Historia Mexicana* 38:2 (1988): 241–82.

———. "Veracruz, the Determining Region: Military Pronunciamientos in Mexico, 1821–1843." In Will Fowler (ed.), *Malcontents, Rebels, and Pronunciados: The Politics of Insurrection in Nineteenth-Century Mexico*. Lincoln: University of Nebraska Press, 2012. 42–67.

Ortiz Escamilla, Juan, and José Antonio Serrano Ortega (eds.). *Ayuntamientos y liberalismo gaditano en México*. Zamora: El Colegio de Michoacán, Universidad Veracruzana, 2007.

Otero, Mariano. *Ensayo sobre el verdadero estado de la cuestión social y política que se agita en la república Mexicana*. Mexico City: Ediciones del Instituto Nacional de la Juventud Mexicana, 1964.

Palti, Elías José. *La invención de una legitimidad: Razón y retórica en el pensamiento mexicano del siglo XIX (Un estudio sobre las formas del discurso político)*. Mexico City: FCE, 2005.

Pani, Erika. "Intervention and Empire: Politics as Usual?" In Will Fowler (ed.), *Malcontents, Rebels, and Pronunciados: The Politics of Insurrection in Nineteenth-Century Mexico*. Lincoln: University of Nebraska Press, 2012. 236–254.

———. *Para mexicanizar el Segundo Imperio: El imaginario político de los imperialistas*. Mexico City: Colegio de México, Instituto Mora, 2001.

Pantoja Morán, David. *El Supremo Poder Conservador: El diseño institucional en las primeras constituciones mexicanas*. Mexico City: El Colegio de México, El Colegio de Michoacán, 2005.

Parcero, María de la Luz. *Lorenzo de Zavala: Fuente y origen de la reforma liberal en México*. Mexico City: UNAM, 1969.

Parra, Plasencia de la. *Independencia y nacionalismo a la luz del discurso conmemorativo (1825–1867)*. Mexico City: Consejo Nacional para la Cultura y las Artes, 1991.

Payne, Stanley. *Politics and the Military in Modern Spain.* Stanford CA: Stanford University Press, 1967.

Payno, Manuel. *Los bandidos de Río Frío.* Mexico City: Porrúa, 1996.

———. *Memoria sobre la revolución de diciembre de 1857 y enero de 1858.* Mexico City: INEHRM, 1987.

Pérez Galdós, Benito. *Fortunata y Jacinta.* 2 vols. Barcelona: Orbis, 1982.

———. *Tormento.* Madrid: Alianza Editorial, 1985.

Pérez Verdía, Luis. *Historia particular del Estado de Jalisco,* vol. 2. Guadalajara: Universidad de Guadalajara, 1988.

Peter, Fabienne. *Democratic Legitimacy.* New York: Routledge, 2009.

Pi-Suñer Llorens, Antonia. "The Crumbling of a 'Hero': Ignacio Comonfort from Ayutla to Tacubaya." In Will Fowler (ed.), *Celebrating Insurrection: The Commemoration and Representation of the Nineteenth-Century Mexican Pronunciamiento.* Lincoln: University of Nebraska Press, 2012. 176–200.

———. "Sebastián Lerdo de Tejada." In Will Fowler (ed.), *Gobernantes mexicanos, vol. 1: 1821–1910.* Mexico City: FCE, 2008. 337–60.

Poinsett, Joel Roberts. *Notes on Mexico, made in the autumn of 1822: Accompanied by an historical sketch of the revolution, and translations of official reports on the present state of that country.* New York: Praeger, 1969.

Portilla, Anselmo de la. *Historia de la revolución de México contra la dictadura del general Santa Anna 1853–1855.* Mexico City: FCE, 1993.

———. *México en 1856 y 1857: Gobierno del General Comonfort.* Mexico City: INEHRM, 1987.

Prieto, Guillermo. *Memorias de mis tiempos.* Mexico City: Editorial Porrúa, 1985.

Pronunciamiento a la Polka. Traduccion libre del plan del general Paredes. Durango: Imp. de Manuel Gonzalez, 1845.

Pronunciamiento en favor de la verdadera opinión general, julio 1835. Mexico City: Imp. por Manuel Fernández Redondas, 1835.

Proust, Marcel. *Remembrance of Things Past (1913–27), book 3 (1920–21),* vol. 2: *The Guermantes Way: Cities of the Plain.* Translated by C. K. Scott Moncrieff and Terence Kilmartin. London: Penguin Books, 1989.

Quinlan, David M. "Issues and Factions in the Constituent Congress, 1823–1824." In Jaime E. Rodríguez O. (ed.), *Mexico in the Age of Democratic Revolutions, 1750–1850.* Boulder: Lynne Rienner Publishers, 1994. 177–207.

Raat, William D. *El positivismo durante el porfiriato (1876–1910).* Mexico City: SepSetentas, 1975.

Racine, Karen. *Francisco de Miranda: A Transatlantic Life in the Age of Revolution.* Wilmington DE: Scholarly Resources, 2003.

Rangel Silva, José Alfredo, and Carlos Rubén Ruiz Medrano. *Discursos públicos, negociaciones y estrategias de lucha colectiva: Aportaciones al estudio de las movilizaciones sociales en México, siglos XVIII y XIX.* San Luis Potosí: El Colegio de San Luis–AHESLP, 2006.

Rapport, Mike. *1848: Year of Revolution.* New York: Basic Books, 2008.

Reed, Nelson. *The Caste War of Yucatán.* Stanford CA: Stanford University Press, 2001.

Reina, Leticia. *Las rebeliones campesinas en México, 1819–1906.* Mexico City: Siglo XXI Editores, 1980.

———. "The Sierra Gorda Peasant Rebellion, 1847–50." In Friedrich Katz (ed.), *Riot, Rebellion, and Revolution: Rural Social Conflict in Mexico.* Princeton: Princeton University Press, 1988. 269–94.

Representación de los ciudadanos de Oaxaca, 23 de agosto de 1835. Mexico City: Imp. Francisco Cay Torres, 1835.

Reséndez Fuentes, Andrés. "Guerra e identidad nacional." *Historia Mexicana* XLVII:2 (octubre–diciembre 1997), 411–39.

Reyes Heroles, Jesús (coord.). *Mariano Otero, Obras.* 2 vols. Mexico City: Porrúa, 1967.

Richmond, Douglas W. (ed.). *Essays on the Mexican War.* College Station: Texas A&M University Press, 1986.

Ridley, Jasper. *Maximilian and Juárez.* London: Phoenix Press, 2001.

Riego, Rafael del, et al. *Representación hecha al rey y a las Cortes, por los generales del ejército de observación Rafael del Riego, Miguel López Baños y Felipe Arco-Agüero.* Mexico City: Oficina de J. M. Benavente y Socios, 1820.

Ripley, R. S. *The War with Mexico.* 2 vols. New York: Burt Franklin, 1970.

Riva Palacio, Vicente. *México a través de los siglos: Historia general y completa del desenvolvimiento social, político, religioso, militar, artístico, científico y literario de México desde la antigüedad más remota hasta la época actual; obra única en su género.* 5 vols. Mexico City: Ballescá, 1880.

Robles, Laura Solares. *La obra política de Manuel Gómez Pedraza 1813–1851.* 2 vols. Mexico City: Instituto de investigaciones Dr José María Luis Mora, Instituto Matías Romero, Acervo Histórico Diplomático de la Secretaría de Relaciones Exteriores, 1999.

Rodríguez O., Jaime E. "Los caudillos y los historiadores: Riego, Iturbide y Santa Anna." In Manuel Chust and Víctor Mínguez (eds.), *La construcción del héroe en España y México (1789–1847)*. Valencia: Universitat de Valencia, 2003. 309–35.

———. "The Constitution of 1824 and the Formation of the Mexican State." In Jaime E. Rodríguez O. (ed.), *The Origins of Mexican National Politics, 1808–1847*. Wilmington DE: Scholarly Resources, 1997. 71–90.

———. *The Independence of Spanish America*. Cambridge: Cambridge University Press, 1998.

———. "The Origins of the 1832 Rebellion." In Jaime E. Rodríguez O. (ed.), *Patterns of Contention in Mexican History*. Wilmington DE: Scholarly Resources, 1992. 145–62.

———. "The Struggle for Dominance: The Legislature versus the Executive in Early Mexico." In Christon I. Archer (ed.), *The Birth of Modern Mexico 1780–1824* (Wilmington DE: Scholarly Resources, 2003). 205–28.

———. "The Transition from Colony to Nation: New Spain, 1810–1821." In Jaime E. Rodríguez O. (ed.), *Mexico in the Age of Democratic Revolutions, 1750–1850*. Boulder CO: Lynne Rienner Publishers, 1994. 97–132.

———. *"We are now the True Spaniards": Sovereignty, Revolution, Independence, and the Emergence of the Federal Republic of Mexico, 1808–1824*. Stanford CA: Stanford University Press, 2012.

Roeder, Ralph. *Juárez and His Mexico*, 2 vols. New York: Viking Press, 1947.

Rojas, Rafael. *La escritura de la independencia: El surgimiento de opinión pública en México*. Mexico City: Taurus, CIDE, 2003.

Romero Valderrama, Ana. "La mirada imparcial: Águila mejicana, 1826–1828." MA thesis, Instituto Mora, 2007.

———. "The Pedracista Alliance. Elections and Rebellions: Re-defining Political Participation in Mexico (1826–1828)." PhD diss., University of St. Andrews, 2011.

Rousseau, J. J. *Discours sur l'origine et les fondements de l'inégalité parmi les homes*. Paris: Éditions Sociales, 1971.

Rovira, Guiomar. *¡Zapata vive! La rebelión indígena de Chiapas contada por sus protagonistas*. Barcelona: Virus Editorial, 1994.

Rugeley, Terry. "The Compass Points of Unrest: Pronunciamientos from Within, Without, Above, and Below in Southeast Mexico, 1821–1876." In Will Fowler (ed.), *Malcontents, Rebels, and Pronunciados: The Politics of Insur-*

rection in Nineteenth-Century Mexico. Lincoln: University of Nebraska Press, 2012. 1–21.

———. *Rebellion Now and Forever: Mayas, Hispanics, and Caste War violence in Yucatán, 1800–1880.* Stanford CA: Stanford University Press, 2009.

———. *Yucatán's Maya Peasantry and the Origins of the Caste War.* Austin: University of Texas Press, 1996.

Runciman, W. G. (ed.). *Weber: Selections in Translation.* Cambridge: Cambridge University Press, 1978.

Salazar Mendoza, Flor de María. "Juan Bustamante's Pronunciamiento and the Civic Speeches that Condemned It. San Luis Potosí, 1868–1869." In Will Fowler (ed.), *Celebrating Insurrection: The Commemoration and Representation of the Nineteenth-Century Mexican Pronunciamiento.* Lincoln: University of Nebraska Press, 2012. 228–46.

———. *La Junta Patriótica de la capital potosina: Un espacio político de los liberales (1873–1882).* San Luis Potosí: Ponciano Arriaga, 1999.

Salinas Sandoval, María del Carmen, Diana Birrichaga Gardida, and Antonio Escobar Ohmstede. *Poder y gobierno local en México 1808–1857.* Zinacantepec: El Colegio Mexiquense, El Colegio de Michoacán, Universidad Autónoma del Estado de México, 2011.

Santoni, Pedro. "The Failure of Mobilization: The Civic Militia of Mexico in 1846." *Mexican Studies/Estudios Mexicanos* 12:2 (Summer 1996): 169–94.

———. "Lucas Balderas: Popular Leader and Patriot." In Jeffrey M. Pilcher (ed.), *The Human Tradition in Mexico.* Wilmington DE: Scholarly Resources, 2003. 41–56.

———. *Mexicans at Arms: Puro Federalists and the Politics of War, 1845–1848.* Fort Worth: Texas Christian University Press, 1996.

———. "Salvas, Cañonazos y Repiques: Celebrating the Pronunciamiento during the United States–Mexican War." In Will Fowler (ed.), *Celebrating Insurrection: The Commemoration and Representation of the Nineteenth-Century Mexican Pronunciamiento.* Lincoln: University of Nebraska Press, 2012. 114–51.

———. "Where Did the Other Heroes Go? Exalting the '*Polko*' National Guard Battalions in Nineteenth-Century Mexico." *Journal of Latin American Studies* 34:4 (November 2002): 807–44.

Schatzberg, Michael G. *Political Legitimacy in Middle Africa: Father, Family, Food.* Bloomington: Indiana University Press, 2001.

Schmitt, Carl. *Legality and Legitimacy*. Translated and edited by Jeffrey Seitzer with an introduction by John P. McCormick. Durham NC: Duke University Press, 2004.

Servín, Elisa, Leticia Reina, and John Tutino (eds.). *Cycles of Conflict, Centuries of Change: Crisis, Reform and Revolution in Mexico*. Durham NC: Duke University Press, 2007.

Sierra, Justo. *Evolución política del pueblo mexicano*. Mexico City: UNAM, 1957.

Silva Herzog, Jesús. *Breve historia de la revolución mexicana*. 2 vols. Mexico City: FCE, 1960.

Simmons, A. John. *Justification and Legitimacy. Essays on Rights and Obligations*. Cambridge: Cambridge University Press, 2001.

Sims, Harold D. *La expulsion de los españoles de México (1821–1828)*. Mexico City: FCE, 1974.

———. *The Expulsion of Mexico's Spaniards 1821–1836*. Pittsburgh: University of Pittsburgh Press, 1990.

Sinkin, Richard. *The Mexican Reform, 1855–1876: A Study in Nation-Building*. Austin: University of Texas Press, 1979.

Smith, Benjamin T. *The Roots of Conservatism in Mexico: Catholicism, Society, and Politics in the Mixteca Baja, 1750–1962*. Albuquerque: University of New Mexico Press, 2012.

Smith, Justin H. (ed.). *Letters of General Antonio López de Santa Anna Relating to the War between the United States and Mexico, 1846–1848*. In *Annual Report of the American Historical Association for the Year 1917*. Washington, D.C., 1920.

Solís Vicarte, Ruth. *Las sociedades secretas en el primer gobierno republicano (1824–1828)*. Mexico City: Editorial ASBE, 1997.

Sordo Cedeño, Reynaldo. "El congreso en la crisis del primer federalismo (1831–1835)." In Josefina Zoraida Vázquez and José Antonio Serrano Ortega (eds.), *Práctica y fracaso del primer federalismo mexicano (1824–1835)*. Mexico City: El Colegio de México, 2012. 111–33.

———. *El congreso en la primera república centralista*. Mexico City: El Colegio de México, Instituto Tecnológico Autónomo de México, 1993.

———. "El Congreso y la guerra con Estados Unidos de América, 1846–1848." In Josefina Zoraida Vázquez (coord.), *México al tiempo de su guerra con Estados Unidos (1846–1848)*. Mexico City: Secretaría de Relaciones Exteriores, El Colegio de México, FCE, 1997. 47–103.

———. "Constitution and Congress: A Pronunciamiento for Legality, December 1844." In Will Fowler (ed.), *Forceful Negotiations: The Origins of the Pronunciamiento in Nineteenth-Century Mexico*. Lincoln: University of Nebraska Press, 2010. 180–202.

Soto, Miguel. *La conspiración monárquica en México 1845–1846*. Mexico City: Editorial Offset, 1988.

Staples, Anne. *Bonanzas y borrascas mineras: El Estado de México, 1821–1876*. Toluca: El Colegio Mexiquense, 1994.

———. "The Clergy and How It Responded to Calls for Rebellion Before the Mid-Nineteenth Century." In Will Fowler (ed.), *Malcontents, Rebels, and Pronunciados: The Politics of Insurrection in Nineteenth-Century Mexico*. Lincoln: University of Nebraska Press, 2012. 68–90.

———. *La iglesia en la primera república federal mexicana (1824–1835)*. Mexico City: SepSetentas, 1976.

———. "Leer y escribir en los estados del México independiente." In *Historia de la alfabetización y de la educación de adultos en México*. 3 vols. Mexico City: SEP, INEA, El Colegio de México, n.d.), 137–87.

———. *Recuento de una batalla inconclusa: La educación mexicana de Iturbide a Juárez*. Mexico City: El Colegio de México, 2005.

Stealey, John E., III (ed.). *Porte Crayon's Mexico: David Hunter Strother's Diaries in the Early Porfirian Era, 1879–1885*. Kent: Kent State University Press, 2006.

Stein, Stanley J., and Barbara H. Stein. *Apogee of Empire: Spain and New Spain in the Age of Charles III, 1759–1789*. Baltimore MD: Johns Hopkins University Press, 2003.

Stern, Steve J. *Battling for Hearts and Minds: Memory Struggles in Pinochet's Chile, 1973–1988*. Durham NC: Duke University Press, 2006.

———. *Reckoning with Pinochet: The Memory Question in Democratic Chile, 1989–2006*. Durham NC: Duke University Press, 2010.

———. *Remembering Pinochet's Chile: On the Eve of London 1998*. Durham NC: Duke University Press, 2006.

Stevens, Donald F. *Origins of Instability in Early Republican Mexico*. Durham NC: Duke University Press, 1991.

Suárez, Federico. *Las Cortes de Cádiz*. Madrid: Rialp, 1982.

Tadeo Ortiz de Ayala, Simón. *Resumen de estadística del imperio mexicano 1822*. Mexico City: UNAM, 1968.

Tamayo, Jorge L. (ed.). *Epistolario de Benito Juárez*. Mexico City: FCE, 1972.

Tanck de Estrada, Dorothy. "La alfabetización: Medio para formar ciudadanos de una democracia 1821–1840." In *Historia de la alfabetización y de la educación de adultos en México*. 3 vols. Mexico City: SEP, INEA, El Colegio de México, n.d.). 111–36.

―――. "Los catecismos políticos: De la revolución francesa al México independiente." In Solange Alberro, Alicia Hernández Chávez, and Elías Trabulse (eds.), *La revolución francesa en México*. Mexico City: El Colegio de México, 1992. 65–80.

―――. *La educación ilustrada 1786–1836*. Mexico City: El Colegio de México, 1977.

―――. "Reformas borbónicas y educación utilitaria 1700–1821." In *Historia de la alfabetización y de la educación de adultos en México*. 3 vols. Mexico City: SEP, INEA, El Colegio de México, n.d. 69–110.

Taylor, William B. *Drinking, Homicide, and Rebellion in Colonial Mexican Villages*. Stanford CA: Stanford University Press, 1979.

―――. *Landlord and Peasant in Colonial Oaxaca*. Stanford CA: Stanford University Press, 1972.

―――. *Magistrates of the Sacred: Priests and Parishioners in Eighteenth-Century Mexico*. Stanford CA: Stanford University Press, 1996.

Tena Ramírez, Felipe. *Leyes fundamentales de México 1808–2002*. Mexico City: Porrúa, 2002.

Tenenbaum, Barbara A. "'Neither a borrower nor a lender be': Financial Constraints and the Treaty of Guadalupe Hidalgo." In Jaime E. Rodríguez O. (ed.), *The Mexican and Mexican American experience in the 19th century* (Tempe AZ: Bilingual Press/Editorial Bilingüe, 1989). 68–84.

―――. *The Politics of Penury: Debts and Taxes in Mexico, 1821–1856*. Albuquerque: University of New Mexico Press, 1986.

―――. "'They Went Thataway': The Evolution of the *Pronunciamiento*, 1821–1856." In Jaime E. Rodríguez O. (ed.), *Patterns of Contention in Mexican History*. Wilmington DE: Scholarly Resources, 1992. 187–205.

Thomson, Guy P. C. "The End of the 'Catholic Nation': Reform and Reaction in Puebla, 1854–1856." In Will Fowler (ed.), *Malcontents, Rebels, and Pronunciados: The Politics of Insurrection in Nineteenth-Century Mexico*. Lincoln: University of Nebraska Press, 2012. 148–70.

————. "Popular Aspects of Liberalism in Mexico, 1848–1888." *Bulletin of Latin American Research* 10:3 (1991), 265–92.

Thomson, Guy P. C., with David G. LaFrance, *Patriotism, Politics, and Popular Liberalism in Nineteenth-Century Mexico: Juan Francisco Lucas and the Puebla Sierra.* Wilmington DE: Scholarly Resources, 1999.

Thomson, Waddy. *Recollections of Mexico.* New York: Wiley and Putnam, 1847.

Tismaneanu, Vladimir (ed.). *Promises of 1968: Crisis, Illusion, Utopia.* Budapest: Central European University Press, 2011.

————. *The Revolutions of 1989.* London: Routledge, 1999.

Tornel y Mendívil, José María. *Breve reseña histórica de los acontecimientos más notables de la nación mexicana.* Mexico City: INEHRM, 1985.

Tornel, José María. *Discurso que pronunció el Ecsmo. Sr. General D. José María Tornel y Mendívil, individuo del Supremo Poder Conservador, en la alameda de la ciudad de México, en el día del solemne aniversario de la independencia.* Mexico City: Imp. de I. Cumplido, 1840.

————. *Manifiesto del origen, causas, progresos y estado de la revolución del imperio mexicano, con relación a la antigua España.* Mexico City: Imp. de Ontiveros, 1821.

Torre Villar, Ernesto de la. *La independencia de México.* Madrid: Mapfre, 1992.

Torre Villar, Ernesto de la (ed.). *Planes en la nación mexicana.* Vol. 5: *1855–56.* Mexico City: Senado de la República–El Colegio de México, 1987.

Trejo, Evelia. *Los límites de un discurso: Lorenzo de Zavala, su "Ensayo histórico" y la cuestión religiosa en México.* Mexico City: FCE, 2001.

Tutino, John. *From Insurrection to Revolution in Mexico: Social Bases of Agrarian Violence 1750–1940.* Princeton: Princeton University Press, 1986.

Tweedie, Mrs. Alec. *Mexico as I Saw It.* London: Hurst and Blakett, 1902.

Valadés, José C. *Alamán: Estadista e historiador.* Mexico City: UNAM, 1977.

Valle Arizpe, Artemio de. *La güera Rodríguez.* Mexico City: Porrúa, 1950.

Van Young, Eric. "In the Gloomy Caverns of Paganism: Popular Culture, Insurgency, and Nation-Building in Mexico, 1800–1821." In Christon I. Archer (ed.), *The Birth of Modern Mexico 1780–1824.* Wilmington DE: Scholarly Resources, 2003. 41–65.

————. *The Other Rebellion: Popular Violence, Ideology, and the Mexican Struggle for Independence, 1810–1821.* Stanford CA: Stanford University Press, 2001.

————. "Of Tempests and Teapots: Imperial Crisis and Local Conflict in Mexico at the Beginning of the Nineteenth Century." In Elisa Servín, Leticia Reina, and John Tutino (eds.), *Cycles of Conflict, Centuries of Change: Crisis, Reform, and Revolution in Mexico*. Durham NC: Duke University Press, 2007. 23–59.

————. "Vidas privadas y mitos públicos: Lucas Alamán y la independencia Mexicana." *Memoria de las revoluciones en México 20/10*, no. 9 (otoño 2010): 43–54.

Varo Montilla, Francisco. "La participación de la tropa en la sublevación del Palmar." *Espacio, Tiempo y Forma, Serie V, Historia Contemporánea*, vol. 15 (2002): 25–40.

Vázquez Mantecón, Carmen. "Espacio social y crisis política: La Sierra Gorda 1850–1855." *Mexican Studies/Estudios Mexicanos* 9:1 (Winter 1993): 47–70.

————. *Santa Anna y la encrucijada del Estado: La Dictadura (1853–1855)*. Mexico City: FCE, 1986.

Vázquez Semadeni, María Eugenia. *La formación de una cultura política republican: El debate público sobre la masonería. México, 1821–1830*. Mexico City: UNAM–Colmich, 2010.

Vázquez, Josefina Zoraida. *Dos décadas de desilusiones: En busca de una fórmula adecuada de gobierno (1832–1854)*. Mexico City: El Colegio de México–Instituto Mora, 2009.

————. "El establecimiento del federalismo en México, 1812–1827." In Josefina Zoraida Vázquez (ed.). *El establecimiento del federalismo en México (1821–1827)*. Mexico City: El Colegio de México, 2003. 19–38.

————. "Iglesia, ejército y centralismo." *Historia Mexicana* 39:1 (1989): 205–34.

————. "In Search of Power: The Pronunciamientos of General Mariano Paredes y Arrillaga." In Will Fowler (ed.), *Malcontents, Rebels, and Pronunciados: The Politics of Insurrection in Nineteenth-Century Mexico*. Lincoln: University of Nebraska Press, 2012. 171–204.

————. *La intervención norteamericana 1846–1848*. Mexico City: Secretaría de Relaciones Exteriores, 1997.

————. *Mexicanos y norteamericanos ante la guerra del 47*. Mexico City: Sep-Setentas, 1972.

————. "México y la guerra con Estados Unidos." In Josefina Zoraida Vázquez (ed.), *México al tiempo de su guerra con Estados Unidos (1846–1848)*. Mexico City: FCE, 1997. 17–46.

Bibliography

————. "El modelo de pronunciamiento mexicano, 1820–1823." *Ulúa* 7 (enero–junio 2006): 31–52.

————. "Political Plans and Collaboration between Civilians and the Military, 1821–1846." *Bulletin of Latin American Research* 15:1 (January 1996): 19–38.

————. "Los pronunciamientos de 1832: Aspirantismo político e ideología." In Jaime E. Rodríguez O. (ed.), *Patterns of Contention in Mexican History*. Wilmington DE: Scholarly Resources, 1992. 163–86.

————. "Two Reactions to the Illegitimate Succession of 1828: Campeche and Jalapa." In Will Fowler (ed.), *Forceful Negotiations: The Origins of the Pronunciamiento in Nineteenth-Century Mexico*. Lincoln: University of Nebraska Press, 2010. 47–73.

Vázquez, Josefina Zoraida (ed.). *El establecimiento del federalismo en México (1821–1827)*. Mexico City: El Colegio de México, 2003.

————. *México al tiempo de su guerra con Estados Unidos (1846–1848)*. Mexico City: FCE, 1997.

————. *Planes en la nación mexicana. Libro dos: 1831–1834*. Mexico City: Senado de la República–El Colegio de México, 1987.

————. *Planes en la nación mexicana. Libro tres: 1835–1840*. Mexico City: Secretaría de Relaciones Exteriores–El Colegio de México, 1987.

————. *Planes en la nación mexicana. Libro cuatro: 1841–1854*. Mexico City: Senado de la República–El Colegio de México, 1987.

Vázquez, Josefina Zoraida, and José Antonio Serrano Ortega (eds.). *Práctica y fracaso del primer federalismo mexicano (1824–1835)*. Mexico City: El Colegio de México, 2012.

Velasco Márquez, Jesús. *La guerra del 47 y la opinión pública (1845–1848)*. Mexico City: SepSetentas, 1975.

Velasco Martínez, Jesús, and Thomas Benjamin. "La guerra entre México y Estados Unidos, 1846–1848." In María Esther Schumacher (ed.), *Mitos en las relaciones México–Estados Unidos* (Mexico City: FCE, 1994), 99–156.

Velázquez, Primo Feliciano. *Historia de San Luis Potosí*. 4 vols. San Luis Potosí: Archivo Histórico del Estado y Academia de Historia Potosina, 1982.

Victoria Gómez, Felipe. *Guadalupe Victoria. Primer presidente de México*. Mexico City: Ediciones Botas, 1952.

Villalobos Velázquez, Rosario. *British Immigrants in the Mining District of Real del Monte and Pachuca 1824–1947: An Approach to Daily Life*. Mexico City: Archivo Histórico y Museo de Minería, 2004.

Villegas Revueltas, Silvestre. "Compromiso político e inversión: El gobierno de Manuel González." In Will Fowler (ed.), *Gobernantes mexicanos, vol. 1: 1821–1910*. Mexico City: FCE, 2008. 361–81.

———. *Deuda y diplomacia: La relación México-Gran Bretaña 1824–1884*. Mexico City: UNAM, 2005.

———. *Ignacio Comonfort*. Mexico City: Planeta, 2004.

———. *El liberalismo moderado en México 1852–1864*. Mexico City: UNAM, 1997.

Villoro, Luis. *El proceso ideológico de la revolución de independencia*. Mexico City: UNAM, 1967.

Ward, Henry George. *México en 1827*. Mexico City: FCE, 1995.

Warren, Richard A. "The Damned Man with the Venerated Plan: The Complex Legacies of Agustín de Iturbide and the Iguala Plan." In Will Fowler (ed.), *Celebrating Insurrection: The Commemoration and Representation of the Nineteenth-Century Mexican Pronunciamiento*. Lincoln: University of Nebraska Press, 2012. 28–49.

———. *Vagrants and Citizens: Politics and the Masses in Mexico City from Colony to Republic*. Wilmington DE: Scholarly Resources, 2001.

Weber, Max. *The Theory of Social and Economic Organization*. New York: Free Press, 1964.

Wheelan, Joseph. *Invading Mexico: America's Continental Dream and the Mexican War, 1846–1848*. New York: Carroll and Graf, 2007.

Zaragoza, José. *Historia de la deuda externa de México 1823–1861*. Mexico City: UNAM, 1996.

Zárate Toscano, Verónica. "Agustín de Iturbide: Entre la memoria y el olvido." *Secuencia*, 28 (enero–abril 1994): 5–27.

———. "Héroes y fiestas en el México decimonónico: La insistencia de Santa Anna." In Manuel Chust and Víctor Mínguez (eds.), *La construcción del héroe en España y México (1789–1847)*. Valencia: Universitat de Valencia, 2003. 133–53.

———. "Porfirio Díaz and the Representations of the Second of April." In Will Fowler (ed.), *Celebrating Insurrection: The Commemoration and Representation of the Nineteenth-Century Mexican Pronunciamiento*. Lincoln: University of Nebraska Press, 2012. 201–27.

Zavala, Lorenzo de. *Ensayo histórico de la revoluciones de México, desde 1808 hasta 1830.* 2 vols. Mexico City: Imp. de Manuel N. de la Vega, 1835.

———. *Obras: El historiador y el representante popular.* Mexico City: Porrúa, 1969.

———. *Obras: Viaje a los Estados Unidos del Norte de América.* Mexico City: Porrúa, 1976.

Zea, Leopoldo. *Positivism in Mexico.* Austin: University of Texas Press, 1974.

Index

Huejotzingo: pronunciamiento of 1833 in, 145, 149, 167, 185; pronunciamiento of 1842 in, 15, 180
Huetamo pronunciamiento (1832), 140
Humboldt, Alexander von, 76–77

Iguala. *See* Plan of Iguala
Imán, Santiago, 158, 304n6
Inclán, Ignacio, 163, 164
indigenous peoples, 136, 141–42, 149, 150–53, 160, 243
insurrectionary contagion, 37–38
Iturbide, Agustín de, 74, 94, 193; as emperor Agustín I, 9, 68, 95, 97; execution of, 104, 162; and Plan of Iguala, 62–63, 68–69, 70, 71–72; pronunciamientos against, 91, 96–98
Iturrigaray, José de, 45, 48

Jalapa pronunciamiento (1829), 115–18, 119, 140, 155, 163. *See also* Plan of Jalapa
Jalisco: agrarian movement in, 155; governmental authority in, 101; pronunciamientos of 1823 in, 121, 128; pronunciamiento of 1824 in, 103–4; pronunciamientos of 1827 in, 121–22, 129; pronunciamientos of 1852 in, 207, 225–27, 302n2
Jarauta, Celedonio Domeco, 205, 293n28, 303n3
Juan Carlos (King of Spain), 5
Juárez, Benito, 84–85, 196–97, 237, 238–39, 301–2n1
Juárez Law, 233
Junta de Notables (1843), 180, 193, 213
Junta Instituyente (1822), 95

Kingsley, Rose Georgina, 134
Knight, Alan, 80

La Acordada pronunciamiento (1828), 112, 121
La Angostura-Buena Vista battle (1847), 221
Lacy, Luis de, 21

La Mesilla valley, 228, 230
Lampazos pronunciamiento (1855), 231
Lanuza, Pedro José, 90
Lara, José Anselmo de, 159, 305n7
Law of Conspirators (1853), 205
legitimacy: as contested and unclear, 17–19, 113, 119, 180–81; in New Spain, 55; political, 85–86; pronunciamientos and, 18–19, 32, 33, 61, 88
Lenin, Vladimir Illich, 37–38
León, Antonio and Manuel, 103
Lerdo de Tejada, Miguel, 235
Lerdo de Tejada, Sebastián, 243–44
Lerdo Law, 233
Ley del Caso, 167, 170
liberalism, 60, 108; creole, 53, 56; popular, 136, 186; and puro-moderado divisions, 234, 235–36, 254–55; and reform period, 84–85, 196–97, 233–36, 238; Spanish, 26, 60, 263n57; triumph of in Mexico, 239
Libya, 7
Life in Mexico (Calderón), 175
Lipset, Seymour Martin, 85
Liss, Peggy, 47
literacy, 79, 276n13
Lobato, José María, 108; pronunciamiento by, 93, 98–99, 103, 121, 129, 284n106, 304n5
local and regional concerns: and Mexican national identity, 79, 80; pronunciamientos about, 12–13, 88, 93, 138–41, 158–59, 211–12, 248, 304–5n7; in War of Independence, 50–51
Locke, John, 47
Lombardini, Manuel María, 227
López Portillo, Jesús, 225
López Uraga, José, 234
Los Olmitos armistice (1840), 157
Lugo, José María, 147
Lynch, John, 43, 47

Madero, Francisco I., 244

Zacatecas: pronunciamiento of 1832 in, 164–65; pronunciamiento of 1833 in, 144–46; pronunciamiento of 1835 in, 157, 171–72, 183, 304n5

Zacatlán de las Manzanas pronunciamiento (1833), 149–50

Zamora pronunciamiento (1830), 121, 128, 284n106

Zapata, Emiliano, 244

Zapatista uprising (1994), 244

Zavala, Lorenzo de, 111, 116, 121; as creole liberal, 53, 56; on Plan of Iguala, 72–73, 89; on Riego's pronunciamiento, 58; and Texas independence, 160–61

Zelaya, Manuel, 3

Zuloaga, Félix, 193, 207, 231, 237, 238, 242

In The Mexican Experience series

*Seen and Heard in Mexico: Children and
Revolutionary Cultural Nationalism*
Elena Albarrán

Railroad Radicals in Cold War Mexico: Gender, Class, and Memory
Robert F. Alegre
Foreword by Elena Poniatowska

Mexicans in Revolution, 1910–1946: An Introduction
William H. Beezley and Colin M. MacLachlan

*Radio in Revolution: Wireless Technology and
State Power in Mexico, 1897–1938*
J. Justin Castro

*Celebrating Insurrection: The Commemoration and Representation of
the Nineteenth-Century Mexican* Pronunciamiento
Edited and with an introduction by Will Fowler

Forceful Negotiations: The Origins of the Pronunciamiento *in
Nineteenth-Century Mexico*
Edited and with an introduction by Will Fowler

Independent Mexico: The Pronunciamiento *in the
Age of Santa Anna, 1821–1858*
Will Fowler

Malcontents, Rebels, and Pronunciados: *The Politics of
Insurrection in Nineteenth-Century Mexico*
Edited and with an introduction by Will Fowler

*Working Women, Entrepreneurs, and the Mexican Revolution:
The Coffee Culture of Córdoba, Veracruz*
Heather Fowler-Salamini

*The Heart in the Glass Jar: Love Letters, Bodies,
and the Law in Mexico*
William E. French

"Muy buenas noches": Mexico, Television, and the Cold War
Celeste González de Bustamante
Foreword by Richard Cole

To order or obtain more information on these or other University of Nebraska Press
titles, visit nebraskapress.unl.edu.

Other works by Will Fowler

Mexico in the Age of Proposals, 1821–1853
Tornel and Santa Anna: The Writer and the Caudillo, Mexico 1795–1853
Santa Anna of Mexico
Latin America since 1780, 3rd edition

CPSIA information can be obtained
at www.ICGtesting.com
Printed in the USA
LVHW030144011218
598842LV00001B/52/P

9 780803 225398